RESEARCH IN MARITIME HISTORY
NO. 13

# "THOSE EMBLEMS OF HELL"? EUROPEAN SAILORS AND THE MARITIME LABOUR MARKET, 1570-1870

Edited By
Paul van Royen,
Jaap Bruijn and Jan Lucassen

International Maritime Economic History Association

St. John's, Newfoundland
1997

ISBN 9780968128831

*Research in Maritime History* is available free of charge to members of the International Maritime Economic History Association. The price to others is US$15 per copy.

Back issues of *Research in Maritime History* are available:

| | |
|---|---|
| No. 1 (1991) | David M. Williams and Andrew P. White (comps.), *A Select Bibliography of British and Irish University Theses about Maritime History, 1792-1990* |
| No. 2 (1992) | Lewis R. Fischer (ed.), *From Wheel House to Counting House: Essays in Maritime Business History in Honour of Professor Peter Neville Davies* |
| No. 3 (1992) | Lewis R. Fischer and Walter Minchinton (eds.), *People of the Northern Seas* |
| No. 4 (1993) | Simon Ville (ed.), *Shipbuilding in the United Kingdom in the Nineteenth Century: A Regional Approach* |
| No. 5 (1993) | Peter N. Davies (ed.), *The Diary of John Holt* |
| No. 6 (1994) | Simon P. Ville and David M. Williams (eds.), *Management, Finance and Industrial Reslations in Maritime Industries: Essays in International Maritime and Business History* |
| No. 7 (1994) | Lewis R. Fischer (ed.), *The Market for Seamen in the Age of Sail* |
| No. 8 (1995) | Gordon Read and Michael Stammers (comps.), *Guide to the Records of Merseyside Maritime Museum* |
| No. 9 (1995) | Frank Broeze (ed.), *Maritime History at the Crossroads: A Critical Review of Recent Historiography* |
| No. 10 (1996) | Nancy Redmayne Ross (ed.), *The Diary of a Maritimer, 1816-1901: The Life and Times of Joseph Salter* |
| No. 11 (1997) | Faye Margaret Kert, *Prize and Prejudice: Privateering and Naval Prize in Atlantic Canada in the War of 1812* |
| No. 12 (1997) | Malcolm Tull, *A Community Enterprise: The History of the Port of Fremantle, 1897 to 1997* |

*Research in Maritime History* would like to thank Memorial University of Newfoundland for its generous financial assistance in support of this volume.

**CONTENTS**



**CONTRIBUTIONS**

# CONTRIBUTORS

ROLAND BAETENS (1935) is Professor of modern history at the University of Antwerp and Dean of the Faculty of Law. He has published on economic and cultural history. His books include *The Chant of Paradise. The Antwerp Zoo: 150 Years of History* (1993); *Album Palaeographicum XVII Provinciarum* (with C. Dekker and S. Dechamps, 1992); *Industriële archeologie in Vlaanderen. Theorie en praktijk* (editor, 1988); and *Nouvelles approches concernant la culture de l'habita* (co-edited with B. Blondé, 1991).

JAAP BRUIJN (1938) is Professor of maritime history at the University of Leiden. He has published on the history of the navy, the Dutch East India Company, whaling and on seamen in particular. His two main publications are *The Dutch Navy of the Seventeenth and Eighteenth Centuries* (1993) and *Dutch-Asiatic Shipping in the 17th and 18th Centuries* (3 vols., 1979-1987, with F.S. Gaastra and I. Schöffer).

KAREL DAVIDS (1952) is Professor of social and economic history at the Free University in Amsterdam. His books include *Zeewezen en wetenschap: De wetenschap en de ontwikkeling van de navigatietechniek in Nederland tussen 1585 en 1815* (1986); *The Dutch Economy in the Golden Age* (1993, co-edited with Leo Noordegraaf); and *A Miracle Mirrored: The Dutch Republic in European Perspective* (1995, co-edited with Jan Lucassen).

PETER EARLE (1937) is Reader Emeritus in economic history at the University of London and writes on social and maritime history. His publications include *A City Full of People: Men and Women of London, 1650-1750* (1994) and *The Last Fight of the Revenge* (1992).

FEMME GAASTRA (1945) is Assistant Professor of history at the University of Leiden and writes on Dutch colonial and maritime history. His publications include *Dutch-Asiatic Shipping in the 17th and 18th Centuries* (3 vols., 1979-1987, with J.R. Bruijn and I. Schöffer); *Bewind en beleid bij de VOC. De financiële en commerciële politiek van de bewindhebbers, 1672-1702* (1989); and *Ships, Sailors and Spices. East India Companies and Their Shipping* (1993, with J.R. Bruijn).

GORDON JACKSON (1934) is Reader in economic history at the University of Strathclyde. He works on the general fields of maritime and urban history, and is writing a maritime history of Scotland. He has contributed to many edited works, and his books include *Hull in the Eighteenth Century* (1972); *The British Whaling Trade* (1978); *The History and Archaeology of Ports* (1983); and, most recently, the co-edited *Glasgow. Vol I: Beginnings to 1830* (1995).

HANS CHRISTIAN JOHANSEN (1935) has been Professor of economic and social history at the University of Odense since 1970. He books and articles on Danish and international economic and social history span the eighteenth, nineteenth and twentieth centuries. Among his books are *Dansk Økonomisk politik efter 1784* (2 vols., 1968-1980) and *Shipping and Trade Between the Baltic Area and Western Europe 1784-95* (1983).

YRJÖ KAUKIAINEN (1940) is Professor of economic history at the University of Helsinki. He has published on maritime history, demographic history and economic and social history, mainly concerning the eighteenth and nineteenth centuries. His recent books include *Sailing into Twilight. Finnish Shipping in an Age of Transport Revolution, 1860-1914* (1991) and *A History of Finnish Shipping* (1993).

T.J.A. LE GOFF (1942) is Associate Professor of history at York University in Toronto. He is the author of *Vannes and its Region: A Study of Town and Country in Eighteenth-Century France* (1981; French translation 1989), and a large number of articles on French economic, maritime and social history.

MARCEL VAN DER LINDEN (1952) is Senior Research Fellow at the International Institute of Social History in Amsterdam. His publications include *Revolutionary Syndicalism. An International Perspective* (1990, co-edited with Wayne Thorpe); *The Formation of Labour Movements 1870-1914. An International Perspective* (2 vol., 1990, co-edited with Jürgen Rojahn); *Social Security Mutualism* (1996); and *Free and Unfree Labour: The Debate Continues* (forthcoming, co-edited with Tom Brass).

JAN LUCASSEN (1947) is Head of Research and Publications of the International Institute of Social History in Amsterdam. Since 1991 he has held a private chair in social history at the Free University of Amsterdam. His books include *Migrant Labour in Europe 1600-1900: The Drift to the North Sea* (1987); *Nieuwkomers, nakomelingen, Nederlanders* (revised edition 1994, with Rinus Penninx); and *A Miracle Mirrored: The Dutch Republic in European Perspective* (1995, co-edited with Karel Davids).

MICHAEL NORTH (1954) is Professor of modern history at the Ernst-Moritz-Arndt-University in Greifswald. A specialist in monetary and financial history and commerce in the early-modern period. His books include *Geldumlauf und Wirtschaftskonjunktur im südlichen Ostseeraum an der Wende der Neuzeit (1440-1570)* (1990); *Kunst und Kommerz im Goldenen Zeitalter. Zur Sozialgeschichte der niederländischen Malerei im 17. Jahrhundert* (1992); *Northwestern Europe in the World Economy 1750-1950* (1993); and *Das Geld und seine Geschichte vom Mittelalter bis zur Gegenwart* (1994).

SARAH PALMER (1943) is Senior Lecturer and Head of the Department of History at Queen Mary and Westfield College, University of London. She is the author of *Politics, Shipping and the Repeal of the Navigation Laws* (1990), and has published a number of articles on maritime themes, including seafaring, shipbuilding and ports.

CARLA RAHN PHILLIPS (1943) is Professor of history at the University of Minnesota. Her research centres on the economic and social history of early-modern Spain. She is the author of *Ciudad Real, 1500-1750: Growth, Crisis, and Readjustment in the Spanish Economy* (1979); *Six Galleons for the King of Spain: Imperial Defense in the Early Seventeenth Century* (1986); and co-author of *The Worlds of Christopher Columbus* (1992).

PAUL VAN ROYEN (1952) is Director of the Institute for Maritime History of the Naval Staff (Royal Netherlands Navy) in The Hague. His research is focussed on the maritime, economic and social history of the Dutch Republic. He was editor of the Dutch journal of maritime history (*Tijdschrift voor Zeegeschiedenis*). He is author of *Zeevarenden op de koopvaardijvloot omstreeks 1700* (1987); and co-author of *50 jaar bestuur in Flevoland, Noordoostpolder en Wieringermeer. Het openbaar lichaam in de Zuiderzee- en IJsselmeerpolders 1937-1987* (1993).

GUSTAV SÆTRA (1953) is Assistant Professor in history at Agder College in Norway. He has published on eighteenth-century political history and local Agder history. His contributions to maritime history comprise articles on Norwegian-Danish trade, shipbrokers and shipping companies in the Agder region. He is also the author of *Shipping and Beyond*, a jubilee book of the shipping company of Arnt J. Mørland in Arendal (1991).

JON THÓR (1944) is Head of the Icelandic Centre for Fisheries History Research. He has written extensively on the history of North Atlantic fisheries, on the history of Iceland's fishery limit and on Icelandic regional history. He was president of the Association for the History of the Northern Seas, 1992-1994, and is currently president of the NAFHA (North Atlantic Fisheries History Association). He is co-editor of *Studia Atlantica* and *North Atlantic Studies*. His books include *British Trawlers in Icelandic Waters 1889-1916* (Icelandic edition 1982; English edition 1992); *British Trawlers and Iceland 1919-1976* (1995); and *Saga Ísfjarðar* (4 vols., 1984-1990).

DAVID WILLIAMS (1940) is Senior Lecturer in economic and social history at the University of Leicester. A specialist in nineteenth-century British maritime and economic history, he is co-editor of *Management, Finance and Industrial Relations in Maritime Industries: Essays in International Maritime and Business History* (1994), and co-editor of *Shipping, Technology and Imperialism* (1996) and *Maritime Europe in the Twentieth Century* (forthcoming).

# Preface

In October 1994 in The Hague, the Institute for Maritime History of the Naval Staff (Royal Netherlands Navy), the International Institute for Social History, and the Department of Maritime History of the University of Leiden hosted a conference on "European Sailors, 1570-1870." This meeting was organized to bring together experts on seafaring labour and the (inter)national labour market for seamen in Europe in the age of sail. The reason for this was our belief that research, particularly comparative research, into maritime labour has been hampered by the absence of an up-to-date overview in the various European countries of the labour market for seafarers. It should be stressed, however, that the organisers were well aware that they were not the first to attempt to get such an overview, as the proceedings of the 1980 International Congress of Maritime History meeting in Bucharest, *Seamen in Society*, show.

In recent years, as studies based upon vague concepts of "global markets," the efficiency of international maritime labour markets or, as a kind of counterpart to the Braudelian Mediterranean, North Sea culture have proliferated, the lack of such an overview is apparent. How can one discuss global concepts without knowing the actual state of affairs in various nations? How can one construct models without at least some hard evidence? And even if one has a few pieces, are they part of the same puzzle? In short, our knowledge for each country is far from uniform, and in many cases far from linguistically accessible. Moreover, much depends on what sources have survived and what kinds of queries put to the material. Since maritime history is not an academic priority in all countries, we have a sketchy and fragmented picture, or sometimes even a total blank. As an example, a question like "how many sailors were employed in any particular period between 1570 and 1870 in any particular trade" posed for some researchers an insurmountable barrier.

Our shared interests in seafaring people were the basis and inspiration for the organisation of the conference on "European Sailors, 1570-1870." In addition, our own research into the various aspects of the Dutch maritime labour market prompted many questions that could only be answered satisfactorily by international comparative research. Because most conferences treating the subject of the maritime labour market tend to lose their way in the dimly-lit alleys of the dockyards, we thought it useful to make up a kind of chartbook to assist our experts in navigating through the dark and vaguely charted backwaters of maritime history. In short, we wanted the various contributions to be structured as a series of national reports, written – as far as possible – in an identical format. To this end the following questionnaire was distributed beforehand:

1. Introduction: "state of the art"
2. Sailing *from* the country concerned
2.1. How many sailors in the mercantile marine, navy, whalers or on subsections of these categories (if possible estimates around 1600, 1650, 1700, 1750, 1800 and 1850); characterisation of each sector (number of ships, tonnage and type of average ships, destination and freight, seasons of sailing, average number of sailors per ship)
2.2. Where did the sailors come from; as far as they came from European countries, per (sub)sector as many socio-economic details as possible on push-regions as well as details such as their age, were they married or not, were they sailing as part of their life- or work-cycle
2.3. Wages and other remuneration: in absolute and in relative terms (difference between pull and push areas)
2.4. Recruitment policies by governmental bodies in push and pull areas (promotive, coercive and preventive)
2.5. Careers of sailors
   1. mobility between the three maritime sectors and other economic sectors (e.g., agriculture, fishing, urban and rural crafts, army)
   2. between the three sectors or their sub-sectors
   3. between the same sector in different countries, vertically within one sector
2.6. Group formation of sailors: culture of sailors, strikes, mutinies
3. Departure *to* another country in order to sail from there
3.1. How many people went to what other countries and to what kind of sailing
3.2. Characteristics of these groups and of the push-region they came from (cf. questions under 2.2. and 2.3.)
3.3. Recruitment policies (cf. under 2.4.)
3.4. Careers of sailors (cf. under 2.5.)
4. Conclusions on major historical developments in the country concerned.

The reason for starting with 1570 is that in the last decades of the sixteenth century the merchant fleets of various European countries were poised on the brink of another stage of expansion. In the years to come, sailing went from being a haphazard enterprise of a few brave sailors to a relatively large-scale and substantial sector. The development of shipbuilding techniques and navigational and sailing skills also contributed to the expansion of shipping. On the eve of the seventeenth century, a maritime network enclosed all European waters and backwaters, while the seas outside Europe were increasingly integrated into this system. Along with this expansion, new branches of shipping developed. For instance, whaling as a specialization came into being. The reason to end the overview in 1870 is quite obvious: by that time, sail was being replaced by steam. Although well into the twentieth century sailing vessels still traversed the seven seas, the fate of sail was sealed: increasingly, the sound of wind in the sails was replaced by the cacophony of steam engines. Other techniques, other skills, and even other men were needed to keep the ships at sea.

Apart from these temporal limits, the project also has geographic and intellectual boundaries. As for the former, we are well aware that not all European countries are included. In particular, it should strike the reader that the Mediterranean is completely omitted. There is a good reason for this: the maritime labour market of the Mediterranean had little to do with that of the Atlantic. The connections were nearly always bilateral. The Venetians sailed to the north, to Bruges, and the Dutch invaded the blue subtropical waters like "insects." By the beginning of the seventeenth century, "the old queen of the world, the Mediterranean, was dethroned by the new king, the Atlantic."[1]

Moreover, it was a matter of logistics, and linguistic and financial possibilities to get together the "expertise" on this subject from all over Europe. Our efforts to bring together an expert on the subject from each European country resulted in this collection of papers by maritime historians. Unfortunately, not all countries, even those facing the Atlantic, are covered. The intellectual boundaries were determined by the actual state of affairs in the various countries and regions involved in this project. In that respect all participants have done what they could to assemble as much material and knowledge as they could, "jeder auf

---

[1]F. Braudel, *The Mediterranean and the Mediterranean World in the Age of Philip II* (2 vols., 4th ed., London, 1981), II, 568.

seine Façon." But we know beforehand that not all literature was covered and not all relevant knowledge will be presented to the reader.

A major point is that all national reports were to be distributed and digested before the conference. With this new intellectual luggage, the experts were to try to construct a coherent picture of the various aspects of maritime labour and to arrive at general conclusions about the historical development of this particular part of the European working class. Four themes were treated during the two days of hard work: the national maritime labour market (session chaired by Paul van Royen); the international maritime labour market (chaired by Jan Lucassen); working conditions (chaired by Femme Gaastra); and career patterns (chaired by Jaap Bruijn). Summing up and conclusions were the tasks of Marcel van der Linden, our external expert on "labour history."

The title of this volume is courtesy of Gordon Jackson. We, however, put the question mark after "Those Emblems of Hell" because of our reasonable doubts on the general validity of this rather negative and stigmatizing characterization.[2]

This fruitful and satisfactory conference on sailors and the maritime labour markets in Europe in the age of sail would have been impossible without the help of the International Institute of Social History, the Rijksuniversiteit Leiden, the Naval Staff of the Royal Netherlands Navy, the Directie van de Oostersche Handel en Reederijen, the Directoraat Generaal voor Scheepvaart en Maritieme Zaken, the staff of the Institute of Maritime History, and the Netherlands Association for Maritime History. We are most grateful to Femme Gaastra of the University of Leiden and Marcel van der Linden of the International Institute of Social History who took care of the session on working conditions and the conclusions, respectively. Our special thanks go to Annemarie Woudstra of the International Institute of Social History, and Heleanne Arnold and Jolanda van Berkum of the Institute for Maritime History for their enormous effort and enthusiasm that helped to make this conference successful.

Paul van Royen
Jaap Bruijn
Jan Lucassen

---

[2]Scottish Record Office, GD 18/5218, Clerke of Penicuik Papers, H. Clerke, London, to J. Clerke, Edinburgh, October 1700.

# The "National" Maritime Labour Market: Looking for Common Characteristics

**Paul C. van Royen**

## Introduction

Seafaring, sailors and ships – in particular in the age of sail – have been stimuli for man's taste for adventure, imagination and longing for the creation of myths. Indeed, many books have been written on seafaring and the romance of the sea – and many will still be written. Yet sailors and seafaring life still seem to remain in a dimly-lit category of history.

"The 'people,' as the ship's company came to be called, remain an anonymous mass, too often neglected...Of all sections of the community, seafaring men and agricultural labourers have been the most ignored and therefore the worst treated," wrote Christopher Lloyd in his study of British seamen. "Only occasionally it is possible to discern...the identity of an individual seaman, to say what he looked like, who was his father, where he came from, because (like the farm labourer) he was usually illiterate and inarticulate."[1]

Evidently, seafaring people in history have left few traces, and those that remain appear to be so vague that historians examining topics like the functioning of a maritime labour market, use of migratory labour aboard, level of wages, or career patterns of individual seamen sometimes get the impression they are dealing with quantum physics or Heisenberg's principle of uncertainty. Reliable information on sailors and seafaring life is scarce and often contradictory. Precise data are even harder to find, let alone to explain and interpret plausibly. This sort of "source vacuum" has led to fascinating but often unrealistic – because seldom backed by reliable proof – stories of the sea. There is a world of difference between Marcus Rediker's *Between the Devil and the Deep Blue Sea* and Nicolas Rodger's *The Wooden World*, or between K. Allard Coles' *Heavy Weather Sailing* and Erskine Childers' *The Riddle of the*

[1]C. Lloyd, *The British Seaman 1200-1800. A Social Survey* (London, 1968), 11.

*Sands*.[2] To get away from the romantic picture of Jack Tar blurred by myths and tales one has at least to attempt to bring together the available knowledge and information thus far gathered on the "people of the sea."

**Sailors and Toneladas**

If we use the concept of the maritime labour market in the sense of the entity of variables, like demand and supply, that determine wages, then several problems arise. First, we hardly know how the maritime labour market functioned. Second, we know very little about supply and demand. And third, data on wages are very scarce. Combining these three problems with the fact that in this volume we attempt to provide a survey of the Western European maritime labour market between 1570 and 1870, the peril of capsizing and sinking before even leaving port is great. C.P. Kindleberger's brave but somewhat premature exercise to get a clear view on sailors and markets might serve as an example of such an unhappy voyage into twilight. Kindleberger put together all the ingredients and research thus far known, along with the concept of the efficiency of the maritime labour market, but ended up painting an unconvincing portrait.[3] Apart from the fact that his book is surely worthwhile reading, it shows clearly that dwelling on the quaysides of maritime history is a dangerous affair. The various articles in *The Market for Seamen in the Age of Sail*, which resulted from a special session at the Eleventh International Congress of Economic History in Milan, Italy, in 1994 prove this.[4]

Between 1570 and 1870 various maritime empires emerged and declined in Western Europe. By the beginning of the period, the Portuguese and Spanish seaborne empires were beginning to wither, while in the north the Dutch, soon to be followed by the English, were to develop more-or-less monopolistic positions in maritime trade and

---

[2]Marcus Rediker, *Between the Devil and the Deep Blue Sea: Merchant Seamen, Pirates, and the Anglo-American Maritime World 1700-1750* (Cambridge, 1987); N.A.M. Rodger, *The Wooden World. An Anatomy of the Georgian Navy* (London, 1986); Kaines Adlard Coles, *Heavy Weather Sailing* (London, 1975); and Erskine Childers, *The Riddle of the Sands* (London, 1915).

[3]C.P. Kindleberger, *Mariners and Markets* (London, 1992).

[4]Lewis R. Fischer (ed.), *The Market for Seamen in the Age of Sail* (St. John's, 1994).

shipping. Other Western Europeans with maritime interests also took part in this overall development, albeit on a much smaller scale. To get an idea of the importance of seafaring as a means of subsistence, some indication of overall employment in this activity might be helpful. In the case of most Western European countries, however, this question seems extremely hard to answer, especially for the sixteenth and the larger part of the seventeenth centuries.

In Spain, the number of sailors employed in the various branches of shipping during the sixteenth century can only be reconstructed through adding the number of *toneladas* and finding an acceptable ratio of sailor and *tonelada*. For France, the possibility of reconstructing overall employment in the maritime sector begins with the reign of Louis XIV. Before 1661 various types of local sources have to be added, while after 1661 an enormous "state-controlled database" provides access to the actual sailors and the labour market. As for the Southern Netherlands, it is only through the scattered numbers of ships that some light is shed on employment. In the case of the Dutch Republic, sources and research concerning employment in the shipping industry seem – from a Dutch perspective, at least – to be in better shape. Part of the estimates of employment are well know, such as the numbers of sailors involved in shipping to the East Indies, and some of the estimates at least have an aura of reliability. For England and Scotland, the reconstruction of overall maritime employment is done on the basis of numbers of ships and tons, but evidently these are very rough. In the case of Denmark, Norway, Finland and Germany, the overall picture generally is the same. Data are scarce and reliable estimates of overall maritime employment are virtually nonexistent.[5] Only information concerning the maritime labour market of Iceland seems to be reliable, but then in this period the number of its sailors could be counted on the fingers of our hands.

## Geography, Demography and the Maritime Labour Market

The simple question "how many sailors were there in your country or region" provides us with a rather scattered pattern. Even harder to answer is the question of what factors influenced this labour market. In the Braudelian tradition, one could ask what role geography played in a

[5]For a survey, see Richard W. Unger, "The Tonnage of Europe's Merchant Fleets, 1300-1800," *American Neptune*, LII (1992), 247-261.

country's process developing as a seafaring state. This approach, however, seems doomed to failure. For instance, one of the causes said to underlie the upsurge of Portugal as a seaborne empire is its position as "Europe's most advanced window on the Atlantic." Although this sounds poetic, it did not mean a thing to most inhabitants. "Even a few miles inland from the coast many people [were] quite uninfluenced by the nearness of the sea," C.R. Boxer stated in his book on the Portuguese seaborne empire. "The peasant in the fields is only conscious of the Atlantic Ocean when trying to protect his vines from the strong sea breezes and the particles of salt which they bring."[6] Moreover, while Portugal's geographic position did not change dramatically, within fifty years its seaborne empire began to crumble.

In short, geography does not imply automatically that seafaring should be a means of subsistence *par excellence*. Moreover, proximity to the sea or the presence of an ancient trading network are no guarantees that a nation will develop a maritime labour market of any importance, as the experience of the Southern Netherlands, and in particular the city of Antwerp, demonstrates. The notion that navigable waters are a *conditio sine qua non* can hardly be regarded as a serious explanation. This is particularly true for Germany, where the absence of contact with the sea did not deter seafaring from becoming the main occupation of a considerable part of the population in the eighteenth century.

Another factor often claimed to be of major importance to the development and structure of the maritime labour market is demography. Indeed, aside from *The Flying Dutchman*, no ship can be sailed without men of flesh and blood – although steel seems to be preferred. Of course, supply and demand are to a certain extent determined by demography. But, although it is often accepted as common knowledge that only relative or absolute overpopulation created the necessary demographic reservoir for the merchant fleets, as well as the navy, fisheries and whaling, the validity of this rather linear and monocausal explanation remains in doubt. It may be that the importance of demography is one of those seafaring myths: goes to sea only because there is no other way to earn one's daily bread.

Viewed from another angle, demography does not help us much to deepen our understanding of the maritime labour market. In most countries this market was but a fraction of the overall labour market, so

---

[6]C.R. Boxer, *The Portuguese Seaborne Empire 1415-1825* (London, 1969), 2 and 14.

the direct influence of demography on supply and demand must have been limited. This view presupposes the very existence of a perfect labour market, but was there such a thing? Indeed, on a local level the demographic factor could play a decisive role. We know that in pre-industrial society demographic shifts had great impacts on the economy, including trade and shipping, and thus on the demand side of the maritime labour market. But these changes were seldom brought about by demography itself.

It is evident that although shipping might have had an enormous economic impact on a country, the number of people directly involved was marginal relative to total population and to the overall numbers of employment. The "guestimates" in the various contributions to this volume make that very clear – and that, I'm afraid, might be the only thing these numbers reveal. Unfortunately, research thus far gives us hardly any clues in this respect. This leaves us with the problem that we still know very little about the factors influencing the maritime labour market. Or again to quote C.R. Boxer (who quotes Orlando Ribeiro): "the seagoing occupations, however important they are (or appear to be) in the framework of the...national economy, can only be classified as limited, fragmentary, and intermittent in comparison with the permanent agricultural labour of the fields."[7] Or to put it differently, maritime employment is marginal in a broader context.

## Economy, Social Environment and the State

Now that we have seen that geographical, physical and demographic factors do not help to explain much about the development and structure of the maritime labour market in the age of sail, let us turn to man-made factors, such as the economy, social setting and the state.

From an economic perspective, the maritime labour market is the "place" where demand and supply intersect. Let us assume that to the actors on both sides of this "place," sailing had economic advantages. For the owners of the ships or the rulers of the state, well-manned ships provided profits or safety, while for the sailors they guaranteed an income that suited them and was in accordance with the advantages or disadvantages of other available means of income. We know, however, that opinions concerning this idyllic market diverge. To Marcus Rediker

[7]Boxer, *Portuguese Seaborne Empire*, 14.

this market was a place of limbo, where the devils of capitalism and class struggle peeped around the corner of anachronism, while to Nicolas Rodger seafaring was a job for those who wanted a relatively easy life.[8] Both views at least give reason to question whether the maritime labour market is the result of our imagination or a form of reality.

Apart from the problem of diverging characterizations of the maritime labour market, there is also no consensus on the profitability of shipping to both the demand and the supply sides of the market. Was shipping a profitable business to the shipowners? Unfortunately, a well-documented answer is hard to find. Most of the archival material suggests the opposite. Shipping was not at all profitable, some historians want us to believe. Ralph Davis solved the problem as follows:

> We cannot say with precision what "profitable" meant to the merchant or the investor of the seventeenth and eighteenth century. It is reasonable to suppose, however, that men would not have invested money in the shipping industry, on a scale that increased almost continuously through two centuries, if they had not been spurred on by the expectation of adequate gains and if on the whole and in the long run those expectations had not been realised. This had surely more importance than lack of evidence which appears to point to a contrary view.[9]

To a certain extent the issue is blurred by the same myth as maritime employment: solely as an investment of last resort.

As for the other side of the labour market – the sailors – we have little more than some scattered data on wages. If compared internationally, these data do not suggest a unified, unifying or efficient European or macro-regional maritime labour market. On the contrary, harmony between demand and supply is hard to find. Wages of sailors are often described as too low to sustain a family. But not all branches

---

[8]P.C. van Royen, "Personnel of the Dutch and English Mercantile Marine (1700-1850). An Introductory Paper," in J.R. Bruijn and W.F.J. Mörzer Bruyns (eds.), *Anglo-Dutch Mercantile Marine Relations 1700-1850* (Amsterdam, Leiden, 1991), especially 103-105.

[9]R. Davis, *The Rise of the English Shipping Industry in the Seventeenth and Eighteenth Centuries* (London, 1962), 383.

of shipping paid that badly. As for the merchant marine, there are indications that seamen were better off. In short, wages in the various branches of shipping differed. But how high were the wages in the various branches and how can these differences be explained? Did skills fix the price? Did sailors need to "network" their way aboard? Was it the availability of labour that made the difference or was it tradition? Was it the relative standard of living that made labour cheap or expensive? Or was it the state or the company that determined wage levels?

The concept of the labour market does not help us very much to explain either wages or their development over time. For instance, the wages paid by the Dutch East India Company remained the same for about a century. During that same period, however, the Dutch labour market changed drastically. Demand increased, rates of mortality rose, numbers of foreigners increased and so did rates of urban unemployment. Everything changed but the wages. In 1665 John de Witt stated "that it was necessary that once for all sailors' pay is fixed as an iron law so that no one can any longer hope for a rise; else the sailor is master and the State at the discretion of the rabble."[10] Soon after, however, wages had to be revised slightly. The example shows that the state tried at least to influence the mechanisms of the labour market.

To solve this problem some historians have posited a bipartite or even a tripartite labour market consisting of various independent segments. In this option, every segment had its own typical wages and its characteristic recruitment pattern. It is evident that this differentiation has led us a long way from the original idea of an undivided and uniform market for sailors in Europe. Apart from the state, local authorities or companies that played their roles, other actors moved about in the backstreets of the harbour districts. Crimps, soul-sellers, press-gangs and women with questionable reputations were more than willing to assist Jack Tar in getting a job.[11] To them, the seaman was a means to earn a living. Seen in a positive way, these figures served as intermediaries between sailor and master, as the "place" where supply and demand met.

[10] C.R. Boxer, "Sedentary Workers and Seafaring Folk in the Dutch Republic," in J.S. Bromley and E.H. Kossman (eds.), *Britain and the Netherlands* (2 vols., Groningen, 1964), II, 148-168, especially 155.

[11] Marc A. van Alphen, "The Female Side of Dutch Shipping: Financial Bonds of Seamen Ashore in the 17th and 18th Century," in Bruijn and Mörzer Bruyns (eds.), *Anglo-Dutch*, 125-132.

Yet not all branches of shipping used their services and crimps and soul-sellers certainly did not decide upon the level of wages. Seen in a negative way, they seduced sailors, only to turn their victims over to cruel and relentless masters.

Because economy and social setting are intertwined, and because seafaring essentially is a social event (single-handed sailing excluded), part of a better understanding of the maritime labour market must be found in the social setting of the sailors. The "structure" – if any – of the maritime labour market in the age of sail differed by country, and various "systems" could coexist peacefully in neighbouring countries. That is to say, the English navy only managed to man its ships with the assistance of press-gangs, while on the other side of the Channel France had a rather sophisticated way of finding sailors for its *Marine Royale*. The navy of the Dutch Republic left it to the free will of the individual sailor. All three "systems" (press-gangs, conscription or free choice) led to times of both abundance and scarcity of labour. The fluctuations of supply and demand over time had little to do with the improvement of working conditions. Moreover, wages hardly changed. What then turned men and boys into deep-sea sailors? Social environment, maritime skills and tradition?

If this were true, then why did sailing as a means of subsistence appear or disappear so suddenly in a region? A most striking example of such a sudden upsurge of maritime activities is supplied by Gravelines in the northwest of France.[12] The mysterious disappearance of sailors in *het Noorderkwartier* (Holland) is an example of the opposite. Both cases leave us with the problem of the role played by tradition and by the presence of maritime skills. Or are we looking at the subject with the wrong type of binoculars?

Perhaps it is wise to formulate the question differently. Maybe we should look first at what kind of maritime activities developed in a certain region and for what reason people participated in these activities? This approach forces us first to draw up an inventory of the various branches of shipping. If it is possible to characterise the special features of a branch of shipping, it might provide more clues on the maritime labour market and the people involved. Coastal fishing for the local

---

[12]Christian Pfister-Langanay, "Gravelines and the Transformation of Its Maritime Life, 1825-1855," in L.R. Fischer, *et al.* (eds.), *The North Sea. Twelve Essays on Social History of Maritime Labour* (Stavanger, 1992), 99-107.

market can be a means of subsistence for one or a whole range of villages in a particular region. Local and regional ties are strong, migratory push and pull factors mean little in the "manning system." Due to the character of the trade itself, the community engaged in this type of fishing is rather introverted. Due also to the control of the necessary skills and techniques for sailing and fishing, the maritime labour force originates from nearby, shows little social mobility and change, and mostly sticks to its trade for generations.

If the type of shipping is less tied to the coast, and shipping has less to do with earning one's daily bread from the sea itself, one might expect different people aboard. These sailors are tied to the ship in a more abstract economic way. They have vital interests in the ship, the ship's company and successful journeys from port to port. It is the money, the wages – not the fish – in which they are interested. They are the "working men who get wet."

The third type of shipping that needs a specific type of sailor is the "martial" branch of sailing: the navy in the first place, but also companies, such as the East India companies, that literally fought their way into long-distance trade. Here the driving force first and foremost might have been the romance of the sea. In this branch of shipping purely economic reasons played a lesser role than in the other two categories. Apart from the dangers of the sea, these sailors took an extra, though calculated, risk. Each of these three global types of shipping had its own specific recruitment patterns, which were influenced by all the specific factors mentioned above: demographic, geographic, economic, social and political.

To the sailor/fisherman the adage "*navigare necesse*" applies. To the sailor/working man, this relation with shipping was less existential: "*navigare necesse*, but not every day, and only as long as it pays." To the sailor/soldier it might have sounded like "*navigare necesse*, as long as the commanding officer says so."

# The International Maritime Labour Market (Sixteenth-Nineteenth Centuries)

Jan Lucassen

## General Characteristics

On early modern European vessels, sailors were the largest single group. In comparison others, such as merchants, soldiers, and craftsmen, were minorities.[1] Before the large-scale introduction of steam, sailors or rowers could be recruited in four different ways: we distinguish between local recruitment and enlistment from elsewhere, and between forced and voluntary recruitment (see figure 1). Most fundamental is the distinction between free and unfree recruitment. Unfree deployment on ships is difficult to realise, except on galleys where the rowers are chained to their benches. Originally, such vessels, mainly men-of-war, were used only occasionally in northern waters – by the Spaniards and the Dutch during the Dutch Revolt, for instance – but as a rule they were confined to the calmer waters of the Mediterranean during spring and summer.[2] Whereas in Antiquity and the Middle Ages galleys were rowed by free men, increasingly during the sixteenth century convicts and even slaves (procured by privateers) were used in the big Ottoman, Venetian and French fleets.[3] In France, 60,000 convicts were sent to the galleys

[1]In this introduction these groups will be dealt with only in passing.

[2]Jaap R. Bruijn, *The Dutch Navy of the Seventeenth and Eighteenth Centuries* (Columbia, SC, 1993), 22 and 35; and J. van Beylen, "Scheepstypen," *Maritieme geschiedenis der Nederlanden*, II (1977), 11-77, especially 20-23.

[3]For Venice and the Ottoman Empire, see Frederick C. Lane, *Venice: A Maritime Republic* (Baltimore, 1973), 364-379, 414-415; and B. Pullan (ed.), *Crisis and Change in the Venetian Economy in the Sixteenth and Seventeenth Centuries* (London, 1968), 152-153. For France, see the work of André Zysberg: "Les galères de France sous le regne de Louis XIV: Essai de compotabilité globale," in Martine Acerra, *et al.* (eds.), *Les marines de guerre européennes XVII-XVIIIe siècles* (Paris, 1985), 402-436; *Les galériens. Vies et destins de 60000 forcats sur les galères de France 1680-1748* (Paris,

between 1680 and 1745. In the eighteenth century sailing ships became the sole type in the Mediterranean and so did the free-born sailor.

**Figure 1**
**Modes of Recruitment for Sea-Going Ships in Europe, Sixteen-Eighteenth Centuries**

| | locally | from elsewhere | |
|---|---|---|---|
| | | nationally | internationally |
| free | fishermen and small merchant vessels | Scandinavia<br>Germany<br>Britain<br>France, Spain, Portugal (part) | Holland<br>Venice (part)<br>Turkey (part) |
| unfree | - | Britain (press)<br>France, Spain (galleys)<br>Russia (lifelong conscription for galleys) | Venice (galleys)<br>Turkey (galleys)<br>Portugal (part) |

*Source*: See text.

The eighteenth century was also distinguished by the demise of the Mediterranean galley and the surge of the oared warship in the Baltic, mainly in Russia, Sweden, and Denmark. Whereas all these nations resorted to conscription, only the Swedish and Danish systems can be characterised as free, while the Russian was definitely unfree. The main reason for this distinction is that the Russians drafted their recruits both for the army and the navy from among their serf population, for life-long service between 1702 and 1793, and between 1793 and 1834 for a twenty-five year period, which in practice meant the same thing. Only in 1834, when the draft was restricted to a *de facto* twelve-year period

1987); and "Le temps des galères (1481-1748)," in Jacques-Guy Petit, *et al.* (eds.), *Histoire des galères, bagnes et prisons XIIIe-XXe siècles* (Paris, 1991), 79-106. For Spain I only found information on the eighteenth century, when the system was no longer important, in Rolf Mühlmann, *Die Reorganisation der spanischen Kriegsmarine im XVIIIe Jahrhundert* (Köln, 1975), especially 39-40 and 126.

(in 1855 this was cut to ten and in 1874 to seven years), can one begin to speak of free labour recruitment.[4] On sailing ships it was possible to use forced labour normally only for one voyage or campaign, such as when Britain introduced the press-gang during wartime emergencies.[5]

Thus, the maritime labour market of the Atlantic (except for Portugal), the North Sea and the Baltic (except Russia) was free; the main distinctions were related to the distance between the sailor's home and the place of embarkation or the domicile of the master.[6] Only fishermen and crews of small coasters did both places usually coincide, while on seagoing craft migratory seamen were common.

In general, three types of migration may be discerned for labourers, including seamen.[7] First, labourers may migrate seasonally (seasonal or circular migration). Most are adult men, who abandon their home for weeks or months (leaving their wives and children to take care of the peasant farm); this migratory labour is combined with various other sources of income, often including cottage industry. In such families, members are interlinked within the "work cycle." The best-known maritime example is whalers. This is true for all countries, except

---

[4]Jan Glete, "Sails and Oars. Warships and Navies in the Baltic during the 18th Century (1700-1815)," in Acerra, *et al.* (eds.), *Les marines de guerre*, 374, claims that the Russians also sent convicts to their galleys. See also Jean Meyer, "Forces navales et puissances économiques," in Paul Adam (ed.), *Seamen in Society* (3 vols., Paris, 1980), II, especially 75-76. Before 1700 Russia also had free recruitment of sailors, both around the White Sea (where serfdom was unknown) and for the galleys on the Sea of Asov and the Black Sea, where free cossacks pulled the oars. Until 1718 foreign (free) sailors also served in the Russian navy. I am grateful to my IISH colleague in Moscow, Irina Novicenko, for this information.

[5]Christopher Lloyd, *The British Seaman, 1200-1860. A Social Survey* (London, 1968).

[6]Jan Lucassen, "Labour and Early Modern Economic Development," in K. Davids and J. Lucassen (eds.), *A Miracle Mirrored: The Dutch Republic in European Perspective* (Cambridge, 1996), 367-409. In the sixteenth century, and probably later, Portuguese naval gunners were recruited from conscripts (*vintaneiros*), Moorish prisoners and men condemned to the galleys. I am grateful to Robert Rowland for this information.

[7]For these distinctions, see J. Lucassen, "The Netherlands, the Dutch and Long-Distance Migration, in the Late Sixteenth to Early Nineteenth Centuries," in N. Canny (ed.), *Europeans on the Move: Studies on European Migration, 1500-1800* (Oxford, 1994), 153-191.

for Scotland where sailors for the whaling fleet were recruited locally.[8] In the sixteenth and early seventeenth centuries, Basque harpooners manned French, English and Dutch ships. After the French in 1643 prohibited Basques from joining Dutch ships, North Frisians took over and nearly monopolized Dutch, North German and Danish whalers.[9] A second type of migration covers several years. This "labour migration" is restricted mainly to young adults, still unmarried but independent of their parents; examples include tramping artisans, servants, soldiers and sailors. In the Dutch Republic, this was the dominant seafaring group. The third type is the immigrant, who has permanent settlement as the objective. Depending on which borders are crossed, we may speak of internal, international or intercontinental migration. As well, we can distinguish between able-bodied seamen changing domicile before or after service on foreign ships (such as a Hamburg sailor migrating permanently to Amsterdam in order to enrol there, or staying there after disembarkation) and the permanent immigrant (men who decide to enrol on the spur of the moment or who deciding to stay in Amsterdam forever after disembarkation). Of course, it is hard to differentiate such men clearly from temporal migrants. Even if sailors marry in a foreign port from which they used to sail, it is by no means certain that they were true permanent immigrants. In this respect it is important to note that the decision to enrol as a sailor can have not only a preconceived but also a concealed objective, such as inexpensive emigration. Many examples of this are known, especially from Europe to America. Both economic and religious factors can cause emigrants to choose this difficult path, such as Spaniards who could not prove that they were fully Catholic by birth.[10]

---

[8]See the contribution by Gordon Jackson to this volume, esp. table 4 ("Greenland").

[9]See several contributions to this volume.

[10]For Norwegians in Amsterdam, see Sølvi Sogner, *Ung i Europa. Norsk ungdom over Nordsjøen til Nederland i tidlig nytid* (Oslo, 1994); Sogner, "Young in Europe around 1700: Norwegian Sailors and Servant-Girls Seeking Employment in Amsterdam," in J.P. Bardet, *et al.* (eds.), *Mesurer et comprendre. Mélanges offerts à Jacques Dupâquier* (Paris, 1993), 515-532; and Sogner, "Popular Contacts between Norway and the Netherlands in the Early Modern Period," in Juliette Roding and Lex Heerma van Voss (eds.), *The North Sea and Culture (1550-1800)* (Hilversum, 1996), 185-198. More generally, see Auke Pieter Jacobs, *Los moviementos migratorios entre Castilla e Hispanoamerica durante el reinado de Felipe III, 1598-1621* (Amsterdam, 1995), 111-120; and the contributions to this volume on England and Scandinavia.

**Table 1**
**Annual Number of Seamen Employed in Selective West European Countries (000 Sailors)**

| | DEN | FRA | SPA | POR | ENG | NET | BEL | GER | NOR | SWE |
|---|---|---|---|---|---|---|---|---|---|---|
| 1550 | | | | 1? | | | 1 | 6 | | |
| | | | | | | | | | | 4 |
| 1575 | | | | | | | | | | |
| | | | | | 16 | | | | | |
| 1600 | | | | 1? | | | 1 | 10 | | |
| | | | | | | 33 | | | | |
| 1625 | | | 30 | | | | 2.5 | | | 3.5 |
| | | | | | | 46 | | | | 5 |
| 1650 | | | | 2? | | | | | | |
| | | 40 | | | | | | | | 6 |
| 1675 | | | | | | | | 10 | | 9 |
| | | | | | 55 | 50 | | 3# | | 5.5 |
| 1700 | | >43 | 40 | 3? | | | | | 7 | 15 |
| 1725 | | | | | | 50 | 1 | | | |
| | | | 40 | | | | | | | |
| 1750 | 10? | | | 4? | 70 | | | | | |
| | | | | | | | | 2.7# | | |
| 1775 | | | | | 70 | 45 | | | | |
| | | >55 | | | | | | | | 16 |
| 1800 | | | | 3? | 95 | | | 3.4# | 14 | |
| 1825 | | | | | | 24 | | 1.5# | | 9 |
| | | | | | | | 1.7 | | | |
| 1850 | | | | | 135* | | | | | 9 |
| | | | | | | 35 | | 3# | | |
| 1875 | | | | | 80* | 20 | | | | |

*Notes*: * excluding steam; # Germany North Sea coast only, according to Michael North, *this volume*, whose figures are low compared with those in Jürgen Brockstedt, "Wirtschaftlicher Aufstieg und soziale Mobilität in deutschen Seefahrtregionen vom 17. bis 19. Jahrhundert. Probleme einer partiellen und abgebrochenen Modernisierung," in Jürgen Bergmann, *et al.* (eds.), *Arbeit, Mobilität, Partizipation, Protest. Gesellschaftlicher Wandel in Deutschland im 19. und 20. Jahrhundert* (Opladen, 1986), 99-158. Portugal: Departures to the East by Africa and Brazil 400-ton and larger vessels until 1630; 600-ton craft thereafter

*Sources*: V. Magelães Godinho, "The Portuguese and the 'Carreira da India,' 1497-1810," in Jaap R. Bruijn and Femme S. Gaastra (eds.), *Ships, Sailors and Spices. East India Companies and Their Shipping in the 16th, 17th and 18th Centuries* (Amsterdam, 1993), 1-47; Walther Vogel, "Zur Grösse der europäischen Handelsflotten im 15., 16. und 17. Jahrhundert. Ein historisch-statistischer Versuch," in *Forschungen und Versuche zur Geschichte des Mittelalters und der Neuzeit. Festschrift Dietrich Schäfer zum siebzigsten Geburtstag dargebracht von seinen Schülern* (Jena, 1915), esp. 280 and 301; J. Lucassen, "Zeevarenden," in L.M. Akveld, S. Hart and W.J. van Hoboken, *Maritieme geschiedenis der Nederlanden* II (1977), 126-158; Jan Glete, Personal communication to J.R. Bruijn, 17 October 1996; and contributions to this volume.

In Europe three periods can be discerned in long-distance migration history between the sixteenth and nineteenth centuries. First, there was a sharp increase in the sixteenth and early seventeenth century; second, there was a slump in the second half of the seventeenth and into the eighteenth century; and finally, there was a rapid rise in the nineteenth century.[11] This periodization was reflected to a great extent in the development of international labour markets for seamen. Moreover, maritime labour markets in western Europe exhibited great differences in magnitude.[12] It is clear from figure 2 that Scandinavia, the German states, Scotland, Ireland, the Southern Netherlands and Portugal used few sailors compared to Holland, England, France and Spain.[13]

On a European level, we should also include in the latter group some Mediterranean nations, like Venice and the Ottoman Empire, as well as Russia from the eighteenth century. In Russia the great majority of sailors were employed by the navy (in 1790 not substantially weaker than the French, then second after the British).[14] Venice and the Ottoman Empire depended heavily on a few Balkan peoples, especially Greeks. Apart from serving in the navies of the great regional powers, it is estimated that in the second half of the eighteenth century there were 615 Greek merchant ships, employing more than 37,000 men.[15]

---

[11]Jan Lucassen and Leo Lucassen, "Introduction," in J. Lucassen and L. Lucassen (eds.), *Migrations, Migration History, History: Old Paradigms and New Perspectives* (Bern, 1997), 9-38.

[12]Although these estimates have many deficiencies, they nevertheless have already a long tradition. See, for example, Walther Vogel, "Zur Grösse der europäischen Handelsflotten im 15., 16. und 17. Jahrhundert. Ein historisch-statistischer Versuch," in *Forschungen und Versuche zur Geschichte des Mittelalters und der Neuzeit. Festschrift Dietrich Schäfer zum siebzigsten Geburtstag dargebracht von seinen Schülern* (Jena, 1915), 268-333; and Meyer, "Forces navales," 82-83. These scholars, however, provide different figures for navies in 1790 than does Bruijn, *Dutch Navy*, 148.

[13]This is not to say, of course, that the number of sailors relative to a country's total population cannot be considerable. Compare, for example, the 12,300 crew in the Norwegian merchant fleet in 1806 with the 880,000 inhabitants in the 1801 census. See Helge W. Nordvik and Jan Oldervoll, "Seafarer and Community in Norway: An Analysis Based on the 1801 Census," in Adam (ed.), *Seamen in Society*, III, 77-87.

[14]Bruijn, *Dutch Navy*, 148.

[15]Nikolai Todorov, *The Balkan City 1400-1900* (Seattle, 1983), 198-200 and 274-276.

The most important seagoing nations can be divided according to their recruitment policies into four groups: mixed systems of free and unfree labour (France, Portugal, Spain, Venice and other Mediterranean countries, at least until the abolition of the galleys); national recruitment of free labour (Scandinavia, Germany and Britain, but with press gangs in emergencies, and to a certain extent France and Spain after the galley period); national recruitment of unfree labour (Russia in the eighteenth and early nineteenth centuries); and international and national recruitment of free labour (Dutch Republic).

## National and International Maritime Labour Markets before 1750

In virtually no western European country before 1700 did the demand for sailors exceed 50,000 men. Only England passed this upper limit at the end of the seventeenth century. Demand in Spain, France and the Netherlands surpassed 30,000. Yet relative to their populations these four were very different. Large countries like France, with twenty million inhabitants in 1700, and medium-rank countries, like Great Britain (half the French total) and Spain (somewhat less) easily outnumbered the Dutch Republic, with about two million by the late seventeenth century. If for the sake of argument we assume that the male working population in all these countries was one-quarter of the total population, this would mean that sailors represented less than one percent in France, roughly two percent in Spain and England, but ten percent in the Dutch Republic.[16] No wonder Dutch skippers were hardly able to recruit their manpower locally or nationally. One could put it slightly differently by saying that Dutch port towns had much less of a national hinterland than their Spanish, French or English cousins. On the other hand, they had enough of a hinterland in the German states, the Southern Netherlands, and elsewhere; it is to these places that they looked for supply. But sheer demand is not enough: favourable wage differentials are necessary as well in order to set migration streams in motion.

Due to the rapid economic development since the late sixteenth century, wages and prices in Holland rose quickly. In the sixteenth

---

[16]Because of the substantially higher immigration of labour to the Dutch Republic compared to the other countries mentioned (see Lucassen, "The Netherlands," and Lucassen, "Labour"), the Dutch percentage was actually below ten percent, but still very likely four times the rates of Spain and Britain.

century wages in Antwerp were still between twenty-five and fifty percent higher than in Amsterdam, but some decades later the roles were reversed and Amsterdam wages surpassed those in Antwerp by twenty percent.[17] The same happened *vis-à-vis* war-stricken Germany. The Dutch maritime labour market, however, was not uniform, but rather highly segmented by destination and duration of voyage. As a rule, the longer the voyage, the lower the payment, the worse the labour conditions, the bigger the risks (especially to health), and the more foreigners on board. These characteristics are based on two fundamental principles: positive discrimination toward kin and neighbours on small vessels and the fact that the bigger the wage differentials, the more prospective sailors were prepared to take big risks.

To a certain extent, these rules can be applied to the Dutch labour market in general during the Golden Age, which in the western core regions depended on immigrants for roughly half its supply.[18] Artisans and common labourers, as well as most servants (generally female), were recruited from an area within a radius of 500 kilometres. Soldiers, often earning as much as the most poorly-paid sailors (those in the navy and the Dutch East India Company), were recruited from as far away as Scotland and Switzerland. No wonder immigrants who arrived from even farther away, like Huguenots, and Sephardic and Ashkenazi Jews, were forced to take more than mere economic risks. As in other countries, Dutch coasters and fishing craft recruited virtually all its crew locally. In contrast, substantial numbers of foreigners served on long-distance ships. Although we lack data for the seventeenth century, on the basis of eighteenth-century figures we can make some estimates.[19]

According to the estimates by Paul van Royen and several other scholars for the first decade of the eighteenth century, between twenty and twenty-five percent of the sailors in the Dutch merchant marine were foreign, mainly on craft trade trading between Archangel in the North and Portugal in the South.[20] Aboard ships bound for the Mediterranean

---

[17]Lucassen, "Labour," 372.

[18]*Ibid.*; and Lucassen, "The Netherlands."

[19]Lucassen, "The Netherlands," 167-169.

[20]P.C. van Royen, *Zeevarenden op de koopvaardijvloot omstreeks 1700* (Amsterdam, 1987), especially 183-184.

and in the triangular trade between Europe, West Africa and the Caribbean, the rate was between thirty and forty percent. The largest foreign component was on Dutch East Indiamen (nearly half); the navy (in the eighteenth century even more than half); and in the whaling fleet. For whalers, it has estimated that eighteenth-century crews may have been two-thirds foreign, mostly from the North Frisian Islands.[21]

The high dependence of the Dutch on foreign labour led to the emergence of the first truly international labour market for sailors in northwestern Europe, preceded only by Venetian recruitment in the eastern Mediterranean. But the Venetians, because of the powerful competition from their Ottoman neighbours, could not afford to depend on free labour recruitment alone. All other labour markets for sailors in the era were still national or even local, outside of Portugal with its imported slave labour. There we can speak of a market, albeit of goods rather than labour, although the goods were alive in this case.

## National and International Maritime Labour Markets, 1750-1870

The dominant economic position of the Netherlands did not last, although the decline was relative rather than absolute and was not as rapid as is often suggested. If we follow the line from Venice, with its international recruitment of free and unfree labour, through the Dutch Republic, with its international recruitment of free labour, the question arises how the next leading nation, Britain, was to solve its recruitment problems.

Perhaps unexpectedly, the new leader solved this problem differently. Although during the eighteenth century its increasing demand for sailors (seventy-five percent) outgrew its population increase (some twenty percent) by a large measure, it still did not reach Dutch levels of the preceding century. According to our rough estimation model, sailors may have represented between three and four percent of the British labour market during the Napoleonic Wars. During the first half of the nineteenth century this share diminished again: Britain's population nearly doubled, whereas the number of sailors increased by only forty percent. Although the pressure to look for sailors was not as severe in Britain, this is not to say that recruitment was only national.

---

[21] C. de Jong, *Geschiedenis van de oude Nederlandse walvisvaart. I: Grondslagen, ontstaan en opkomst 1612-1642* (Pretoria, 1972), 81; and Brockstedt, "Wirtschaftlicher Aufstieg."

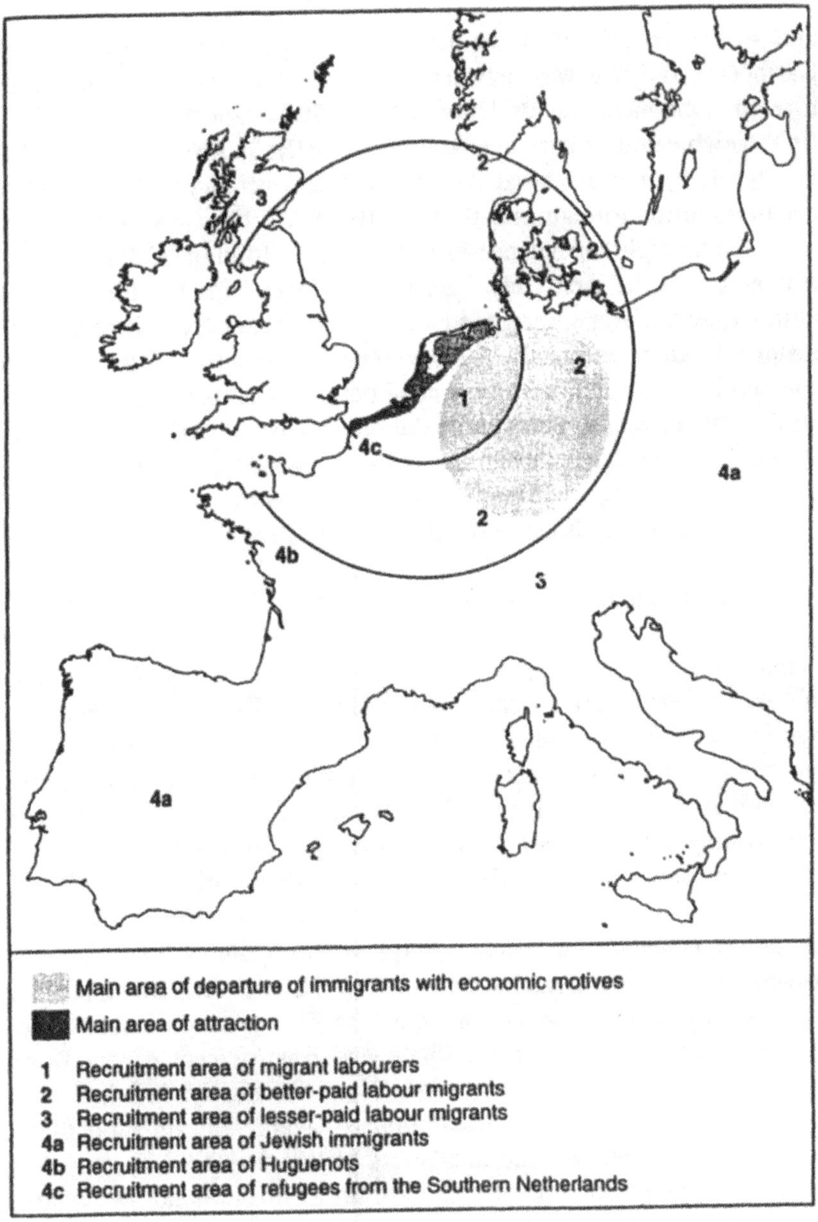


*Figure 1*: Resources for the Dutch Labour Market, Seventeenth to Nineteenth Centuries.

*Source*: Courtesy of the author.

To understand this last point, we need briefly to examine British migration history during the seventeenth and eighteenth centuries. Unlike the Netherlands, Britain experienced emigration. Again contrary to the Dutch experience, it was hardly integrated within a North Sea system.[22] Even before the rapid growth of English shipping in the seventeenth century, England was exporting people to Ireland, and later to the Caribbean and North America. According to E.A Wrigley and R.S. Schofield, net out-migration increased from about 250,000 in the second half of the sixteenth century, to 350,000 in the next half century and 365,000 in the second half of the seventeenth century, before dropping to 265,000 and 255,000 in the first and second halves of the eighteenth century. Net out-migration continued in the nineteenth century, as they did for Scotland, to the advantage of the expanding overseas lands.[23]

Although intensive migrations occurred between Scotland and Scandinavia and the Baltic in the seventeenth century, England sent its masses westwards and southwards and hardly received any migrants from the continent. The internationalisation of the Danish labour market in the eighteenth century did not compensate for developments in Britain.[24]

The conclusion is clear. While Britain's demand for sailors could normally be met domestically, this was impossible during wars. Because foreign labour could not easily enter the British labour market, there was no well-trodden path for recruiters in emergencies. Impressment, even of foreign sailors by chance in British harbours, was thus the only solution. In the later years of the Napoleonic wars, twenty-five percent of sailors in the navy had been recruited voluntarily, compared with seventy-five percent by compulsory methods. The percentage of forced recruits was about fifteen percent foreign and sixty percent British. Earlier in the war, the relationship may have been fifty-fifty.[25]

---

[22]For the argument that follows, see Jan Lucassen, "The North Sea: A Crossroad for Migrants?" in Roding and Heerma van Voss (eds.), *North Sea and Culture*, 168-184.

[23]E.A. Wrigley and R.S. Schofield, *The Population History of England, 1541-1871: A Reconstruction* (London, 1981), 221 and 227. In my own work, I have pointed to differences between these reconstructions and the results of recent migration history. The overall trend, however, may be correct.

[24]Lucassen, "The North Sea."

[25]Lloyd, *British Seaman*, 196.

In normal times, Britain did not have to rely on foreigners and thus had no reason to stimulate an international labour market for sailors. On the contrary, the employment of foreign mariners was officially banned until 1850, and Britain adopted a policy to build a "national nursery" after the French and Danish examples. While foreigners were eager to join British ships, it was mainly to emigrate cheaply to the US. These short-term sailors came in particular from Scandinavia.[26] This hidden emigration made the British maritime labour market look more international than the eight-percent share until the 1880s suggests.[27]

At the end of the sailing era, a different type of internationalisation of the maritime labour market began, originating in the US and Asia. Increasing global demand for sailors, enhanced by imperialism and intensified colonisation, caused shifts in the supply structure. Consistent with what we have seen about British emigration are estimates of between 60,000 and 100,000 British seamen employed in the US. An increasing proportion no longer sailed within Europe or between Europe and elsewhere, but rather stayed in the Pacific, Indian Ocean or the South Atlantic. An example, of course, was the coolie trade.[28]

Early initiatives of the Dutch East India Company to employ Chinese and Lascar sailors in the intra-Asiatic trade, and from 1781 on fleets between Europe and Asia, were adopted also by other nations, in particular by Britain in the late nineteenth century.[29] But also more peripheral European nations supplied sailors for ships of the greater nations. The Greek census of 1879, for example, listed not only some

---

[26]See Lewis R. Fischer, "The Sea as Highway: Maritime Service as a Means of International Migration, 1863-1913," in Klaus Friedland (ed.), *Maritime Aspects of Migration* (Köln, 1989), 293-307.

[27]See Sarah Palmer and David M. Williams, "British Sailors 1775-1870," *this volume*.

[28]Kenneth McPherson, *et al.*, "The Social Expansion of the Maritime World of the Indian Ocean: Passenger Traffic and Community Building 1815-1939," in Friedland (ed.), *Maritime Aspects*, 427-440.

[29]J.R. Bruijn and J. Lucassen (eds.), *Op de schepen der Oost-Indische Compagnie. Vijf artikelen van J. de Hullu, ingeleid, bewerkt en voorzien van een studie over de werkgelegenheid bij de VOC* (Groningen, 1980), 22; and Palmer and Williams, "British Sailors."

16,000 seamen and 2000 naval seamen but also 5180 "seamen abroad."[30] Contrary to this employment of common sailors from other countries (including non-European areas), there was a movement of masters: during the Dutch Republic, Dutch skippers went to Danzig, and in the nineteenth century European mates worked on American vessels.

## The Emergence of International Labour Markets

The internationalisation of the European maritime labour market took place in three different phases.[31] The first phase took place in the heydays of first Venice and then the Dutch Republic. Both maritime powers depended, because of their small territories and high wages to a great extent on foreign labour. The second phase was marked by a stagnation or even possibly a decline in internationalisation. This took place when Britain took international maritime leadership; Britain recruited largely within its own borders, voluntarily in peacetime and by compulsion in times of war. In the third phase, which began at the dawn of the steam era, the labour market became more international, now on a world rather than a European scale. This is the epoch in which we are still living and which in the second half of the twentieth century is characterised by a decreasing share of ships owned in Europe, manned by crews mainly from the southern or eastern rim of Europe and even more from Africa and Asia, albeit still to a great extent commanded by European officers. Yet there are no direct links between the first and the third phase and, consequently, the development of an international and even global maritime labour market is not a linear process.[32]

---

[30]Todorov, *Balkan City*, 331. According to Gelina Harlaftis, *A History of Greek-Owned Shipping. The Making of an International Tramp Fleet, 1830 to the Present Day* (London, 1996), 170, in 1879 the estimated number of Greek seamen on Greek deep-sea vessels was 12,370. Thus, Todorov's figures should be used with caution.

[31]I consider this conclusion to be generally consistent with the outcome of the debate on the "efficiency" of maritime labour markets, which started with Charles P. Kindleberger, *Mariners and Markets* (New York, 1992) and was continued in Lewis R. Fischer (ed.), *The Market for Seamen in the Age of Sail* (St. John's, 1994); for a summary of the debate, see especially the introduction by Lewis R. Fischer.

[32]Julia Adams, "Trading States, Trading Places: The Role of Patrimonialism in Early Modern Dutch Development," *Comparative Studies in Society and History*, XXXVI (1994), 348-349; and Davids and Lucassen (eds.), *A Miracle Mirrored*, 450-453.

# Career Patterns

## Jaap R. Bruijn

Jens Jacob Eschels had a varied life at sea. His children, grandchildren and friends were interested in it, and in his old age he wrote his memoirs. Is Eschels' life also of interest to maritime historians who want to study labour patterns in the age of sail? The question will be answered in the affirmative in this essay.

Born in 1757 on the Northern Frisian island of Föhr – near Schleswig and ruled by the king of Denmark – Eschels went to sea at the age of eleven. Under the guidance of a seafaring uncle he was enroled in Amsterdam for the Dutch whaling fleet. Starting as a junior cabin boy, after seven consecutive whaling voyages Eschels in 1776 switched in Copenhagen to a Danish whaler, where the financial rewards were greater. Meanwhile he had become an able seaman who spent winters at home supporting his family. In 1778 he stopped whaling and turned to the mercantile marine, not returning home for more than a decade. He sailed from Amsterdam, and later from Hamburg and Altona. At the age of twenty-four he became a captain, when his own superior died during the voyage. Eschels sailed in European, Mediterranean and Caribbean waters. He married in 1784 and six years later, as a widower, he remarried and settled in Altona. In 1797 he left the sea and became a shopkeeper, a tobacco manufacturer and a consultant on shipping. He died in 1842, seven years after his memoirs were published.[1]

Eschels' life contains all the elements usually ascribed to a successful seaman: maritime background, early entry, promotion, various sorts of voyages, marriage and a further life ashore. But not every young lad met the same Dame Fortune. Still, Jens Jacob was not exceptional. Many seamen could have told similar stories, and several did.[2]

---

[1]Jens Jacob Eschels, *Lebensbeschreibung eines alten Seemannes* (Hamburg, 1995).

[2]Some Dutch examples from the same period include P.A. Liefhebber and J.P. Ambriola (eds.), *De avonturen van Dirk Kooger. Belevenissen van een Texels zeeman (1780-1847)* (Texel, 1979); J.R. Bruijn and E.S. van Eyck van Heslinga (eds.), *Maarten Schaap, een Katwijker ter koopvaardij (1782-1870). Een biografie en een dagboek* (Amsterdam, 1988); J. Klatter (ed.), *Een Groninger zeeman in Napoleontische tijd. Zee-*

In a quantitative sense it is impossible to gauge how typical Eschels was. There were tens of thousands of them. In the other chapters of this book one can find rough estimates for different countries. But figures about the seafaring labour force do not provide insight into the labour pattern of the individual seaman. The vast majority of these men remain anonymous for the maritime historian and remain obscured within the totality of a crew. Yet a contemporary could have known who was on board each vessel at its port of departure, for it was common international practice to register the names of those enroled. In every port city a public official was in charge of such registration. The navies, and in some cases the East India companies as well, kept their own records. Standard data on each enlisted man included name, rank, wage, place of origin and sometimes the age. The purpose of this registration in muster lists and payrolls is obvious. Moreover, it could be used by relatives of lost seamen who wanted to claim unpaid wages. The fate of Eschels' father, for instance, was traced in the Dutch East India company's books by his brother, who was also a seaman. Father Eschels, as it turned out, had not survived his voyage to Batavia in 1778.[3]

For historical research into the careers of seamen most of this information is no longer available. The records were often discarded after they had served their purpose, or they did not survive housekeeping by later authorities – a universal problem, it seems. Only parts or clusters of muster lists and payrolls, mainly from the eighteenth century onwards, are still extant. One can also discover seamen and information about their seafaring or private lives in notarial and orphanage records or in lawsuits. The mass of paperwork surrounding privateering and prize jurisdiction can also be a rewarding source, especially in Great Britain and France. When using this material one hopes to discern the patterns of seamen's lives. Some young man, however, died on board or in a foreign port, deserted, made only one voyage, or never got involved in a lawsuit. These men remain unknown. Research based on sources like these has become more common in recent years and has provided more insight into the labour patterns of seamen. Some results are

---

*en landreizen van K.J. Kuipers* (Zutphen, 1980); and J.A. van der Kooij (ed.), *Uit het leven van de zeeman. Dagboekfragmenten en reisverslagen uit de 18de en 19de eeuw* (Bussum, 1976).

[3]Eschels, *Lebensbeschreibung*, 179.

presented in the following chapters, but a few generalizations are offered in this introduction.

**A Young Man's Profession**

If we consider men below the age of thirty as young, then it is obvious that seafaring was a young man's profession. This is a fair conclusion, especially considering that the average marriage age in those days was often twenty-five or older. Two-thirds to three-quarters of the crew, excluding officers, were younger than thirty. At an age when it was common for most children to look for paid labour, boys of twelve or a few years more also went to sea. At a younger age it was as an unpaid apprentice to an officer or a close relative.[4] Entry at an older age could also happen, but usually it was then a second option after disappointment with a land occupation or it was connected with a desire to emigrate.

The sea was often the only choice possible. In many communities there was little if any alternative employment. In Norwegian coastal settlements, on Föhr or in Katwijk, a village amidst the dunes of Holland, it was a case of following the fathers' example. T.J.A. Le Goff states in his contribution that about half the French skilled seamen were the sons of seamen. In communities with options for agriculture or other manual work, the choice of the sea was often based upon family tradition. The lure of the sea also brought boys from other parts of a country to the coast and to seafaring. The sheer lack of alternatives often made the navy or an East India company the last resort for even the urban sector of the populace.

Most youths completed their apprenticeships or their years as ship's boy and became ordinary seamen. Then a division began to take place between those who learned some navigational skills or who got employed as assistants to petty officers like the sailmaker or the carpenter, and those who remained unskilled. The majority of the latter group sooner or later turned their backs on the sea and looked for unskilled posts ashore. The first group, however, remained loyal to the sea much longer, and its members were promoted to the ranks of petty officers and even captain. The navy was the exception. Eschels is a

[4]There is evidence in the following chapters, as well as in M. Rediker, *Between the Devil and the Deep Blue Sea. Merchant Seamen, Pirates, and the Anglo-American Maritime World, 1700-1750* (Cambridge, 1987), 300.

perfect example of this career pattern. He bought navigational instruments and books, and went to school during the winter.[5] Substantially more than half the officers and captains were older than thirty years. Captains were not necessarily older than their officers. Luck – something Eschels had – family tradition and the right relations could provide the first position on board even to men in their early twenties.

Those who reached the higher ranks retired from the sea at a later age than most of their unskilled colleagues. The reasons for their decision to return to life ashore were obvious: time for a change, a desire to start a family, sufficient savings or the possibility of good land occupation were among the leading ones.

The career pattern in the navies, however, differed on one essential point. The officer corps was, in general, not open to the rank and file. In most periods only sons of those who belonged to the upper classes would become cadets and join the ranks of officers.[6] The other opportunities for promotion were in principle the same as in the mercantile marine, whaling and the fisheries. The number of seamen on naval vessels, as well as on East Indiamen, was always many times greater than in any other trade. That has to be taken into account.

The apparent paradox in the image of nineteenth-century sailors as old tars commanding not only a complex assortment of skills but also as rascals and drunkards existed for previous centuries as well, at least for long-distance voyages.[7] But no authors or poets, as Kipling did around 1900, have evoked the image so eloquently. Still, many youngsters went to sea, but for most it was a brief phase. Eschels belonged to the skilled minority, a fact that makes his memoirs of great interest.

## Government Interference

The young boy who opted for the sea was free in his decision. Of course, the situation at home and in his community helped to shape the

---

[5]Eschels, *Lebensbeschreibung*, 58 and 73.

[6]See, for example, N.A.M. Rodger, *The Wooden World. An Anatomy of the Georgian Navy* (London, 1986); and J.R. Bruijn, *The Dutch Navy of the Seventeenth and Eighteenth Centuries* (Columbia, SC, 1993).

[7]This image has been further developed in Yrjö Kaukiainen's paper presented at the Second Congress of Maritime History, held in Amsterdam and Rotterdam in June 1996.

decision and the type of seafaring chosen. No government authority was involved. At a later stage, however, this could be different for two reasons. Absolute rulers wanted to ensure that their navies were adequately manned. And in time of war, even in liberal states, public leaders tried to compel seamen to serve in their enlarged fleets.

In the Nordic countries, the kings of Sweden and Denmark both introduced a registration of seamen or a sort of conscription. In 1634 the Swedish king introduced in the coastal districts registration for youths and adults. The districts were allotted quotas for the navy. In 1682 the system was improved. Finland, for instance, had to deliver 1200 to 2000 men during the sailing season, a figure later decreased to 600. In the Danish empire conscription forced a proportion of eighteen year-olds to serve in the navy. After 1674 one out of five Norwegian males did so.[8]

From the late sixteenth century onwards Spanish monarchs tried to get a grip on their seafarers through registration and various enticements. This process is described in more details in Carla Rahn Phillips' chapter. Louis XIV of France and his minister Colbert imposed their regime of naval conscription with the "système des classes," the different categories of seamen. The conscription registers have now become a magnificent source for maritime historians.

The Dutch Republic and Britain were not familiar with such registration on behalf of their navies. But their authorities could interfere with the labour patterns of their sea-going compatriots in time of war. The system of impressment in Britain is well-known. It could have long-lasting effects on one's career. Dutch interference was only indirect and short-lived. If a shortage of naval manpower was feared, a spring embargo was imposed on nearly all other seafaring. A seaman looking for an immediate post was thus forced to opt for naval service, but he could also wait until the embargo was lifted, always before the end of summer. Moreover, the merchant and whaling fleets were regularly permitted to sail after the shipowners had delivered their so-called fifth man or had paid the equivalent in cash. Hence, the impact of war via coercion upon a seaman's career was only slight in the Netherlands.

---

[8]J. Glete, "Sails and Oars. Warships and Navies in the Baltic during the 18th Century (1700-1815)," in M. Acerra, *et al.* (eds.), *Les marines de guerre européennes XVII-XVIIIe siècles* (Paris, 1985), 369-401; and O. Rian, "State and Society in Seventeenth-Century Norway," *Scandinavian Journal of History*, X (1985), especially 350-352.

The establishment of standing navies with a permanent labour force in all ranks and a requirement of some special education for naval service took place during the transition from sail to steam. That was a mid-nineteenth century development, which evened out the opportunities for western seamen to have a free choice of labour. No state would then interfere with pressure or force on behalf of its navy.

## Horizontal Mobility Between the Different Seafaring Trades

It goes without saying that as a result of state regulations many seamen – except those in the Netherlands and northern Germany – spent some time in naval service, at least from the late sixteenth century until the end of the Napoleonic era. Given the British Royal Navy's high and regularly changing demand for manpower, seamen in Britain in particular must have been frequently and often involuntarily on warships. The mercantile world always had to reckon with that. This movement or transfer was temporary, and did not recur after 1815.

Not much is known as yet about the mobility of seamen between the various branches of shipping. But some positive remarks in the chapters of this book suggest that seamen were often loyal to their trade and their ships. An example of loyalty to naval service is the so-called "Holmens faste stok," a permanent corps of naval personnel, established in 1615. Its members served at sea and in the naval dockyard, and they had their private homes in a special district of Copenhagen. When reaching the age of retirement, these men received a naval pension. An Icelandic fisherman had no other options; he could rarely consider fishing his main occupation. Livestock raising was a typical priority well into the nineteenth century.

Some authors point to a change in the labour pattern at sea that was related to the age of the mariner. After some time young lads would have preferred deep-water voyages. As they grew older these men transferred to shorter trips near their home ports. This distinction is perhaps more valid for the nineteenth century than for the earlier period, for Dutch evidence from around 1700 does not corroborate this kind of mobility. Dutch merchant seamen and whalers almost never joined the navy or the Dutch East India Company. Instead, these seamen and whalers stuck to their familiar routes in European waters and the Arctic. They might change their master or sail to the Baltic instead of Archangel or Lisbon. An occasional switch to whaling was also a likely option.[9] An important cause of mobility was pay. Wages in the mercantile marine and whaling were the top and the risks to life often minimal. Another typical Dutch feature was the separation between seamen from seafaring communities and those from the casual labour market. The lack of any recruitment system in the navy and the massive demand for manpower from the East India company were important in this respect.

A type of mobility not yet mentioned was the transfer of seafarers between ships of different nationalities. This was a phenomenon most common among Scandinavians, Germans and Italians. Once again Eschels is a good example: he sailed on Dutch, Danish and Hamburg vessels. But many English and Dutch mariners sailed under foreign flags, and several instances are cited in this book. In the Dutch case, mostly skilled persons left their homes for one specific job abroad. They did not leave at random. A number of merchant captains, sometimes accompanied by the core of their crew, migrated to a neutral country when the Republic was at war. This occurred during the Nine Years' War (1689-1697), for example, and a recent study found sixty-five Dutch masters on Danzig and ninety-four on Stockholm registers.[10]

## Upward Mobility

It is generally assumed that life ashore offered fewer opportunities for upward mobility or promotion than at sea. This assumption has to be restricted to those men who managed to acquire skills in demand on ships. As a petty officer or officer a man would earn wages and extra remuneration often not available to skilled artisans on land.

The better chances for promotion implied the occurrence of vacancies. Work at sea could be risky: fatal accidents could happen and diseases claimed their victims. Certain types of shipping were more prone to infectious diseases than others. The West Indies had a particularly bad reputation, as did the Asian trades in the seventeenth and

---

[9]P.A. Boon, *Bouwers van de zee. Scheepvaart op het Westfriese platteland, c. 1680-1720* (The Hague, 1996); and P.C. van Royen, *Zeevarenden op de koopvaardijvloot omstreeks 1700* (Amsterdam, 1987). See also Karel Davids' contribution to this volume.

[10]T. Ufkes, "Nederlandse schippers op Danziger en Stockholmse handelsschepen, 1670-1700," *Tijdschrift voor Zeegeschiedenis*, XV (1996), 25-57.

eighteenth centuries. Rising several grades in the shipboard hierarchy was not exceptional for a good seaman. Dangerous whaling voyages could also provide unexpected promotions.

Apart from the hazards of shipboard work and life, war was another factor. One author remarks that war could even "rejuvenate" the stock of seamen in naval and mercantile seafaring.[11] Impressment in Britain brought landfolk involuntarily in contact with sea; a number of them stayed when the conflict was over. Naval wars were frequent in the seventeenth as well as the eighteenth century.

For a long time a seaman's education consisted of practical training at sea and attendance at local private schools during the winter. In some countries, such as Scotland, local authorities appointed teachers of navigation around 1700. Huge organisations like the East India companies tested the knowledge of their mates before the departure of their vessels. Naval authorities required certain levels of experience before their cadets and lieutenants were promoted. It took a long time, however, before the Dutch navy created a form of institutionalized education for its officers. The first school was founded at Amsterdam in 1749, in cooperation with the East India Company, and it lasted well into the nineteenth century. Then the state created systems of examinations for masters and mates in the merchant marine. Certificates were also introduced. In the fisheries these requirements were adopted at an even later date.

Seafaring was an international business. Crews of most vessels were composed of a mixture of nationalities, in France and Spain as well in Britain and Denmark. In some countries the state stipulated that the number of foreigners had to remain below a certain level. Spain was perhaps the first country to do so in 1568. Such limits, expressed as a percentage of total crew size, were soon forgotten in wartime. Some authors doubt whether the apparently indispensable foreign mariners had equal opportunities to get promoted. In the lower ranks there was little discrimination, but how open were the positions of officers and captains to foreigners? One is inclined to assume that the situation began to change in the eighteenth century. Prior to this, abundant examples show that foreigners were not disbarred from the higher ranks. The unstable boundaries in the Habsburg and Bourbon empires, and in the Baltic, made the distinction between compatriots and aliens rather vague. Navies

---

[11]See T.G.A. Le Goff's contribution to this volume.

closed their officer ranks first. A Danish naval officer in the eighteenth century was of Danish birth, for instance. The last resort for a foreign seaman with officer's ambitions was probably Dutch shipping, which so permanently and heavily relied on an influx of people from abroad.

**Life after Sailing**

Seafaring was mainly a young men's profession, as we have seen. Sarah Palmer and David Williams suggest that ten years was a fair average in the mid-nineteenth century British merchant fleet. The so-called "old tars" hung on and occupied the higher positions, but if they survived, these people also settled ashore. It is impossible to trace them as a group. In individual cases their whereabouts and occupations can sometimes be followed. Eschels is just one such case. Nonetheless, for certain seafaring communities research on a higher level than the individual has now been done.[12]

Family life was more common for seamen than generally assumed. Many mariners married in their twenties and were not among the dissolute group that spent much of their wages in taverns and brothels. How deeply they could care about their own lives and that of their families is illustrated by the numerous seamen's boxes in the Netherlands. Membership in this mutual insurance arrangement was not restricted to masters and mates, but was also open to the ordinary seaman. The later shipmasters' societies, however, were aimed at one specific category of seaman.[13]

By and large, insurance was probably rather unknown among seafarers. After an accident resulting in the loss of one or more bodily functions, a mariner had to rely on the charity of his shipowner or his local community. In most navies it became the practice that lasting mutilation caused by naval service was compensated by an allowance in the form of a lump sum or payment of small monthly or weekly instalments. In Spain, France, Denmark and Sweden, some benefits were available. The age of retirement from the Spanish navy was set at sixty.

In the last stage of his life ashore an old tar was not any different from a landlubber. He had to live on his savings, rely on his family or

---

[12]See Boon, *Bouwers van de zee*.

[13]See Davids' essay in this volume.

seek support from charities. In the age of sail hardly any pension or allowance was available. Even a well-off master could run into trouble. Maarten Schaap, for instance, almost did. After forty-six years at sea, this inhabitant of the little maritime community of Katwijk retired in 1841 at the age of fifty-nine. He had been in command of the largest vessels plying to the Dutch East Indies, and had very carefully saved and invested his earnings. He could not expect to live another twenty-nine years, or to be rather unlucky with his investments. At his death in 1870, he owned only his little house and a few small bonds, the interest from which was his sole source of income.[14]

---

[14]Bruijn and Van Eyck van Heslinga (eds.), *Maarten Schaap*, 45-54.

# Labour Conditions

Femme Gaastra

There can be no doubt that labour conditions for sailors during the age of sail in the sixteenth to the nineteenth centuries were characterized by great variations. There were differences in time, between or even within countries or regions, and according to the categories of shipping. It made a great difference if a sailor joined the navy, a merchant vessel, or a fisherman craft.

The working skills needed to handle a sailing vessel, whatever its size or trade, were basically the same, which made it in principle possible for sailors to move from trade to trade. Only when more specialized skills were needed in, for example, fishing, whaling or fighting, was it difficult to make such a switch. In practice, however, sailors seem to have been more traditional and were inclined to stay in a certain type of trade. It has been suggested that the labour market for sailors was imperfect and that a segmentation in markets or recruitment patterns along regional lines more or less "dictated" the trade in which a sailor would end up. But it might well be that individual choices made by newcomers on the labour market were in the first instance influenced by labour conditions – not only the material gain that was to be expected but also the non-material side.

## Wage-Earning Proletarians?

It was already common in Europe by the seventeenth century to pay sailors in money, either in monthly wages or fixed rates for a certain voyage. Because of this dependence on wages, Marcus Rediker called seamen one of the first groups of collective labourers:

> In historical terms the collective laborer did not possess traditional craft skills, did not own any means of production, such as land or tools (and therefore depended completely upon wages), and labored among a large number of like-situated people.

In short, the sailor was the exemplification of the "proletarian of the period of manufacture."[1]

But even if we accept Rediker's ideas about the wage-earning seamen, we must admit that his picture is not complete. It may have been true for sailors in deep-sea trades, for those serving in the large chartered companies or perhaps even the navy. These sailors were recruited in port cities and they can indeed be called proletarians. But for those far removed from the centres of economic activity or in the coastal trades, the situation was different. The Finnish "peasant ships," as mentioned in Yrjö Kaukiainen's contribution to this volume, were only manned by three or four men, often ordinary farm hands; these men represented another, perhaps more traditional, type of worker.

In other branches of the maritime sector sailors were paid for their service, but often only for a short period or during a certain season. Their income did not come wholly from maritime work. Instead, they earned income from a plurality of sources, some of which might be maritime or even agricultural. Such combinations of two or more sources of income were still dominant among seafarers in the countryside of West Friesland, for instance, in the early eighteenth century.[2]

There are other factors as well that cast doubts upon whether the concept of "collective worker" can be applied to all sailors. A regular wage according to fixed standards has been traditional in deep-sea shipping and in the navy, but in other trades, like the fishery, pay per voyage or by shares was typical. As Tim Le Goff remarks, between 1725 and 1743 only forty to forty-five percent of maritime workers were paid monthly wages. The proliferation of wage labour in France during the eighteenth century changed this situation, and by 1800 wage-earners were in the majority. Such a development might indicate that there was a gradual shift to full-time sailors, as has been postulated for the Dutch situation, only later in the century.[3]

---

[1]Marcus Rediker, *Between the Devil and the Deep Blue See. Merchant Seamen, Pirates, and the Anglo-American Maritime World, 1700-1750* (Cambridge, 1987), 78.

[2]P.A. Boon, *Bouwers van de zee: zeevarenden van het Westfriese platteland, c. 1680-1720* (The Hague, 1996), 152-155.

[3]J.L. van Zanden, *The Rise and Decline of Holland's Economy. Merchant Capitalism and the Labour Market* (Manchester, 1993), 39; and Boon, *Bouwers van de zee*, 184-185.

Finally, it should be emphasized, as has been done in a number of the contributions to this book, that even if the sailors were paid a wage, this was often not the only source of income. Sailors sometimes got a bonus after a voyage, were allowed to carry some private commodities, or shared in prize money. And, of course, sailors were fed and housed during their voyage.

It is thus not easy to make comparisons between the level of income in the several categories of maritime activity, or to make comparisons between wages in different European countries. It is remarkable that in many lands the wage level was stable during the greater part of the seventeenth and eighteenth centuries. In wartime, demand and shortages could suddenly arise, and so could wages. Remuneration rose in most European countries at the end of the eighteenth century not only because of wars but also because of inflation, which threatened real incomes.

The picture arising from the contributions to this book confirms the notion that nominal wages were highest in the Dutch Republic. This seems to be especially the case compared with Germany and Scandinavia, thus providing a possible "pull-factor" for seafarers from these regions to try to get a job on Dutch ships. But there are remarkable differences in the payments between the various branches of shipping.

The Dutch East India Company (VOC) and the Dutch navy paid less than the merchant marine or whaling. Sailors who entered the service of the VOC were assured of a minimum service time of two years, and often they served considerably longer.[4] If sailors in the Netherlands were said to have a low profile, then it applies especially to this sector: to enter the service of the VOC and go "to the Indies" was sometimes regarded as shameful. This negative connotation in the Netherlands was in sharp contrast with the situation in Sweden. The Swedish Company paid more than the average wage for sailors, and serving on board Swedish East Indiamen or Chinamen was regarded as

---

[4]According to the rules of the Company, experienced sailors had to sign for three years, and others normally for five, but in practice a small part of the crew returned to Europe within two years. See K.L. van Schouwenburg, "Het personeel op de schepen van de Kamer Delft der VOC in de eerste helft van de 18de eeuw," *Tijdschrift voor Zeegeschiedenis*, VII (1988), 76-93.

a most profitable job because a number of other privileges were provided in addition to high wages.[5]

So we have two different extremes, depending upon our point of view. If we consider the sailor as a wage-earning proletarian, a collective worker even before the Industrial Revolution, then the seamen on VOC vessels had the lowest profile, while those on Swedish ships to Asia stood at the top in earnings and respectability. If, however, we look at the degree of wage dependency, i.e., of proletarianization, then the extremes are between the seafarers in deep-sea trades and those serving in on coastal craft or in the fisheries.

## Non-material Labour Conditions

Logbooks kept by the officers of ships do not very often provide a lively portrait of the harsh life aboard. But the second mate of the *Voorberg*, Jacobus Arkenbout, could not ignore the extreme circumstances to which the crew of this VOC vessel was exposed. The officers of the *Voorberg*, sailing in the English Channel in October 1786, gave in to protests from the sailors and decided to terminate the voyage to Batavia and to return to the roads of Texel.[6] The ship leaked, the carpenters could not find the cause, and the sailors were compelled to pump continuously. Some days earlier the officers had rejected the crew's request to return, but they now concluded that the vessel was indeed in such poor condition that it was unfit for a long voyage. Even after it made it to Texel, the social protest of the sailors and soldiers continued, although this did not escalate into a strike or mutiny. The sailors asked to be released from their service, for which they had to submit a written petition to the directors of the VOC. Many apparently did not have high expectations of their employer and deserted instead. While the *Voorberg* was anchored at Texel, no fewer than 119 men out of a crew of 310 jumped ship.

---

[5]C. Koninckx, "The Swedish East India Company (1715-1732)," in J.R. Bruijn and F.S. Gaastra (eds.), *Ships, Sailors and Spices. East India Companies and their Shipping in the 16th, 17th and 18th Centuries* (Amsterdam, 1993), 135.

[6]Maritieme Museum "Prins Hendrik," "Journaal ofte dagregister van den Sous Luijtenant ter zee Jacobus Arkenbout, geduurende deszelfs dienst presteering aan boord van het S.E. Oostindisch Compagnies Voorberg. This log covers the period 24 December 1784 (first departure from Texel) to 16 December 1786 (when the ship was declared unfit for the voyage after the failure of the second attempt to sail out of the English Channel).

They had good reasons to escape from the service of the VOC this way. The *Voorberg* had already made an attempt in December 1785 to sail to Batavia with 356 men on board. But it was damaged by a heavy storm and had to take refuge at Dartmouth, after the loss of the masts and rigging. During this short but eventful voyage forty men drowned, and some dead bodies had been found between the chests under the decks. During the stay in Dartmouth, ninety-six men died due to illness, and the ship was held in quarantine for several months. It is understandable that those who had survived the first "voyage to disaster" and were still on board when the ship tried to make its passage to Batavia for the second time did not want to risk a third attempt, even on another craft.

The problems the *Voorberg* encountered were exceptional, not so much because the ship and its crew were victims of the hazards of the sea – that could occur to any ship or sailor – but because the number on board was exceptionally high, as was the desperation and unwillingness to serve their employer. Social protest or collective action, even mutinies could and did occur. But in a hierarchical and even a military-like concern like the VOC, these goals were not easy to accomplish.[7]

Conditions on board have been compared to "total institutions," such as military camps, prisons or even cloisters, and have been studied by sociologists rather than historians.[8] It is obvious that labour conditions for sailors differed in some basic elements from most other professions, even from soldiers or monks. Apart from the fact that a ship can be considered a "total institution," where the place of work and the place of living are the same, V. Aubert and O. Arner mention four other aspects: the place of work is physically isolated from the family; the degree of turnover among seamen is much larger than in occupations on land; the positions on board are more graded and specialized than in other occupations, leaving few people on board in exactly the same position; and promotion starts in the lower ranks and follows a somewhat formalized scheme, based on qualifications and skills. Perhaps the last two factors are more valid for the twentieth century than for the age of sail, since for the greater part of the crews of East Indiamen or men-of-

---

[7]See J.R. Bruijn and E.S. van Eyck van Heslinga, *Muiterij. Oproer en berechting op schepen van de VOC* (Haarlem, 1980), 25-26.

[8]Vilhelm Aubert and Oddvar Arner, "On the Social Structure of the Ship," *Acta Sociologica*, III (1958), 200.

war, there was almost no way to rise to the officers' ranks. Still, as Peter Earle observes in his contribution, those in the lower ranks also knew a number of ways to increase earnings and prestige.

It is clear once again that there was a great variation among trades, and hence the consequences of these factors must have been different as well. These differences – the period of separation from home and family, the way in which discipline on board was administered, or the possibility of attaining a higher position – must have influenced the choice of an individual sailor in opting for a certain trade as much as wages or other forms of remuneration did.

Finally, it can be observed that the high turnover rate of the industry gave a special role to the labour market and the mediators between employer and labourer. The labour market was not only a place for newcomers but also a place where time and again professional sailors had to offer their labour, and where employers could recruit from a standing pool of skilled workers.

# Maritime Labour in the Netherlands, 1570-1870

**Karel Davids**

## Introduction

Although the study of the history of maritime labour in the Netherlands has made great strides in the past twenty years, a survey of the development of the labour market between 1570 and 1870 still is necessarily incomplete. First of all, research on the seventeenth and eighteenth centuries has been more extensive than inquiries on the period before 1600 or the era after 1800; labour in the Dutch navy and mercantile marine after 1825 has up to now hardly been studied at all. Second, most pre-1800 studies have concentrated on the navy, the East India Company (VOC) and whaling rather than on the fisheries or the merchant marine. Third, inquiries on maritime labour until recently were more concerned with themes like geographical origins, mortality rates or wage levels than with analyses on a micro-level of the mechanisms that made the maritime labour market operate as it did. Career patterns, labour cycles, earnings, marriage rates, age distribution or reproductive behaviour of seamen – to mention but a few salient topics – are as yet still insufficiently known. Fourth, the movement of foreign maritime labour to the Netherlands has received more attention than the flow of Dutch maritime labour abroad. These biases are to some extent reflected in the following survey.

The survey starts with an overview of aggregate data on maritime labour in the Netherlands. This section summarizes the evidence available on such general aspects as levels of employment; the size, structure and productivity of shipping; the geographic origins of crews; and the movement of Dutch labour abroad. Having sketched the parameters of the maritime labour market at large, I will then take a closer look at the operation of the labour market itself. Starting from the model of the "segmented labour market," which at present holds sway in the study of labour in the early modern Netherlands, I will attempt both to integrate the findings so far and to pinpoint the principal issues that require further research. This survey naturally leads to the conclusion, I will argue in the final section of this essay, that the study of maritime labour in the Netherlands is now especially in need of more micro-level research.

## Size and Structure of the Dutch Maritime Sector

### Employment Levels

Because of the work by J.R. Bruijn and J. Lucassen, we have a rough estimate of employment levels in the Dutch maritime sector at various points in time between the early seventeenth century and the first quarter of the nineteenth century. The estimated figures are given in table 1.

**Table 1**
**Employment in the Dutch Maritime Sector,**
**c. 1610-1825**

| Branch of Shipping | 1610 | 1630/40 | 1680 | 1725 | 1770 | 1825 |
|---|---|---|---|---|---|---|
| Navy | 3,000 | 8,000 | 3,500 | 3,500 | 2,000 | 5,000 |
| Merchant Marine | 21,500 | 25,500 | 22,500 | 22,000 | 21,000 | 17,000 |
| East India Company | 2,000 | 4,000 | 8,000 | 11,000 | 11,500 | - |
| Whaling | - | 1,500 | 9,000 | 9,000 | 6,000 | - |
| Sea Fisheries | 6,500 | 7,000 | 6,500 | 4,000 | 4,000 | 2,000 |
| Totals | 33,000 | 46,000 | 50,000 | 49,500 | 44,500 | 24,000 |

*Sources*: J.R. Bruijn and J. Lucassen, *Op de schepen der Oost-Indische Compagnie. Vijf artikelen van J. de Hullu* (Groningen, 1980), 14; and J.R. Bruijn, "Zeevarenden," *Maritieme Geschiedenis der Nederlanden*, III (1977), 157.

All these estimates relate to "normal" periods in the history of Dutch shipping, that is, eras when the total level of employment or the ratio between different branches did not suddenly change as a result of the outbreak of large-scale war and the expansion of the Navy and privateering that went with it, as happened during the three Anglo-Dutch wars of the seventeenth century (1652-1654, 1665-1667, 1672-1674), the wars with France in the age of Louis XIV (1672-1678, 1688-1697, 1702-1713) and the Napoleonic Wars. Employment levels in the Navy during the Anglo-Dutch Wars and the Nine Years' War, for instance, peaked at over 20,000 men and in the War of the Spanish Succession still reached 14,000-17,000 men. The number of seamen employed on Zeeland privateers during the latter war varied probably between 4500 and 7000.[1] The extra demand from the Navy and privateering was only in part balanced by a temporary reduction in activities in other branches of shipping, such as whaling or the sea fisheries. Thus, total levels of employment in the Dutch maritime sector in times of large-scale war up to the early nineteenth century far outstripped the "normal" limits of about 44,000-50,000 seamen.

Although estimates of total employment in the Dutch maritime sector for later dates in the nineteenth century are still lacking, employment in the merchant navy can (on the basis of data collected by H. Wijn) be assumed to have risen steadily to almost 30,000 by 1860 and to have collapsed dramatically to about 15,000 by the mid-1870s. Thus, the overall level of employment in the Dutch merchant marine (including the East India trade) at its nineteenth-century peak was probably as high as the normal level of employment in the merchant navy and the VOC combined during the seventeenth century. Employment in the Navy, after peaking at 6000-8000 during the Belgian conflict in the 1830s, settled down around 4000-5000 by 1850.[2]

## Size, Productivity and Sailing Patterns

The most important source of employment for maritime labour in the Netherlands was evidently the merchant marine. What was the overall size of this fleet? Table 2 provides the most informed estimates available so far; vessels in the Asia and Atlantic trades are included from 1824. The total tonnage of the Dutch carrying fleet in the seventeenth and eighteenth century was still larger, as part of the carrying capacity was provided by ships employed in the Asia and Atlantic trades, which are

---

[1]J.R. Bruijn, *The Dutch Navy of the Seventeenth and Eighteenth Centuries* (Columbia, SC, 1993), 131; and J.Th.M. Verhees-van Meer, *De Zeeuwse kaapvaart tijdens de Spaanse Successieoorlog 1702-1713* (Leiden, 1986), 47.

[2]H. Wijn, "Aanmonstering en arbeidsplaats ter koopvaardij in de 19de eeuw: een reconstructie," *Leidschrift*, I (1984), 39; and Bruijn, "Zeevarenden," 153.

not included in table 2. The size of the VOC fleet showed considerable growth up to the eve of the Fourth Anglo-Dutch War (1780-1784); its total tonnage has been estimated at about 24,000 tons in 1686 and 115,000 tons in 1780. The tonnage employed in the Atlantic trades probably also expanded in the eighteenth century, but certainly remained much smaller than that owned by the VOC, perhaps on the order of some 20,000 tons.[3]

**Table 2**
**Estimated Size of the Dutch Merchant Marine, 1636-1860**

| Year | Estimated Tonnage |
|---|---|
| 1636 | 310,000 |
| 1670 | 368,000 |
| 1750 | 365,000 |
| 1824 | 131,000 |
| 1860 | 479,000 |

*Sources*: J.R. Bruijn, "De vaart in Europa," *Maritieme Geschiedenis der Nederlanden*, II (1977), 200; P.C. van Royen, *Zeevarenden op de koopvaardijvloot omstreeks 1700* (Amsterdam, 1987), 15; J.V.Th. Knoppers, "De vaart in Europa," *Maritieme Geschiedenis der Nederlanden*, III (1977), 227; R.T. Griffiths, *Industrial Retardation in the Netherlands 1830-1850* (The Hague, 1979), 93; H. Wijn, "Aanmonstering en arbeidsplaats ter koopvaardij in de 19de eeuw: een reconstructie," *Leidschrift*, I (1984), 44-47; Lewis R. Fischer, "Around the Rim: Seamen's Wages in North Sea Ports, 1863-1900," in Lewis R. Fischer, *et al.* (eds.), *The North Sea. Twelve Essays on Social History of Maritime Labour* (Stavanger, 1992), 60.

Tonnages and numbers of ships differed sharply by trade, as estimates for 1636, 1700/1710 and 1750 attest (see table 3).

---

[3]F.S. Gaastra, *De geschiedenis van de VOC* (2nd ed., Zutphen, 1991), 119; and I.M. Dillo, *De nadagen van de Verenigde Oostindische Compagnie 1783-1795. Schepen en zeevarenden* (Amsterdam, 1992), 42. The total number of vessels employed in various branches of the Atlantic trade in the eighteenth century has been estimated at 110-125 per year; the average tonnage of ships (mainly used as slavers) of the largest shipowning company in the Atlantic trade, the *Middelburgse Commercie Compagnie*, was 160 tons; see P.C. Emmer, "Suiker, goud en slaven. De Republiek in West-Afrika en West-Indië 1674-1800," *Algemene Geschiedenis der Nederlanden*, IX (Haarlem, 1980), 469; and W.S. Unger, "Bijdragen tot de geschiedenis van de Nederlandse slavenhandel, II De slavenhandel der Middelburgsche Commercie Compagnie 1732-1808," *Economisch-Historisch Jaarboek*, XXVIII (1961), 109-110.

**Table 3**
**Estimated Numbers of Ships (N) and Average Tonnage per Ship (AT) in the Dutch Merchant Fleet by Trade, 1636, 1700/1710, 1750**

| Trade | 1636 | | 1700/1710 | 1750 | |
|---|---|---|---|---|---|
| | N | AT | AT | N | AT |
| Baltic | 400 | 200 | 290 | | |
| Norway | 350 | 200 | 334 | | |
| Baltic + Norway | | | | 870 | 300 |
| Archangel | 50 | 240 | 404 | 33 | 460 |
| North Germany | 150 | 40 | 104 | | |
| Dover, London and Coal trade | 100 | 80 | | | |
| Rest England and Scotland | 50 | 60 | | | |
| Great Britain | | | 148 | | |
| Ireland | | | 174 | | |
| England and the Channel | | | | 81 | 54 |
| Northwest France | 140 | 80 | | | |
| Calais | 10 | 40 | | | |
| France | | | 228 | 248 | 140 |
| Southwest France | 300 | 200 | | | |
| Spain | | | 364 | | |
| Portugal | | | 350 | | |
| Mediterranean | | | 326 | | |
| Spain, Portugal and Mediterranean | 200 | 300 | | 216 | 230 |

*Sources*: Bruijn, "De vaart in Europa," 200; Van Royen, *Zeevarenden*, 170; and Knoppers, "De vaart in Europa," 227.

Estimates of the average size of crew per ship (AC) and the total employment of seamen by trade (TE) which are available so far all pertain to the seventeenth and early eighteenth centuries. Table 4 gives an overview. On the basis of estimates of tonnages and crews in the 1630s and his own data on the Dutch merchant marine between 1700 and 1710, Paul van Royen has made a case for the thesis that tons (or rather lasts, with one last being equal to two tons) carried per man in the early eighteenth century in all trades, and thus productivity per man, was considerably higher than seventy years before, although the exact reasons for these gains are still unclear (see table 5).[4]

**Table 4**
**Size of Crew per Ship and Employment by Trade, c. 1630-1640, 1680 and 1700-1710**

| | 1630/1640 | | 1680 | 1700-1710 |
|---|---|---|---|---|
| Trade | AC | TE | TE | AC |
| Baltic | 10 | 4,000 | 4,000 | 12 |
| Norway | 12 | 4,200 | 4,000 | 14 |
| Archangel | 20 | 1,000 | 1,200 | 17 |
| North Germany | 5.3 | 800 | 800 | 4 |
| Dover, London and Coal Trade | 7 | 700 | | |
| Rest England and Scotland | 6 | 300 | | |
| England/Great Britain | | | 500 | 8 |
| Ireland | | | | 9 |
| Northwest France | 6.8 | 950 | | |
| Calais | 5 | 50 | | |
| Southwest France | 11.7 | 3,500 | | |
| France | | | 4,000 | 10 |
| Spain | | | | 17 |
| Portugal | | | | 14 |
| Mediterranean | | | | 23 |
| Spain, Portugal and Mediterranean | 30 | 6,000 | 6,000 | |

*Sources*: J. Lucassen, "Zeevarenden," *Maritieme Geschiedenis der Nederlanden*, II (1977), 132; Bruijn, "De vaart in Europa," 200; and Van Royen, *Zeevarenden*, 24-25 and 183.

Crew sizes in other branches of shipping (excluding the fisheries) were higher than in the mercantile marine. Ships in the Atlantic trades carried sixteen to twenty men in the 1610s, but much higher numbers in the eighteenth century: the complement of slavers of the Middelburgse Commercie Compagnie was twenty-five to forty-four men, and of West Indiamen in the 1720s even sixty. The total number of ships employed

[4]Van Royen, *Zeevarenden*, 179. See also J.R. Bruijn, "Productivity, Profitability and Costs of Private and Corporate Dutch Ship Owning in the Seventeenth and Eighteenth Centuries," in James D. Tracy (ed.), *The Rise of Merchant Empires. Long-Distance Trade in the Early Modern World 1350-1750* (Cambridge, 1990), 177-178.

per year in the trade to Africa, the West Indies and Dutch Guyana in the eighteenth century has been estimated at 110-125. Whaling ships normally had crews of forty-two. The number of whalers sent to the Arctic expanded from ten to twenty per year before 1640, via forty or fifty in the middle decades of the century, to levels of 150-200 between 1680 and 1770 (and even higher in the 1680s and 1720s), before collapsing to virtually nil in the last quarter of the eighteenth century.[5]

**Table 5**
**Lasts Carried per Man by Trade, 1636 and 1700/1710**

| Trade | 1636 | 1700-1710 |
|---|---|---|
| Baltic | 10 | 12.8 |
| Norway | 8.3 | 12 |
| Archangel | 6 | 6.7 |
| North Germany | 3.75 | ? |
| England/Great Britain | 5 - 5.7 | 9 |
| France | 4 - 5.9 | 12.1 |
| Spain, Portugal and Mediterranean | 5 | 7.7 |

*Source*: Van Royen, *Zeevarenden*, 179.

In the East India trade, outward-bound vessels equipped by the VOC were always far more heavily manned than homeward-bound craft and this discrepancy became even more pronounced over time. While the average number of voyagers on the former – including seafarers, soldiers, craftsmen as well as passengers – increased from 184 in the period 1602-1730 to 252 between 1730 and 1795, the mean number on the latter – sixty percent of whom were seafarers – fluctuated narrowly between 105 and 120 men. Productivity per man in the VOC, in common with developments in the merchant navy, also exhibited substantial growth: average tons per homeward-bound vessel increased from 443 in the 1600s via 537 in the 1630s and 702 in the 1700s to a peak of 1002 in the 1770s. The evolution of the total number of ships owned by the VOC, however, did not correspond at all with the expansion of total

[5]J.P. van de Voort, *De Westindische plantages van 1720-1795. Financiën en handel* (Eindhoven, 1973), 48; Emmer, "Suiker, goud en slaven," 469; C. de Jong, "Walvisvaart," *Maritieme Geschiedenis der Nederlanden*, III (1977), 339-340; and L. Hacquebord, *Smeerenburg. Het verblijf van Nederlandse walvisvaarders op de westkust van Spitsbergen in de zeventiende eeuw* (Amsterdam, 1984), 76-79.

tonnage from about 24,000 in the 1680s to 115,000 by 1780. The number of VOC ships increased from 125 in 1680 to 161 in 1725, but dropped to 118 in 1775. The size of the fleets sent to Asia varied as well: from eight per year in the 1600s to twenty-three in the 1660s, down to twenty in the 1690s, up to thirty-seven or thirty-eight in the 1720s and 1730s and down again to twenty-nine in the second half of the eighteenth century. In the nineteenth century, the average tonnage of East Indiamen was smaller than in the last hundred years of the VOC's existence: the most common type of vessel employed in the 1830s, the frigate, measured on average no more than 582 tons. Crew size declined to some forty men. The number of ships sailing to the East Indies meanwhile increased to about 100 in the mid-1830s.[6]

The complement on warships of course differed according to the rate of the vessel. First-rate warships in the Second or Third Anglo-Dutch Wars carried 400-500 men, but the normal type of vessel in the Dutch Navy after 1713, a fifth-rate frigate (forty to forty-eight guns), had crews of no more than 200 in peacetime and 225 during wars. Complements of privateers varied just as widely. During the War of the Spanish Succession the smallest Zeeland privateer carried twenty man, the largest 350; a twenty-six-gun privateer had a crew of 180.[7]

The shipping industry was by 1700 to a large extent a year-round business. Even in winter the carrying trade did not come to a full halt. Nonetheless, a seasonal pattern continued. Maritime activities, whether commercial or naval, were normally less intensive in wintertime than between March and November. The whaling season was restricted to the period between late April and early September. Archangel fleets in the seventeenth century left the Texel in the beginning of May or the end of July and departed from Russia in early October at the latest. Fleets

---

[6]J.R. Bruijn, "De personeelsbehoefte van de VOC overzee en aan boord, bezien in Aziatisch en Nederlands perspectief," *Bijdragen en Mededelingen betreffende de Geschiedenis der Nederlanden*, XCI (1976), 221; J.R. Bruijn, *et al.* (eds.), *Dutch-Asiatic Shipping in the 17th and 18th Centuries* (3 vols., The Hague, 1979-1987), I, 144-149 and 177; Gaastra, *De geschiedenis*, 115 and 118; Griffiths, *Industrial Retardation*, 94; and F.J.A. Broeze, *De Stad Schiedam. De Schiedamsche Scheepsreederij en de Nederlandse vaart op Oost-Indië omstreeks 1840* (The Hague, 1978), 11 and 119.

[7]J.R. Bruijn (ed.), *De oorlogvoering ter zee in 1673 in journalen en andere stukken* (Groningen, 1966), 204-209; Bruijn, *De Admiraliteit van Amsterdam in rustige jaren 1713-1751* (Amsterdam, 1970), 134; and Verhees-Van Meer, *De Zeeuwse kaapvaart*, 47.

bound for the Mediterranean in the second half of the seventeenth century usually sailed in armed convoys, leaving Dutch ports in spring (the small one) or in the autumn (the large one), after the return of fleets from Archangel and the East Indies. VOC fleets bound for Asia normally left around Easter, in September or October and around Christmas. The vast majority of seamen who sailed in Dutch ships from a port in the Netherlands could expect to be home within a few months or at most a year. Only seafarers who enlisted on VOC vessels had to contract for longer periods. Of those in the lower ranks who returned, 17.5% did so within a year of departure, fifty-seven percent within two years, and sixty-seven percent within three years.[8]

## Geographic Origins of Seamen, Dutchmen and Foreigners

The vast demand for labour on Dutch ships was never wholly satisfied by seamen born and bred in the Netherlands. Indeed, many jobs in the Dutch maritime sector, like many posts in other areas of the Dutch economy between 1600 and 1870, were filled by foreigners. But the proportion of foreigners in the Dutch maritime sector was not spread evenly in time, branch of shipping or rank.[9]

In the late sixteenth century, the variations by branch of shipping were striking indeed. Recent research by Jaap Bruijn has indicated that on vessels of the Admiralty of Zeeland around 1600 the share of foreigners among petty officers and common seamen was about forty-nine percent. The Spanish Netherlands supplied fourteen percent of the crews; England and Germany 8.5% each; Scandinavia and the Baltic eight percent; and Scotland six percent. But the composition of crews on expeditions to the East Indies fitted out in Amsterdam in 1599/1600 was

[8]Van Royen, *Zeevarenden*, 59; S. Hart, "Amsterdam Shipping and Trade to Northern Russia in the Seventeenth Century," *Mededelingen van de Nederlandse Vereniging voor Zeegeschiedenis*, XXVI (1973), 11 and 20; J.I. Israel, "The Phases of the Dutch *Straatvaart*, 1590-1713: A Chapter in the Economic History of the Mediterranean," in Israel, *Empires and Entrepots. The Dutch, the Spanish Monarchy and the Jews, 1585-1713* (London, 1990), 155; Bruijn, *et al.* (eds.), *Dutch Asiatic Shipping*, I, 62 and 147; and K.L. van Schouwenburg, "Het personeel op schepen van de kamer Delft der VOC in de eerste helft der achttiende eeuw," *Tijdschrift voor Zeegeschiedenis*, VII (1988), 76.

[9]For an overview, see J. Lucassen, *Dutch Long Distance Migration. A Concise History 1600-1900* (Amsterdam, 1991), 10-16.

completely different: 766 out of the 836 seamen whose geographic origin is known (or ninety-one percent) came from Holland, Friesland or other parts of the Dutch Republic. The proportion of Germans was no more than 5.1%, and from the Spanish Netherlands 1.9%. And the States-General around 1600 even took measures to lure Dutch seamen who had entered service on ships fitted out in the Spanish Netherlands back to the United Provinces.[10]

During the seventeenth and early eighteenth centuries the Navy and the VOC alternated in their relative attractiveness to foreign labour. Whereas the proportion of foreigners among the crews of East Indiamen (according to random samples in 1637 and 1661) grew from twenty-nine percent in the late 1630s to forty-two percent in the early 1660s, their share among petty officers and common seamen on vessels of the Admiralties of Zeeland and Amsterdam around 1670 (as far as the evidence of payrolls of two ships is anything to go by) amounted to just about twenty-five percent. By the end of the seventeenth century the tables appear to have turned: whereas the percentage on VOC ships in the period 1680-1720 hovered around twenty-two or twenty-six percent, the proportion on Zeeland men-of-war during the Nine Years' War and the War of the Spanish Succession (according to samples of crews of two men-of-war in 1694 and 1709) reached thirty-seven and forty-five percent, respectively. The Navy thereafter remained in the lead. While the proportion of foreigners on VOC ships again grew rapidly from the 1720s, their share among petty officers and seamen of naval vessels rose to even higher levels. While the percentage on East Indiamen increased from thirty-eight percent around 1730 to almost fifty percent about 1750, and fluctuated between forty-four and fifty-three percent during the rest of the century, samples taken from payrolls of warships of the Admiralties of Amsterdam, Zeeland and the Noorderkwartier in 1720/1733, 1769/1772 and 1772/1775 reveal proportions of foreigners of fifty, sixty-one and seventy percent. It was not until the nineteenth century that the

---

[10]Bruijn, *The Dutch Navy*, 55; H.A. van Foreest and A. de Booy (eds.), *De vierde schipvaart der Nederlanders naar Oost-Indië onder Jacob Wilkens en Jacob van Neck (1599-1604)* (2 vols., The Hague, 1980-1981), II, 196-203; and A.P. van Vliet, *Vissers en kapers. De zeevisserij vanuit het Maasmondgebied en de Duinkerker kapers (ca. 1580-1648)* (The Hague, 1994), 76.

share of foreigners on Dutch warships finally declined: to about thirty-five percent around 1820 and a mere 3.5% in the mid-1850s.[11]

The origins of foreigners employed by the Admiralties and the VOC changed as well. Englishmen, Scotchmen and Flemings, who figured so prominently among crews of Zeeland warships around 1600, hardly appeared at all on payrolls of warships in the later seventeenth and eighteenth centuries. Scandinavians and Germans, by contrast, showed up in ever greater numbers from the end of the seventeenth century onwards. In the samples of 1694, 1709, 1720/1733, 1769/1772 and 1772/1775 cited above, the proportion of seamen from Scandinavia and the Baltic amounted to ten, fourteen, twenty-four, sixteen and twenty-three percent, and that of seafarers from Germany to seven, twelve, nineteen, thirty-one and thirty-five percent. The pattern in the East India trade was somewhat different. Whereas the numbers of seamen from Denmark and Schleswig-Holstein entering VOC service in the course of the eighteenth century showed a relative decline, the share of Germans strongly increased, especially after 1740. These Germans to an ever-greater extent originated from the interior rather than the coastal regions: 17.6% of all seamen recruited by the VOC in 1790/1791 were from the German interior, as against only three percent around 1700. Moreover, the Chamber Zeeland of the VOC in the eighteenth century attracted growing numbers from the Austrian Netherlands and France.[12]

On VOC vessels, crews in the second half of the eighteenth century increasingly consisted of Asian seamen. Employment of Asian sailors first started in the War of the Spanish Succession, when the supply of Europeans dried up. It was long considered a temporary expedient, to be restricted solely to shipping in Asian waters. But when rising mortality rates in Asia in the later eighteenth century led to acute manning problems, the restrictions were progressively abandoned. From the 1740s, the VOC began to recruit Indian seamen ("Moors") on a regular basis, mainly from Bengal and Gujarat. In the 1750s, Chinese sailors entered the Company's service as well. Javanese were first hired in 1778. In the late 1780s, Indian, Chinese and Javanese seamen

---

[11]Bruijn and Lucassen, *Op de schepen*, 139; Bruijn, *The Dutch Navy*, 133, 201; and Bruijn, "Zeevarenden," 154.

[12]Bruijn and Lucassen, *Op de schepen*, 139; Bruijn, "De personeelsbehoefte," 245-246; and Bruijn, *et al.* (eds.), *Dutch-Asiatic Shipping*, I, 157.

comprised two-thirds of the crews of VOC craft in Asian waters, in proportions of roughly ten, fifty and forty percent, adding up on average to 2000 men. By then, the Directors had also abandoned their ban on Asian seamen on ships bound for Europe. It was no longer uncommon to see Asian sailors arrive in Dutch ports.[13]

**Table 6**
**Geographical Origins of Crews of Whalers, 1612-1825**

| | 1612-1639 % | 1640-1664 % | c. 1700-1825 % |
|---|---|---|---|
| Amsterdam | 5.1 | 9.3 | |
| Holland North of Y | 42.9 | 46.9 | |
| Rest of Northern Provinces | 8.2 | 30.8 | |
| South Holland | 10.4 | 6.3 | |
| Zeeland | 1.0 | 0.5 | |
| Other Provinces | 2.1 | 0.2 | |
| Total Dutch | 69.7 | 94.0 | 34.7 |
| (French) Basque Region | 26.9 | 2.8 | |
| North Germany | 2.3 | 2.4 | |
| German and Danish Wadden Islands | | | 23.1 |
| Rest of Germany | | | 39.4 |
| Other | 1.1 | 0.8 | 2.6 |
| Total Foreign | 30.3 | 6.0 | 65.1 |
| Total | 525 | 1061 | 1896 |

*Note*: Only seamen of known origins included in this table.

*Sources*: 1612/1639 and 1640/1664: L. Hacquebord, *Smeerenburg. Het verblijf van Nederlandse walvisvaarders op de westkust van Spitsbergen in de zeventiende eeuw* (Amsterdam, 1984), 66; 1700-1825: C. de Jong, *Geschiedenis van de oude Nederlandse walvisvaart* (Pretoria, 1972), I, 81.

---

[13]Dillo, *De nadagen*, 95-109; Bruijn, *et al.* (eds.), *Dutch Asiatic Shipping*, I, 152-153; and C.A. Davids, "Navigeren in Azië. De uitwisseling van kennis tussen Aziaten en navigatiepersoneel bij de voorcompagnieën en de VOC, 1596-1795," *Tijdschrift voor Zeegeschiedenis*, IX (1990), 10.

Aside from the sea fisheries, which before the 1750s in all probability recruited their personnel almost exclusively domestically, the other branches of shipping to varying degrees also relied on the use of foreign labour.[14] Whaling displayed a pattern not unlike the Navy: a relatively high proportion of foreigners in the beginning of the seventeenth century, a decrease in the middle decades of the century and a renewed growth during the eighteenth century. Table 6 summarizes the figures available so far, based on samples from notarial archives and the registers of the Amsterdam shipping master. Among the foreigners, two groups stand out: the Basques – hired in the early phase of Dutch whaling because of their specialist skills – and seafarers from the German and Danish Wadden Islands (from common seamen up to *commandeurs*), who entered Dutch whaling in growing numbers from the 1680s. P. Dekker has estimated that the number of seamen from Föhr on Dutch whalers peaked around 1760 at 1100-1200 annually.[15]

There is no doubt that the mercantile marine employed foreign manpower as well. The evolution of the share of foreigners is still in dispute, however. According to A.M. van der Woude, the proportion of foreigners in the Dutch merchant marine by the early eighteenth century had probably risen to about forty percent. Paul van Royen has argued that, while the percentage on ships commanded by masters from Amsterdam might have been close to fifty, the share of foreigners on ships commanded by masters from North Holland, Friesland and the Wadden Islands amounted to no more than twenty to twenty-five percent. It should be noted that if Van der Woude's estimate is accepted, this would imply that the share of foreigners among seamen in the Dutch mercantile marine around 1700 was actually much higher than among crews of Dutch East Indiamen between 1680 and 1720 (twenty-two to twenty-six percent). By 1774-1775, Van Royen found the share of foreigners among crews on merchantmen in Amsterdam increased to about sixty percent. For crews of Zeeland ships employed in the slave trade between Africa and the West Indies between 1732 and 1802 (under

[14] Bruijn and Lucassen, *Op de schepen*, 20. But according to a contemporary estimate in 1829, the herring fisheries by then employed a substantial number of foreigners, too; see Bruijn, "Zeevarenden," 158.

[15] Hacquebord, *Smeerenburg*, 67-68; and P. Dekker, "Föhrer Seeleute bei der niederländischen Walfangfahrt besonders im 18. Jahrhundert," *Nordfriesisches Jahrbuch*, Neue Folge, XIV (1978), 130 and 150.

the aegis of the Middelburgse Commercie Compagnie), W.S. Unger has calculated the percentage of foreigners at thirty-five. Both the evidence gathered by Van Royen and Unger show that the vast majority of foreigners came from Scandinavia, Northwestern Germany and the German Baltic coast; the proportion of seamen from England or the Spanish (Austrian) Netherlands was negligible.[16]

**Table 7**
**Ratio between Dutchmen and Foreigners Among Petty Officers and Common Seamen Mustered on Dutch Merchantmen, 1814-1839**

| Port and Period | Trade | Dutch & | Foreign % | Total |
|---|---|---|---|---|
| Amsterdam 1814/26 | all | 72 | 28 | 9415 |
| Amsterdam 1821/22 | all | 60 | 40 | 2982 |
| Amsterdam 1836 | East-India | 50 | 50 | 587 |
| Dordrecht 1836 | East-India | 65 | 35 | 147 |
| Rotterdam 1839 | East-India | 97 | 3 | 67 |

*Sources*: Bruijn, "Zeevarenden," 157; F.J.A. Broeze, *De Stad Schiedam. De Schiedamsche Scheepsreederij en de Nederlandse vaart op Oost-Indië omstreeks 1840* (The Hague, 1978), 148; and P.C. van Royen, "Moedernegotie en kraamkamer. Schippers en scheepsvolk op de Nederlandse vrachtvaart in Europese wateren vanaf de zeventiende tot in de negentiende eeuw," *Tijdschrift voor Zeegeschiedenis*, IX (1990), 57.

The pattern that emerges thus far did not change substantially during the first quarter-century after the Napoleonic Wars. Research on the composition of crews of merchantmen in the period 1814-1839, based on samples of muster rolls from Amsterdam and other leading ports, has revealed that the proportion of foreigners among petty officers and

[16]A.M. van der Woude, "De contractiefase van de seculaire trend in het Noorderkwartier nader beschouwd," *Bijdragen en Mededelingen betreffende de Geschiedenis der Nederlanden*, CIII (1988), 393; P.C. van Royen, "De zeeman en de seculaire trend. De Nederlandse vrachtvaart als bron van werkgelegenheid omstreeks 1700," *Bijdragen en Mededelingen betreffende de Geschiedenis der Nederlanden*, CIV (1989), 216; Van Royen, "Manning the Merchant Marine: The Dutch Maritime Labour Market," *International Journal of Maritime History*, I (1989), 16 and 19-20; Van Royen, "Moedernegotie en kraamkamer. Schippers en scheepsvolk op de Nederlandse vrachtvaart in Europese wateren vanaf de zeventiende tot in de negentiende eeuw," *Tijdschrift voor Zeegeschiedenis*, IX (1990), 57; and Unger, "Bijdragen," 22-23.

common seamen (with an odd exception) remained in the range of twenty-eight to fifty percent (table 7). There was a shift in the origins of foreigners, though. While the proportion of Germans increased, the Scandinavian share tended to decline. In 1774-1775, Northwest Germany, the German Baltic coast and Scandinavia supplied fifty-two, thirteen and twenty-seven percent of foreign manpower on ships mustered in Amsterdam; samples of 1814/1816, 1824/1826 and 1821/1822 showed that the German share had risen to just over seventy percent and that the Scandinavian had declined to fourteen (in the first two samples) and twenty-two percent (in the final one).[17]

The share of foreigners in the merchant navy did not begin to show an overall decline until the latter part of the nineteenth century. Table 8, based on statistics for all petty officers and seamen mustered on Dutch merchantmen in Dutch ports between 1875 and 1899, provides an overview. The decline coincided with a decrease in recruitment of foreign labour in other sectors of the Dutch economy.[18]

**Table 8**
**Ration between Dutchmen and Foreigners Among Petty Officers and Common Seamen Mustered on Dutch Merchantmen in Dutch Ports, 1875-1889**

| Period | Dutch % | Foreign % | Mean Number Mustered per Year |
|---|---|---|---|
| 1875/1879 | 80.2 | 19.8 | 14,622 |
| 1880/1884 | 78.3 | 21.7 | 15,445 |
| 1885/1889 | 84.0 | 16.0 | 15,107 |
| 1890/1894 | 87.4 | 12.6 | 19,921 |
| 1895/1899 | 89.3 | 10.7 | 20,451 |

*Source*: C.A. Davids, *Wat lijdt den zeeman al verdriet. Het Nederlandse zeemanslied in de zeiltijd, 1600-1900* (The Hague, 1980), 14.

The ratio between Dutchmen and foreigners varied not only by time and branch of shipping but also by rank. Aside from the odd exception, like Basque harpooneers on Dutch whalers in the early seventeenth century, foreigners in general were much better represented in the lower than the higher ranks. The vast majority of naval officers,

---

[17]Van Royen, "Moedernegotie," 57; and Bruijn, "Zeevarenden," 157.

[18]Lucassen, *Dutch Long Distance Migration*, 15-16.

masters and *commandeurs* of whaling ships and masters and mates of merchant vessels in the seventeenth, eighteenth and nineteenth century were Dutch. The same holds true for the VOC. Whereas the share of foreigners among common seamen on ships of the Chambers Hoorn and Enkhuizen of the VOC in the period 1700-1795, for example, amounted to nearly forty percent, their proportion of petty officers was less than twenty-five percent and among officers no more than eight percent. In the Chamber Zeeland, foreigners in the eighteenth century comprised forty-six percent of the crews, but just fourteen percent of officers in 1736/1740 and twenty-three percent in 1772/1779. Asian mariners hardly ever served in a capacity other than common seaman.[19]

## Origins of Dutch Seamen

With respect to the origins of seafarers in the Netherlands, the picture is somewhat less clear. But research conducted by Van Royen, Bruijn, P. de Buck, J.Th. Lindblad, P. Boon, Van der Woude and others allows us to discern several broad trends.

First, the importance of Holland north of the Y as a reservoir of seamen tended to decline. A comparison between the composition of crews of East Indiamen enlisted at Amsterdam in 1599/1600 and crews of merchantmen (including East Indiamen) mustered at Amsterdam between 1814 and 1826 illustrates the point: in the former case, thirty-four percent of the Dutch seamen originated from a town or a village to the north of the Y; in the latter no more than three to six percent. As for the timing of the decline, it can be inferred that the process did not begin until after 1650 and was more protracted and varied than has previously been assumed. Van der Woude and Van Royen agreed that in the first

[19]Bruijn, *The Dutch Navy*, 181-182; Van Royen, *Zeevarenden*; Van Royen, "Moedernegotie;" R. Prud'homme van Reine, "Een gevangenenlijst van zeelieden uit 1689," *Tijdschrift voor Zeegeschiedenis*, V (1986), 24; Hacquebord, *Smeerenburg*, 69; J.R. Bruijn and C.A. Davids, "Jonas vrij. De Nederlandse walvisvaart, in het bijzonder de Amsterdamse, in de jaren 1640-1664," *Economisch- en Sociaal-Historisch Jaarboek*, XXXVIII (1975), 161-164 and 169; J.K. Beers and C. Bakker, *Westfriezen naar de Oost. De kamers der VOC te Hoorn en Enkhuizen en hun recruteringsgebied* (Hoorn, 1990), 93; E. van der Doe and A. Wiggers, "Varen voor de kamer Zeeland van de VOC. Enige opmerkingen over zeevarenden aan boord van de Zeeuwse schepen in de 18e eeuw," *Zeeuws Tijdschrift*, XXXVII (1987), 212-213; V. Enthoven, "De Verenigde Oostindische Compagnie in Zeeland," *Archief van het Zeeuwsch Genootschap der Wetenschappen 1989*, 101; and Davids, "Navigeren in Azië," 10.

half of the seventeenth century Holland north of the Y (the Noorderkwartier and Westfriesland) supplied nearly half of all native-born seamen in the Dutch Republic. Whereas Van der Woude argued, however, that the decline began in the second half of the seventeenth century and had largely been completed by 1740, Van Royen pointed out that the Noorderkwartier and Westfriesland still provided one-third of the Dutch crew in the mercantile marine in 1700-1710 and thirteen percent of the petty officers and common seamen mustered on Dutch merchantmen in Amsterdam in 1774-1775. The decline almost certainly began faster in the Noorderkwartier than Westfriesland, and proceeded more quickly among the lower ranks than the higher. The spread of facilities for education in navigation, such as training for the ranks of master, mates or naval officer, reached its greatest extent in Holland north of the Y during the very period that the region's share among petty officers and common seamen steadily diminished – the second half of the eighteenth century. While the Noorderkwartier and Westfriesland between 1760 and 1795 supplied merely eleven or twelve percent of the lower ranks of East India crews fitted out by the Chambers Hoorn and Enkhuizen of the VOC, they still provided sixty percent of the officers.[20]

Second, a similar decline, though at a lower level, took place in Zeeland. In contrast with the seventeenth and early eighteenth centuries, Zeeland by 1770 was seldom able to provide seamen for the warships equipped in Flushing. Victor Enthoven has shown that in the eighteenth

---

[20]Van Foreest and De Booy, *De vierde schipvaart*, II, 196-201; P.C. van Royen, "Recruitment Patterns of the Dutch Merchant Marine in the Seventeenth to Nineteenth Centuries," in Lewis R. Fischer, *et al.* (eds.), *The North Sea. Twelve Essays on Social History of Maritime Labour* (Stavanger, 1992), 19 and 21-22; Bruijn, "Zeevarenden," 157; A.M. van der Woude, *Het Noorderkwartier. Een regionaal-historisch onderzoek in de demografische en economische geschiedenis van westelijk Nederland van de late Middeleeuwen tot het begin van de 19e eeuw* (2nd ed., Utrecht, 1983), 366-395; Van Royen, "Manning the Merchant Marine," 16; Van Royen, "Moedernegotie," 57; P. Boon, "De sociale en economische positie van schippers in het Westfriese dorp Schellinkhout rond 1700," *Mededelingen van de Nederlandse Vereniging voor Zeegeschiedenis*, XXXIX (1979), 4-14; Boon, "Zeelieden te Schellinkhout omstreeks 1700," *Tijdschrift voor Zeegeschiedenis*, VI (1987), 107-123; Boon, "Dutch Connections to Scandinavia. The Case of the Westfrisian Seaman Abroad and At Home," in Mette Guldberg, *et al.* (eds.), *Facing the North Sea. West Jutland and the World* (Esbjerg, 1993), 87-101; C.A. Davids, *Zeewezen en wetenschap. De wetenschap en de ontwikkeling van de navigatietechniek in Nederland 1585-1815* (Amsterdam, 1986), 330-331; and Beers and Bakker, *Westfriezen*, 57, 62 and 66.

century the Chamber Zeeland of the VOC relied more than any other on recruitment from outside its home province. And although the local supply recovered slightly in the second half of the century, Zeeland never regained its former stature as a seafaring region. In samples of seamen for the nineteenth century, its share was pitifully small.[21]

Third, in the northern part of the Netherlands there was a gradual eastward shift in the supply area of seamen. While the importance of the west coast of Friesland and the western Wadden Islands (Texel and Vlieland) slowly declined at the end of the eighteenth and the beginning of the nineteenth centuries, Terschelling held its own and the shares of the eastern Wadden Islands, Ameland and Schiermonnikoog, and especially of the eastern part of Groningen increased. The percentage of seamen from Friesland on merchant ships mustered in Amsterdam dropped from thirty-seven percent in 1774-1775 to seventeen percent in the samples of 1814/1816 and 1824/1826, and to thirteen percent in the sample of 1821/1822. The proportion of Groningers, by contrast, grew from four percent to twenty-five and twenty percent, respectively. Groningen also dramatically enlarged its share of the total number of masters, from almost none in 1700 to close to one-half in the 1850s.[22]

Fourth, the most constant areas of supply of seamen in the Netherlands between 1590 and 1870 appear to have been the city of Amsterdam and the crescent-shaped region along the rivers Nieuwe Maas, Noord and Lek in South Holland, running from Maassluis via Rotterdam to Dordrecht. The former area usually contributed ten percent or more of the masters, petty officers and common seamen in any of the samples available so far, while the latter area normally provided a few percent less. Neither Amsterdam nor the district around Rotterdam suffered in the eighteenth and early nineteenth centuries from a terminal decline in seafaring population like that which befell Zeeland and Holland north of the Y. Indeed, the number of seamen in the region

---

[21]Bruijn, *The Dutch Navy*, 55, 133, 201; Enthoven, "De Verenigde Oostindische Compagnie," 101-102; and Bruijn, "Zeevarenden," 154.

[22]P. de Buck and J.Th. Lindblad, "De scheepvaart en handel uit de Oostzee op Amsterdam en de Republiek, 1722-1780," *Tijdschrift voor Geschiedenis*, XCVI (1983), 43; Van Royen, "Recruitment Patterns," 21; Bruijn, "Zeevarenden," 157; Van Royen, *Zeevarenden*, 105; Van Royen, "Moedernegotie," 56; and C.A. Davids, "Technological Change and the Professionalism of Masters and Mates in the Dutch Mercantile Marine, 1815-1914," *Collectanea Maritima*, V (1991), 289 and 296.

around Rotterdam in the mid-nineteenth century may well have been larger than before.[23] But because the history of maritime labour in the Rotterdam area is still unstudied, this hypothesis can not yet be proven.

Finally, recruitment in some regions and branches of shipping was much more urban-centred than in others. More than half the native seamen and petty officers enlisted by the Admiralty of Zeeland in 1600 and 1669 originated from the city of Flushing. In the eighteenth century, Flushing and Middelburg jointly supplied more than two-thirds of all native seamen and craftsmen recruited by the VOC's Chamber Zeeland. Among the seamen and craftsmen recruited by the VOC in the eighteenth century in Holland (two-thirds to three-quarters of all crew were from the Dutch Republic), the urban background was even more pronounced: ninety percent came from one of the nineteen principal cities. In 1821/1822, the proportion of urbanites among Dutch seamen enlisted at Amsterdam for the Atlantic and Asia trades was fifty-nine percent, as against forty-five percent among the total group of Dutch seamen enrolled on merchantmen in Amsterdam. The share of urban recruits reached its greatest extent in the eighteenth and nineteenth century Navy: sixty-eight percent around 1725, eighty-four percent in the 1760s and more than seventy-five percent in the 1820s and 1850s.[24]

## Dutch Seamen Abroad

Movements of Dutch seamen abroad were much rarer than flows in the opposite direction. Dutchmen in the period 1570-1800 seldom served on

---

[23] Bruijn, "De personeelsbehoefte," 243; P. Dekker, "Commandeurs ter walvisvaart uit het gebied van Maasmond en Lekstreek in de achttiende eeuw," *Rotterdams Jaarboekje*, Eighth series, V (1977), 265-311; A.M. van der Woude, "De weerbare mannen van 1747 in de dorpen van het Zuiderkwartier van Holland als demografisch gegeven," *AAG Bijdragen*, VIII (1962), 35-76; and Van der Woude's comparison between South Holland and Holland north of the Y in *Het Noorderkwartier*, 369. On the growth of the number of masters organised in *zeemanscolleges*, see Davids, "Technological Change," 289 and 296. For the high proportion of seamen from South Holland (over thirty percent) on East Indiamen enlisted in Rotterdam and Dordrecht in the 1830s, see Broeze, *De Stad Schiedam*, 148. For a discussion of crews of warships in 1821 and 1856, see Bruijn, "Zeevarenden," 154.

[24] Bruijn, *The Dutch Navy*, 55, 133; Enthoven, "De Verenigde Oostindische Compagnie," 102; Bruijn, "De personeelsbehoefte," 237-238; and Bruijn, "Zeevarenden," 154 and 157.

foreign vessels. The scattered data available so far suggest that movements to other countries were spasmodic, short-lived and restricted in scope. In contrast to the foreign labour recruited for Dutch ships, seamen from the Netherlands who moved abroad – with the exception of those in the first wave in the 1590s – seem generally to have been skilled and to have been concentrated in the higher ranks.

The first wave, at the end of the sixteenth century, went to the Spanish Netherlands. Seamen from the United Provinces joined privateers and Spanish men-of-war based in Flemish ports in such large numbers as to give the States-General genuine cause for alarm. A second, smaller wave consisted of specialists hired to serve on the first Danish whalers after 1620. The third migration, starting in the 1670s and lasting until the early 1700s, was larger, broader and more varied in destination. Dutchmen were now occasionally also recruited as officers in the Danish Navy and navigators on Danish East Indiamen. Immigration of seamen from the Dutch Republic – mostly masters, mates and bosuns from Vlieland, Terschelling, Amsterdam and Friesland – into Danzig, which had been under way since the early sixteenth century, peaked between about 1678 and 1698. But the largest flow went to Russia, as a result of a recruitment drive organized by Czar Peter I. In 1698, Cornelis Cruys, a high official of the Admiralty of Amsterdam engaged as admiral of the Russian Navy, took 231 seamen from the Dutch Republic for service in Russia. Another 175 were recruited in 1703-1704. Both groups included not only common sailors, but also a few dozen captains, lieutenants, mates, gunners and surgeons. A fourth peak occurred shortly after the end of the War of the Spanish Succession. Seamen from Holland comprised about twenty percent of all foreigners (who made up more than forty percent of the crews) on private Indiamen and Chinamen fitted out in Ostend in the period 1715-1732; on ships of the Ostend East India Company, chartered in 1722, their share of the foreign element was about ten percent. The outbreak of another war between Russia and Sweden in the 1740s brought another wave of Dutch seamen into Russian service. By the middle of the eighteenth century, Dutchmen also for the first time crossed the North Sea to find employment in the British herring fisheries. The sixth, and last, wave took place during the 1760s and 1770s. A few seamen from Schiermonnikoog, Ameland, Den Helder and Huisduinen were hired as *commandeurs* on Hamburg whalers; in the peak year, 1767, seven out of fifty-four whalers equipped from Hamburg were commanded by Amelanders. And finally, seafarers from the Dutch Republic around 1770 once again moved to Russia to serve in the war against the Turks.[25]

Whether the movement of Dutchmen to foreign countries in the nineteenth century was more common than before 1800 is as yet hard to say. Eric Sager's data on the merchant marine of Atlantic Canada reveal that in the period 1863-1914 at least a small percentage of the crews of its fleets originated from the Netherlands.[26] Dutch mariners may have enlisted on other foreign ships as well. But the full reconstruction of flows of Dutch labour to other merchant marines in the nineteenth century – including the period 1815-1863 – awaits further research.

## The Operation of the Dutch Maritime Labour Market

Having outlined the basic features of the maritime labour market in the Netherlands between around 1570 and 1870, let us now take a closer

---

[25]Van Vliet, *Vissers*, 76; R.A. Stradling, *The Armada of Flanders. Spanish Maritime Policy and European War, 1568-1668* (Cambridge, 1992), 157-158 and 179; Sune Dalgaard, *Dansk-Norsk hvalfangst 1615-1660* (Copenhagen, 1962), 102-105 and 286-287; Bruijn, *The Dutch Navy*, 92; J. Parmentier, "Vogel Phoenix's rejse til Bantam 1677-1679," *Handels- of Søfahrtsmuseet på Kronborg årbog 1985*, 115-116; F.C. Berkenvelder, "Some Unknown Dutch Archivalia in the Gdańsk Archives," in W.G. Heeres, *et al.* (eds.), *From Dunkirk to Danzig. Shipping and Trade in the North Sea and the Baltic, 1350-1850* (Hilversum, 1988), 148; M. Bogucka, "Recruitment of Seamen for Gdansk ships in the 16th-18th Centuries," *Northern Seas Yearbook 1994*, 14-15; T. Ufkes, "Vlielanders, Friezen en andere Nederlanders te Danzig. Zeventiende en achttiende eeuwse gegevens in het burgerboek en de geloofsbrieven," *Jaarboek van het Centraal Bureau voor Genealogie*, XL (1989), 163-184; C.A. Davids, "On the Diffusion of Nautical Knowledge from the Netherlands to North-Eastern Europe, 1550-1850," in Heeres, *et al.* (eds.), *From Dunkirk to Danzig*, 232; *Russen en Nederlanders. Uit de geschiedenis van de betrekkingen tussen Nederland en Rusland 1600-1917* (The Hague, 1989), 97, 99 and 110; K. Degryse and J. Parmentier, "Maritime aspects of the Ostend trade to Mocha, India and China (1715-1732)," in J.R. Bruijn and F.S. Gaastra (eds.), *Ships, Sailors and Spices. East-India Companies and their Shipping in the 16th, 17th and 18th Centuries* (Amsterdam, 1993), 144; Bruijn and Lucassen, *Op de schepen*, 20 and 27; Wanda Oesau, *Hamburgs Grönlandfahrt auf Walfischfang und Robbenschlag* (Glückstadt, 1955), 192-205; P. Dekker, "De Amelander walvisvaart," *It Beaken*, XXXVI (1974), 210-211; and R.B. Prud'homme van Reine, *Jan Hendrik van Kinsbergen 1735-1819* (Amsterdam, 1990), 53.

[26]Eric W. Sager, *Seafaring Labour: The Merchant Marine of Atlantic Canada 1820-1914* (Montréal, 1989), 148-149.

look at the operation of the market itself. How was labour mobilized? How did the labour market actually function?

It is now generally assumed that the maritime labour market in the Netherlands (in common with the market for labour in other sectors of the Dutch economy) between the early seventeenth and late nineteenth centuries was not homogeneous, but consisted in fact of two segments: an internal segment, containing a core of labourers with more-or-less regular ties to particular employers, and an external segment, consisting of a flexible mass of casual labour and migrant workers. The former included a large part of the workforce of the merchant marine active in European waters and (up to the end of the seventeenth century at least) of the whaling industry, plus the higher ranks in the Navy, the West India trade and the VOC, while the latter comprised the remainder of the seafaring labour force. Labour for the internal segment was largely recruited from maritime communities in Holland, Zeeland, Friesland, Groningen and the Wadden Islands. Labour for the external segment was partly recruited from the permanent urban population in Holland and Zeeland, as well as from migrant workers from abroad, especially from Germany and Scandinavia.[27] The proportion between the internal and external segments and between the Dutch and foreign elements in the external segment varied over time.

Mobility between the internal and external segments was low. The higher ranks were virtually closed to foreigners. Van Royen has shown that around 1700 it was hard for a foreigner in the Dutch merchant marine even to reach the rank of bosun, let alone mate or master. Movement of seamen from maritime communities into the segment of the labour market where casual labour dominated was also rare, as data on employment patterns of seafarers subscribing to seamen's boxes in Holland attest. Members of seamen's boxes rarely if ever joined the Navy, the VOC, or West Indiamen. Of the forty-four contributors to the box in Broek in Waterland in 1658 whose employment during the year is known, twenty-one sailed to France, ten to the Baltic and seven to Archangel, while six went whaling. Among the seventy-seven contributors in 1660, twenty-three went to France, eighteen to the Baltic,

[27]See Lucassen, "Zeevarenden," 130-136; Davids, *Wat lijdt den zeeman*, 14-17; Bruijn and Lucassen, *Op de schepen*, 11-29; A. Knotter, "De Amsterdamse scheepvaart en het Noordhollandse platteland in de 16de en 17de eeuw. Het probleem van de arbeidsmarkt," *Holland*, XVI (1984), 281-291; and Van Royen, *Zeevarenden*, 139-150.

six to Norway, two to the Mediterranean and twenty to the whaling grounds off Spitsbergen; a mere eight joined the VOC. Specialization in whaling and short-sea merchant shipping was also evident among members of three other insurance boxes of seamen in Holland in the first half of the eighteenth century (see table 9). This was the very period when demand for sailors in the Dutch Navy, privateering (during the War of Spanish Succession) and the VOC was higher than ever.[28]

**Table 9**
**Specialization by Branch of Shipping of Members of Seamen's Boxes in Holland**

| | Seamen's Box | | | | | | |
|---|---|---|---|---|---|---|---|
| Branch of Shipping | Westwoud | | Hem | | Graft | | |
| | 1700 | 1710 | 1703 | 1710 | 1703 | 1715 | 1740 |
| Whaling | 1 | 6 | 20 | 11 | 42 | 24 | 24 |
| Herring fishing | 1 | | | 1 | 7 | 1 | 5 |
| West Indies/Africa | | | 1 | | 5 | 1 | 1 |
| France/Portugal | 5 | 3 | 8 | 1 | 5 | 2 | 1 |
| Mediterranean | | | | 1 | | | 1 |
| Russia | | 1 | | | 2 | 5 | |
| North Sea/Baltic | 6 | 6 | 18 | 13 | 2 | 2 | 4 |
| whaling + Portugal | | | 9 | | 2 | 3 | |
| West Indies + Russia | | | | | | 2 | |
| Portugal + Russia | | | | | | 2 | |
| France + Baltic | | 6 | | 2 | | | 1 |
| Other Combinations | 4 | 1 | 1 | 4 | 2 | 4 | 1 |
| Total Members | 17 | 23 | 57 | 33 | 67 | 46 | 38 |

*Sources*: See text.

Recruitment methods differed between the two segments of the labour market. Seamen in the internal segment were normally recruited through networks of personal relations, centered upon maritime communities in villages and ports. Crews of merchantmen (and certainly the higher ranks) were often composed largely of people from the same

[28]Van Royen, *Zeevarenden*, 139-149 and 232-235; C.A. Davids, "Seamen's Organisations and Social Protest in Europe, c.1300-1825," *International Review of Social History*, XXXIX (1994), 159-160; Van Royen, "Recruitment Patterns," 18; J.C. van der Does, "Een eigenaardige assurantie," *Tijdschrift voor Geschiedenis*, XLIII (1930), 60; and Boon, "Zeelieden," 112.

locality as the master. In the external segment, by contrast, supply and demand were – since the late seventeenth century at least – brought together through the agency of private or government-appointed brokers, called *makelaars ter zeevaart*, *besteder van zeevarende lieden* or *verhuurder van matrozen*, who in ports commonly relied on the services of crimps or lodginghouse keepers (*volkhouders*, *slaapbazen*, *zielverkopers*). Amsterdam had at least nine private *makelaars* around 1700 and eight in 1870; in Rotterdam, the number of brokers appointed by the local government rose from one in the seventeenth century to four in 1749 and eight by 1870. The number of crimps was certainly much larger. Recruitment of Javanese and Chinese seamen for the VOC in Asia was arranged through the intermediary of native brokers. There were several brokers active in Batavia in the 1780s.[29]

Although the methods used by crimps often tended more towards compulsion than friendly persuasion (especially after 1740, when demand for able seamen increasingly outran supply), enlistment on warships, whalers, VOC vessels or West Indiamen in the Netherlands always remained essentially voluntary. The Dutch Navy never resorted to impressment. In times of acute need, the authorities chose to attract additional labour by offering bounties, introducing wartime wage increases, imposing temporary embargoes on merchant shipping, whaling or privateering, or recruiting fixed numbers of men by private shipowners (under threat of embargoes) rather than outright coercion. In the nineteenth century the Navy slowly built a more stable workforce by enlisting seamen for a fixed term (two to four years in 1800, five after 1821) instead of recruiting them by the voyage.[30]

In contrast to seamen in the internal segment of the market, workers in the external segment did not develop any durable, formal organisation. Although the dozens of riots and work stoppages by sailors in the Navy or the VOC during the seventeenth and eighteenth centuries betrayed a higher level of preparation and informal organisation than has sometimes been claimed, common seamen in these branches of shipping

---

[29]Van Royen, *Zeevarenden*, chapter 3 and 146; J.R. Bruijn, *Het gelag der zeelieden* (Leiden, 1978), 5-9, 20, 25-27; and Dillo, *De nadagen*, 105-106.

[30]M. van Alphen, "The Female Side of Dutch Shipping. Financial Bonds of Seamen Ashore in the 17th and 18th Centuries," in J.R. Bruijn and W.F.J. Mörzer Bruyns (eds.), *Anglo-Dutch Mercantile Maritime Relations 1700-1850* (Amsterdam, 1991), 127-128; Bruijn, *The Dutch Navy*, 130 and 195-199; and Bruijn, "Zeevarenden," 168.

in the period under discussion never established a permanent association, let alone a trade union.[31] In the internal segment of the labour market, however, the period 1570-1870 saw the rise of two new types of seamen's organisations: insurance boxes and shipmasters' societies.

The total number of known seamen's boxes (*zeevarende beurzen, bootsgezellenbeurzen* or *budels van assurantie*) established in the Netherlands is forty-three, a figure that must be regarded as a minimum.[32] The first was founded in the fishing village of Maassluis in Holland in 1613, while the last was founded in Hoogkarspel in Westfriesland in 1829. As table 10 shows, the creation of these insurance boxes peaked during the final phase of the war between the Republic and Spain (the 1630s and 1640s) and during the Nine Years' War and the War of Spanish Succession. The majority arose in villages and towns in the Noorderkwartier and Westfriesland.

**Table 10**
**Insurance Boxes of Seamen in the Netherlands**

| Period | Number of New Foundations |
|---|---|
| 1610-1629 | 5 |
| 1630-1649 | 23 |
| 1650-1669 | 4 |
| 1670-1689 | 1 |
| 1690-1709 | 4 |
| 1710-1729 | - |
| 1730-1749 | 1 |
| 1750-1769 | 1 |
| 1770-1789 | - |
| 1790-1809 | - |
| 1810-1829 | 1 |
| Date Unknown | 3 |
| Total | 43 |

*Source*: See text.

[31] Davids, "Seamens' Organisations," 159-161.

[32] The numbers given here are higher than the preliminary ones in Davids, "Seamens' Organisations," 153. Additional information was provided by P. Boon, "West Friesland and the Sound (1681-1720). Sound Toll Tables and the Facts in West Friesland," in Heeres, *et al.* (eds.), *From Dunkirk to Danzig*, 174, and personal communication from drs. P. Boon. I am grateful to drs. Boon for sharing his extensive knowledge of *bootsgezellenbeurzen*.

Seamen's boxes included masters, mates and common seamen. The principle of the boxes was that in exchange for dues paid each time they left port – the amount varied according to the destination – members were entitled to benefits if they fell victim to a particular misfortune. Originally, seamen's boxes confined themselves to providing subsistence allowances to seamen held in captivity by privateers. Some also furnished money to cover travel expenses for the voyage home after release. In the second half of the seventeenth century insurance boxes widened their package of services to include disability benefits and compensation for personal property lost in combat or by shipwreck. When the number of claims by members of insurance boxes in the countryside of North Holland declined due to a drop in seafaring activities in the eighteenth century, the funds in the seamen's boxes were often at the behest of village authorities re-allocated for communal purposes, like poor relief, education or repair of churches.[33]

Shipmasters' societies (*zeemanscolleges*) developed in the Netherlands in the late eighteenth century. Whether the first one, *De Blaauwe Vlag* founded in Amsterdam in 1795, had some connection with an insurance box of VOC officers established in Amsterdam in 1750 is as yet unclear. The total number of *zeemanscolleges* founded up to 1881 was at least sixteen.[34]

Shipmasters' societies essentially can be described as separate insurance boxes for masters. Their chief purpose was to provide pensions and other allowances to masters and their families. Yet it was not uncommon for them to assume a variety of other functions as well. They could accelerate the flow of information in the industry by encouraging members to transmit data on ships sighted at sea to owners and other interested parties ashore, or promote the long-term advancement of seafaring by subsidizing navigation schools, founding libraries and reading rooms or collaborating in the gathering of data for scientific research. As a result, they could help to enhance the corporate spirit of shipmasters, the technical competence of their members and the status of the profession of sea captain in general.[35]

---

[33]Davids, "Seamens' Organisations," 153-154.

[34]Davids, "Technological Change," 289; and Davids, "Seamen's Organisations," 156.

[35]Davids, "Technological Change," 289-291.

To what extent the segmented structure of the maritime labour market was also reflected in differences in nominal income levels is as yet hard to gauge. The size of wage differentials and their variation in the course of time are not as precisely established as one would wish. While levels in the Navy and the VOC are reasonably well known – and in fact, except in wartime, throughout much of the seventeenth and eighteenth centuries scarcely varied at all – data on wages in the merchant navy and other branches of shipping are much more difficult to find. Tables 11 and 12 sum up the evidence available so far for wages of selected ranks of seafarers.

**Table 11**
**Monthly Rates of Pay in the Dutch Navy, 17th-19th Centuries (guilders)**

| Rank | Admiralty and Year | | | | |
|---|---|---|---|---|---|
| | Zeeland 1621 | Navy, second half 17th c. | Amsterdam from 1725 on | Zeeland c. 1770 | Navy, first half 19th c |
| First Mate | 24 | 34-36 | 36 | 36 | 48 |
| Second Mate | | 30 | 30 | 30 | 36 |
| Bosun | 14 | 20-22 | 22 | 22 | 26 |
| Quartermaster | 12 | 13-14 | 15 | 14 | |
| Carpenter | 16 | 28-30 | 28 | 30 | 46 (max.) |
| Sailmaker | | 14-16 | 18 | 25 | 30 (max.) |
| Steward | 12 | 18-22 | 18 | 20 | |
| Cook | 12 | 18-21 | 18 | 20 | 20-22 |
| Able Seaman | 8 | 10-11 | 11 | 9-12 | 13-15 |
| Ordinary Seaman | 6 | | | | 11 |
| Boy | 3 | 4-7 | 4-7 | 6-7 | |

*Sources*: Bruijn, "Zeevarenden," 171; Bruijn, *The Dutch Navy*, 58, 199; and Lucassen, "Zeevarenden," 141.

It can be cautiously inferred that the wages of the highest ranking mates (almost exclusively Dutchmen) were in general about three times as high as those of able seamen (who were to a greater extent recruited from the pool of casual and foreign labour), with the difference being somewhat larger in the VOC and somewhat smaller in the merchant marine employed in Europe. Moreover, wages in the lower ranks of the merchant marine in Europe were in the seventeenth and eighteenth centuries higher than those paid by the Navy and the East-India Company, even though the wage level in the Navy (in line with the overall trend in wages in the Dutch Republic) underwent a substantial increase between the 1620s and 1650s. While the level of wages of common seamen showed an overall rise in the early nineteenth century, the gap between wages in the lower ranks of the merchant marine (both in the European and outer-European trades) and those of the navy apparently became even larger than before. Monthly rates of pay of able seamen in the whaling industry were in the later seventeenth and eighteenth century probably higher than in the Navy, the East-India Company and even the mercantile marine: eighteen-twenty guilders.[36]

**Table 12**
**Monthly Rates of Pay in the VOC and the Merchant Marine, 17th-19th Centuries (guilders)**

| Rank | Branch of Shipping, Period, Trade | | | | | |
|---|---|---|---|---|---|---|
| | VOC | Merchant Shipping | | | | |
| | c. 1650-1740 | 1700-1710 | 1774/75 | c. 1815-1830 | | |
| | | Europe | Europe | Europe | Atlantic | Asia |
| Master | 60-80 | | | | | |
| First Mate | 48-50 | 32 | 31.6 | 25-40 | 35-50 | 70-75 |
| Second Mate | 32-36 | | | 15-25 | 26-40 | 45-50 |
| Bosun | 22-26 | | 23.4 | 24-29 | 28-32 | 30-45 |
| Quartermaster | 14 | | | | | |
| Carpenter | 38-48 | 32 | 31.7 | 25-36 | 26-50 | 50-56 |
| Sailmaker | 18-20 | | | | 25 | 25-34 |
| Steward | 20-24 | | | | | |
| Cook | 20-24 | 25 | 19.8 | 10-25 | 25-35 | 30-40 |
| Able Seaman | 11-12 | 10-15 | 14.5 | 18-20 | 18-20 | 20 |
| Ordinary Seaman | 7-11 | | | 12-16 | 12-18 | 14-18 |
| Boy | 4-6 | 5-8 | | | | |

*Sources*: J.R. Bruijn, *et al.* (eds.), *Dutch-Asiatic Shipping in the 17th and 18th Centuries* (3 vols., The Hague, 1979-1987), I, 210-211; Paul C. van Royen, "Recruitment Patterns of the Dutch Merchant Marine in the Seventeenth to Nineteenth Centuries," in Lewis R. Fischer, *et al.* (eds.), *The North Sea. Twelve Essays on Social History of Maritime Labour* (Stavanger, 1992), 17; P.C. van Royen, "Mariners and Markets in the Age of Sail: The Case of the Netherlands," in Lewis R. Fischer (ed.), *The Market for Seamen in the Age of Sail* (St. John's, 1994), 54; and Bruijn, "Zeevarenden," 171.

And wages did not necessarily equal earnings. On the one hand, actual earnings of individual seamen could be lower than the wages to

[36]De Jong, *Geschiedenis*, 309-310.

which they were formally entitled due to deductions for fines or personal expenses or for medical care aboard. On the other hand, earnings could be higher than wages thanks to all sorts of additional benefits which seamen could gain in the course of a voyage or a term of service as a result of their own enterprise or the collective efforts of the crew, notably bounties, shares in a catch, shares in prize money or income from private trade. There is no reason to dismiss these sources of income *a priori* as insignificant. In 1742 and 1743 sailors in Amsterdam rioted against new rules by which the VOC tried to abolish opportunities for private trade in exchange for a lump sum paid on return, even though this "cursed" lump sum amounted to no less than thirteen times an ordinary seaman's monthly wage.[37] If the additional sources of income were *not* insignificant, it follows that a comparison between nominal income differences between internal and external segments of the labour market cannot be based solely on an examination of wage differentials.

If wages did not equal earnings, it further follows that data on wage levels – even if calculated in real terms – are not sufficient to warrant conclusions about whether or not seamen were able to marry, reproduce and support families (to say nothing of the possibility that seamen's incomes might be in fact have been supplemented by their wives). In contrast with a current assumption about the implications of the relatively low level of wages in the Navy or the VOC, Hart's data on seamen in mid-seventeenth century Amsterdam show that large numbers of seamen in the casual labour pool married. Riots against naval authorities during the Anglo-Dutch Wars time and again turn out to have been led by seamen's wives. And the majority of *zielverkopers* up to about 1725 were wives of seamen who had enlisted in the Navy, the VOC or the West-India trade.[38] There is thus every reason to push the micro-analysis of the operation of the labour market on this point further than has been done to this point.

[37] Lucassen, "Zeevarenden," 140-143; Bruijn, "Zeevarenden," 172-174; De Jong, *Geschiedenis*, 91-108; Verhees-Van Meer, *De Zeeuwse kaapvaart*, 54-55; Bruijn, *The Dutch Navy*, 135; and Davids, "Seamens' Organisations," 160.

[38] Lucassen, "Zeevarenden," 144; Lucassen and Bruijn, *Op de schepen*, 16 and 18; S. Hart, "Zeelieden te Amsterdam in de zeventiende eeuw. Een historisch-demografisch onderzoek," in S. Hart, *Geschrift en getal* (Dordrecht, 1976), 193-208; R.M. Dekker, *Holland in beroering. Oproeren in de 17de en 18de eeuw* (Baarn, 1982), 56; and Van Alphen, "The Female Side," 128.

The causes for the variation in the proportion between the internal and external segments of the labour market and between the Dutch and foreign elements in the external segment in the course of time also deserve closer scrutiny. Jan Lucassen has drawn attention to the importance of changes in the traditional labour cycle in the countryside of Holland north of the Y as a possible explanation for its population decline after 1650 (which Van der Woude in turn suggested as a possible reason for the decrease in the supply of labour from maritime communities in the Noorderkwartier and Westfriesland). The size of population in Holland north of the Y may have declined, Lucassen argued, because opportunities for peasants or labourers to generate a sufficient income by moving through a linked series of by-employments throughout the year (including seafaring or fishing during the summer) declined considerably in the second half of the seventeenth century. Van Royen on the other hand has hypothesized that the disappearance of seamen from Holland north of the Y was rather a consequence of the "enormous demand for manpower [between 1680 and 1720] from all different branches of shipping in the Dutch Republic combined with the dangers and vicissitudes of life on board." The area, in short, was drained of people because of the heavy demands of seafaring. To explain the shifts in shares of foreigners and Dutchmen in the external segment of the maritime labour market, Bruijn and Lucassen have suggested that at least three variables should be considered: employment opportunities in high-wage jobs in other sectors of the Dutch economy; the evolution of real wages; and the size of demand for low-wage labour in the shipping industry, notably the VOC. The share of Dutchmen among VOC personnel peaked, they argued, in the period between the 1660s and 1720s when employment opportunities in high-wage jobs in other sectors of the Dutch economy declined, real wages increased and demand from the VOC rapidly expanded.[39] To assess the validity of these different theses, further micro-level studies are urgently needed. These inquiries should specifically address such issues as the actual operation of the labour cycle in Holland (including possibilities of substitution of lost employment opportunities), the mortality rates in different branches of

---

[39]Van der Woude, *Het Noorderkwartier*, 396-397; J. Lucassen, *Naar de kusten van de Noordzee. Trekarbeid in Europees perspektief, 1600-1900* (Gouda, 1984), 159-164; Van Royen, "Manning the Merchant Marine," 26; and Bruijn and Lucassen, *Op de schepen*, 24-29.

shipping, the reproductive behaviour of seamen and the actual earnings of VOC employees compared to labour elsewhere in the Dutch economy.

## Conclusion

This survey of the development of the maritime labour market in the Netherlands between 1570 and 1870 has revealed a number of features that compared with other countries in Europe are particularly of note. First of all, a rapid expansion up to the middle of the seventeenth century was followed by a long period of stabilisation to the end of the eighteenth century; after a rapid decline around 1800, a strong recovery set in during the second quarter of the nineteenth century. Second, a large share of total employment in the seventeenth and eighteenth centuries was provided by the Dutch East India Company, particularly after 1680. Third, there was a significant shift in the origins of seafarers in the Netherlands: while Holland north of the Y and Zeeland (for reasons which are still not fully understood) showed a long-term decline as reservoirs of seamen, the central regions around Amsterdam and Rotterdam held their own and the northeastern periphery became ever more important in the period between 1700 and 1850. Fourth, a large part of the labour supply in the Dutch maritime sector was always recruited from abroad, though the proportion between Dutchmen and foreigners varied significantly by branch of shipping, rank and over time. Fifth, the movement of Dutchmen abroad always paled by comparison with the flow in the opposite direction.

To understand these trends, the concepts and theory of the segmented labour market are of great importance. But these can only be used fully, I have argued in the last section, if the aggregate perspective is supplemented by detailed analyses at a micro-level. The proposition launched by Baud, Engelen and Knotter for the study of changing labour relations as a whole is valid for maritime history as well: the most interesting new insights can be obtained by focusing on the level of households, family networks and life courses of individuals.[40]

---

[40]Michiel Baud, Theo Engelen and Ad Knotter, "Preface," in Baud, Engelen and Knotter (eds.), *Economic and Social History in the Netherlands 6. Family Strategies and Changing Labour Relations* (Amsterdam, 1994), 8; and Jan Kok, "Revealing Family Strategies using Life Course Analysis," *ibid.*, 109-127. A recent model study of this kind is Piet Boon, *Bouwers van de zee. Zeevarenden van het Westfriese platteland c. 1680-1720* (The Hague, 1996).

# English Sailors, 1570-1775

**Peter Earle**

## Introduction

English shipping in the middle of the sixteenth century was at a low ebb, "a meagre coastal traffic, a fishery of moderate scale, a trickle of carrying trade with the Low Countries, Spain, Portugal, France and the Baltic," as Ralph Davis described it.[1] The three decades from 1570, however, were marked by considerable expansion, driven by the rapid growth of the east coast coal trade, the revival of trade to the Mediterranean and the development of oceanic fishing off Iceland and the Newfoundland Banks. After 1600, voyages to the Indian Ocean became a regular feature of maritime life, while colonization in North America and the West Indies triggered a huge expansion in Atlantic trade.

The growth of these trades doubled tonnage between the 1580s and the 1640s, but as yet posed little threat to the Dutch, who remained the common carriers of Europe. English ships were notable for their strength and fighting abilities, not for their cheapness. Such powerful ships, bristling with men and guns, were suitable for the dangerous waters south and west of Cape Finisterre. But in the bulk carrying trades of the North Sea and the Baltic these expensive ships found it very difficult to compete with the lightly-manned Dutch flyboats.[2]

In the four decades after 1650 tonnage doubled again, with rapid growth in many long-distance trades, above all to America and the West Indies, where the rise of the plantation also encouraged rapid expansion in the slave trade from West Africa. Such growth was counterbalanced to some extent by stability or decline in oceanic fishing and whaling.

---

[1]Ralph Davis, *The Rise of the English Shipping Industry in the Seventeenth and Eighteenth Centuries* (London, 1962), 2. This book is the main source for this introduction.

[2]*Ibid.*, 11; and Violet Barbour, "Dutch and English Merchant Shipping in the Seventeenth Century," *Economic History Review*, II (1930).

Nearer home, slower growth in the coal trade was compensated by rapid expansion in the carriage of timber and marine stores from Norway and the Baltic, suggesting that the English were at last becoming competitive in the carriage of bulky low-value cargoes. The other major development after 1650 was the impact of the Navigation Acts, which provided English and colonial shipping with a virtual monopoly of the colonial carrying trade, driving out the once dominant Dutch.[3] In peacetime at least, the manning requirements of the legislation were also observed so that at least three-quarters and probably far more of the sailors on English ships were natives of England or its colonies.

Growth did not continue with the same vigour into the eighteenth century. French competition made inroads into Mediterranean commerce, while New England skippers took over much of the trade in salt cod from Newfoundland to Europe. The east coast coal trade grew very slowly until the 1730s, while trade to Norway and the Baltic also went through a period of difficulty. Only the long-distance trades to the Americas and the east were still buoyant, though growth in the tobacco trade tended to benefit Scottish rather than English shipping, a shift in geographic emphasis reflected in the rise in importance of northwestern English ports such as Liverpool and Whitehaven.

This period of comparative stagnation came to an end with peace in 1748, which ushered in a quarter of a century of very rapid growth. The chief beneficiaries were once again the colonial and East Indian trades, the tea trade from China growing particularly rapidly. Demand for new shipping also led to a recovery in trade with the Baltic, while whaling in the Greenland Seas, which had been abandoned for decades, now rose to employ over fifty ships a year by the early 1770s.[4] This period was also characterized by the beginnings of the Industrial Revolution which led, among other things, to growth in the coastal trades and in the import of iron from Sweden and Russia.

The period 1570 to 1775 thus saw immense changes in the possibilities and nature of employment for English sailors. In 1570, such prospects were few in number and, with the exception of the oceanic fisheries, largely confined to the coastal waters of England and of western and northwestern Europe. In 1775, such waters were still the

---

[3]On this subject see L.A. Harper, *The English Navigation Laws* (New York, 1939).

[4]Gordon Jackson, *The British Whaling Trade* (London, 1978).

only maritime experience of many English sailors, but there were also thousands of seafaring men who could boast like the old tar John Seagerts that they had "been in almost all habitable parts of ye world."[5]

Very little is known about the lives of these men. English historians have tended to neglect sailors, especially those in the merchant service.[6] Some work has been done on numbers, manning ratios, crew size and wages. But little has been done on where the sailors came from, their training and career structure, discipline, mortality or collective behaviour. Historians such as Ralph Davis, Geoffrey Scammell, Marcus Rediker and Jon Press certainly have something to say on these subjects, while the present author is also working on the "social history" of sailors, but overall the gaps in our knowledge are very large.[7]

**How Many Sailors?**

Contributors were asked how many sailors there were at benchmark dates. One can start with the surveys of ships and sailors ordered by the Privy Council in the late sixteenth and early seventeenth centuries (see table 1). The most complete in 1582 records just over 16,000 sailors and fishermen, about 0.5% of the population.[8] There was no similar survey for the late seventeenth century, so historians have been forced to use contemporary estimates by Petty and King, who put the number of sailors at 48,000 and 50,000, respectively.[9] Such numbers are probably

---

[5]Great Britain, Public Record Office (PRO), High Court of Admiralty (HCA) 13/83.

[6]For surveys of recent work, see Peter N. Davies and Sheila Marriner, "Recent Publications and Developments in the Study of Maritime Economic History," *Journal of Transport History*, Third Series, IX (1988); and David M. Williams, "The Progress of Maritime History, 1953-93," *ibid.*, Third Series, XIV (1993).

[7]Davis, *Rise*, chapters 6 and 7; G.V. Scammell, "Manning the English Merchant Service in the Sixteenth Century," *Mariner's Mirror*, LVI (1970); Marcus Rediker, *Between the Devil and the Deep Blue Sea. Merchant Seamen, Pirates, and the Anglo-American Maritime World, 1700-1750* (Cambridge, 1987); and Jon Press, *The Merchant Seamen of Bristol, 1747-1789* (Bristol, 1976).

[8]PRO, State Papers (SP) 12/156, nos. 45 and 46. Some allowance has been made for Wales, which was omitted from the survey.

[9]John Ehrman, *The Navy in the War of William III* (Cambridge, 1953), 110-111.

too high but, as they stand, indicate a three-fold increase since the late sixteenth century, so that by the 1680s seamen represented about one percent of the populace, a figure never reached again in the period.

**Table 1**
**Sailors and Shipping Tonnage**

| Year | Tonnage | Sailors | Ton/Man |
|---|---|---|---|
| 1582 | 68433 | 16119 | 4.25 |
| 1686 | 350000 | c. 50000 | 7.0 |
| 1773 | 581000 | 52789 | 11.0 |

*Sources*: 1582: tonnage from L.A. Harper, *The English Navigation Laws* (New York, 1939), 322; sailors from Great Britain, Public Record Office (PRO), State Papers (SP) 12/156, no. 46. The total has been inflated by 4.9% to include an estimate for Wales; see Harper, *English Navigation Laws*, 323, fn. 6. 1686: tonnage from Ralph Davis, "Merchant Shipping in the Economy of the Late Seventeenth Century," *Economic History Review*, Second Series, IX (1956), 72, fn. 5; sailors from John Ehrman, *The Navy in the War of William III* (Cambridge, 1953), 110-111. 1773: tonnage and sailors from Harper, *English Navigation Laws*, 329 and fn. 28.

**Table 2**
**Regional Distribution of Sailors**

| | 1582 | | 1792 | | % |
|---|---|---|---|---|---|
| Region | N | % | N | % | Inc |
| Northeast | 2180 | 13.5 | 18197 | 20.8 | 835 |
| East Anglia | 2952 | 18.3 | 4820 | 5.5 | 163 |
| Southeast | 1888 | 11.7 | 4347 | 5.0 | 230 |
| London | 1325 | 8.2 | 30200 | 34.5 | 2279 |
| South | 983 | 6.1 | 2414 | 2.8 | 246 |
| Southwest | 5461 | 33.9 | 11658 | 13.3 | 213 |
| Wales | 790 | 4.9 | 3296 | 3.8 | 417 |
| Northwest | 536 | 3.3 | 12637 | 14.4 | 2358 |
| Total | 16115 | 99.9 | 87569 | 100.1 | 543 |

*Notes*: Northeast: Northumberland, Durham, Yorks and Lincs; East Anglia: Suffolk, Norfolk and Cambridgeshire; Southeast: Essex and Kent; South: Sussex and Hampshire; Southwest: Dorset, Devon, Cornwall, Somerset and Gloucester; Northwest: Cheshire, Lancashire and Cumberland.

*Source*: For 1582: PRO SP12/156 No. 46, omitting the London "wherrymen." Welsh sailors have been estimated as in table 1. For 1792: BL, Add. Ms. 38432. This lists tonnage port by port and "the number of sailors usually employed therein," so that real totals would be less since not all ships would be at sea at once.

Eighteenth-century evidence is more abundant and shows that, despite a considerable increase in shipping tonnage after 1750, there was little if any increase on the 1680s figure before 1775. Indeed, if David Starkey's estimates are correct, there was a fall in numbers from the late seventeenth century which was only made up after 1750.[10] The main reason for this stability was the improvement in manning ratios, which is shown in table 1 and will be discussed in the next section.

The period was also marked by considerable change in the distribution of sailors between regions (see table 2). The growth in the Northeast reflects the rise of the coal trade and would have been concentrated in the period up to 1700, since the trade grew more slowly afterwards and there was a big improvement in manning ratios. The rise of the Northwest is dominated by Liverpool, which was second only to London as a sailortown by the second half of the eighteenth century. But the rapid expansion of the Northwest coal trade was also important, Whitehaven having nearly as many sailors as Bristol in 1792. The increase in London's sailors was probably not quite as great as shown in the table, since the 1582 figure seems too low, but there certainly was a phenomenal growth, as London increasingly dominated English foreign trade in the seventeenth century. Most of this growth in numbers probably occurred before 1700, since London's percentage of England's shipping tonnage fell in the eighteenth century and its share of the labour-intensive fishing and coastal trades fell even faster. Meanwhile, growth in the numbers of sailors in London and the northern counties was balanced by a relative decline of the leading regions of the 1580s, East Anglia and especially the Southwest, a region almost synonymous with English maritime expansion in Elizabethan times.

One large group has so far been omitted from this survey, the men who served in the Royal Navy (RN). It will be more realistic to estimate peacetime numbers, since wartime conditions confuse the issue. Every war saw relaxation of the manning requirements of the Navigation Acts, leading to recruitment of foreign sailors. War also interfered with trade so that often fewer merchant ships were at sea and these were not

---

[10]David J. Starkey, "War and the Market for Seafarers in Britain, 1736-1792," in Lewis R. Fischer and Helge W. Nordvik (eds.), *Shipping and Trade, 1750-1950: Essays in International Maritime Economic History* (Pontefract, 1990), 29 and 41. His figures show only about 35,000 sailors in the 1730s. His 1773 figure is consistent with that in Harper, *English Navigation Laws*, 329, used in table 1.

manned as fully as in peacetime. Finally, merchant vessels, privateers and the RN all employed large numbers of landsmen in wartime.

Sailors in the RN are possibly included in the total given above for 1582 but, in any case, the numbers were very small. In 1580, for instance, there were only ten royal ships in commission, which probably employed about 1000 sailors.[11] A hundred years later, the Restoration navy normally employed some 3000-4000 men in peacetime. Growth continued into the eighteenth century, with numbers around 10,000 between 1713 and 1739 and 15,000 after the Seven Years' War.[12] The peacetime navy thus made a far greater demand on the nation's stock of seamen than in the seventeenth century but, even so, it is unlikely that peacetime numbers in the navy and merchant service combined ever exceeded 70,000 in the two centuries considered.

## Manning Ratios and Crew Size

English shipping made great gains in tons carried per man employed, as can be seen in table 1. The figure was about four tons in 1582, seven in 1686 and eleven in 1773. These are of course very crude figures, reflecting simply the tonnage of shipping divided by the number of sailors. The improvement is, however, confirmed in specialist studies and should be seen as a major gain in productivity, caused mainly by an increase in the size of ships. James Shepherd and Gary Walton analysed Lloyd's *Register of Shipping* for 1764 and found a steady improvement related to size, with ships between fifty and ninety-nine tons carrying less than ten tons per man, while ships of more than 300 tons carried over twenty tons per man.[13]

---

[11]M. Oppenheim, *A History of the Administration of the Royal Navy. Vol. I: 1509-1660* (London, 1896), 118.

[12]For the Restoration Navy, see J.D. Davies, *Gentlemen and Tarpaulins: The Officers and Men of the Restoration Navy* (Oxford, 1991), 12 and 69; for the eighteenth century, see Christopher Lloyd, *The British Seaman 1200-1860. A Social Survey* (London, 1968), 286-288. See also Starkey, "War and the Market for Seafarers," for detailed estimates for the period after 1736.

[13]James F. Shepherd and Gary M. Walton, *Shipping, Maritime Trade and the Economic Development of Colonial North America* (Cambridge, 1972), 75. See also Davis, *Rise*, 73.

The merchant fleet of 1582 was minuscule, with only twenty vessels over 200 tons, but ships got larger in the seventeenth century, the earliest and biggest increase coming in colliers and timber ships which were both quick to adopt the Dutch-type cheap bulk carriers. The average size of colliers quadrupled in the course of the seventeenth century to about 250 tons, while ton/man ratios rose from ten or less in the late sixteenth century to well over twenty by 1700. There was to be further improvement in the eighteenth century.[14]

The cheap operation of colliers depended on readily available cargoes, comparatively quick turnaround times, and the relative absence of predators, so that ships did not have to carry large crews to defend themselves. Few other trades shared all these advantages. In most other coasting trades, there was not sufficient cargo to justify the use of large vessels. In colonial trades, there might be enough cargo but loading was so slow that it rarely paid to employ very large craft. And all long-distance trade was sufficiently dangerous to require large numbers of guns and the men to work them to fend off predators.

Conditions changed in the eighteenth century. Turnaround times and cargo availability improved, encouraging the use of larger ships in a wider range of trades. From the 1720s and 1730s, piracy also became less of a problem, thus enabling craft in Mediterranean and colonial waters to reduce their crews to the minimum needed to sail them.[15] Such changes allowed vessels to get bigger and to use smaller crews, but few could match the ton/man ratios of twenty and more already achieved by colliers and timber ships by 1700. Most long-distance trades improved their ratios from well under ten in the seventeenth century to around fourteen or fifteen by the end of our period, but the average was kept down by craft engaged in the short trades to Europe and even more by the great mass of coasters with very small crews but also very little carrying capacity.[16]

Ton/man ratios do not by themselves tell us much about crew size. This obviously varied enormously, reflecting as it did both the size

---

[14]Harper, *English Navigation Laws*, 335-336.

[15]Shepherd and Walton, *Shipping*, chapter 5 and appendix 3.

[16]For some figures based on Mediterranean passes and Seamen's Sixpences, see Davis, *Rise*, 71. The analysis in Shepherd and Walton, *Shipping*, appendix 3, based on colonial shipping returns, shows lower ratios but the same trend to higher ton/man ratios.

of the ships and the manning ratios in different trades. Some idea of the variety can be seen in table 3, which is based on a survey made in 1703, augmented by estimates for colliers and other coasters from different sources. Life must have been very different for sailors in East Indiamen, which averaged some 500 tons at this date and were likely to be away from home for at least two years, than for the typical master, man and boy who worked the small coasters and were seldom away from their home port for more than a month. They were all sailors, however, and we will now see from where they came.

**Table 3**
**Crew Size in Different Trades, 1703**

| Trade | No. Ships | No. Men | Avg. Crew |
|---|---|---|---|
| East India | 21 | 1800 | 85.7 |
| Mediterranean | 50 | 1590 | 31.8 |
| Africa | 48 | 1359 | 28.3 |
| Barbados/Leeward Islands | 85 | 1691 | 19.9 |
| Virginia, Maryland, Penn. | 125 | 2489 | 19.9 |
| East Country | 67 | 960 | 14.3 |
| Portugal | 175 | 2074 | 11.8 |
| Ireland and Scotland | 28 | 311 | 11.1 |
| Coal Trade | | | 8.5 |
| Holland | 47 | 237 | 5.0 |
| Coasters | | | 2.8 |

*Source*: British Library, Add. 4539, f. 104, for all except the coal trade, which is based on figures for 1703 in M.W. Flinn, *The History of the British Coal Industry. Vol. 2, 1700-1830: The Industrial Revolution* (Oxford, 1984), 180, and coasters, which comes from data on vessels leaving Chichester in 1732 in T.S. Willan, *The English Coasting Trade, 1600-1750* (Manchester, 1938), 17.

## Geographical Origins of Sailors

Little is known of the social or geographical origins of English sailors, which in any case probably changed considerably in the two centuries studied.[17] Numbers roughly trebled between the 1580s and the 1680s,

[17]For speculation on the origins of sailors, see Scammell, "Manning the English Merchant Service," 136-139; Davis, *Rise*, 153; and Rediker, *Devil and the Deep Blue Sea*, 13 and 155.

which would have required a widening of the network of recruitment. Most of this period was marked by great hardship for the English poor, so that one might expect an expanding merchant service to attract young hopefuls born far from the sea. But after the 1680s numbers hardly grew at all while conditions generally were much easier for the poor, a situation which probably made the sea service largely self-recruiting, with the great majority of young sailors being boys "bred to the sea," the sons and nephews of men who were sailors or fishermen themselves.

**Table 4**
**County/Country/Town of Birth of Sailors**

| County/Country | Number | % | Town | No. |
|---|---|---|---|---|
| London | 227 | | London | 227 |
| Devon | 125 | | Yarmouth | 66 |
| Yorkshire | 113 | | Newcastle | 56 |
| Kent | 102 | | Bristol | 34 |
| Norfolk | 102 | | Plymouth | 30 |
| Northumbria | 94 | | Whitby | 27 |
| Dorset | 72 | | Dover | 23 |
| Durham | 50 | | Ipswich | 22 |
| Somerset | 48 | | Dartmouth | 21 |
| Cornwall | 41 | | Weymouth | 21 |
| Suffolk | 40 | | Poole | 15 |
| Essex | 40 | | Hull | 14 |
| Other Coastal counties | 118 | | King's Lynn | 13 |
| Inland Counties | 69 | | Exeter | 12 |
| | | | Sunderland | 11 |
| ENGLAND | 1241 | 83.3 | Greenwich | 10 |
| Scotland | 92 | | | |
| Ireland | 35 | | | |
| Wales | 30 | | | |
| Channel Islands | 20 | | | |
| BRITISH ISLES | 1418 | 95.2 | | |
| Scandinavia | 19 | | | |
| Low Countries | 12 | | | |
| Other Europe | 16 | | | |
| North America | 13 | | | |
| Other overseas | 12 | | | |
| OVERSEAS | 72 | 4.8 | | |
| TOTAL | 1490 | | | |

*Note*: The analysis includes all deponents who styled themselves "nauta," "mariner," etc. in the introduction to their deposition and gave their place of birth. It does not include surgeons and ships' carpenters, nor does it include "landsmen" even though they might have been earning their living on the sea. The volumes searched cover the period 1665-1720, but most of the cases come from the shorter period 1685-1705, when deponents were quite regularly asked to state their place of birth.

*Source*: PRO, HCA 13/75-86.

It would be difficult to test this hypothesis, but it is possible to analyze the geographical origins of sailors, since deponents in the High Court of Admiralty were sometimes asked to state their place of birth. Table 4 analyses the answers of some 1500 sailor deponents living in England, Scotland or Wales who supplied this information between 1665 and 1720. The main feature apparent in this table is that sailors were overwhelmingly drawn from the maritime counties or from London. Only sixty-nine of the sailors born in England (5.6%) came from counties with no coastline while, including the Londoners, a minimum of 912 (73.5%) were born in port towns or coastal villages.[18] Most of those born outside England also came from port towns, so that one can conclude that at least three-quarters of sailors working in England were born within sight of the sea and ships. Who their fathers were cannot be discovered from this source, but it seems probable that most were people of the sea themselves.

## Wages

English sailors were usually paid either by the month or the voyage, such "run wages" being normal in the coasting trades and on the short routes to Europe and the Baltic. Sailors hired in the colonies were also often paid a fixed sum for the run home. Run wages were attractive for shipowners since they fixed an important element in costs, but they were a gamble for the sailor, as a witness from the Newcastle coal trade pointed out in 1692. He claimed to have made the round trip from London in as little as eighteen days and as long as nineteen weeks, though the average was about six weeks.[19]

Sailors' pay was subject to deductions for such things as clothes or drink bought from the ship's stores, damage attributed to the individual or the crew as a whole, and fines incurred for such offences as stopping ashore without leave. These deductions occasionally left a sailor with no pay at all, as could such disasters as shipwreck or capture.

---

[18]The true figure would be higher, since some deponents did not name their town or village of birth and many village names have been so mangled by the clerks that they cannot be identified. There were also many deponents who came from villages two or three miles from the sea but not actually on it.

[19]PRO, HCA 13/80, 9 July 1692, evidence of Henry King.

On the positive side, many seamen enhanced their pay by private trading, especially in the colonial trades.[20]

Peacetime monthly wages for common seamen are set out in table 5. They rose fairly steadily during the long period of inflation up to the middle of the seventeenth century and then stabilized at around twenty-five shillings a month for the rest of the period. Column B provides an index of wages and column C an index of the cost of living (1570s = 100). Column D is created by dividing B by C and is an index of the "real" earnings of seamen. These kept up adequately with inflation until 1650 and then leaped ahead during the period of rapid expansion in shipping between 1650 and 1690. Stable wages were thereafter paralleled by very little inflation until the renewed rise in prices after 1750 began to eat into the sailors' earlier gains.

**Table 5**
**Peacetime Wages of Common Seamen**
**(in shillings per month)**

| | A | B | C | D |
|---|---|---|---|---|
| Period | Wages | Wages Index | C of L Index | B/C |
| 1570s | 10 | 100 | 100 | 100 |
| 1603-29 | 18 | 180 | 162 | 111 |
| 1630-49 | 20 | 200 | 196 | 102 |
| 1654-55 | 24 | 240 | 178 | 135 |
| 1667-71 | 29 | 290 | 184 | 158 |
| 1679-88 | 25 | 250 | 186 | 134 |
| 1730s | 25 | 250 | 176 | 142 |
| 1764-70 | 25 | 250 | 207 | 121 |

*Source:* 1570s wages: Scammell, "Manning the English Merchant Service," 141; other wages: Ralph Davis, *The Rise of the English Shipping Industry in the Seventeenth and Eighteenth Centuries* (London, 1962), 135-137. Cost of living recalculated (1570s = 100) from E.H. Phelps Brown and Sheila V. Hopkins, "Seven Centuries of the Price of Consumables Compared with Builders' Wage-rates," *Economica* (1956), 194-195. Marcus Rediker, *Between the Devil and the Deep Blue Sea. Merchant Seamen, Pirates, and the Anglo-American Maritime World, 1700-1750* (Cambridge, 1987), appendix 3, has a wages table for 1700-1750 which shows slightly higher rates than Davis but the same pattern of stability.

[20]Sometimes such trading was at the cost of lower wages.

Wartime wages were much higher as the navy, privateers and merchant shipping competed for the services of seamen. In the seventeenth century typical wartime rates rose to thirty-five or forty shillings a month, but these were nothing compared to the rates current after 1689, which were usually in excess of fifty shillings and sometimes as high as sixty or seventy.[21] This was very good pay indeed and explains why sailors took such pains to avoid the press, since even in peacetime seamen in the navy got paid a little less than merchant seamen and there was no increase in pay in wartime.

There was a hierarchy on board ship – each step upwards carrying greater pay – which had few parallels in landbound occupations. In the 1680s, when peacetime rates for common seamen had stabilized at around twenty-five shillings a month, a boy starting out was often paid nothing for his first voyage and then paid progressively more as he gained in age and experience. William James of Poole, who was sixteen, had been paid five, ten, twelve, thirteen and sixteen shillings a month on his last five voyages.[22] Eventually, a boy would be deemed a man and would receive the wages of a foremastman or common seaman, ranks which also provided some scope for increases for ability and seniority around the twenty-five shilling average. The next stage would be quartermaster, or gunner's or bosun's mate, and then gunner or bosun at wages between thirty and forty shillings per month. Mates' pay varied, depending on the size of ship and the number of mates, from about fifty-five to 100 shillings. For a fortunate minority there was the glory of becoming master, with pay which became standardized from 1650 at 120 shillings per month, although it might be enhanced by commissions, trading profits and often a share in the freight, since many masters were part-owners of their ships. Few sailors became masters unless they had good connections ashore or some capital, but many men of ability ended up as mates at rates that put them on the same level as skilled artisans.

## Some Characteristics of the Careers of English Sailors

Some boys going to sea started as unpaid apprentices to officers who contracted to teach them navigation and other skills; many of these

---

[21]Wartime rates from Davis, *Rise*, 135-137.

[22]PRO, HCA 13/80, 29 May 1692.

apprentices had capital or connections which ensured them fairly rapid promotion. The majority, however, began as cabin boys, ship's boys or servants to the officers. Some of these lads were very young, as can be seen from table 6, which tabulates the ages at which deponents said they went to sea. The most common starting ages were between twelve and fifteen, the same ages as were normal in land-based occupations. And a substantial minority, mainly young men "bred" to other trades, did not go to sea for the first time until they were in their twenties or later.

**Table 6**
**Age at Going to Sea**

| Age | No. | Age | No. |
|---|---|---|---|
| 8 | 2 | 16 | 14 |
| 9 | 2 | 17 | 13 |
| 10 | 8 | 18 | 13 |
| 11 | 16 | 19 | 2 |
| 12 | 24 | 20-24 | 22 |
| 13 | 29 | 25-29 | 10 |
| 14 | 26 | 30 & over | 9 |
| 15 | 30 | | |

*Note*: Median = 15 (220 cases). The oldest were two men who went to sea as cooks when they were forty-four and fifty, respectively.

*Source*: PRO, HCA 13/75-86. Some deponents stated the age at which they went to sea; others stated how long they had been at sea, together with their age, when they made their deposition.

Once youngsters completed their apprenticeships or their period of service as boys, promotion was rapid for those with connections or ability. Many young men became bosuns or even mates in their teens, while the median age for becoming a master was only twenty-four, although many had to wait rather longer (see table 7).

Officers tended to stay longer in the service than common seamen, but overall sailors were young men, as can be seen in the analysis of the ages of deponents in table 8.[23] This shows a median age

[23]For a similar age structure based on depositions between 1700 and 1750, see Rediker, *Devil and the Deep Blue Sea*, 300. See also Scammell, "Manning the English Merchant Service," 138, for the ages of sailors in the late sixteenth century.

for common sailors of only twenty-seven, which may be rather higher than the reality, since witnesses were often called simply because they had long experience at sea.

**Table 7**
**Age on Becoming Master**

| Age | No. | Age | No. |
|---|---|---|---|
| 19 | 1 | 27 | 3 |
| 20 | 6 | 28 | 2 |
| 21 | 5 | 29 | 1 |
| 22 | 7 | 30 | 3 |
| 23 | 9 | 31 | 1 |
| 24 | 3 | 33 | 1 |
| 25 | 8 | 34 | 2 |
| 26 | 6 | 35 | 1 |

*Note*: Median = 24 (59 cases).

*Source*: See table 6.

**Table 8**
**Age Structure of Sailor Deponents**

| Age | Captains % | Officers % | Sailors % |
|---|---|---|---|
| Under 20 | 0.0 | 1.2 | 16.1 |
| 20 - 24 | 3.8 | 14.2 | 18.2 |
| 25 - 29 | 15.9 | 21.6 | 22.6 |
| 30 - 34 | 19.7 | 23.9 | 16.5 |
| 35 - 44 | 35.3 | 25.5 | 13.6 |
| 45 - 54 | 17.5 | 9.8 | 8.1 |
| 55 - 64 | 6.9 | 2.9 | 3.8 |
| 65 & over | 0.9 | 0.9 | 1.1 |
| | 100.0 | 100.0 | 100.0 |
| Lower quartile | 30 | 27 | 21 |
| Median | 38 | 32 | 27 |
| Upper quartile | 45 | 40 | 35 |
| No. of cases | 320 | 656 | 715 |

*Note*: "Captains" include masters, commanders, etc. "Sailors" include mariners, foremastmen, seamen, cooks, stewards, boys, apprentices, etc. "Officers" include everyone else.

*Source*: See table 6.

One reason for the low median age of sailors was early death through accident, disease and violence; around five percent of Bristol's sailors were lost every year according to Jon Press.[24] Loss by mortality was reinforced by the fact that sailors often saw the sea as a "life-cycle" job and moved to other occupations in their thirties and forties. Many sailors were married and such men often drew on their wives' experience and skills to set up small businesses, such as alehouses, lodging houses or slop shops selling seamen's clothing. There was also much work available for shore-based sailors rigging and fitting-out ships. But most retired sailors probably did manual labour, engaging in such jobs as construction, porterage and general labouring.[25]

During their years at sea, sailors were likely to have had a wide variety of experience. In wartime most would have had some service in the RN, often serving a year or two in royal ships between more lucrative voyages on merchantmen, depending on the vagaries of the press. Many also served on privateers, especially those based in London and southern and southwestern ports. In the merchant service itself, sailors often chopped and changed, from ship to ship, trade to trade, or even from country to country, many sailors spending some of their lives working on the ships of the Dutch or other seafaring nations. But judging from the snatches of biography often included in depositions, most showed at least some loyalty either to a particular trade or to a ship, like Samuel Atkinson of Newcastle who said that "where he likes the ship and the master he cares not where he goes."[26]

Finally, we should note that much of a sailor's life was not spent at sea at all. Much time was spent in port, fitting-out, waiting for a wind, or loading and unloading. For instance, charter-parties allowed forty to forty-five days for loading in the Canaries, seventy to eighty in the West Indies and eighty to 100 in Virginia and Maryland.[27] And much time was spent without a ship between voyages, either voluntarily as the sailor drank or otherwise consumed his wages or involuntarily

---

[24]Press, *Merchant Seamen*, 11.

[25]For London-based sailors, see Peter Earle, *A City Full of People: Men and Women of London, 1650-1750* (London, 1994), 80-82.

[26]PRO, HCA 13/83, f.74.

[27]Davis, *Rise*, 241, 280 and 287.

because there was no work. Sir William Petty estimated in the 1670s that only half of the country's population of sailors was at sea at any one time, probably an under-estimate but not outrageously so judging by individual experience as revealed in depositions.[28]

## Group Formations of Sailors

Most writers on sailors and the sea emphasize one aspect of the group behaviour of sailors: the solidarity and instinctive response to orders of a ship's company who know their safety depends on acting as a team. A few writers, notably Marcus Rediker, also stress a different form of collective behaviour rooted in the inherent contradictions between the priorities of the men as wage-earning workers and of the captain as the representative of capital and indeed himself often a capitalist and part-owner of the ship.[29]

In merchant ships there clearly were such contradictions, as can be seen from the many lawsuits brought by crews against captains, most of which relate to unpaid wages. Sailors wanted their due no less than men in landbound occupations, who were also constantly suing those who had failed to pay them. Sailors often acted as a group in negotiating improved wages or conditions from captains who made changes in the voyage "contrary to his agreement," it being necessary in such cases to gain "the good likeing of the mariners and company aboard."[30]

It seems wrong however to see such collective behaviour as a real precursor of the conflict between labour and capital of the nineteenth century. The hierarchical organization of a crew, with its possibilities of promotion, meant that only a minority of sailors had no chance of bettering themselves, and the majority were cynically aware that such betterment came more quickly for those with no reputation for being "obstinate." A culture of conformity rather than of conflict must also have been encouraged by the small numbers in most crews, rarely more

---

[28]Ehrman, *Navy*, 110-111. Starkey, "War and the Market for Seafarers," calculates from Seamen's Sixpence records that sailors averaged 9.67 months work a year between 1740 and 1766.

[29]Rediker, *Devil and the Deep Blue Sea*, especially chapters 2 and 3.

[30]PRO, HCA 13/81, 17 August 1693.

than thirty even in long-distance trades and more commonly between ten and twenty with a tendency to get smaller over time.[31]

This was a face to face society where, after a day or two at sea, everybody knew everyone else's business only too well, not the most suitable environment for class struggle (although it was a ready breeding ground for other forms of struggle). Cooping men up together in a small ship for weeks or months is hardly conducive to total harmony and individual dislikes or hatreds were common enough, leading to bullying and fights and, in the common case of animosity between captain and mate, to serious breakdown in the efficient operation of the ship.

Little work has been done on discipline in merchant ships, though the subject has attracted attention from historians of the Royal Navy. This work suggests that there was an increase over time in both strictness and the severity of punishment, which meant a deterioration in the sailor's lot from the "brisk paternalism" of the Commonwealth navy to the reported savagery of the navy of the 1790s.[32] Ralph Davis believed that, on merchant ships too, discipline "grew harsher with the passage of time," a belief echoed by Marcus Rediker.[33] The evidence for such views is difficult to assess since it relies mainly on dramatic quotation from cases of sailors bringing charges of brutality or arbitrary treatment against their captains or other officers. That such cases could be successfully brought suggests a limitation to the despotism of a harsh or bullying captain, a point well made by Bernard Capp in his discussion of discipline in Cromwell's navy.[34]

On the other hand, such depositions, exaggerated though they doubtless were, do make it clear that beatings of various kinds and the confinement of sailors "in irons" were fairly common on merchant ships,

---

[31]By the end of the period, the only ships likely to have crews of more than thirty were East Indiamen, slavers and whalers; it is striking that the first two were notorious for bad shipboard relations.

[32]See Bernard Capp, *Cromwell's Navy: The Fleet and the English Revolution, 1648-1660* (Oxford, 1989), 213-230; Davies, *Gentlemen and Tarpaulins*, 95-99; and N.A.M. Rodger, *The Wooden World: An Anatomy of the Georgian Navy* (London, 1986), chapter 6.

[33]Davis, *Rise*, 154; and Rediker, *Devil and the Deep Blue Sea*, especially chapter 5.

[34]Capp, *Cromwell's Navy*, 222-225.

the point at issue normally being whether in the particular case such punishments had been unfair or "excessive." Old sailors in the merchant service no less than in the RN felt that if there was no punishment there would be no authority. "If it was not lawfull for them soe to correct the men," said Captain John Higgins, a veteran of the Archangel trade, "they would not obey, and twould be impossible to carry a ship to sea for often ['sometimes' crossed out] the men are soe mutinous, negligent and troublesom that they must be drubbed before they do their duty." Another witness in this case of 1706 echoed the words of Captain Higgins but added that mariners were much more troublesome "of late years than formerly."[35]

This may have been true but it would be extremely difficult to prove, just as it would be to prove conclusively that discipline "grew harsher with the passage of time." What seems probable is that authority on the great majority of merchantmen was characterized by "brisk paternalism" rather than savage discipline, since sailors were free agents who had no need to sign on a ship with a bad reputation and had the fairly easy option of desertion if they found out too late that they had agreed to serve under a tartar of a captain. They also had the rather harder option of mutiny.

The word "mutiny" can mean anything from an open revolt to a fairly minor questioning of authority; it is often used in this lesser sense in contemporary documents. Nevertheless, open revolt was not unusual in English merchant shipping. The men might refuse to sail in a leaky ship, until they had received their wages or, during wartime, until a convoy had been formed. More seriously, many merchant ships were seized at sea by a rising of the men; Marcus Rediker found sixty such cases in the first half of the eighteenth century and there were plenty in the late sixteenth and seventeenth centuries as well.[36] If caught, mutineers would be ready with justifications of their behaviour – maltreatment, an unseaworthy ship, overwork, shortage of water or provisions, "a frantick captain," non-payment of wages and so on – and these were no doubt important factors in persuading men to join a conspiracy. Yet the relatively high level of mutinies in this period does not necessarily reflect very harsh conditions for sailors. What it does reflect is the

---

[35]PRO, HCA 13/82, f. 336v; and HCA 13/83, f. 409.

[36]Rediker, *Devil and the Deep Blue Sea*, 227-228, and appendix E.

existence of an alternative to the hard work of the merchant service in piracy and buccaneering. When these died down in the 1720s and 1730s, so did the incidence of mutiny at sea.

Mutiny at sea was very rare in the RN, the most important incident being the naval revolt of 1648 which was a product of the complex state of English politics rather than a sign of discontent among the sailors. Mutiny in port, on the other hand, was so common as to be virtually endemic. Sailors refused to sail, rioted and even marched on the offices of the Navy Board in London, usually because they had not been paid, although complaints against the press, poor victuals and lack of leave were often contributory factors.[37] In his study of the RN during the Seven Years' War, N.A.M. Rodger found mutiny so institutionalized that he was able to draw up a set of rules which governed the way it would take place. No mutiny should take place at sea or in the presence of the enemy; no personal violence should be employed; and mutinies should "be held in pursuit only of objectives sanctioned by the traditions of the service."[38] The authorities ashore played by the rules as well, usually doing what they could to meet the sailors' demands and rarely punishing the mutineers, such conciliatory behaviour being very similar to the treatment accorded to those in landward occupations who rioted in pursuit of what were often seen to be legitimate grievances.

## Conclusion

During these two centuries Britain became the possessor of the world's largest trading fleet and the world's most powerful navy. This expansion in shipping tonnage appears to have posed few manning problems in peacetime, though in wartime there was always a serious shortfall which was met by the employment of landsmen and foreigners and by allowing ships to go to sea short of their full complement.[39] Government made repeated efforts to increase the number of sailors but, with the exception

---

[37]See Capp, *Cromwell's Navy*, 286-292 and chapter 2 for the revolt of 1648. See also Davies, *Gentlemen and Tarpaulins*, 82, 137, 147-149 and 225-226; and Rodger, *Wooden World*, 237-244.

[38]Rodger, *Wooden World*, 238.

[39]For a study of the sources of extra manpower in eighteenth-century wars, see Starkey, "War and the Market for Seafarers."

of the Navigation Acts, these probably had little effect. Instead, the operation of the laws of supply and demand were sufficient to produce the numbers of sailors required. Pay, including food and "lodging," compared favourably with alternative occupations, at least outside London, and it rose faster than inflation during most of the period, rising particularly fast in the third quarter of the seventeenth century, when there was the greatest need for increased numbers.

By 1700, the numbers of sailors had reached a plateau of around 50,000 and there was to be little further growth before 1775 as a result of the reduction in manning ratios. The trade of sailor now became largely self-recruiting, as sons followed fathers to the sea from England's ports and coastal villages, though there was always a trickle of recruits from inland areas. The skills required of the sailor changed very little in this period and they were handed down from generation to generation. So too was an accumulated knowledge of the world's shipping lines and seaports and of those many "customs of the sea" which governed everything from differential pay rates to how best to manage a mutiny.

# British Sailors, 1775-1870

**Sarah Palmer and David M. Williams**

This study of English sailors between 1775 and 1870 follows the structure suggested by the editors. Participants were invited to address a series of specific questions and the paper considers these in turn. The extent of coverage of particular issues varies, however, according to their relevance in the British context and the source material. This paper follows on from that of Peter Earle, which covers the two previous centuries. Where possible it builds on his earlier survey, although material available for addressing the questions which were the focus of the conference is not always complementary for the two periods.

In the setting of a review of European sailors, it may be appropriate to commence by stressing the special features of the British experience. First and foremost, Britain is an island, separate from the mainland. Irrespective of the fact that in consequence Britain has a very lengthy coastline – in fact, the longest of any European nation – and, as Gordon Jackson has shrewdly observed, the unique feature of ports facing east and west, this insular character gave a special impetus to maritime activity of all kinds and ensured that the naval rather than military dimension was emphasised in strategic policy.[1] During the period of this paper, Britain became the undisputed maritime world power in both mercantile and naval terms. In great part this was due to the wealth and technological lead associated with being the first country to industrialise. Britain was the leader in the utilisation of steam power, including the maritime dimension, where it was the most successful innovator. All these features have a bearing on the maritime labour force, not least the last mentioned, for Britain alone of all the countries under review from the mid-nineteenth century had a growing proportion of its maritime labour force employed in steam. In 1851, 7.5% of persons employed on fishing and trading vessels were to be found in

[1] G. Jackson, "The Changing Structure of British Trade, Shipping and Ports 1700-1850," in J.R. Bruijn and W.F.J. Mörzer Bruyns (eds.), *Anglo-Dutch Mercantile Marine Relations 1700-1850* (Leiden, 1991), 43-55.

steam; by 1881, the figure was 47.2%.[2] While the focus in this paper is on seamen in the "age of sail," it must be recognised that the growing proportion of seamen employed in this different setting – unique among European nations in its extent – had an impact on all who worked afloat. For many reasons, the British experience has certain special features.

**British Sailors: Sources and Historiography**

The scholarly study of the British maritime labour force is of relatively recent origin, arguably of but the past three or four decades. Such a statement may elicit some surprise. A search of computerised bibliographies utilising the key words "seamen" or "sailors" would generate a considerable volume of references to works published before 1950. But further investigation of this output would prove less rewarding. So-called histories of British "seamen" invariably turn out to be accounts of the careers or notable exploits of "personalities" justly famed for their prowess in naval battles or exploration. "Seamen" and "sailors" are conceived of as terms embracing seafarers of every class or station and not in the more specific sense of the labour force as distinct from officers and masters and mates. In the naval context there are earlier studies purporting to be of "tarpaulins" or the lower deck but few, if any, directly address social and economic issues. Historical studies of maritime labour in the merchant sector are notable by their absence. This neglect of the history of sailors was highlighted by Christopher Lloyd in *The British Seamen 1200-1860: A Social Survey*, published in 1968. Lloyd knew that he was breaking new ground, for he observed that:

> there has been so little written about the British seamen himself. The "people," as the ship's company came to be called, remain an anonymous mass...Of all sections of the community, seafaring men and agricultural labourers have been the most ignored and therefore the worst treated.[3]

---

[2]Great Britain, House of Commons, *Parliamentary Papers* (*BPP*), "Annual Statements of Trade and Navigation" and "Annual Statements of Navigation and Shipping."

[3]C. Lloyd, *The British Seaman 1200-1860. A Social Survey* (London, 1968), 11.

For its attempt to reverse past neglect, its broad chronological sweep and its avowed, though not entirely successful, intent to embrace both naval and mercantile, Lloyd's book merits attention. Yet in many respects it was an anachronistic study, with its "social history" drawing more on the ethos of Trevelyan and the Edwardian era than that of its decade of publication. Indeed, if one were to search for a turning point in the academic study of maritime labour, as in so many other fields of maritime history, it would be the work of Ralph Davis, who was the first to address the maritime sector as an economic historian, and the role and experience of labour was a theme in his seminal *Rise of the English Shipping Industry in the Seventeenth and Eighteenth Centuries*, which appeared in 1962, some six years before Lloyd's book.[4] Davis was a major contributor to the development of economic and social history in the post-World War II era which, alongside the expansion of higher education generally, led to the growth of post-graduate research in all fields of history, including the maritime sector.

Since the early 1960s, and the publication of Davis' seminal work, contributors to the history of English maritime labour number well into double figures and their research has immeasurably enhanced our understanding.[5] Yet – and this is to recognise the spirit and ambition of Lloyd's approach – no scholar has directly addressed the theme of maritime labour *as a whole*. The many valuable studies comprise assessments of facets of the labour force: numbers, composition, wages, conditions of service, legal status, welfare, unionisation and the attitudes of government and society towards seamen. Moreover, all such contributions have appeared as articles or conference papers rather than in book form. Even Jon Press, Alston Kennerley and Conrad Dixon, authors of lengthy and distinguished doctoral theses, have chosen to publish their research as papers rather than as books or monographs.[6] In this respect

---

[4]R. Davis, *The Rise of the English Shipping Industry in the Seventeenth and Eighteenth Centuries* (London, 1962).

[5]Contributors include Burton, Cox, Dixon, Jones, Kennerley, McCord, Palmer, Press, Rowe, Ville and Williams. Citations of their many studies appear in subsequent footnotes.

[6]J.P. Press, "The Economic and Social Condition of the Merchant Seamen of England 1815-1854" (Unpublished PhD thesis, University of Bristol, 1978); C.H. Dixon, "Seamen and the Law: An Examination of the Impact of Legislation on the British

the initiative of a conference/workshop is a major spur to synthesis, which until now has only been attempted in a very general or chronologically limited fashion.[7]

The sectoral or fragmentary approach of so many scholars can hardly be explained in terms of limited sources. Researchers on the period after 1750 are well served with official records on maritime matters and there is much which relates to seamen; so much so, that the "sectoral" rather than the "overall" approach may have seemed to be the most prudent. The extent of official documentation is explained by the long-standing importance of overseas commerce in the contexts of international relations, customs income and the pursuit of naval power. In the nineteenth century, alongside these traditional concerns, new influences gave further impetus to government investigation and data collection. The huge expansion of maritime activity, concern over commercial policy, the abandonment of impressment for naval service, humanitarianism and the general debate over the role of the state were all issues which promoted interest in maritime affairs and consequently the output of material at an official and unofficial level. At the official level, the establishment of the Marine Department of the Board of Trade in 1851 was a significant development in the assembly of records.[8] Two other factors which influenced both the flow and character of this output are a growing fascination with the contemporary "science" of statistics and the practical consideration of cheaper and more efficient printing associated with technological progress.[9] All these varied influences promoted the fuller documentation of maritime affairs and, within this,

---

Merchant Seaman's Lot" (Unpublished PhD thesis, University of London, 1981); and A. Kennerley, "British Seaman's Missions and Sailors' Homes, 1815 to 1970" (Unpublished PhD thesis, CNNA, 1989).

[7]See, for example, David M. Williams, "Industrialisation, Technological Change and the Maritime Labour Force: the British Experience 1800-1914," *Collectanea Maritima*, V (1991), 317-330; and Williams, "'A Period of Transition:' Personnel in the British Mercantile Marine in the First Half of the 19th Century," in Bruijn and Mörzer Bruyns (eds.), *Anglo-Dutch Mercantile Marine Relations*, 115-124.

[8]J.H. Wilde, "The Creation of the Marine Department of the Board of Trade," *Journal of Transport History*, First series, II (1956); and R. Proughty, *The Transformation of the Board of Trade, 1830-1855* (London, 1957).

[9]M.J. Cullen, *The Statistical Movement in Early Victorian Britain* (New York, 1975).

the seamen's experience. The growth in the volume of material is of particular relevance in the context of a review of maritime labour in the century or so after 1775, since the fuller and more reliable data from the mid-nineteenth century give rise to the process of backward extrapolation on those themes and questions where material on earlier periods is unavailable.

## The Number of Sailors and the Pattern of Recruitment

British maritime activity underwent remarkable expansion in the period from the mid-eighteenth century to the 1870s. Naval activity, trade values (and more important, trade volumes), registered tonnage and the number of seamen all underwent huge increases. The precise magnitude of these changes, their timing and the relationship between them is difficult to ascertain. As Davis observed, "the pathway through the shipping statistics of the seventeenth and eighteenth century is a slippery and often misleading one," and it might be added that the traveller does not reach safer ground until well after the mid-nineteenth century.[10] This is true of official statistics of imports and exports, as well as ships and men. In this instance, where the concern is with the maritime labour force, the principal problems lie with merchant seamen, for the data on naval personnel are full and relatively accessible. Not so for the mercantile marine, where material is only to be gleaned from a variety of official records, all assembled for different reasons. In consequence, as D.J. Starkey observes, "employment levels are therefore difficult to measure with any precision."[11] Given the contrast between the availability and the interpretational problems of the naval and mercantile data, it is proposed to examine the sectors separately and then to endeavour to form some conclusions on the benchmark dates selected by the editors.

Data on the number of men in the Royal Navy is readily available in the Navy Board's returns and are discussed in the works of

---

[10]Davis, *Rise of the English Shipping Industry*, 395.

[11]D.J. Starkey, "War and the Market for Seafarers in Britain, 1736-1792," in L.R. Fischer and H.W. Nordvik, *Shipping and Trade, 1750-1950: Essays in International Maritime Economic History* (Pontefract, 1990), 27-28.

Lloyd, N.A.M. Rodger, Starkey and Michael Lewis.[12] Few definitional problems exist other than the distinction between "number borne" and "number mustered." "Numbers borne" represent the personnel who were on the ships' books, either as part of the complement or as supernumeraries. They include all ranks and marines. "Number mustered" represent the numbers actually on board and were thus always slightly lower than "numbers borne." The figures quoted in table 1 are of "numbers borne." They reveal the quite remarkable fluctuations in numbers between times of peace and war. A further feature of wartime was the employment of seamen in privateering. Numbers engaged in this sector reached as high as 8000 in some years. The implications of wartime demands on the market for seafarers in Britain have been discussed by Starkey.

**Table 1**
**Number Borne in the Navy, Selected Years, 1750-1855**

| | |
|---|---|
| 1750 | 11,691 |
| 1755 | 33,612 |
| 1760 | 85,658 |
| 1765 | 15,863 |
| 1770 | 14,744 |
| 1775 | 15,230 |
| 1780 | 91,566 |
| 1785 | 22,826 |
| 1790 | 20,025 |
| 1795 | 96,001 |
| 1800 | 128,930 |
| 1810 | 142,098 |
| 1826 | 28,607 |
| 1835 | 21,141 |
| 1846 | 36,181 |
| 1851 | 32,914 |
| 1855 | 61,246 |

*Note*: The figures are monthly averages of "numbers borne."

*Source*: C. Lloyd, *The British Seaman 1200-1860. A Social Survey* (London, 1968), appendix table 3.

[12]N.A.M. Rodger, *The Wooden World: An Anatomy of the Georgian Navy* (London, 1986); and Michael Lewis, *A Social History of the Navy* (London, 1960).

In contrast to the navy, data on the mercantile marine for much of the eighteenth century are sketchy and rely heavily on the records of the payment of Seamen's Sixpences, a levy of sixpence per month taken from the wages of mariners to support the Seamen's Hospital in Greenwich.[13] There are considerable difficulties in the interpretation and manipulation of material from this source. From the late eighteenth century, government began to collect data on the merchant marine in a more systematic fashion, most notably with the establishment of the Register of Shipping in 1786.[14] Yet the figures of merchant seamen from this period flatter to deceive, and Valerie Burton has concluded that the published returns before 1895 "were not true accounts of the number employed." The deficiencies in official figures arise from the manner and form of collection. These are well known and need only to be summarised here. Before 1835, figures were collected by the Registrar of Shipping. Owners registering new vessels were required to provide a statement of the number of men they intended to employ. The Registrar's calculation of the total numbers of men took no account of any subsequent changes in crewing levels; even more seriously, the figures included all ships – as though all would be in employment at any one time. Again there were lags in deleting ships lost, broken up or "sold abroad." Such flaws led to considerable over-recording – perhaps as much as twenty to twenty-five percent by the 1830s. Working in the opposite direction was the exclusion of masters, which may have led to under-recording of about ten percent. The establishment of a Register Office of Merchant Seamen in 1835 – the purpose being the creation of a Register to be drawn on by the navy in time of war – and the introduction of the Register ticket system in 1844, which stated that no British seamen should set out on an overseas voyage without a ticket, did not improve matters. Official figures were based on the number of tickets issued with no names being removed from the Register other than those of seamen who had died at sea. Figures were thus increasingly overstated by as much perhaps as thirty percent by 1850. In 1853, the Board of

---

[13]R. Davis, "Seamen's Sixpences. An index of Commercial Activity, 1697-1828," *Economica*, XXIII (1956), 328-343. See also Starkey, "War," 41.

[14]On records of numbers of seamen from the late eighteenth century, see N. Cox, "The Records of the Registrar General of Shipping and Seamen," *Maritime History*, II (1972), 168-188; and V.C. Burton, "Counting Seafarers: The Published Records of the Registry of Merchant Seamen," *Mariner's Mirror*, LXXI (1985), 305-320.

Trade – which from 1850 oversaw the office of the Registrar General of Seamen – abolished the ticket system as expensive and ineffective. In 1854, a new Register was commenced but this was discontinued in 1856, when the Board decided that a Register could be maintained through the preservation of Crew Lists. Even then problems were encountered and successive attempts to refine the figures gave rise to "virtually five separate statistical series" between 1849 and 1914.[15]

The above account of official recording is certainly depressing and might even be characterised as defeatist, but it serves to indicate the very real minefield of the statistics on the merchant service. All that can be done is to present in tables 2 and 3 some of the data available and to stress reservations and qualifications.

**Table 2**
**Men Serving in Foreign and Coastal Vessels, 1750-1790**

| | |
|---|---|
| 1750 | 33,040 |
| 1760 | 36,213 |
| 1770 | 43,243 |
| 1780 | 39,108 |
| 1790 | 52,802 |

*Note*: Based on data derived from Seamen's Sixpences.

*Source*: D.J. Starkey, "War and the Market for Seafarers in Britain, 1736-1792," in L.R. Fischer and H.W. Nordvik, *Shipping and Trade, 1750-1950: Essays in International Maritime Economic History* (Pontefract, 1990), 40-41.

Table 2 presents data on the second half of the eighteenth century. The credence to be accorded the figures is debatable. They exclude fishermen, who along with persons employed in inland navigation comprised between 4000 and 7000 workers over the period. This apart, it is likely that the Sixpence data underestimate numbers serving. Davis tentatively estimated numbers of seamen and those in the fisheries at 70,000 or 80,000 around mid-century – though the Sixpence data plus fisheries put the total around 40,000.[16] Likewise in 1792, when the

[15]Burton, "Counting Seafarers," 312-313.

[16]"On the Eve of the Seven Years' War (1756-63), The Much Larger Merchant Fleet, May Have Had, Along with the Fisheries, 70,000 or 80,000 Seamen." Davis, *Rise of the English Shipping Industry*, 323.

Sixpence data, together with those employed in fisheries totalled 59,464, a contemporary estimate placed the number of men in the merchant navy at 87,569.[17] Such discrepancies hardly inspire confidence.

From the late eighteenth century, data were collected in a more systematic fashion but, as indicated, their reliability is open to grave doubt. Figures derived from the Registrar of Shipping and later the Registrar of Seamen provide the totals for the merchant marine depicted in table 3. It is known, however, that all such figures embody considerable over-counting and need to be discounted at an increasing rate in the first half of the nineteenth century.

**Table 3**
**Number of Seamen in the Merchant Service**

| | |
|---|---|
| 1700 | 105,037 |
| 1815 | 162,603 |
| 1820 | 159,210 |
| 1830 | 133,649 |
| 1840 | 165,527 |
| 1850 | 193,170 |
| 1860 | 171,592 |

*Note*: Includes fishermen employed on vessels over fifteen tons.

*Sources*: 1800: Lloyd, *The British Seaman*, 285. Other figures: Great Britain, House of Commons, *Parliamentary Papers* (*BPP*), "Annual Statements of Trade and Navigation" and "Annual Statements of Navigation and Shipping."

The conclusion to be drawn from the above discussion is that in counting the maritime labour force we have no firm data other than for the Royal Navy. Any attempt to quantify numbers in the merchant service or the maritime labour force as a whole are, at best, "guesstimates." But for the benchmark dates of mid-eighteenth century, 1800 and mid-nineteenth century, the following suggestions are offered for numbers of merchant seamen. For the mid-eighteenth century we are inclined towards Davis's lower estimate of 70,000.[18] For 1800, around 95,000 – arrived at by discounting the 1800 figure in table 3 by some

[17]Lloyd, *The British Seaman*, 285.

[18]It is appreciated that this figure exceeds that implied in Peter Earle's paper.

ten percent. For 1850, around 150,000 – through discounting the figure in table 3 by twenty percent. We would stress the "guesstimate" character of these figures. Combining such estimates with the more reliable naval statistics would provide figures on the maritime labour force as a whole – *but for any one time only* – as one of the few firm conclusions from this discussion is that Royal Navy totals fluctuated wildly according to the state of international relations.

## Wages and Remuneration

Wages (or "pay," in the case of naval service) are self-evidently only one element of remuneration. The value of provisions or victuals has always to be allowed for, while volunteer bounties, prize monies, catch shares, primage allowances and proceeds from private trading also contributed according to circumstances. Less obviously, in the case of the Navy, non-contributory pensions earned by continuous service, as well as the quality of available medical care, should perhaps also be counted as part of the reward to naval seamen, though few served the twenty years required to qualify. In addition, whether serving on a merchantman or a naval vessel, the tight accommodation on board at least saved the rent the seaman would have paid if lodging ashore. Offsetting these rewards, however, were a variety of hidden costs, which for the merchant seaman included until 1851 the forced "Seaman's Sixpence" and the discount paid to cash an advance note.[19]

Naval provisioning was based on standard rations but, with the exception of Lascar seamen, diet on merchant vessels was unregulated throughout this period, apart from statutory obligations introduced in 1844 relating to drinking water, which subsequent legislation extended to anti-scorbutics. A study by Dixon, which surveys the evidence on the food supplied to seafarers, shows that variations between vessels and over time make it impossible to develop estimates of the monetary value to seafarers of the foodstuffs supplied. But British perceptions of lower or higher victualling standards in certain national fleets (for Scandinavia and the United States, respectively) have implications for the internation-

---

[19]C.J. Bartlett, *Great Britain and Sea Power 1815-1853* (Oxford, 1963); J.S. Bromley (ed.), *The Manning of the Royal Navy: Selected Public Pamphlets 1693-1873* (London, 1974); and Jon Press, "Wages in the Merchant Navy," *Journal of Transport History*, Third series, II (1981), 37-52.

alisation of the labour market, while contrasts between mercantile and naval standards, as between ship and shore, must be judged factors in maritime recruitment. No specialist study of the issue has yet been done, though Rodger, writing of the mid-eighteenth century, guesses that "with a reasonable proportion of fresh provisions the men of the Navy probably ate something nearer a balanced diet than many of their contemporaries ashore," while Bartlett, considering Royal Navy conditions a century later, suggests that these compared badly both with standards on merchantmen and on American warships, yet judges that "there had been no small improvement in the Royal Navy since 1797."[20]

Basic rates of pay for the Navy in the mid-eighteenth century were established a hundred years earlier in 1653. The able seamen received 22s.6d. per lunar month net of fixed deductions. Until the 1760s this rate seems to have been relatively competitive with peacetime wages in merchant ships. Thereafter, it fell rapidly behind and the lag – in a period of inflation – was a major cause of naval unrest in the 1790s. Wage increases were one outcome of the mutinies, and in 1806 able seamen's wages were established at 32s. and ordinary seamen's at 25s.6d. net per month. They remained roughly at this level until the mid-nineteenth century. Scales for the distribution of prize money were adjusted in 1808 toward favouring the lower decks. In 1816 this more equitable scale was revoked, but in 1834 the claims of admirals and captains were again reduced. Given peacetime conditions, this was an aid to recruitment rather than an advance in remuneration, but the significance of prize money earlier on, while difficult to evaluate, is clearly not to be discounted.[21]

Payment based on time served was also typical on long-distance merchant vessels, though those who worked on slavers, privateers and whalers were paid shares of the outcome of the venture. In coastal trades, such as the shipping of coal from northeastern ports to London, or where the passage was routine and of short duration, payment was by

---

[20]Conrad Dixon, "Pound and Pint: Diet in the Merchant Service 1750-1980," in Sarah Palmer and Glyndwr Williams (eds.), *Charted and Uncharted Waters* (London, 1982), 164-180; Rodger, *Wooden World*, 87; and Bartlett, *Great Britain*, 311.

[21]N.A.M. Rodger, "Shipboard Life in the Georgian Navy, 1750-1800, The Decline of the Old Order," in L.R. Fischer, *et al.* (eds.), *The North Sea: Twelve Essays on the Social History of Maritime Labour* (Stavanger, 1992), 29-41; Lewis, *Social History*, 300; Bartlett, *Great Britain*, 311; and Bromley (ed.), *The Manning*, 163, n. 1 and 359, n. 1.

voyage. Wages were agreed at the time of signing on, rates varying according to the destination, and with advance notes issued in those cases where a voyage of several months was anticipated. The most systematic study of British merchant navy wage rates to date is that by Press for the period 1815-1854, but studies of early-nineteenth century London shipowners by S.P. Ville and Palmer also contain information on wages. In considering the period 1847-1854, Press makes detailed use of the post-1844 Crew Agreements in the Public Record Office Series BT98, which include details of wages. Prior to these years evidence is more fragmentary. Wages are known to have risen during wartime (in the Crimean War years they almost doubled), but in peace, according to Press, "the general picture is one of stable wage levels," with average monthly wages of able seamen at 45s-50s and of ordinary seamen at 30s-35s. Within this general picture, there were variations reflecting, Press argues, traditional regional labour market disparities, local supply conditions including the impact of unionisation, and the effect of high wage rates in North American ports which tended to push up outward rates on the passage. Press attributes this last element to the control of the maritime labour market by crimps, but it seems as likely to reflect general labour shortages in America. Although Press' work necessarily deals primarily with conditions on sailing vessels, he pays some attention to wages on steamships, noting the comparatively higher rates paid here on shorter routes as against levels on sailing vessels.[22]

**Government Policy and Recruitment**

Stephen Jones has observed that "the press gang manned the Navy directly and the merchant service indirectly."[23] Until 1815 recruitment to the two services was inextricably linked; in wartime the requirements of the Navy for experienced seamen could not be met by the recruitment

---

[22]David M. Williams, "'Advance Notes' and the Recruitment of Maritime Labour in Britain in the Nineteenth Century," in Lewis R. Fischer (ed.), *The Market for Seamen in the Age of Sail* (St. John's, 1994), 81-100; Press, "Wages;" Simon P. Ville, *English Shipowning during the Industrial Revolution, Michael Henley and Son, London Shipowners 1770-1830* (Manchester, 1987); and Sarah Palmer, "John Long; A London Shipowner," *Mariner's Mirror*, LXXII (1986).

[23]Stephen Jones, "Blood Red Roses: The Supply of Merchant Seamen in the Nineteenth Century," *Mariner's Mirror*, LVIII (1972).

of volunteers, hence the need for impressment and, for Jones, the attraction of the merchant service for men seeking to avoid this. Yet as J.S. Bromley notes, the shipping interest tended to regard impressment as a source of artificial labour shortage because it forced seamen into hiding. These differing interpretations of the impact of impressment on the manning of the two services highlight the point that historical understanding of the basis of recruitment in the late eighteenth and early nineteenth centuries is still very limited. Indeed, even determining the proportion of volunteers to pressed men is fraught with difficulty.[24]

Nevertheless, it is clear that for the most part recruits to the two services were drawn from a common pool, though the wartime suspension of the Navigation Act in 1793, in order to lift limits on the employment of foreign nationals on British merchant vessels, temporarily widened this. These regulations were briefly suspended in 1825 in response to labour unrest, but it was not until 1850, in the wake of the repeal of the Navigation Acts – 1854 in the case of the coasting trade – that it became possible to employ foreign seamen freely, though in the event the proportion of these serving in the British merchant marine, at around eight percent, was fairly insignificant until the 1880s. In peacetime, recruitment to the Navy reverted to a wasteful "hire and discharge" system, whereby the national fleet consisted of vessels manned by crews who served only for the period of the commission, nominally five years but typically three years. The prime source of recruits continued to be the merchant navy but, with re-introduction of impressment in wartime increasingly regarded as a political impossibility and the impact of the repeal of the Navigation Laws on the merchant marine the subject of uncertainty, at mid-century the issue of manning came to the fore. The creation of the Royal Navy Reserve in 1859 marked the statutory beginning of the transition to a continuous service standing Navy backed by a voluntary force, serving also to further widen the distinction between the mercantile and naval services.[25]

In the merchant marine, crews were signed on to serve for the duration of the voyage, to be replaced as necessary as death, injury and

---

[24]J.S. Bromley, "The British Navy and Its Seamen After 1688: Notes for an Unwritten History," in Palmer and Williams (eds.), *Charted and Uncharted Waters*; and Rodger, *Wooden World*, 145-204.

[25]R. Taylor, "Manning the Royal Navy: The Reform of the Recruiting System 1852-1862," *Mariner's Mirror*, XLIV (1958); and Bartlett, *Great Britain*, 304-310.

desertion took their toll. In the long-distance trades, it was the practice to issue a credit note as an advance on a month's wages to enable the seafarer to settle lodging debts and to equip himself. This was the "Advance Note," which led to the use of a financial intermediary – the crimp – in order to cash it. At the end of the voyage the delayed settlement of the wage bill generated a further connection in the need for credit until paying off was complete. From this system of pre- and post-payment developed the role of the crimp as a labour agent with a pecuniary interest in finding berths. Technically there was no need for an intermediary – there was nothing to prevent a man from signing on directly – but the use of a crimp was favoured by masters, despite the fact that crimps appear to have been paid a commission, presumably because it saved effort and helped to ensure that men who signed on did in fact turn up at the time of sailing. In so far as the entire system rested on the Advance Note, it can be concluded that prior payment was a central feature of the British recruitment system as far as long-distance trades were concerned.[26] The mode of recruitment for voyages of shorter duration has not as yet received sufficient scholarly attention to enable us to comment further here, other than to note that evidence from larger ports should not be taken as representative of all ports.[27]

Work on recruitment has tended to concentrate on mechanisms and social welfare aspects and has thrown little direct light on the issues of "push" and "pull." (An exception here is Burton's work on apprenticeship, which in part deals with a compulsory element in employment, dispensed with at mid-century).[28] Outside maritime history, however, in the wider ocean of British economic historiography, one can note

---

[26]Davis, *Rise of the English Shipping Industry*, 133-158; Conrad Dixon, "The Rise and Fall of the Crimp 1840-1914," in S. Fisher (ed.), *British Shipping and Seamen 1630-1960: Some Studies* (Exeter, 1984), 49-67; Sarah B. Palmer, "Seamen Ashore in Late Nineteenth Century London," in P. Adam (ed.), *Seamen in Society* (Paris, 1980); and Williams, "'Advance Notes.'"

[27]On recruitment in small ports, for example, see Aled Eames, *Ships and Seamen of Anglesey, 1588-1918* (Anglesey, 1973); Eames, *Ventures in Sail* (Caernarfon, 1987); and E. Hughes and A. Eames, *Portmadog Ships* (Caernarfon, 1976).

[28]V.C. Burton, "Apprenticeship Regulation and Maritime Labour in the Nineteenth Century Merchant Marine," *International Journal of Maritime History*, I (1989). See also E.G. Thomas, "The Old Poor Law and Maritime Apprenticeship," *Mariner's Mirror*, LXIII (1977).

increasing recognition of regional disparities in the pace and direction of economic development and a concomitant understanding of the persistence of local economies, as indeed reflected in wage variations.[29] On this basis it can be hypothesised that within Britain there were regions where lack of alternative sources of employment produced a push towards maritime employment; others where pull dominated because maritime skill was a recognised adjunct of regional industrial specialisation; and still others which offered both a range of alternative employment opportunities and intense labour competition, where both "push and pull" elements can be detected.

## The Careers of Sailors

Evidence on the careers of sailors is not generally forthcoming for the period under review. There are two possible sources for the study of career patterns; first, the biographies and autobiographies of seamen and second, official documentation. The former are limited in number, and by their nature tend to be exceptional both in their appearance and in the careers they relate.[30] Utilising the records of the Registrar General of Seamen and the Crew Agreements, available from the 1830s and 1860s, respectively, is a theoretical rather than practical possibility.[31] Not until the introduction of Continuous Discharge Certificates at the beginning of

---

[29]A useful summary of the literature is provided by Eric Richards, "Margins of the Industrial Revolution," in Patrick O'Brien and Roland Quinault (eds.), *The Industrial Revolution and British Society* (Cambridge, 1993).

[30]Examples of biographies and autobiographies of seamen are John Howell (ed.), *Life and Adventures of John Nicol* (Edinburgh, 1822); V. Lovett Cameron (ed.), *The Log of a Jack Tar; or, the Life of James Choyce, Master Mariner* (London, 1897); S. Childers (ed.), *A Mariner of England* (London, 1990); and Joshua Marsden, *Sketches of the Early Life of a Sailor* (Hull, [1812?]).

[31]Were all the records of the Registrar General of Seamen and the Crew Agreements to be assembled in data bases it would be possible to undertake searches of seamen and their careers from the mid-nineteenth century. The task is currently impracticable though not inconceivable. On the respective records see Cox, "The Records of the Registrar General of Shipping and Seamen;" Burton, "Counting Seafarers;" K. Matthews, "Crew Lists, Agreements and Official Logs of the British Empire," *Business History*, XVI (1974); and L.R. Fischer and E.W. Sager, "An Approach to the Quantitative Analysis of British Shipping Records," *Business History*, XXII (1980).

the twentieth century is a study of seafaring careers really feasible.[32] In consequence, for the period 1775-1870 evidence of career patterns is fragmentary, but some observations can be made on the length and pattern of careers, status and movement in and out of seafaring.

Although men of all ages were to be found in the maritime labour force, seafaring was primarily a young man's trade. Rodger's work on the age of naval ships' companies shows that almost eighty percent of ordinary seamen and landsmen were under the age of twenty-five, with the majority in the sixteen to twenty bracket. For able seamen, a slightly older profile prevailed, but some seventy-five percent were thirty or under, with the twenty-one to twenty-five age group being most common. Press presents a similar picture in the merchant service, where from a sample of seamen between 1815 and 1854 he shows that the most common age band was twenty to twenty-five and then twenty-five to thirty. Such age profiles imply that seafaring careers tended to be of short rather than long duration. In many ways this is to be expected; a seafaring life may provide certain freedoms and an opportunity "to see the world," but it also involves sacrifices, such as the loss of contact with home and family, subjection to shipboard discipline and, to use a phrase coined by Dixon, not least that of living as "an involuntary monk."[33] As a general rule, usually sooner rather than later, human nature settles for a more stable and standardised life experience. It is thus likely that most sailors tended to serve part-time rather than full-time careers at sea. How long was the average seafaring career? The short answer is that we do not know. But through extrapolations of the intake needed annually to maintain numbers suggested by the Liverpool Committee of Shipowners in the early 1870s, the careers of merchant seafarers averaged around ten years.[34] How relevant such a figure is for the preceding century is conjectural but, if we accept that seafaring is

---

[32]On the introduction of Continuous Discharge Certificates, see Dixon, "The Rise," 49-67.

[33]Rodger, *The Wooden World*, 360-361; Press, "The Economic and Social Condition," appendix; and Dixon, "The Rise," 50.

[34]The Liverpool Committee of Shipowners suggested in 1873 that some 16,000 new seamen per year were needed to cope with annual wastage. At that time the number of seamen in the merchant service was around 170,000. See Thomas Brassey, *British Seamen* (London, 1877), chapters 1 and 2.

most likely to be a life for the young and single; that many entrants to seafaring were in their mid-teens; and that the age of marriage for males in the early and mid-nineteenth century was between twenty-three and twenty-five, then the estimate of a ten-year career has a ring of veracity. In considering the length of seafaring careers, a variety of influences have to be taken into account: physical fitness was clearly significant in employment in sail. Marital status must also have had some bearing. And it is again worth remembering that both men pressed into the Royal Navy and boys from institutional backgrounds – orphans or offenders – apprenticed into the merchant service were involuntary entrants to maritime employment.

Whatever the average seafaring career, there were workers who left the sea after but one voyage and some who served longer than average, and even lifetime, careers at sea. No analysis has been undertaken of extended careers, but Press has suggested that young merchant seamen were mainly in foreign trades and that as they grew older transferred to the "home" or coasting trades. Dixon provides a variant to this, believing that youngsters began in coasting, went deep-sea as they became more mature, and later returned to shorter hauls and coasting as fitness waned. Marriage also influenced the decision to limit "time away."[35] These theses are certainly worthy of serious consideration, but it must be accepted there is little in the way of supporting data on age and marital status. Burton has undertaken work on such issues, but her study is set in the late nineteenth century when employment in steam changed both the nature of maritime labour and the seagoing labour force. Even so, her findings that seafarers employed in the home trade were on average older than their counterparts in foreign trade, and that married men formed a higher proportion of the coasting as compared with the foreign-going workforce, are of interest in this context.[36] One further feature arising from Burton's findings, mentioned merely to stimulate debate – for it relates to the end of the nineteenth century – is that in 1891, forty-six percent of merchant seafarers were married or

---

[35]For discussion of these issues see Ville, *English Shipowning*, 92-94.

[36]Burton, "Counting Seafarers," 316; Valerie Burton, "The Myth of Bachelor Jack: Masculinity, Patriarchy and Seafaring Labour," in Colin Howell and Richard Twomey (eds.), *Jack Tar in History: Essays in the History of Maritime Life and Labour* (Fredericton, 1991), 179-198.

once married.[37] Rodger, in his eighteenth-century naval context, returns a far lower figure of around twenty percent.[38]

A factor which may have influenced the length of career is status. Were there career structures that enabled the entrant to progress in rank and earning capacity? In both the merchant and Royal navies entrants, providing they persevered and acquired the necessary skills, could progress from the lowest levels to petty officers or, in the merchant trade, to the positions of bosun, sailmaker and carpenter. And while the hurdle was somewhat higher, men could also progress to officer rank. In the Navy there were opportunities to "rise to the quarter deck" as a ranking officer. Such promotion was far easier in time of war. In the eighteenth-century mercantile marine, the move from mate to captain was perhaps the most difficult, as masters often required capital as well as skill. In the mid-nineteenth century the introduction of statutory requirements for masters and mates imposed new demands on those seeking to advance.[39]

Finally in the context of careers, what of transfers within and in and out of seafaring? Down to the end of the period of the French wars, transfers between the navy and mercantile service would appear to have been frequent and common – logically so, given the navy's fluctuating demand.[40] Such moves were less common after 1815. In terms of moving in and out of seafaring, little study has been undertaken, but it is possible that in the trade of small ports in peripheral areas there may have been a seasonal dimension. As for what employments seafarers followed on leaving the sea, this again is unresearched: it is known that some retained a maritime connection by working in fishing, dock work,

---

[37]Burton, "The Myth," 187.

[38]"The evidence suggests that the proportion of the officers and men of the Navy who were permanently married was no more than a fifth or a quarter, disproportionately concentrated among the officers, petty officers and older seamen." See Rodger, *Wooden World*, 78.

[39]C. Jeans, "The First Statutory Qualifications for Seafarers," *Journal of Transport History*, Third series, VI (1973), 248-267; and Valerie Burton, "The Making of a Nineteenth Century Profession: Shipmasters and the British Shipping Industry," *Journal of the Canadian Historical Association* (1990), 97-118.

[40]Starkey, "War," 25-42.

port trades and carpentry, but most probably entered the general labour force.

**Culture and Organisation**

The culture of English sailors in the sense of a particular set of values or lifestyle has not been a significant topic of academic study in the period under review. True, such themes as life ashore between voyages, educational and religious influences, desertion, lower deck unrest in the navy and organisation and militancy amongst merchant seamen have all been subjects of research – and will be considered in due course – but generally historians of the final century or so of the age of sail have eschewed the study of sailors' culture in its widest form. While for the early and mid-eighteenth century there are the seminal studies of Marcus Rediker and Rodger and, for the twentieth century, those of A. Carew and T. Lane, the intervening 150 years lack similar coverage, other than a paper by R.D. Foulke comparing literary images and the realities of life in sail at the end of the nineteenth century.[41] Yet scholars researching the late eighteenth and nineteenth centuries have hardly been idle, and in three areas – seamen ashore, organisation of maritime labour and contemporary perceptions of seamen – significant research has been undertaken.

Research into the seaman's life ashore is fuller than studies of his work experience afloat, for it was between voyages that the life of the seaman came into contact with, and impinged upon, society as a whole. As a consequence, other than in time of war or more particularly national peril, contemporary attention tended to focus on the seamen "in their midst" rather than the worker out of sight "afloat the sea." The resulting documentation has encouraged study. Thus, the relationship of seamen with boarding housekeepers and crimps has been examined by Dixon and Palmer. Both view the role and function of the crimp in a far more objective fashion than that taken by many contemporaries and in this

[41] M. Rediker, *Between the Devil and the Deep Blue Sea. Merchant Seamen, Pirates and the Anglo-American Maritime World, 1700-1750* (Cambridge, 1987); Rodger, *Wooden World*; A. Carew, *The Lower Deck of the Royal Navy, 1900-1939: The Invergordon Mutiny in Perspective* (Manchester, 1981); T. Lane, *Grey Dawn Breaking. British Merchant Seafarers in the Twentieth Century* (Manchester, 1986); K. Weibust, *Deep Sea Sailors. A Study in Maritime Ethnology* (Stockholm, 1969); and R.D. Foulke, "Life in the Dying World of Sail," *Journal of British Studies*, III (1963), 105-136.

sense align themselves with international studies which view the crimp primarily as an element in the labour market. The contemporary perception of the crimp and the concern and response to the position and lifestyle of the seafarer, particularly by evangelicals, have been the theme of Kennerley's research into the Sailors' Homes and Seamens' Missions movements. Such movements are historically significant both for their practical provision and the insight they give into nineteenth century attitudes to the maritime labour force. Kennerley has also published important studies of educational provisions for seafarers, though these impinged upon only a minority of the maritime labour force.[42]

Attitudes to seamen in the final century or so of the age of sail have been examined by D.M. Williams and Burton.[43] It would be true to say that for much of the period under review contemporary views of seamen, other than the unqualified, heroic perception of times of war, varied between the extremes of seeing him as a simple innocent exposed to temptation and exploitation or as a degenerate, brutalised misfit. As always, while some sailors fit the extremes of the definition, no doubt a greater number fell between. Yet, however appropriate or otherwise nineteenth-century images of seafarers may have been, such views influenced the pattern of official regulation and private charitable provision, which served to improve the seafarer's lot over time.

---

[42]Dixon, "The Rise;" Palmer, "Seamen Ashore;" Judith Fingard, *Jack in Port: Sailortowns on Eastern Canada* (Toronto, 1982); A. Kennerley, "British Seaman's Missions;" Kennerley, "British Seamen's Missions in the Nineteenth Century," in Fischer, *et al.* (eds.), *The North Sea*, 79-98; Kennerley, "Seamen's Missions and Sailors' Homes: Spiritual and Social Welfare Provisions in British Ports in the Nineteenth Century," in Stephen Fisher (ed.), *Studies in British Privateering, Trading Enterprises and Seamen's Welfare, 1770-1900* (Exeter, 1987), 121-165. On the more general theme of Seamen's Missions see Roald Kverndal, *Seamen's Missions: Their Origins and Early Growth* (Pasadena, 1986). On education, see A. Kennerley, "Navigation School and Training Ship: Educational Provision in Plymouth for the Mercantile Marine in the Nineteenth Century," in Stephen Fisher (ed.), *West Country Maritime and Social History: Some Essays* (Exeter, 1980), 53-77; and D.G. Bovill, "The Proprietary Schools of Navigation and Marine Engineering in the Ports of the North East of England, 1822-1914," *History of Education Society Bulletin*, XLIV (1989), 10-25.

[43]See for example Burton, "The Myth;" David M. Williams, "Henry Mayhew and the British Seamen," in Stephen Fisher (ed.), *Lisbon as a Port Town, the British Seamen and Other Maritime Themes* (Exeter, 1988), 111-128; and Williams, "Mid-Victorian Attitudes to Seamen and Maritime Reform: The Society for Improving the Condition of Merchant Seamen, 1867," *International Journal of Maritime History*, III (1991), 101-126.

What of the voice and actions of the seamen themselves? In terms of personal statements or presence at official enquiries, seafarers have the lowest of profiles in the period under review. But like all workers, if they acted communally, seafarers could voice opinions and endeavour to influence their condition. Maritime labour with its transitory, dispersed and fragmented labour force is especially difficult to organise, a characteristic borne out by both historical and current experience. Yet labour could and did present a united front when circumstances provided the opportunity. Hence the mutinies of the late 1790s when, in time of war, the naval fleets were lying anchored at the Nore and Spithead.[44] Similarly, there was the often militant stance of seamen in the northeast coal trade, who enjoyed the unique advantage of being a concentrated body engaged in a regular trade essential to London's comfort and well being. The attempts of labour to exploit and capitalise on such situations have been much studied, especially in the context of the northeastern experience.[45] Liverpool, too, with its exceptional dependence on maritime activity, was a place where seamen could make their presence felt.[46] The outcome of such protests was at best local and transitory. Seafaring labour in the age of sail, though occasionally voicing its grievances through riot, mutiny or industrial action, and sometimes participating in more general social protest, was unable to organise permanently and thus had no lasting impact.

In concluding this section on the culture of sailors it is perhaps worth emphasising that for all the common elements of their experience,

---

[44]Still the basic texts for the study of these momentous events are Conrad Gill, *The Naval Mutinies of 1797* (Manchester, 1913); G.E. Manwaring and Bonamy Dobree, *The Floating Republic* (London, 1936).

[45]See a whole series of studies: S. Jones, "Community and Organisation – Early Seamen's Trade Unionism on the North East Coast, 1768-1844," *Maritime History*, III (1973), 35-62; N. McCord and D.E. Brewster, "Some Labour Troubles of the 1790s in North-Eastern England," *International Review of Social History*, XIIII (1968), 366-383; McCord, "Tyneside Discontents and Peterloo," *Northern History*, II (1967), 99-111; and McCord, "The Seamen's Strike of 1815 in North East England," *Economic History Review*, Second series, XXI (1968), 127-143. More general studies of conflict in the northeast are D. Bean, *Tyneside* (London, 1971); and T.P. MacDermott, *Centuries of Conflict. The Story of Trade Unionism on Tyneside* (Newcastle, 1965).

[46]R.B. Rose, "A Liverpool Sailor's Strike in the 18th Century," *Transactions of the Lancashire and Cheshire Antiquarian Society*, LXVIII (1958).

seamen are not an homogenous body. Age, marital status, length of voyage, size of ship, nature and character of the crew, temperament of master or owners, the community from which he hailed, and port of embarkation are but some of the factors which determined the attitude and lifestyle of the mariner. Between the extremes of the seaman bidding a brief good-bye to wife and family before embarking on his regular bi-monthly trip between a northeastern coal port and London, and the young, single, seamen setting sail on a first voyage to the Americas, East Asia or Australia, there was a literal world of difference. Likewise, the contrasting experience of the boy, sailing from his small home port in the company of local acquaintances, and that of the orphan apprentice thrust into a forecastle with rough, sea-worn strangers. Culture, career patterns and lifestyle are not experiences which lend themselves to generalisation.

## Nationals Serving in Foreign Registered Shipping

Information on British seamen serving in foreign vessels or departing to other countries in order to sail from there is limited, a situation that likely arises from the fact that such features were uncommon. Unlike other European workers, British labour could not cross over land frontiers in search of employment in another country. British seamen could only travel to ports abroad by sea, and if we accept that few workers could afford passage money, it is apparent that all British seamen left Britain as seamen, mostly in British vessels. Moreover, their terms of engagement invariably embraced an outward voyage and a return to a British port. Of course, once abroad, seamen could leave by agreement or more commonly by desertion. They were then free to seek new berths. Many, without doubt signed on to colonial vessels, but there is little evidence of widespread service on foreign ships. The one exception is in the case of United States' vessels. In the first half of the nineteenth century, large numbers of British seamen joined American vessels, which offered better pay and provisions albeit with sterner discipline. There were contemporary claims that the crews of American vessels operating in the North Atlantic comprised chiefly of British and to a lesser extent Scandinavians, and there were estimates of sixty to 100,000 British seamen employed in the US. Such claims seem likely to be exaggerated and there are problems of definition of nationality, but a sizeable British presence clearly existed despite American navigation laws.[47] Likewise, British seamen served with the early US Navy. This instance apart, it would seem that British seamen served in British vessels and that such vessels were almost entirely manned by British seamen. Even after the repeal of the Navigation Laws allowed owners to employ foreign seamen freely, the number of foreigners employed represented less than ten percent until the last quarter of the century when they rose rapidly.[48] Yet official figures of seafaring labour took no account of the use of Lascars, who from the 1780s had been employed on vessels in the Indian trade. Although there are no official figures before 1888, Lascars, according to Dixon, may have comprised two to three percent of the "Empire seagoing workforce" between 1830 and 1880.[49] Lascars were recruited overseas, in India. Where other foreigners joined British ships is unclear, but presumably they were hired in overseas or changed ships after arrival in Britain on foreign vessels. As for seamen travelling to Britain to gain seafaring employment, there are instances in mid-century of Scandinavians crossing to Hull to find berths on British sailing vessels, but the reporting probably reflects its exceptional nature.[50]

## Sailors and the State

Throughout the period under consideration the state took a considerable interest in the sailor. This attention was generated by one central concern: the defence of the realm. As long as the merchant navy was

---

[47]David M. Williams, "The Rise of United States Merchant Shipping on the North Atlantic, 1800-1850: The British Perception and Response," in Clark G. Reynolds (ed.), *Global Crossroads and the American Seas* (Missoula, 1988), 73-74.

[48]Sarah Palmer, "The British Merchant Seaman in the Age of Free Trade: Government and British Maritime Labour 1815-1860," *Collectanea Maritima*, V (1991), 305-316.

[49]Conrad Dixon, "Lascars: The Forgotten Seamen," in Rosemary Ommer and Gerald Panting (eds.), *Working Men Who Got Wet* (St. John's, 1980), 265-277, suggests that Lascar employment exceptionally may have reached as high as eight percent in the 1850s due to increased demand for seamen associated with gold rushes, the Crimean War and the Indian Mutiny.

[50]See *BPP*, 1878 [205], XVI, Select Committee on the Merchant Seamen Bill, questions 2513-2516. William Tulley, shipowner of Hull, quoted the case of penniless Scandinavian seamen arriving in the port seeking employment.

regarded as the "nursery of seamen" for the Royal Navy, government could never consider relations between shipowners and their workforce as purely a private commercial concern. Indeed, the justification for the entire protective code of the Navigation Laws was as a means to this end, but even after their abolition in 1849, governments continued to regard the employment conditions of seafarers as a legitimate field for intervention. As Palmer has argued elsewhere, "no section of the labour force found itself in so much routine contact with officialdom as the men who went to sea after 1850."[51]

Under the registry requirements associated with the Navigation Laws, the entire crew of coasting vessels and three-quarters of the crew of a foreign-going vessel had to be British subjects. Shipowners were also compelled under an 1825 Act, re-enacted in 1835, to take on apprentices, with the number regulated according to the size of vessel.[52] The 1835 Act also instituted a national Registry of Seamen. In 1844 the General Merchant Seamen's Act required every seaman to have a register ticket, but this proved impossible to implement efficiently and was abolished in 1853.[53] Two years before this a much older scheme, the privately-managed contributory pension system established in the early eighteenth century (the Merchant Seamen's Fund), had been wound up, with the power to distribute the wages and effects of deceased seamen transferred to government. This was among a number of responsibilities acquired at this time by a new administrative body, the Marine Department of the Board of Trade. Others relating to seafarers included the creation of a system of examination for masters and men; the establishment of shipping offices at which crews of foreign-going British vessels were engaged and discharged; a savings bank scheme; and a programme for the remittance of wages. The context for these changes, as also for the imposition of more severe penalties for desertion or indiscipline, has been shown by Williams to be related to evidence from British consuls suggesting low standards of seamanship, and concern about the rise of US shipping on the North Atlantic, which included the perception that

---

[51]Sarah Palmer, *Politics, Shipping and the Repeal of the Navigation Laws* (Manchester, 1990), 171.

[52]See Burton, "Apprenticeship Regulation."

[53]Jon Press, "The Collapse of a Contributory Pension Scheme: The Merchant Seamen's Fund, 1747-1851," *Journal of Transport History*, New Series, V (1979).

the British seafarer was inferior in terms of skill and moral quality to his American counterpart.[54] The repeal of the Navigation Laws and the threat of even greater foreign competition, – plus, it must be said, a growing concern over safety at sea – added further impetus to the introduction of measures to promote respectability among seafarers. In the event, the replacement of the sailing vessel by the steamer, and with it the introduction of more permanent modes of employment, arguably did more to alter the status of seafarers than such measures.

## English Sailors 1775-1870: Summary and Conclusion

During the period 1775-1870, British maritime labour greatly increased in numbers and importance. To the nation, seamen became of greater significance – economically and strategically – than any other sector of the labour force, a feature revealed in the continuous concern of government with "ships and men." Scholarly study, primarily in the past three decades, has immeasurably increased our knowledge and understanding of this important group of workers. Thus, reviewing the substantial modern research product has proved a rewarding exercise. But it has also been a frustrating experience: far too often it has not been possible to provide satisfactory answers to the issues listed in the "guidelines." In part, such failings reflect the deficiencies of the contemporary statistical sources and consequent problems of interpretation. Even so, the gaps in our knowledge over such basic issues as numbers, age structure and career patterns are painfully apparent.

Reviewing the literature has also raised the issue of the contexts of study. One is that of the need to study the overall maritime labour force and here one is aware of the very real separation that exists in Britain between scholars researching the navy and the mercantile marine. But perhaps of greater significance is the need to place seafarers in the context of the labour force and society as a whole. There is a danger that in emphasising the particular features of maritime labour, scholars lose sight of the fact that seamen are but one sector of the workforce. Seafaring labour was different from other work and seamen were

[54]Williams, "The Rise." This summary of legislation has drawn on the "Report to the President of the Board of Trade on the Legislation Concerning Merchant Ships and Seamen during the Last 40 Years," *BPP* (XXV) 1876, 337-357. See also Conrad Dixon, "Legislation and The Sailor's Lot," in Adam (ed.), *Seamen and Society*.

different from other workers, and in this sense the seaman was separate, "apart." But seafaring and seamen were also "a part" of the wider world of labour, nationally and, perhaps uniquely for labour in the period, internationally. It is encouraging to note that many recent studies of British sailors reveal an appreciation of such contexts. The workshop convened in the Netherlands will undoubtedly promote this essential, wider view of seafaring labour.

# Scottish Sailors[1]

## Gordon Jackson

How many sailors were there in Scotland? The simplest questions are always the most difficult to answer. We do not know for most of the period of sail how many men were involved. Naturally the number varied from season to season, week to week, and was seriously disrupted by trade fluctuations and wars, while the total desiring employment, including those between jobs and those lost in the Baltic, was doubtless greater than the number actually employed. This grand total of men who might call themselves sailors was never assessed and cannot now be estimated with any degree of confidence. The easiest and probably the most sensible way of envisaging changes in the mercantile marine is to count ships, or tons, employed; and by this imperfect measure there was only a handful of Scottish sailors until the early eighteenth century. A government-inspired survey in 1656 revealed only eighty vessels of more than twenty-five tons in the whole of Scotland. The number was probably depressed by the Civil War, and T.C. Smout has estimated the number of active Scottish ships at between 200 and 300 for the two decades preceding the Union with England in 1707.[2] In the latter year there were 14,485 tons of Scottish shipping: less, Smout points out, than that possessed by the English port of Whitby. Moreover, the Scottish ships were still very small, reflecting the poor quality of many harbours, the relative poverty of shipowners, and the difficulty of filling ships trading from diminutive ports with fragile hinterlands of self-sufficient crofters. Indeed, before the Union many of the larger foreign-going vessels were Dutch-owned. Nor were Scottish vessels – commonly Dutch-built – kept in the best of condition, as one crew found when they sank off Heligoland in 1680: "the ship is lost," it was said, "for being keepen so long

[1]I am grateful to the British Economic and Social Research Council for supporting a programme of research into aspects of Scottish maritime history, c. 1780-1830, on which this work is partly based. My work has benefitted from discussions with five of my past and present postgraduates: Dr. M. Whitehead, Dr. J. Kinloch, Mr. J. Matthews, Mr. E. Graham, and Mrs. C. Hill.

[2]T.C. Smout, *Scottish Trade on the Eve of the Union* (Edinburgh, 1963), 53-55.

at sea; the ship grew so leaky that it was impossible for the seamen to keep her any longer above water."[3]

By far the largest part of Scottish foreign trade in 1707 was with northern Europe, and most was consequently pursued from long-established ports on the east coast. This is where the sailors mostly lived, heavily concentrated in Leith and its creeks, with smaller communities in Aberdeen, Dundee and Montrose, and the much smaller ports specialising in the export of coal from the Firth of Forth, though the vessels involved in the short-haul coastal trade were often rowing boats drawn from the fisheries.[4] Some of the smaller west coast ports also owed their rising status to coal following the opening of the Ayrshire field. Ayr, Ardrossan, Irvine and associated shipping places – Saltcoats, for instance, was built after 1686 in the "precinct" of Irvine – first came to prominence shipping coal to Ireland in return for provisions.[5] It must be stressed that for much of the sailing era the coal/provision trade with Ireland was a most important component of the west of Scotland's total trade, and that until the 1820s this was counted as *foreign* trade. There was also the important, but unquantifiable, smuggling carried on with the Isle of Man, chiefly in fishing wherries that were often owned and crewed in Ireland.[6]

One of the strongest elements of growth after the Union was the coastal trade with England, and since vessels of both countries were involved it becomes difficult – if not impossible – to quantify the number of seamen contributed by each country. One thing seems clear, however: as with some of the English east coast ports, there was a tendency for vessels to be supplied by the northern partners rather than by London and the southern coasts, and for both owners and crews to have Aberdeen, Dundee or Leith as their home ports. This was especially so when sailing lines developed towards the end of the eighteenth

---

[3]*Ibid*, 58.

[4]See, for instance, D.G. Adams, "Trade in the Eighteenth and Nineteenth Centuries," in G. Jackson and S.G.E. Lythe (eds.), *The Port of Montrose* (Tayport, 1994), 138.

[5]B.F. Duckham, *A History of the Scottish Coal Industry* (Newton Abbot, 1970), 223-225.

[6]L.M. Cullen, "Smuggling in the North Channel in the Eighteenth Century," *Scottish Economic and Social History*, VII (1987), 11-13.

century. The chief one in Scotland was aptly called the Dundee, Perth and London Shipping Company, not the London, Perth and Dundee. The reason was simple. With agricultural improvement in their hinterland, the rise of factory-based textile industries and the extension of the local market for consumer goods, the people of Aberdeen, Dundee and Leith had a greater interest in trade with London than *vice-versa*. Scotland was heavily dependent on trade via English ports, not least because that was a cheaper and easier way for a country still short of capital – and probably also of maritime expertise and labour – to obtain foreign imports and to export its manufactures to both foreign and colonial markets. It was also the case that Scottish vessels engaged in Baltic trade went down to the Tyne for a load of coal and were classified as coasters. Those engaged in cross-trading as part of a round trip disappeared with their crews from the official record until they returned home.[7]

It was not only the eastern ports which pursued some measure of European trade. A fair proportion of it by the mid-eighteenth century had its *raison d'être* in the west of Scotland, generated principally in Glasgow and its industrial hinterland, which from the 1770s was shipping goods in small sailing vessels through the Forth and Clyde Canal and transhipping in the rising port of Bo'ness which was in effect Glasgow's third port, its gateway to Europe.[8] By the early nineteenth century a noticeable amount of trade passing through the Leith Custom House also originated in Glasgow but employed Leith ships and labour. But while the east of Scotland remained wedded to European trade Glasgow – operating until the early nineteenth century through its satellites, Port Glasgow and Greenock – put its resources increasingly into transatlantic trade, and in so doing created a new trading pattern which was to lead to its dominating position in Scottish trade and shipping and to its well-deserved appellation, "Workshop of the Empire." Metal goods and textiles were manufactured to support the transatlantic production of a miscellany of goods, but chiefly sugar, tobacco and eventually cotton. Defoe was so alarmed at Glasgow's progress after the Union that he forecast that the English colonies would soon become Scottish.

---

[7]G. Jackson, *The Trade and Shipping of Dundee, 1780-1850* (Dundee, 1991), 65-66.

[8]The most recent work on the development of Glasgow's trade and shipping, and its relationship with local industry, may be found in T.M. Devine and G. Jackson (eds.), *Glasgow. Vol. I: Beginnings to 1830* (Manchester, 1995).

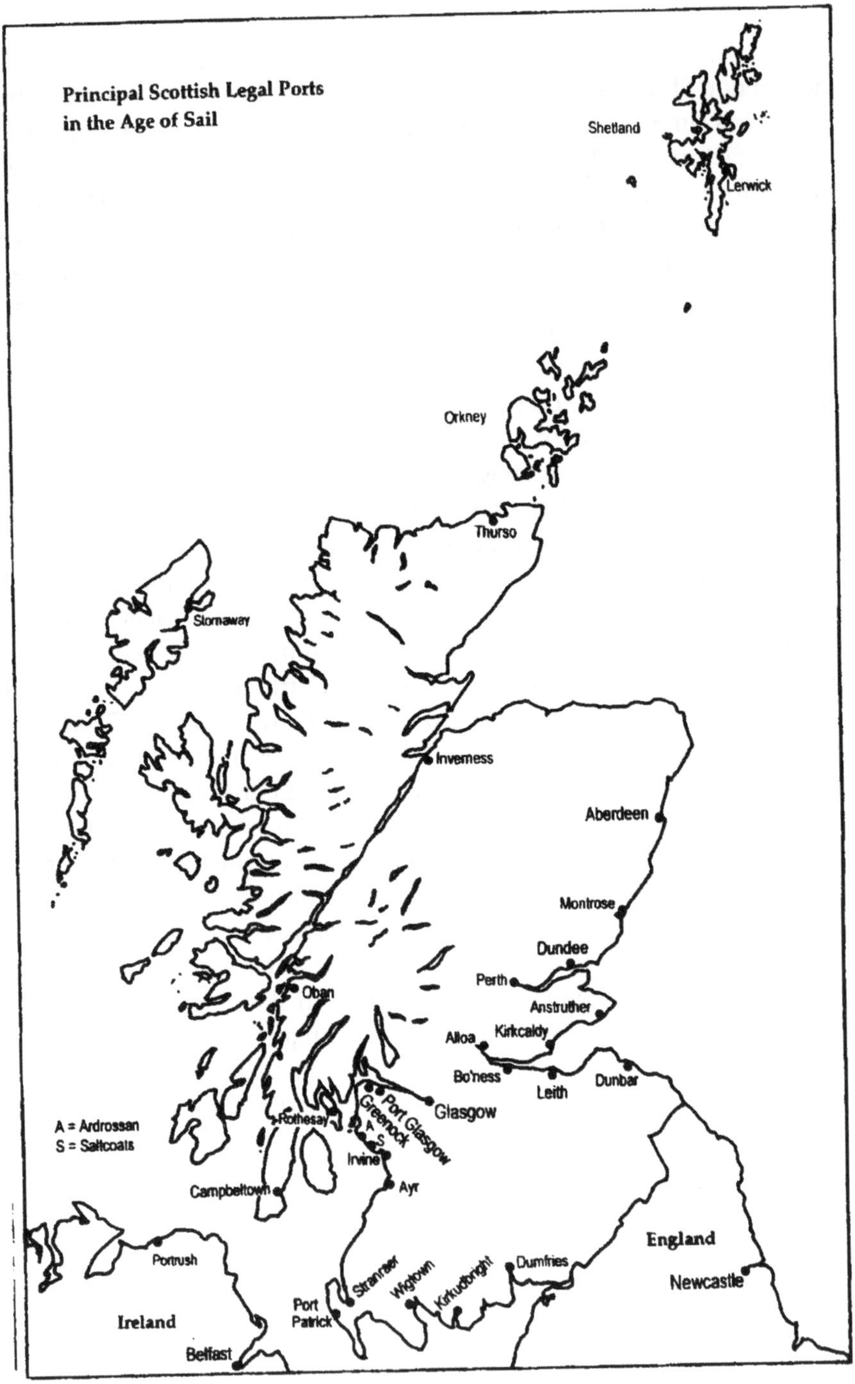


*Source*: Courtesy of the author.

These developments in the early eighteenth century had momentous implications for mercantile labour, as Postlethwayt argued while reviewing British trade in 1757:

> By this encrease of commerce, the Scots are much encreased in shipping; and they not only purchase but build ships of their own continually, especially for the West India trade and for the Southern commerce; an article which is necessarily followed by an encrease of seamen.[9]

Yet it was not until 1772 that the government required estimates of seamen throughout the empire as part of detailed Customs Reports on the state of trade and shipping preserved in the Public Record Office as Customs 17. Every vessel was recorded once a year on entering its "home" port from foreign or coastal trade, or from fishing, so that, despite the shortcomings of the figures, and problems of interpretation, we have a *rough* guide to the relative status of ports and the growing number of vessels and sailors during the expansion of the "Industrial Revolution" period. Vessels and crews "belonging" to all but the most moribund of Scottish ports for the year 1775 are shown in appendix table 1. By this time the foreign trade of Glasgow was beyond compare, and the number of seamen thought to be employed was almost forty percent of the national total. If we add in the Clyde coal ports (Ayr and Irvine) and the "service" and fishing port of Campbeltown we have a very substantial proportion of the Scottish mercantile marine.

It must, however, be remembered that the Irish component of foreign trade offered mariners employment opportunities more akin to short-haul coastal than to long-haul foreign trade. Like this Irish trade, the legal coastal trade was structured quite differently from foreign trade. Much of it carried coal and such things as slate, stone and lime. Ignoring the Irish trade, there was only a small western coal and provision trade with the tiny Highlands and Islands communities; the Glasgow and west of Scotland industrial region was self-sufficient in coal. By contrast the urban centres on the east coast did not have adjacent coal deposits and supplies were drawn coastwise from the Forth ports and increasingly

---

[9]M. Postlethwayt, *Britain's Commercial Interest Explained and Improved* (2 vols., London, 1757), I, 60.

from the Tyne and Wear. Moreover, coal exports formed part of the over-all trading activity of foreign-going vessels, and "triangular trading" down the coast was very common. But the most surprising thing at first sight is the large share of total activity taken by fishing, which employed a third of total manpower. Although there were plenty of crofter fishing boats and salmon cobbles round the coast, the fishing fleet was boosted by the inclusion of whalers with crews of forty or more, and the large Dutch-type busses engaged in the production of salt herring for the Baltic market. Fishing had been stimulated after the Union by bounties as part of the "pacification" programme.

The chief problem with these figures is that vessels trading more than once at a port might have two different crews, which would involve under-counting, while the same man might be counted in both coastal and fishing vessels, or in two different foreign-going vessels, involving over-counting. Both masters and men attempted to obtain maximum work by mixing coastal and foreign voyages; some vessels and men entered in both whaling and foreign or foreign and coastal trades, while others did not enter their home port during the year. If we consider change over the next ten years (see appendix table 2), it is obvious that the "industrial" ports were gaining slightly and that fishing was actually diminishing in importance. Evidence from Montrose and Dundee as well as from the west coast seems to indicate that fishing was indeed being squeezed between the demands of war for impressed fishermen and the demands of shipowners for more seamen, quite apart from any natural diminution of the fish stock. It is not even clear whether it is justifiable to count fishermen as a separate category of mariners, and the practice of so doing was abandoned in 1787.

If the problem of assessing the number of mariners required to man ships "belonging" to a specific port is fraught with difficulty, would the Registration Act of 1786 make for greater accuracy? The local Registrar of Shipping was from 1788 ordered to assess the number of men required to man all the vessels on the Register on 30 September each year. Appendix table 3 shows these figures for 1790, 1795, 1800 and 1805, during which, despite the upsets of war, the number of seamen grew strongly to an estimated 15,160 in 1805. In fact 15,000, give or take, is about the number recorded for some considerable time after 1800, but unfortunately we have no precise or systematic recording of seamen for Scotland between the Napoleonic War and the 1850s.

It is also the case that, unlike the earlier ships *belonging* and trading, these were ships *registered* but *not necessarily trading*, so there were likely to be more of them. While it was still common for ships to operate regularly from their own port, those on the east coast frequently moved up and down the coast and those in the west were increasingly likely to be involved in trips to or from Liverpool or Whitehaven as the transatlantic trades grew more complex. Some ports, such as Montrose and Campbeltown, had a tradition, like Whitby in England, of ship-owning which exceeded the requirements of the home port, and some local vessels were infrequent visitors. In the early eighteenth-century boom the trade of Glasgow was regularly serviced by the ships of Ayr, Irvine and Saltcoats. With the eclipse of Aberdeen by Dundee many of the former's vessels regularly traded to and from the Tay, and this, again, was part of coastal trade as far as Aberdeen was concerned and reduced the demand for sailors – and mercantile capital – in Dundee.[10] The confusion between foreign and coastal trade was clearly admitted in Aberdeen: "our vessels, calculated for the Baltic, generally go in the Coasting trade all the winter, and the Baltic trade all the summer."[11] What the men did is not stated, though we know from many sources that they also moved between trades.

Another attempt by the Registrar General was to assess the number of seamen engaged in different trades (see appendix table 4). As is to be expected, the Baltic trades were important, but by far the greatest employer of seamen was the Irish trade. If to this we add the transatlantic trades, it is obvious why Glasgow's ports employ such a large number of seamen.

There is one very important and novel feature of the assessments contained in appendix table 4: they recognise foreign seamen. So much is written about the Navigation Laws that it is commonly assumed that foreign ships and seamen could not trade in Scottish ports. Of course this is untrue. Scotland had always made use of Scandinavian vessels in the wood trade and Leith in particular made increasing use of foreigners after the Napoleonic war. By 1850, 686 foreign sailing vessels (60,251 tons) entered Leith compared with 322 British vessels (38,516 tons). Foreign vessels entering Bo'ness measured almost four times the tonnage

---

[10] *Aberdeen Harbour. Evidence and Proceedings in the Committee of the House of Commons in Regard to the Aberdeen Harbour Bill, 1839* (reprinted Aberdeen, 1839), 37-59. Their "Ships Laid On" appear regularly in the *Dundee Advertiser*.

[11] *Ibid*, 72. Masters with expertise in foreign trades often did not take their vessels coastwise.

of British ones. Even Glasgow had forty-two percent of tonnage entering in foreign bottoms. This does not include imperial trade, in which foreign vessels were negligible, but even in European trades Scotland's ratio of foreign vessels – and hence employment for foreign seamen – was very high compared with Hull, which was one of the leading English European-trade ports. Foreign tonnage entering Scotland as a whole in 1850 was forty-five percent, compared with Hull's twenty-two percent.[12] More problematic was the extent to which foreigners were used on board Scottish vessels. A quarter or fifth of the crew (depending on the period) could, in theory, be foreign, but since this would mean only one man on a typical-sized vessel there were few foreigners in service except to cover emergencies when men died or were left behind for various reasons in foreign ports. We know about them chiefly through accidents. When a gale blew overboard the galley of *Victoria* of Dundee in 1836 there was a foreigner in it; when *Esker* was caught in heavy seas in 1840 the five men washed overboard included two from Copenhagen and one from Hamburg.[13] Occasionally officials were strict: in 1823 an American barque arriving from Bremen to carry bounty linens to the US was reported for having five Americans, three Swedes and two Frenchmen among its crew in contravention of the law.[14]

The increase in foreign tonnage does not imply a collapse of the Scottish marine. Compared with the 2581 vessels and 210,295 tons registered in Scotland in 1805, there were 3516 and 449,746 tons in 1841 and 3432 and 491,395 tons in 1850. It was simply that the Scottish sailing marine was not growing fast enough, which may reflect to some extent the indirect use of cheaper crews and vessels from less-developed economies. The chief reason, however, was that Scottish owners were turning to steam, especially in coastal trade. The very sharp decline in sail activity from c. 1860 is apparent in the tonnage and direction of trade of vessels clearing from Glasgow in appendix table 5, while the aggregate experience of sail in Glasgow is shown in figure 2. Para-

---

[12] *British Parliamentary Papers (BPP)*, 1851 (92), LII, 201-205. By comparison, Hull's tonnage entering was not much less than half that of the whole of Scotland.

[13] *Dundee Advertiser*, 30 December 1836 and 30 October 1840.

[14] The captain blamed desertions for the three Danes and increased work – they left America in ballast – for the two Frenchmen. The outcome is unknown. Dundee Regional Archives (DRA), CE/70/1/16, Customs Letter Books, 14 October 1823.

doxically, the tonnage of sail owned in Glasgow grew to 571 vessels and 572,568 tons in 1895, but these were chiefly over 1000 tons and engaged in the last of the long-distance sail trades, such as those operated to South America and Australasia by the General Shipping Company of Glasgow.[15] Those trading at their home port amounted to less than 100,000 tons.

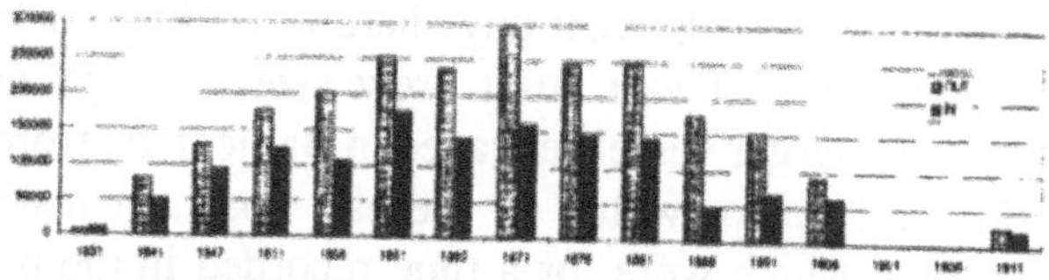

*Figure 2*: Sail Vessels Entering and Clearing Glasgow with Cargo, Foreign Trade, 1831-1911 (tons).

*Source*: Figures are for the Harbour of Glasgow and exclude Port Glasgow and Greenock, from which trade was gradually attracted up-river. The growth of activity to c. 1850 reflects this transfer. Data are not available for 1901 and 1906. See G. Jackson and C.W. Munn, "Trade, Commerce and Finance," in W.H. Fraser and C.W. Munn (eds.), *Glasgow. Vol. II: 1830-1912* (Manchester, 1996), 52-95.

For most of the sailing era Scottish ships were, then, relatively few in number and small in size. Well into the nineteenth century, when Pollok and Gilmour of Glasgow were building 700- to 1000-ton vessels in their Canadian yards, the typical vessel was still less than 100 tons. Their crews were correspondingly small. Unfortunately, as in so many aspects of seamen's lives, fortuitous information is all that is available. Even where we know the size of crews, we rarely know either the tonnage or the rig, and sometimes not even the trade, all of which determine optimum crew size. Interest – even among shipowners – generally lay in the number of seamen rather than ton/man ratios, labour efficiency, or even total manning costs. There were attempts to change rigs to reduce crew size, but the experience of Montrose, where chopping and changing vessels was a common pursuit, shows that most crews were so small that there was often little to be gained by it. Some of the best evidence regarding crews in European trade covers Leith, for

[15] *BPP*, "Annual Statement of Navigation," 1895, table 44; and Strathclyde Regional Archives (SRA), T-CN 6/5, Clyde Navigation Trust Accounts and Statistics, 1895-1896.

1734-1742. The records of Leith Trinity House contain 193 voyages in these years, with crews ranging from three to eight per vessel:[16]

| | | | | | | |
|---|---|---|---|---|---|---|
| Crew size | 3 | 4 | 5 | 6 | 7 | 8 |
| No. of Vessels | 16 | 53 | 47 | 43 | 13 | 21 |

Since few vessels went anywhere other than to Europe, this is fairly representative of east coast crew sizes, though not perhaps of Clyde crews. As larger vessels engaged in Baltic trade from mid-century, crew sizes went up to twelve on the east coast, at least according to victualling bills which were for a time recorded in the port books, and in this case we also know the tonnage because it was included, being necessary to judge the accuracy of the bills. Between 1743 and 1770 crews fell between four and twelve in number, with three-quarters of the crews consisting of four to six men (or youths).[17] No Scottish trader was larger than 100 tons, though, broadly speaking, there were efficiency gains associated with size. These were not, however, related absolutely to vessel size, and there may have been good reasons for some relative under- or over-manning of which we are ignorant. Suffice it to say that between 1743 and 1770 vessels up to sixty-nine tons could be sailed with a minimum crew of four, and each extra ten tons up to ninety required one more man:

| | | | | | | | |
|---|---|---|---|---|---|---|---|
| Tons burthen | <40 | 40-50 | 50-60 | 60-70 | 70-80 | 80-90 | 90-100 |
| Minimum crew | 4 | 4 | 4 | 5 | 6 | 7 | 7 |
| tons/man ratio | 10:1 | 13:1 | 15:1 | 14:1 | 13:1 | 13:1 | 14:1 |

This reveals the interesting fact that the clearest gains in tons per man was in vessels under seventy tons, and thereafter there was actually a decline in the ratio as vessels got bigger. In other words, because these vessels were all relatively small, a certain minimum crew was necessary for safety in specific trades, but an increase might be necessary for certain rigs (three masts required more men than two), difficult voyages

---

[16]Scottish Record Office (SRO), GD226/7/2, 7, Records of Trinity House of Leith.

[17]SRO, E/504, Port Books for the eastern ports, 1743-1770. I owe these figures to my Research Assistant and student, Dr. Janet Kinloch.

or cumbersome and dangerous cargoes.[18] Evidence for Montrose, which is somewhat better, supports that for Leith. In the eighteenth century, forty-ton brigantines usually carried a master and four or five men; 110-ton vessels usually six to ten; and both sloops and schooners carried four or five. Almost always one crew member was a boy, and government encouragement of apprenticeship – to boost the number of common seamen suitable for the press during the Napoleonic wars – raised the number of boys to two out of the average crew of six employed in thirty-four vessels engaged in Montrose's foreign trade in 1808.[19] In Dundee in the first third of the nineteenth century we find the most common vessels on the coast, the sloops, with approximate crew levels of six for eighty-ninety tons, five for seventy-eighty tons, three for forty-fifty tons, and two for the seventeen-ton *Pitlour*, wrecked with fifty sacks of flour off St. Andrews in 1825. By contrast, the smacks of the coastal lines usually carried six to eleven men. The foreign trade also had its share of diminutive vessels, with one carrying a crew of only two and another only three. The largest number carried seven men: brigs under 200 tons usually carried seven to eight but could go up to twelve, and those over 200 tons usually had twelve to fourteen. The whalers, though no longer constrained by law, still carried around fifty. The only port for which crewing details are available for the entire fleet is Dundee, and then only for 1824:[20]

| Crew Size | 1 | 2 | 3 | 4 | 5 | 6 | 7 | 8 | 9 | 10 | 11 | 12 | 13 | 14 | 15 | 16 |
|---|---|---|---|---|---|---|---|---|---|---|---|---|---|---|---|---|
| Foreign-going | 0 | 1 | 1 | 1 | 10 | 10 | 14 | 11 | 4 | 7 | 1 | 5 | 0 | 3 | 0 | 1 |
| Coastal | 0 | 8 | 25 | 5 | 9 | 7 | 1 | 0 | 1 | 4 | 7 | | | | | |

One thing is fairly clear from the crew sizes: outside the coastal smack trade and the distant foreign trades employing vessels over 100 tons, there was little hope of a cook or anything approaching seaborne banquets. Nevertheless, though doubtless there were masters who fed their crews rubbish, and cooks who were old, drunken and/or dirty, or who simply could not cook, the amount of food provided does not seem

---

[18]SRO, E/504.

[19]Jackson and Lythe (eds.), *Port of Montrose*, 155.

[20]*Dundee Register and Directory 1824-1825* (Dundee, 1824), 46-53. Regrettably, no other *Directory* contains crew sizes.

unduly low in the instances where records have survived. Victualling bills from the mid-eighteenth century offer few surprises. Vessels always carried an adequate supply of salt meat (which is why the victualling bills were required), and usually also fresh meat, barley and oatmeal, cheese and butter. Whether any of it could be cooked adequately in tiny vessels, some of which – at least in the coastal trade – had no decks, is another matter. Of greater interest are a small number of letters and accounts of master mariners which indicate the purchase of food in foreign ports. The best set of papers, of a Glasgow shipmaster called William Lang, in the West Indian and Iberian trades, reveals regular opportunist purchases of fresh meat and vegetables and a special concern for fresh fruit, though it must be confessed that Lang was thought by his owners to spend too much of their profits.[21]

About the wages of men in the sailing fleet there is again very little that can be confidently attributed to the whole marine. They varied with the trade. Long-haul men received more than coastal men, and some – commonly in the coastal trade – were paid by the voyage and others – in foreign trade – by the month. It would not be too much of a generalisation to suggest that around £1 per month was typical of short-haul time wages for much of the eighteenth century. Offerings in the transatlantic trade were greater and could be £2 or as much as £2.50 per month. Things changed for a time with the Napoleonic wars. Certainly £2.50 was thought reasonable in the 1820s in Dundee. But Lenman found that some able seamen on the east coast were accepting £2 per month in the 1840s, and *Sappho*, out of Glasgow, was paying them £2. 5s. per month for Indian and East Asian voyages.[22] Scoresby reckoned that allowing for differences between ports, whaling men had a complicated wage structure based on a minimum sum plus bonuses for catches according to their status, which could work out at £25 for the voyage for a common seaman to £95 for the first mate and £250 for the master.[23] It was expected of whaling men that they would make up their income

[21]SRO, CS 96/648/5, W. Lang, Journal of Journeys in Spain.

[22]B. Lenman, *From Esk to Tweed; Harbours, Ships and Men of the East Coast of Scotland* (Glasgow, 1975), 184; and SRA, TD ARD [gowan] 12/4/1-4. I owe details of *Sappho* to Dr. Margaret Whitehead.

[23]W. Scoresby, *An Account of the Arctic Regions, with a History and Description of the Northern Whale Fishery* (2 vols., London, 1820), II, 201.

from other earnings between seasons, and many served in the Baltic after a rest from their exertions. The ships, too, filled in the off-season as profitably as could be arranged.[24] Occasionally one reads of the despair of the man who arrived back in port too late to catch his whaler, and there was – at least in Montrose – a sort of waiting list for places in whalers should men not turn up. This kind of regularity of employment for good men, which can be traced because we know the names of whaling seamen during the bounty years, went some way to consolidate the small communities from which they derived.

Most Scottish ports were, by English or Glasgow standards, small indeed, and recruitment was often very localised. Even so, those which experienced significant growth in the eighteenth century had difficulty finding sufficient labour in the local community. Until the steamer took over some of Glasgow's coastal distribution trade from 1812, at least part was carried by fishermen from recipient communities offering fish and rural products in exchange. Men from smaller places down the Clyde estuary hoped to sail from Greenock or Port Glasgow, where trade was increasingly concentrated, though here the more usual transfer of activity was sometimes reversed when colliers were sent to the herring fishing.[25] By the nineteenth century ships in the Indian and East Asian trades appear to have been crewed largely in Greenock or Port Glasgow, indicating their attractions for the men of those places that were declining as ports. Several marginal ports had more ships and men than they needed. The Kirkcudbright Shipping Company, for instance, could not employ its single ship in its home port just after the Napoleonic wars. In the 1830s Aberdeen shipowners were asserting that they often sailed their vessels into and out of Dundee, so the major linen port was availing itself of maritime labour and capital from its northern neighbour.[26] Until quite late in the eighteenth century the port books regularly distinguished between vessels having the same name – and small ports

---

[24]"The Greenland Ships," it was said of Peterhead, "have gone out to the Baltic for several years...[and] they are generally freighted for London, or some of the King's dockyards...None of them bring their cargoes to Peterhead." Quoted by R.C. Michie, "North-East Scotland and the Northern Whale Fishing, 1752-1893," *Northern Scotland*, III (1977-1978), 69.

[25]E.J. Graham, *The Shipping Trade of Ayrshire, 1689-1791* (Ayr, n.d.), 15.

[26]*Aberdeen Harbour*, 39 and 58.

were not inventive in this matter – by appending "of...," and commonly they were "of" a place which was not a port of registry at all, but a "creek" within a port where trading was not usually allowed. For instance, iron and brass wire from Stockholm destined for Glasgow was sent to Bo'ness in 1700 in a vessel "of Pittenweem" (a creek of Anstruther);[27] iron from St. Petersburg arrived in Port Glasgow in the *Ann* "of Airth" (a creek of Bo'ness); and Greenock shipped goods in the *Mary Margaret* "of Inverkip," a hamlet on the Clyde.[28]

All ports were within reach of fishing communities, which were always good sources of labour, especially with fluctuations in fishing and the onset of bad weather. It has been suggested that in the 1780s the crews of as many as twenty coastal sloops belonging to Montrose switched between grain and coal in the summer and fish in the winter.[29] Crofters from south of the Tay were similarly among those seeking employment in the Dundee whaling fleet, and when Dundee's Union Whale Fishing Company advertised for apprentices in the 1820s they asserted that "stout lads from the country will be preferred."[30] Campbeltown, on the Mull of Kintyre, one of the leading Scottish fishing towns, made use of both local rural and Irish labour resources in its fishing and offered both rural and fishing labour with its merchant ships to the trade of the Clyde.[31] All along the coast inhabitants of tiny villages moved easily between crofting, fishing, whaling and coastal or foreign voyages. Recruitment was often very localised, which was a principal cause of

---

[27]Mitchell Library, Glasgow, MSS Dept, Adam Montgomerie's Letter Book, Montgomerie to J. Bryson and Co., 16 May 1700.

[28]SRO, E504/15/1, E504/28/1, Port Books of Greenock and Port Glasgow, 1743-1744. A harbour at Inverkip was proposed in 1700 but not built; *Acts of the Parliament of Scotland*, X, 231.

[29]D.G. Adams, "'Abundant with all kinde of fishes'. Sea Fishing before 1800," in Jackson and Lythe (eds.), *Port of Montrose*, 230.

[30]G. Jackson, "Montrose Whaling," in Jackson and Lythe (eds.), *Port of Montrose*, 223. The Aberdeen Whaling Company had used almost identical words in 1790; see W.R.H. Duncan, "Aberdeen and the Early Development of the Whaling Industry, 1750-1800," *Northern Scotland*, III (1977-1978), 55.

[31]Cullen, "Smuggling," 13, points to a strong contribution of Irish expertise and labour in the long-distance fishery from both Campbeltown and Greenock.

some of the more distressing accidents at sea, for in fishing and whaling tragedies hit the same family or village more than once.

The ease with which labour was recruited – sometimes for short periods or seasonal operations – is an indication of the lack of alternative employment opportunities in the old fishing villages of the east coast. On the other hand, there was a general lack of cheap labour as industrialisation drove up its price, and this also was a reason to employ part-time labour from the fisheries or farming. Sometimes it was full-time labour, but only for a limited number of years, as young men went out to make some money and then returned to the land – perhaps to dead men's boots – or, as sometimes happened, to land-based jobs associated with port activities. About the regularity of employment very little is known. Can we assume that short-haul men were youths or family men with more interest in home-based steady jobs? The "whole town" turned out when whalers left, and disasters in the Arctic always brought a flood of emotions and fears for starving children. But when *Susanna*'s crew was paid for a voyage to St. Eustatius in 1754, only the master and three men were counted for nine months; three were paid for five months; two for four months; and three for three months.[32] In the 1840s *Sappho*'s crew to East Asia were chiefly in their twenties, unmarried, and footloose, with a heavy turn-over in foreign ports, especially after the discovery of gold in Australia.[33]

It is easy enough to talk about men walking into a harbour looking for a berth to America, but actually getting to America was by no means easy and was the cause of much anxiety in ports as trade initiatives appeared from the seventeenth century onwards. There were never, it seems, enough masters, and this may, indeed be a cause for constraints to trade during the Industrial Revolution, and was one of the good reasons for shifting to the greater productivity of steam vessels.

The training of ship's officers was always difficult. It is clear from surviving crew lists – and there are not all that many – that sons followed fathers through the generations, but nepotism needs nephews and while port books and shipping registers show a great affinity of names between masters, merchants and owners, recruitment of good men

---

[32]SRO, CS96/646, Journal of William Lang for the brigantine *Susanna*, 22 October 1754.

[33]SRA, TD ARD 12/4/2-4, Log Books of *Sappho*, 1840-1853.

was a matter for careful thought. Money was a good substitute for blood. Apprenticeships for two to four years may have been more common than the few surviving papers suggest, but apprenticeships offering at least the prospect of decent rewards carried premiums beyond the reach of the poorer sort of people. Moreover, even where there was enthusiasm for the sea, the Scottish marine may not have been large enough for boys to be trained on the job, and any serious expansion brought a surge of interest in the alternative "academic" training in navigation, and at the same time an interest in making ship's officers out of poorer boys. Trinity House School of Leith (the port of Edinburgh) appointed its first teacher of mathematics in 1680, and his successors continued to offer navigation and "plain sailing."[34] Since marine education was essential for successful trading, the city of Edinburgh also appointed schoolmasters in navigation and "vulgar" mathematics. Montrose – by no means a great port – supported marine education before appointing in 1718 a "Professor of Mathematics" who taught "arithmetic in all its parts, geometry, trigonometry, plain and spherical navigation, astronomy and book keeping."[35] Edinburgh at least had the experience of centuries of trading into Europe. For Glasgow the learning process in the transatlantic voyage to the English colonies – still alien territory though the Scots were infiltrating them with gusto – was more complicated. Glasgow men had little or no experience here, the Glasgow fleet was tiny, the mariners few, and Trinity House noticeably absent. Adventures to Barbados, it was said, had failed through want of ships or expertise. It was left to the City Council to initiate marine education, appointing a "Professor of Navigation" in 1681, opening subsidised navigation schools in 1695 and 1707, and giving a Captain Davies his freedom, *gratis*, in 1695 "in respect he is a person qualified to be useful to this burgh in voyages to Africa and America."[36] Glasgow could also draw on the small ports of the Clyde estuary – chiefly dealing in coal and provisions with Ireland – for a steady supply of masters and mariners. Ayr was teaching navigation and geography from 1727 with "maps and globes; the knowledge of which...is highly necessary for forming the man of

---

[34]J. Mason, *The History of Trinity House of Leith* (Edinburgh, 1957), 163.

[35]Jackson and Lythe (eds.), *Port of Montrose*, 83-84.

[36]*Glasgow Records*, IV, 21 September and 7 December 1695, and 18 September 1707.

business." Saltcoats parish school was also teaching navigation from the 1740s and by the end of the century was reflecting the relative value of knowledge by charging twice as much – one guinea – for navigation as for bookkeeping and four times as much as for arithmetic. "The success of this programme of instruction," it has been said, "is evident in the number of Ayrshire captains who commanded Virginiamen across the Atlantic."[37] More than a little knowledge was a great thing, as Dundee discovered in the 1830s when it was trying without much success to break into the southern European fruit trade in which vessels had to make fast passages and the masters had also to be able to purchase suitable fruit.[38] A shortage of appropriately experienced masters was one of several reasons why many smaller ports continued into the nineteenth century to import or export goods coastwise and rely on larger ports for foreign-going expertise.

It is, however, at least possible that the provision of academic training for seamen indicates not only a relative shortage of apprenticeships but also their high cost. Many navigation schools in Britain, and certainly those in Glasgow and Edinburgh, seem to have been educating poor boys for the sea at minimal cost to please merchants and shipowners rather than shipmasters. In other words, while many a master was the son or even – in one Dundee example – the father of the shipowner, steps were being taken to recruit more widely as trade expanded in the late seventeenth and early eighteenth centuries. Certainly Montrose Council, in the early nineteenth century if not before, was subsidising marine education for poor boys as "a most essential piece of education in a seaport town."[39]

Whatever a boy's background, the sea was never an easy calling, and it was as hard for potential masters as for mariners. An interesting light is thrown on a number of aspects of training in the case of Henry Clerke, son of a mercantile and landowning family of substance in the east of Scotland. He was sent to an Edinburgh navigation school in the 1690s, and then apprenticed to a master who could give a wide range of

---

[37]Graham, *Shipping Trade of Ayrshire*, 20.

[38]*Dundee Advertiser*, 18 July 1834 and 18 December 1835; and Jackson, *Dundee*, 20.

[39]Quoted by Adams in Jackson and Lythe (eds.), *Port of Montrose*, 83.

voyage experiences from the Baltic to the Mediterranean.[40] Enthusiasm soon turned sour. He learned a good deal about trade, and visited the rigging, but the crew treated him with less respect than he thought he deserved. So did the captain's wife, and his appearance suffered. "At present," a friend told his father, "his equipage is so ordinary that he appears no more than a common seaman [than] which nothing can make his advancement more difficult here."[41] And as for the common seamen, they were rogues, thieves and villains. In London a gentleman would rather send his son to Virginia as a slave than put him to sea. "Mast men" were, as the Spaniards said, nothing but "baptised beasts." But at least they were men who worked hard as they moved towards being "too old at thirty." "Seamen experience hardship and danger, work like horses, do not respect the Sabbath and curse and swear, and whoever desires to see an emblem of Hell, let him go aboard a ship and there he shall see it to the life."[42] Henry Clerke gave up the sea. "An emblem of Hell" would seem to contradict what we have just said about a lack of beastliness, but there were always the Clerkes of this world who expected an easy living and whose susceptibilities were offended by those two great enemies of polite society, the drink and the curse. It is also a reminder that many masters were no better than their crews. Indeed, many men slipped from master to mate more easily than they rose in the first place; certainly some masters working for the Dundee, Perth and London Shipping Company not only drank but were foolish enough to do it when their directors were on board. It is interesting comment on seamen's behaviour that this company at least would not tolerate on its expensive steamers what was still acceptable on its sailing vessels.

Whatever government might have hoped, most apprentices were in effect cheap labour as much as, or more than, potential masters; their chances of promotion and eventually leaving the sea as brokers, shipowners or merchants planning their country houses excite the emotions rather than the intellect. Even those who might graduate from the navigation section of Montrose's Council School to the quarter-deck

---

[40]Details from SRO, GD 18/5218, Clerke of Penicuik Papers, John Clerke's letters.

[41]SRO, GD 18/5218, J. Galloway, London, to J. Clerke, Edinburgh, July 1700.

[42]SRO, GD 18/5218, H. Clerke, London, to J. Clerke, Edinburgh, October 1700.

were, it was alleged in 1759, a rough lot, who must be segregated because they assaulted and abused boys in the English and Writing schools and beat up the janitor.[43] A more telling constraint on their promotion, however, was doubtless the almost universal expectation that the master must purchase shares in his ship unless – which was very common if not quite universal – his father or brother owned it. Even in whaling, where apprenticeship to one of the officers was the traditional method of rising to the top, the apprentices required by law were sometimes poor boys and sometimes cheated. In 1788 the Marine Society, which aimed at equipping poor boys for the sea, and particularly the Navy, complained to the Board of Trade that boys fitted out by them "appeared to have been discharged from Greenland Ships since the last Season. We suspect there have been many more in the same situation...as the practice of turning them adrift after the voyage is admitted to be very general."[44]

The expected progress of a man on the way to the top was outlined in great detail in a case brought against William Lang, a Glasgow shipmaster, in the Scottish Admiralty Court, the Scottish Court of Session and eventually the House of Lords, in which it is said, *inter alia*:[45]

> Merchants in established business buy a ship and cargo and take by the hand a young man who has been mate or perhaps master of a small vessel whom they think well of...They intrust him with the care of the cargo and assume him a partner to a certain extent in order to secure his diligence by his self interest...This is attended with advantage to all parties. The young man is set into the world and into business. He gets trust and credit in the eyes of mankind which helps him on. He gains

---

[43]Jackson and Lythe (eds.), *Port of Montrose*, 84.

[44]For a recent account of the early activities of the Marine Society, see J.S. Taylor, *Jonas Hanway: Founder of the Marine Society* (London, 1985). The quote is from PRO, BT 6/94, Minutes of the Board of Trade, ff. 34-37, Letter from Samuel Thornton, 28 February 1788.

[45]SRO, CS 96/231/W.3/1, and House of Lords Record Office, Alexander Wilson and Robert Pollock versus William Lang, 1766.

> experience and acquaintance with an opportunity of gaining character and by that means lays a foundation for his future fortune.

But what of those who did not have William Lang's apparent ability to buy a mastership – or have it bought for him? Can it be argued that common seamen might learn the trade and that obvious ability might gain promotion? It is an attractive thought, and the occasional references to the most remarkable fêtes of navigation – and general competence – by those on whom authority was thrust imply that maybe the system did not always employ the best masters. Take, for instance, the case of John Wesley, mariner in the Dundee brig *Neilson*, sent on a round trip with linen to Jamaica, sugar from Havana to St. Petersburg and flax back to Dundee.[46] Fever struck the vessel in the Caribbean, and Wesley – "a very young man" – took it from Havana to Elsinore in two months and, after quarantine there, on to St. Petersburg, again making good time. As an act of charity he brought home the effects of the dead men, and in consequence of their "disagreeable effluvia" they were sunk by the Customs men in the deepest part of the River Tay and the ship was once more quarantined. As a result of all this the round trip took nine months instead of seven, but not bad going for a young man pursued by fever. What happened to him is not recorded.

From time to time we come across those who did not make the grade and the troubles that beset them. David Balfour, for instance, son of a coachman to a petty laird in Forfarshire, was at the age of ten apprenticed for four years to a Dundee shipmaster. Three months after his indentures ended he was pressed and served eleven years in the Navy before his release in 1813, when he returned – as a seaman – to Dundee. After three or four years he was attracted by better prospects in Greenock, and sailed from there for seven or eight years before returning once more to Dundee. Perhaps he should have come home sooner; his wife, whom he had married when they were both sixteen, was less faithful than he thought. He stabbed her. There was local sympathy and he would have been charged only with manslaughter had he not, after

---

[46]DRA, CE 70/1/16. Customs Letter Books, Collector to Board, 27 November 1821. See also Jackson, *Dundee*, 70.

twenty-eight years at sea, been so poor that he had to go next door to borrow the knife with which the deed was done![47]

Nowhere was the acquisition of skilled knowledge involved in navigation easy, and nowhere, perhaps, was it more difficult than in the whaling trade. Finding the Arctic was the easy part. Catching the whales and processing their blubber offered the promise of relatively rich rewards for all levels of labour, but carried the danger of frostbite, broken bones, dreadful cuts and a winter of poverty. When Edinburgh began whaling in 1683 Dutch harpooners were put in one whaler and Scotsmen in another, "so that they think it both their concerns to do their utmost," but there was little skill transferred.[48] When Glasgow made its second attempt at whaling in 1727, the importance of experience was stressed by George Bogle, learning to be a merchant in Holland:[49]

> The Greenland Fishery is but a very precarious Trade, yet there is more probability of the company's succeeding in it when they use the right means...in short the encouraging of foreigners to settle in Scotland, and to learn us the many arts and mysteries we are still ignorant of.

In this case Dutch masters, officers and equipment – and some, apparently, from Hamburg – were obtained, though at a cost, since the Dutch agent was hauled before a Court lest he invest in a foreign company. He was "so much chagrined and discouraged by the hard usage he met with from the judges, as to the men's wages, that he had no heart to write" and declined to take up a share in the Glasgow venture.[50] Whaling was a major enterprise involving long voyages and complex

---

[47]Balfour's life history and full reports of the trial are in *Dundee Advertiser*, May 1826.

[48]SRO, GD 18/2568, Clerke of Penicuik Papers, G. Campbell to Sir John Clerke, 30 April 1683.

[49]SRA, George Bogle's Letter Book, Bogle, Leiden, to Robert Bogle, Glasgow, 16 February 1727; see also G. Jackson, *The British Whaling Trade* (London, 1978), 40-47.

[50]SRA, George Bogle's Letter Book, Bogle, Leiden, to Robert Bogle, Glasgow, 20 May 1727.

operations, but the truth is that in the early eighteenth century there was not even a uniform ability in ordinary fishing throughout Scotland. In the Clyde estuary fishing had virtually collapsed owing to the lack of expertise among indigenous Ayrshire fishermen: "the principal reason," it was said in 1771, "may be that the Highland sailors and rowers are more expert at the business than ours."[51] Such confessions of inadequacy were no idle boasting. The Scots really were deficient in maritime experience even at simple levels, and so far as whaling was concerned they did not learn very quickly. The average catches of whalers in the 1750s were proportional to the number of foreigners in the crew (presumably as officers), with nine foreigners being the optimum number. At the same time there was a consistent discrepancy between the performance of whaling captains, with only half of the forty men involved in the 1740s catching more than two whales, and five catching thirty-four percent of the total catch.[52] The learning curve in the whaling trade became astronomical when profits rose towards the end of the century and it may be that around mid-century it was enthusiasm rather than innate ability that was lacking among the sort of people who might expect to enter the rather limited numbers of officers or masters of merchantmen. Certainly Scottish vessels were out-performing English ones in the early nineteenth century, though again it was the case that some masters always did better than others.

The "fast sailers" so prominently advertised among "Ships Laid On" for the Baltic or America doubtless owed much to the extent to which their build and sail pattern was appropriate for the winds, seas and even ports in which they operated. Nonetheless, the master was important. Some men were known to be faster sailers than others, as they judged more accurately the amount of sail to set, or the moment to tack, and as Dundee vessels commonly raced from the Baltic with cargoes of flax for the linen mills, voyage times were a matter of comment in the *Dundee Advertiser*. But they were to some extent limited by the quality of their crews and the extent to which they worked as a team. There is evidence that masters of good crews endeavoured to keep them together,

---

[51]Quoted in Graham, *Shipping Trade of Ayrshire*, 26.

[52]G. Jackson, "Government Bounties and the Establishment of the Scottish Whaling Trade, 1750-1800," in J. Butt and J.T. Ward (eds.), *Scottish Themes* (Glasgow, 1976), 57-59.

and when one considers the smallness of most crews, and of the maritime communities from which they were usually drawn in Scotland, it is not surprising that crews often stuck together. In the case of coastal sloops, with two or three men and a boy, they were commonly related, and being a master was by no means as grand as it sounds. Since in the eighteenth century the average Scottish ship was around 100 tons and its crew around six, there were opportunities for an affinity of interest between members of a small society in which social divisions were not yet fully developed. Since shipowning had not fully emerged as an independent occupation there must be doubts about the universal application of a capitalist-proletariat distinction.

The benevolence with which government treated the whole British whaling trade, with substantial subsidies up to £2 per ton from the 1730s to the 1820s, was to encourage labour rather than capital. Maritime activity – whaling, fishing and even the coastal trade – was a "nursery for seamen" for a navy which government was increasingly inclined to use but reluctant to fund on a permanent basis until the 1830s. Oil could always be imported; seamen, in time of war or bluster, were not so easily come by. So a great imperial – or imperialist – power required a great mercantile marine – the kind of perverse logic which assumes that pheasants exist to employ gamekeepers. When whaling was undermined by gas companies, the trade argued that "Every branch of shipping which can find employ for 10,000 seamen must be valuable at all times, but more particularly so in times of peace."[53] Indeed, as naval warfare grew in importance and outbreaks of peace might lead to 20,000 unemployed seamen seeking foreign employment beyond the reach of the press gang in the next war, a fanciful scheme was proposed to send the Royal Navy to the Arctic in peacetime, employing 250 vessels, 17,000 seamen and 1500 non-commissioned officers. It is of some interest that this document also notices one of the basic labour problems supposed to exist in whaling:

> the present method of carrying on the Whale Fishery is not a proper inducement to seamen (in time of Peace) to embark; for the voyage seldom exceeds four or five months and the wages per man not more than £7 or £8

---

[53]British Library, Add. MS. 38, 367, ff. 107-110, "Whale Ship Owners versus the Gas Companies," 1817.

> the voyage and as the benefit arising from the Bounty... centres on the owners and masters only, the seamen after deducting extra clothes and liquor, etc., which he is obliged to equip himself with on account of the severity of the climate, he has little or nothing left for his support the remaining seven months.[54]

He could, on the other hand, sign on for the Baltic, or carry coals to Ireland.

Wages generally rose in wartime for those who avoided the press. Even in whaling, where there was theoretical protection from the press gang, costs rose. A Board of Trade memorandum in 1776 suggested that:

> if the differences in the costs of the outfit in times of peace and war, and of the wages and difficulty or facility of obtaining seamen, are considered, it will clearly appear that a Bounty of 30 shillings [per ton] in time of peace is at least equal to 40 shillings in time of war.[55]

As the trade grew so did the difficulty in maintaining labour discipline, to the point where owners' representatives complained to the Board of Trade 1789 that:

> The alarming conduct of the seamen employed in the Fishery in contempt of the most solemn contracts, by disregard of command, is become so serious as to require an investigation; the uncertainty of success from the caprice of their dispositions has checked the spirit of adventure.[56]

---

[54]British Library, Add. MS. 38, 332, f. 253, "Plan for employing discharged navy men in the whaling trade." Unfortunately there is no provenance or date for this MS, though context suggests shortly after peace in 1763.

[55]PRO, BT 6/93/115.

[56]PRO, BT 6/94, f. 90, Memorial of Merchants in the Greenland Trade, April 1789.

There is some evidence that the supply of men was not matching demand, though this should not be a surprise since war with suppliers of oil in America and Europe was one of the stimulants to the trade. Men were needed most when they were least available.

It was obvious soon after the Napoleonic wars that Scotland did not have enough seamen or, indeed, master mariners. Heavy use had been made of foreign vessels during the war, and the Scottish fleet had failed to grow at the same speed as Scottish trade. At least on the coastal side this pressure was released over the next two decades by growth in the sailing fleet and a substantial gain in efficiency associated with the move to steam, when both masters and crews did a great deal more work, in terms of ton-miles, on the Clyde, Forth and Tay. But in the interval there was a shortage, and that led to labour militancy. In the whaling fleet, for instance, the law demanded manning in the port of certification, since anything else would open the way to frauds on the bounty system. This had not been much of a problem until the press gang was partially replaced by bounties for seamen to be "recruited" for the navy by mercantile communities. It was a sensible arrangement, since a "hot press" could result in a vessel losing all or most of its competent seamen, with consequent danger to the vessel and its remaining crew. The new system allowed vessels to hand over crew members or substitute landsmen, whose inexperience at sea might not be too serious a problem in a battleship. In fact there was so much competition for labour between owners, and so many mariners disappeared into the navy, that whaler owners petitioned the Board of Trade because they "find it out of their power to man their ships with seamen, without raising the wages to a higher rate than their trade will afford."

At this stage owners turned to an almost untouched but potentially good source of labour outside the normal competitive labour system. While Scottish crofters traditionally drifted in and out of mercantile activity, the same was not true of Orkney or the Shetlands, where poor land and over-population produced a crofter society barely subsisting off the land and landowners whose wealth depended on their tenants' supplementary fishing. There was no opportunity for the islanders to engage as normal sailors in their own communities, and it was difficult for them to break their traditional ties and go to the mainland. But English whaler owners in particular, competing with industrialists as well as with other shipowners for labour, cast envious eyes on this potential source of cheap labour which their vessels had to pass on their outward and homeward voyages, and which might save them a month or more in victuals on the round trip. The Bounty Act prohibited its employment and earlier requests for permission to recruit in Orkney and Shetland had been refused by a government not prepared to change the law because of potential fraud, and reluctant to upset northern lairds who resented the "escape" from their lands of labour, especially the fishermen.[57] Nevertheless, the acute shortage of maritime labour in the 1790s was such that the law was softened and lairds realised their ability to contract their younger men to whaler owners at less than the going-rate but at a greater profit than they obtained from the over-fishing of local waters. Indeed, the cost difference was such that when they were first employed in the hey-day of whaling, some owners thought it worth foregoing a £300 bounty because they could make it up on savings on wages and victuals. There is no evidence that this level of shortage was effective in Scotland in the 1790s, but in 1803, for instance, Montrose could not find enough sailors for *Eliza Swan* and sought permission for six Orkneymen.[58] Pressure then appears to have been released, for although the number of islanders engaged in the English fleet increased during the war, it was apparently not until 1820 that another Scottish request was made, for *Hero* of Montrose.[59]

The ending of the bounty in 1824, when owners were, for the first time since 1733, free to hire their crews wherever they wished, coincided with another rise in maritime wages. Scottish vessels immediately began to make up their complement in Stromness or Lerwick, where merchants such as the Hay family came to dominate the supply of labour, chiefly for the major English ports such as London and Hull and on the basis of lowest possible wage and highest possible ability. From 1825, when whaling was no longer as popular with mainland sailors, not least because Arctic conditions worsened and catches declined, islanders gradually took over the lowest paid whaling. They made a valuable

---

[57]PRO, BT 5/8, Minutes of the Board of Trade, 13 February 1793 and 22 March 1793.

[58]SRO, C 503, Customs Letter Books, Collector to Board, 8 January 1803. It was open to an owner to recruit in the northern islands so long as he was prepared to forego the bounty.

[59]SRO, C 503, 14 April 1820. It is of course possible that Scottish vessels recruiting in the islands have simply escaped notice in the usual sources, but bounty certificates reveal no difficulty in filling whaling berths in Scotland during the Napoleonic wars.

contribution to the industry during its twenty-five year decline. In return, the impact of their wages created a money economy in the islands which changed their social structure. The local newspaper estimated in 1825 that wages were worth £50,000 per annum to the islands' economies, though the historian of this subject estimates it more conservatively at around £10,000 per annum for Shetland alone. As much as a sixth of the male population of Shetland was engaged in whaling for English and Scottish ports for perhaps a quarter of a century.[60] It is not surprising that the islanders were not popular with Scottish sailors, and during the final stages of whaling there were many adverse comments about the undernourished, physically inadequate and easily demoralised youngsters from Shetlands; "we can depend upon our English crew," the surgeon wrote when *Diana* was in trouble in 1867, "but these Shetland men cause us a world of trouble."[61]

For seamen outside the whaling trade life was perhaps more complicated. Seamen were not generically fools, and being aware of the value of their labour, and particularly their enhanced bargaining power as a ship was about to leave port, they endeavoured to avoid situations which would upset their earnings and applied pressure to masters or owners when they could. In 1791, for instance, four sailors from *Elizabeth* of Greenock were arrested in Norway, with eight others, for mutiny "to oblige their masters to raise their wages, etc."[62] Seamen very sensibly withdrew labour from vessels destined for potential enemy countries when wars were clearly imminent, though in reverse, it was not unknown for seamen to conspire with masters to so delay sailing from the Baltic that they were forced to over-winter and remain on the ship's payroll and eat at their owner's expense. It was alleged, for instance, by the Edinburgh owner of *Jenny Crawford of Bo'ness*, that he had sent it with cargo to Bremen and instructed the master to proceed with an arranged cargo to Dover, "yet, the crew being hired by the month and not by the run or voyage, the master finding the crew not averse to

---

[60]The material on Shetland is taken chiefly from R.J. Smith, "Shetland and the Greenland Whaling Industry, 1780-1870," *Northern Scotland*, XII (1992), 67-87.

[61]C.E. Smith Harris (ed.), *From the Deep of the Sea, being the Diary of...C.E. Smith* (London, 1922), 164. Many of his stronger comments on Shetland men were edited out of the printed diary.

[62]PRO, BT 6/189.

winter there," delayed until his vessel was frozen in and they did not reach Dover until May 1741.[63] This was doubtless an exceptional case which found its way to the Scottish High Court of Admiralty as the owner tried to recover his lost profit and six months' victuals and maintenance for the crew, though there must have been similar possibilities of squeezing money out of an owner paying by the month. On the other hand, Glasgow's eighteenth-century domination of the tobacco trade owed something to the forcing down of crew costs by cutting turnaround times.[64] Intense pressure from labour was only really possible in the fraught circumstances of war when the press gang removed men from the mercantile marine and raised the value of those remaining, or when labour became scarce, as in the 1820s when shipping in Scotland expanded faster than in Britain as a whole.

There were grumbles around Scottish ports late in 1824, but the most substantial action appears to have started in the rather cosy and unrepresentative atmosphere of the Dundee-London packet service, in a port where locally-owned shipping grew from 165 vessels and 17,945 tons in 1824 to 225 vessels and 27,150 tons in 1828, and where seamen employed rose from around 1500 to about 2000. Packet services running to timetable and races between specially-built and very expensive fast smacks had been introduced along the Scottish east coast in the last decade of the eighteenth century as an increasingly wealthy Scotland sought from England – and particularly London – foreign and colonial luxuries which the Scottish ports were too inexperienced or poor to import for themselves, and as the industrial products of Dundee and the Forth ports were distributed southwards and, via the Forth and Clyde Canal, to Glasgow and on to America. But above all these vessels carried live animals, fresh foodstuffs and passengers, and for the latter there was introduced in 1825 the "fine new fast-sailing smack London," with two "large and commodious" cabins, ten state rooms, dressing rooms and new-fangled water closets. The smacks' regular operations demanded a fast turnaround in port, which made permanent crews both possible and desirable; and these crews were, relatively speaking, in a sellers' market, further encouraged by competition between two local companies and

---

[63]SRO, RH 15/38/59, High Court of Admiralty, John Carmichael, owner, versus John Mathie, master, 17 July 1741. I owe this reference to Dr. Janet Kinloch.

[64]R.F. Dell, "The Operational Record of the Clyde Tobacco Fleet, 1747-75," *Scottish Economic and Social History*, II (1982), 9-13.

intruders from outside. In January 1825, the *Dundee Advertiser* announced that "The seamen employed in the trade between Dundee and London have struck for an advance of wages. The demand, which is considered reasonable, under all the circumstances connected with that hard-working class of mariners, will, it is believed, be complied with." It was complied with, but in this case the Dundee companies formed the expected "shipping ring" and in identical words announced that:

> in consequence of the high rate of seamen's wages, provisions, and almost everything connected with shipping, they have found it necessary to make a small advances on the freight of goods carried by their vessels between this place and Perth, London and Glasgow.[65]

The success of the packet men encouraged the blue-water men, and towards the end of the year the Dundee Seamen's Provident Union was formed, partly, it was said, with the laudable view of guarding against the consequences of shipwrecks and other disasters incident to a seafaring life; but chiefly, we are afraid, for the purpose of being able to dictate to their employers the rates of their wages, and secure a monopoly to their members of the most lucrative posts which the trade of the port affords in their line.[66] Their intentions have been so far developed, by the refusal of some of them to sail in certain vessels, because they found individuals employed on board who did not belong to the Union. One of the more notable confrontations arose when the brig *Scotsman* was prepared to sail on its maiden voyage to Jamaica in February 1826. A seaman called Haggard who had been on board for four days refused to sign articles of agreement which stipulated a wage of fifty-five shillings per month "or whatever rate of wages the crews of three other vessels then loading for foreign parts should receive:" in other words, being forced to sail before the true level of wages was revealed. Haggart walked off the ship and promptly – and unsuccessfully – sued the master for four days' wages, while the rest of the crew – who had also walked off after signing the articles – were arrested for

---

[65]*Dundee Advertiser*, 6 January, 31 March and 27 November 1825; and Jackson, *Dundee*, 33.

[66]*Dundee Advertiser*, 19 January 1826; and Jackson, *Dundee*, 72-73.

desertion and eventually took the brig to sea.[67] Trouble of this kind continued until 1829, with owners or masters reluctant to take crewmen to court because of the loss of time involved, but a growing determination to use the law – which imprisoned seamen for up to a month for refusing to sail or subsequently to work – may have owed something to provocative disobedience shown by two members of *Scotia*'s crew as it was being hauled out of the harbour: they stood motionless and silent, and laughed in the master's face. They went to prison, and doubtless meditated on the relative value of high principles and lost wages.[68]

In conclusion, one or two general points might be made. First, to talk of master mariners and mariners as two different species may not be appropriate for all Scottish ports at all times. Many shipowners are described as mariners in the ship registers; forty-seven of them owned eleven percent of the tonnage registered in Dundee in 1824-1825, and another four described themselves as "mariners and shipowners." A couple of mariners built and owned one of the more remarkable Dundee vessels, a "vessel designed to be rowed with paddles" using their own labour as the power. Second, life at sea may have been brutish but it was generally short, not because death occurred but because men were often too old at thirty. It was a young man's profession. The old men stayed at home to fish or collect harbour dues. They were supported if need be by Glasgow City Council on the west coast, Trinity House in Leith, and assorted charities along the coast. Some managed to save money. Advances in wages were not uniformly lost to the tavern. Some, it is alleged, smuggled on the side. And one or two – that we know about – conspired to sink their vessel for the sake of the insurance. Others took up collections in the whaling fleet for the widows of deceased crewmen, or were drowned trying to rescue their friends.

It was undoubtedly a hard life. Total loss, either of vessel or life, was probably less common than serious hardship that stopped short of total loss. In the American trades, for instance, heavy weather was a recurrent theme. In 1821, for instance, *Hind* of Dundee took 135 days

[67] *Dundee Advertiser*, 2 February 1826.

[68] *Ibid.*, 3 March 1829.

to reach New York, and the master subsequently wrote a vivid account of the near disasters:[69]

> On the 1st January we were taken by a heavy squall, which made us cut away our square mainsail, foresail, fore-topsail and main topgallant sail, after every exertion had in vain been made to furl or reef them. After we were hove to, two tremendous seas broke over us which carried away two of our standing stanchions, all the rails and bulwarks, drove the longboat out of the chocks, washed the jolly boat overboard, stove the cookhouse and did other damage which rendered the vessel a wreck on deck. On the 11th we lost our main yard in a gale. On the morning of the 20th, the ice carried the vessel right out of our anchorage. We then let go our best bower anchor; but the safety of the ship obliged also to let it go and run on the safest point of Sandyhook [the bar on the southern side of Lower New York Bay]. The following morning a large mass of ice carried the ship right off, after the tide had fallen three feet. We reached New York on the 1st February. The cargo is not materially damaged and the crew though they suffered from the cold are all well.

A shanty once called *Eliza Swan* the "Battler of Montrose." For seamen, too, it was a battle with the elements as well as, occasionally, the employers. There was also a battle with "society" that is not yet over. It was commonly said that seamen belonged to a world of their own, cut off from civilised life. In the whaling trade many volumes have been filled with tales of suffering and heroism and hard work. The same is true of many blue-water men, and coasting men were not without their scares and scars. We have noted the eighteenth-century comment on "beasts," which could be replicated in the last days of serious sail. Why were sailors so regarded? What do the condemnations amount to? There were some horrible incidents at sea. The Scottish High Court of Admiralty occasionally considered piracy, murder and sodomy; but rarely were offences at sea "serious." In part they are the usual problems

---

[69] *Ibid.*, 7 March 1822, letter from Captain William Boyack.

of confined relationships. The troubles mentioned in the log of *Sappho*, for instance, on two voyages to East Asia, were breaches of discipline at a low level: talking-back, incompetence, and desertion, the latter seen as evidence of "untrustworthiness."

More seriously, in the eyes of polite society, sailors had a tendency to cock a snoot at social control. They were not polite. "The trade and inhabitants, and consequently the houses, are increasing swiftly," John Wesley wrote of Greenock in 1772, "and so is cursing, swearing, drunkenness, Sabbath-breaking, and all manner of wickedness."[70] Ten years later when two Greenock Tidesmen were dismissed for being "most exceptional in their behaviour" – drink – they were thought "as able to gain a subsistence by their former employment in the seafaring way as any in the Port."[71] In the same vein, one of the few early references to seamen in Montrose laments the "extravagances" in 1694 of "strangers seamen and others concerned with shipping by drinking whole nights in taverns," so the sale of liquor to foreign seamen after sunset was banned.[72]

Certainly in the 1840s whaler owners, who earlier had praised the qualities of their men, were beginning to talk of them as the dregs of society. Towards the end of the nineteenth century the General Shipping Company kept report books on their senior crew members and apprentices in the Far Eastern trade. What the misdemeanours add up to is a mixture of lack of decency and more serious incidents which might – but never do – threaten the safety or good order of the ship. Some men were "impudent;" some were dirty, especially the cooks; some were deceitful; some were thieves; some were lazy; more were "dense" or slow. Long-distance crews were more troublesome than others. Refusal to work was common – as it had been on *Sappho* – and the threat of desertion worried masters. But this was almost always in Asian ports, not on the high seas. For much of the age of sail, sailors in the East and West Indian trades were not particularly healthy, and it may not be too surprising that getting them out of their bed was sometimes difficult. Above all, demon drink lurked in every locker, or, to be more exact, in

---

[70]*Journal of the Reverend John Wesley* (London, 1906), III, 467.

[71]SRO, CE 1/17, Scottish Board of Customs Minute Books, 3 October 1782.

[72]S.G.E. Lythe, "Early Modern Trade," in Jackson and Lythe (eds.), *Port of Montrose*, 101.

every port. So did naughty women. And seamen were given to using what is now called "language." When the Greenock Seamen's Friend Society set up in 1820 to promote "the temporal and spiritual interests of Seamen trading to this Port" it was satisfied with bibles, tracts and "recommending stranger seamen on their arrival to well-regulated boarding houses."[73] The implication here is crimping in the long-haul trades, with opportunities for corruption, and that things would get better under the Bethel flag. Perhaps in general they did, but in the General Shipping Company they appeared to degenerate as sail neared its end in the 1890s and one wonders how the ships managed to reach Australia.

Perhaps we are reading what Victorian prudery expected to read of sailors who were not prudes. Sailors may have been superstitious – is this also overdone? – but there is little evidence that they were religious. Captains might fly the Bethel flag and import landward social graces, but *Diana*, at least, when caught in the ice, abandoned the prayer meeting! As for being a de-humanised sub-species, there seems little evidence from available diaries and reports if we read between the drink, "language" and "insolence." Surviving logs and diaries suggest that the elementary human goodness which emerged with whaling tragedies reflects a maritime community certainly hard but not quite so sordid as we like to think. We need to rehabilitate as well as count the sailors.

---

[73]"Constitution," *Sailor's Magazine*, I (1820), 185-186. I owe this to Dr. A. Kennerley.

**Appendix Table 1**
**Number and Tonnage of Vessels and Number of Seamen in Principal Scottish Ports, 1775**

| | Foreign Trade | | | Coastal Trade | | | Fishing | | | Total | | |
|---|---|---|---|---|---|---|---|---|---|---|---|---|
| Port | No. | Tons | Men | No. | Tons | Men | No. | Tons | Men | No. | Tons | Men |
| Aberdeen | 65 | 4,390 | 340 | 86 | 4,590 | 398 | 3 | 170 | 48 | 154 | 9,150 | 786 |
| Ayr | 4 | 290 | 29 | 9 | 49 | 18 | 13 | 551 | 117 | 26 | 890 | 164 |
| Alloa | 20 | 965 | 94 | 82 | 3,115 | 366 | 0 | 0 | 0 | 102 | 4,080 | 460 |
| Anstruther | 11 | 810 | 75 | 5 | 105 | 12 | 0 | 0 | 0 | 16 | 915 | 87 |
| Bo'ness | 40 | 3,690 | 253 | 73 | 3,110 | 246 | 0 | 0 | 0 | 113 | 6,800 | 499 |
| Campbeltown | 55 | 2,406 | 271 | 19 | 301 | 76 | 65 | 3,223 | 738 | 139 | 5,930 | 1,085 |
| Dumfries | 1 | 60 | 7 | 12 | 346 | 37 | 2 | 74 | 17 | 15 | 480 | 61 |
| Dunbar | 8 | 820 | 57 | 8 | 250 | 25 | 6 | 1,042 | 163 | 22 | 2,112 | 245 |
| Dundee | 22 | 1,830 | 140 | 38 | 1,629 | 152 | 1 | 364 | 48 | 61 | 3,823 | 340 |
| Inverness | 1 | 60 | 5 | 10 | 450 | 45 | 0 | 0 | 0 | 11 | 510 | 50 |
| Irvine | 65 | 4,295 | 433 | 13 | 467 | 61 | 17 | 770 | 180 | 95 | 5,532 | 674 |
| Kirkcaldy | 37 | 4,010 | 288 | 27 | 850 | 95 | 15 | 45 | 75 | 79 | 4,905 | 458 |
| Leith | 51 | 6,330 | 415 | 42 | 3,080 | 221 | 3 | 269 | 126 | 96 | 10,379 | 762 |
| Montrose | 16 | 1,170 | 95 | 57 | 1,665 | 175 | 1 | 30 | 12 | 74 | 2,865 | 282 |
| Oban | 5 | 207 | 20 | 6 | 232 | 20 | 9 | 335 | 81 | 20 | 774 | 121 |
| Orkney | 0 | 0 | 0 | 15 | 538 | 49 | 4 | 147 | 45 | 19 | 685 | 194 |
| Perth | 10 | 570 | 54 | 11 | 540 | 56 | 0 | 0 | 0 | 21 | 1,110 | 110 |
| Pt Gl./Greenock | 213 | 19,164 | 1,677 | 43 | 1360 | 162 | 134 | 6,200 | 1,293 | 390 | 26,724 | 3,132 |
| Rothesay | 0 | 0 | 0 | 3 | 63 | 8 | 16 | 712 | 153 | 19 | 775 | 161 |
| Stornaway | 0 | 0 | 0 | 0 | 0 | 0 | 16 | 638 | 150 | 16 | 638 | 150 |
| Stranraer | 0 | 0 | 0 | 5 | 134 | 16 | 12 | 598 | 137 | 17 | 732 | 153 |
| Wigtown | 0 | 0 | 0 | 18 | 370 | 42 | 1 | 35 | 8 | 19 | 405 | 50 |
| Total | 635 | 51,448 | 4,302 | 606 | 23,919 | 2,355 | 318 | 15,903 | 3,391 | 1,559 | 91,270 | 10,048 |

*Source*: Public Record Office (PRO), Customs 17.

**Appendix Table 2**
**Number of Seamen in Foreign, Coastal and Fishing Trades, 1775-1785**

| | 1775 | | | | 1781 | | | | 1785 | | | |
|---|---|---|---|---|---|---|---|---|---|---|---|---|
| Port | Fng | Coast | Fish | Total | Fgn | Coast | Fish | Total | Fgn | Coast | Fish | Total |
| Aberdeen | 340 | 398 | 48 | 786 | 281 | 208 | 62 | 551 | 258 | 225 | 106 | 589 |
| Ayr | 29 | 18 | 117 | 164 | 59 | 9 | 7 | 75 | 80 | 9 | 9 | 98 |
| Alloa | 94 | 366 | 0 | 460 | 97 | 212 | 0 | 309 | 174 | 223 | 0 | 397 |
| Anstruther | 75 | 12 | 0 | 87 | 53 | 26 | 0 | 79 | 80 | 46 | 0 | 126 |
| Bo'ness | 253 | 246 | 0 | 499 | 167 | 477 | 0 | 644 | 299 | 528 | 40 | 867 |
| Campbeltown | 271 | 76 | 738 | 1,085 | 130 | 92 | 376 | 598 | 158 | 139 | 501 | 798 |
| Dumfries | 7 | 37 | 17 | 61 | 5 | 0 | 0 | 5 | 7 | 46 | 0 | 53 |
| Dunbar | 57 | 25 | 163 | 245 | 43 | 32 | 164 | 239 | 18 | 20 | 215 | 253 |
| Dundee | 140 | 152 | 48 | 340 | 104 | 141 | 46 | 291 | 182 | 256 | 0 | 438 |
| Inverness | 5 | 45 | 0 | 50 | 20 | 30 | 8 | 58 | 23 | 52 | 0 | 75 |
| Irvine | 433 | 61 | 180 | 674 | 287 | 48 | 36 | 371 | 458 | 111 | 85 | 654 |
| Kirkcaldy | 288 | 95 | 75 | 458 | 162 | 85 | 75 | 322 | 299 | 95 | 74 | 468 |
| Kirkudbright | 10 | 30 | 0 | 40 | 4 | 45 | 5 | 54 | 15 | 43 | 9 | 67 |
| Leith | 415 | 221 | 126 | 762 | 400 | 200 | 36 | 636 | 430 | 280 | 0 | 710 |
| Montrose | 95 | 175 | 12 | 282 | 93 | 224 | 0 | 317 | 165 | 214 | 46 | 425 |
| Oban | 20 | 20 | 81 | 121 | 4 | 28 | 66 | 98 | 9 | 34 | 60 | 103 |
| Orkney | 0 | 49 | 45 | 194 | 0 | 50 | 42 | 92 | 0 | 52 | 6 | 58 |
| Perth | 54 | 56 | 0 | 110 | 30 | 84 | 0 | 114 | 41 | 92 | 0 | 133 |
| Pt Gl./Greenock | 1,677 | 162 | 1,293 | 3,132 | 2,522 | 214 | 839 | 3,575 | 2,143 | 344 | 835 | 3,322 |
| Port Patrick | 23 | 0 | 0 | 23 | 31 | 4 | 0 | 35 | 34 | 8 | 0 | 42 |
| Rothesay | 0 | 8 | 153 | 161 | 39 | 44 | 243 | 326 | 110 | 79 | 382 | 571 |
| Stornaway | 0 | 0 | 150 | 150 | 0 | 0 | 72 | 72 | 0 | 0 | 74 | 74 |
| Stranraer | 0 | 16 | 137 | 153 | 9 | 15 | 72 | 96 | 37 | 22 | 60 | 119 |
| Wigtown | 0 | 42 | 8 | 50 | 5 | 67 | 0 | 72 | 42 | 57 | 0 | 99 |
| Total | 4,302 | 2,355 | 3,391 | 10,048 | 4,561 | 2,380 | 2,174 | 9,115 | 5,082 | 3,019 | 2,502 | 10,603 |

*Note*: The table for 1781 is partially illegible.

*Source*: See table 1.

**Appendix Table 3**
**Crews of Vessels Registered in Scottish Ports, 30 September 1790-1805**

| Port | 1790 No. | 1790 Tons | 1790 Men | 1795 No. | 1795 Tons | 1795 Men | 1800 No. | 1800 Tons | 1800 Men | 1805 No. | 1805 Tons | 1805 Men |
|---|---|---|---|---|---|---|---|---|---|---|---|---|
| Aberdeen | 176 | 13,309 | 905 | 198 | 14,516 | 1,073 | 281 | 23,235 | 1,585 | 267 | 27,874 | 1,684 |
| Ayr | 33 | 2,423 | 190 | 37 | 2,450 | 187 | 44 | 3,256 | 237 | 58 | 4,813 | 356 |
| Alloa | 109 | 6,577 | 481 | 108 | 6,480 | 418 | 100 | 6,341 | 378 | 123 | 9,141 | 511 |
| Anstruther | 39 | 2,392 | 198 | 51 | 2,871 | 213 | 46 | 2,128 | 167 | 52 | 2,585 | 194 |
| Bo'ness | 160 | 11,712 | 873 | 146 | 9,324 | 669 | 130 | 8,406 | 550 | 168 | 12,023 | 704 |
| Campbeltown | 82 | 4,662 | 728 | 75 | 3,982 | 766 | 75 | 3,496 | 618 | 81 | 3,780 | 471 |
| Dumfries | 19 | 943 | 71 | 26 | 1,038 | 88 | 29 | 1,190 | 95 | 40 | 1,795 | 131 |
| Dunbar | 23 | 2,771 | 238 | 17 | 2,069 | 181 | 16 | 1,584 | 162 | 22 | 1,374 | 89 |
| Dundee | 115 | 8,168 | 679 | 125 | 8,508 | 643 | 123 | 8,741 | 641 | 138 | 12,220 | 963 |
| Inverness | 36 | 1,944 | 173 | 41 | 2,083 | 197 | 42 | 2,143 | 177 | 66 | 4,248 | 298 |
| Irvine | 98 | 7,807 | 646 | 84 | 6,105 | 506 | 82 | 5,783 | 448 | 99 | 8,105 | 577 |
| Kirkcaldy | 94 | 9,326 | 624 | 98 | 10,498 | 680 | 97 | 11,248 | 690 | 116 | 12,870 | 742 |
| Kirkudbright | 19 | 756 | 62 | 33 | 1,267 | 109 | 35 | 1,514 | 162 | 37 | 1,572 | 107 |
| Leith | 161 | 16,990 | 1,205 | 143 | 15,348 | 948 | 134 | 13,894 | 899 | 177 | 21,802 | 1,406 |
| Montrose | 102 | 5,865 | 571 | 113 | 6,318 | 530 | 112 | 6,555 | 506 | 142 | 10,052 | 729 |
| Oban | 25 | 1,008 | 105 | 16 | 638 | 91 | 18 | 904 | 79 | 49 | 156 | 152 |
| Perth | 28 | 1,995 | 175 | 29 | 2,038 | 147 | 31 | 2,429 | 151 | 39 | 2,968 | 171 |
| Pt Gl./Greenock | 438 | 40,323 | 3,571 | 386 | 34,321 | 2,759 | 467 | 45,109 | 4,589 | 501 | 53,017 | 3,969 |
| Port Patrick | 10 | 447 | 52 | 10 | 445 | 47 | 4 | 173 | 21 | 5 | 184 | 21 |
| Rothesay | 76 | 3,883 | 739 | 77 | 3,968 | 650 | 92 | 4,504 | 958 | 92 | 4,881 | 667 |
| Stornaway | 45 | 1,765 | 200 | 51 | 1,963 | 232 | 50 | 1,759 | 208 | 67 | 2,298 | 279 |
| Stranraer | 13 | 693 | 61 | 27 | 1,433 | 129 | 38 | 1,688 | 157 | 33 | 1,382 | 119 |
| Wigtown | 37 | 1,564 | 139 | 35 | 1,262 | 107 | 34 | 1,197 | 97 | 41 | 1,586 | 113 |
| Total | 2,006 | 150,749 | 13,041 | 2,014 | 142,694 | 11,785 | 2,125 | 160,506 | 13,868 | 2,581 | 210,295 | 15,160 |

*Source*: See table 1.

**Appendix Table 4**
**Number of British and Foreign Seamen Involved in Specific Trades, 1790-1805**

| | 1790 | | | | 1795 | | | | 1800 | | | | 1805 | | | |
|---|---|---|---|---|---|---|---|---|---|---|---|---|---|---|---|---|
| | In | | Out | | In | | Out | | In | | Out | | In | | Out | |
| Country | Brit | Fgn | Brit | Fgn | Brit | Fgn | Brit | Fgn | Brit | Fgn | Brit | Fgn | Brit | Fgn | Brit | Fgn |
| Denk/Nwy | 639 | 690 | 566 | 105 | 78 | 1181 | 408 | 496 | 204 | 1840 | 510 | 894 | 669 | 2236 | 1288 | 1106 |
| Russia | 1143 | 0 | 240 | 0 | 917 | 0 | 608 | 0 | 1036 | 0 | 672 | 0 | 1495 | 10 | 1142 | 19 |
| Sweden | 462 | 0 | 376 | 0 | 353 | 28 | 482 | 22 | 222 | 120 | 139 | 59 | 196 | 14 | 133 | 127 |
| Poland | 266 | 19 | 15 | 9 | 52 | 0 | 38 | 0 | 211 | 0 | 202 | 0 | 61 | 0 | 70 | 0 |
| Prussia | 1,420 | 23 | 298 | 5 | 581 | 37 | 161 | 24 | 1,314 | 355 | 632 | 281 | 1,691 | 117 | 843 | 227 |
| Germany | 404 | 7 | 643 | 0 | 230 | 0 | 155 | 49 | 716 | 143 | 739 | 36 | 14 | 8 | 161 | 0 |
| Holland | 711 | 18 | 590 | 12 | 14 | 42 | 0 | 0 | 0 | 362 | 0 | 99 | 0 | 263 | 0 | 0 |
| Flanders | 12 | 0 | 15 | 0 | 0 | 0 | 0 | 0 | 0 | 0 | 0 | 0 | 0 | 0 | 0 | 0 |
| France | 99 | 7 | 120 | 15 | 0 | 5 | 0 | 0 | 0 | 0 | 0 | 0 | 0 | 28 | 0 | 0 |
| Spain | 90 | 0 | 106 | 0 | 66 | 0 | 103 | 0 | 0 | 18 | 0 | 0 | 0 | 144 | 0 | 21 |
| Portugal | 228 | 5 | 145 | 6 | 174 | 0 | 138 | 20 | 179 | 0 | 52 | 0 | 307 | 23 | 252 | 7 |
| Italy | 105 | 0 | 56 | 0 | 22 | 0 | 36 | 0 | 15 | 0 | 25 | 15 | 20 | 41 | 0 | 9 |
| Ireland | 9014 | 7 | 5802 | 0 | 15892 | 0 | 14894 | 6 | 4956 | 16 | 6729 | 4 | 7911 | 0 | 7103 | 0 |
| Greenland | 824 | 0 | 845 | 0 | 353 | 0 | 352 | 0 | 378 | 0 | 379 | 0 | 724 | 0 | 724 | 0 |
| Europe | 15469 | 776 | 9841 | 152 | 18836 | 1299 | 17435 | 617 | 9357 | 2854 | 10183 | 1388 | 13191 | 2934 | 11861 | 1542 |
| BNA | 85 | 0 | 0 | 0 | 105 | 0 | 409 | 0 | 508 | 0 | 833 | 0 | 493 | 0 | 916 | 0 |
| USA | 499 | 169 | 655 | 150 | 45 | 160 | 0 | 145 | 466 | 508 | 457 | 407 | 267 | 385 | 203 | 416 |
| W Indies | 925 | 0 | 1377 | 0 | 614 | 0 | 858 | 0 | 1420 | 17 | 1710 | 0 | 1404 | 0 | 2088 | 0 |
| Total | 16988 | 945 | 11905 | 302 | 19600 | 1459 | 18702 | 778 | 11751 | 3379 | 13183 | 1795 | 15380 | 3337 | 15121 | 1966 |

*Source:* See table 1.

**Appendix Table 5a**
**Sailing Vessels Entering Glasgow, Foreign Trade, with Cargo, Years Ending June 1831-1911 (tons)**

| From | 1831 | 1841 | 1847 | 1851 | 1856 | 1861 | 1866 | 1871 | 1876 | 1881 | 1886 | 1891 | 1896 | 1911 |
|---|---|---|---|---|---|---|---|---|---|---|---|---|---|---|
| Northern Europe | 3536 | 6233 | 6452 | 7079 | 279 | 7505 | 35358 | 35542 | 12993 | 4968 | 4867 | 7970 | 7298 | 452 |
| Nearby Europe | 1803 | 7025 | 5304 | 19462 | 4740 | 3731 | 15832 | 6249 | 6543 | 4834 | 2665 | 11162 | 9393 | 1590 |
| Spain | 796 | 1092 | 1182 | 1886 | 3814 | 6387 | 5367 | 6005 | 2,352 | 1356 | 806 | 66 | 110 | 0 |
| Portugal | 1477 | 2412 | 2497 | 3313 | 3189 | 6064 | 5583 | 1964 | 353 | 1419 | 0 | 0 | 205 | 0 |
| Gib/Med | 553 | 6374 | 8462 | 19239 | 23529 | 21517 | 16431 | 17268 | 20116 | 7388 | 3601 | 3221 | 1588 | 99 |
| Africa | 0 | 191 | 760 | 760 | 2137 | 1341 | 3183 | 1106 | 1262 | 1393 | 397 | 483 | 704 | 0 |
| East Indies | 0 | 0 | 1158 | 2166 | 897 | 2280 | 2321 | 1749 | 2606 | 1465 | 400 | 0 | 0 | 0 |
| China/Japan/Pac. | 0 | 649 | 2253 | 2181 | 2145 | 1225 | 2619 | 3164 | 851 | 594 | 0 | 0 | 0 | 0 |
| Australia & NZ | 0 | 0 | 0 | 0 | 0 | 0 | 0 | 0 | 999 | 0 | 1032 | 2522 | 11366 | 6010 |
| BNA | 485 | 12398 | 22682 | 22271 | 19091 | 28336 | 31575 | 47449 | 33895 | 65193 | 12966 | 14677 | 17376 | 1492 |
| USA | 0 | 4610 | 34392 | 36368 | 37379 | 81843 | 8550 | 22054 | 43897 | 37647 | 7217 | 8794 | 2819 | 1589 |
| West Indies | 1312 | 10772 | 6241 | 5254 | 2836 | 5025 | 4968 | 8799 | 12370 | 12789 | 6579 | 6590 | 8141 | 1062 |
| S. America, East | 0 | 146 | 4543 | 458 | 0 | 647 | 129 | 1509 | 568 | 1142 | 2011 | 5335 | 1437 | 2390 |
| S. America, West | 0 | 182 | 0 | 2909 | 6901 | 9543 | 8931 | 8793 | 9050 | 3968 | 6584 | 6257 | 2938 | 7391 |
| Total In | 9962 | 52084 | 95926 | 123346 | 106937 | 175444 | 140847 | 161651 | 147855 | 144156 | 49125 | 67077 | 63375 | 22075 |

*Note:* Figures for 1901 and 1906 are not available.

*Source:* Strathclyde Regional Archives (SRA), T-CN 6, Clyde Navigation Trust Accounts and Statistics.

**Appendix Table 5b**
**Sailing Vessels Clearing Glasgow, Foreign Trade, with Cargo, 1831-1911**

| From | 1831 | 1841 | 1847 | 1851 | 1856 | 1861 | 1866 | 1871 | 1876 | 1881 | 1886 | 1891 | 1896 | 1911 |
|---|---|---|---|---|---|---|---|---|---|---|---|---|---|---|
| Northern Europe | 974 | 5895 | 2723 | 6242 | 3065 | 2384 | 4325 | 12494 | 10036 | 9836 | 6159 | 14411 | 8499 | 1628 |
| Nearby Europe | 1000 | 11142 | 14079 | 10265 | 22418 | 13673 | 7230 | 2115 | 8314 | 4664 | 3547 | 981 | 625 | 1375 |
| Spain | 704 | 190 | 1321 | 4488 | 2716 | 4957 | 2761 | 2211 | 4484 | 2405 | 956 | 531 | 387 | 129 |
| Portugal | 1079 | 2550 | 2468 | 5955 | 4050 | 3804 | 4280 | 1153 | 1737 | 726 | 163 | 0 | 352 | 0 |
| Gib/Med | 1771 | 5806 | 8583 | 12287 | 9931 | 17454 | 14326 | 21343 | 15801 | 6423 | 3226 | 0 | 1000 | 0 |
| Africa | 0 | 1500 | 854 | 3006 | 3401 | 6733 | 8210 | 4614 | 3253 | 9699 | 2909 | 5478 | 2646 | 0 |
| East Indies | 0 | 8185 | 8501 | 15868 | 19891 | 37769 | 44502 | 66241 | 16408 | 41828 | 11860 | 0 | 489 | 0 |
| China/Japan/Pac. | 259 | 2627 | 3972 | 8328 | 9894 | 6830 | 13174 | 21243 | 11845 | 11849 | 5175 | 0 | 0 | 0 |
| Australia & NZ | 0 | 3311 | 2844 | 4678 | 19714 | 15408 | 18919 | 19191 | 41688 | 61945 | 88825 | 72668 | 51526 | 1235 |
| BNA | 860 | 10891 | 19860 | 24413 | 28594 | 32645 | 31060 | 35794 | 23063 | 33628 | 5021 | 5032 | 3799 | 1026 |
| USA | 137 | 6812 | 32960 | 48970 | 37690 | 52541 | 17718 | 27377 | 15227 | 22369 | 11580 | 12106 | 1292 | 12377 |
| West Indies | 448 | 16213 | 25875 | 23808 | 26823 | 37894 | 39533 | 43937 | 41410 | 6975 | 6692 | 8292 | 3709 | 756 |
| S. America, East | 0 | 6673 | 5763 | 3950 | 6444 | 15724 | 22360 | 24977 | 34080 | 28776 | 20403 | 26637 | 15646 | 4437 |
| S. America, West | 0 | 927 | 0 | 8014 | 5453 | 4765 | 7602 | 13309 | 17455 | 8861 | 8918 | 6335 | 2705 | 3810 |
| Total In | 7232 | 82722 | 129703 | 176441 | 200621 | 252680 | 236000 | 295999 | 244801 | 249984 | 175434 | 152471 | 92,675 | 26773 |

*Source*: See table 5a.

# Iceland

J. Th. Thór

Strange as it may seem for an island nation, the sailor's profession is a relatively new occupation in Iceland. To be sure, Icelanders have been a seagoing people from the country's settlement in the late ninth century, but mostly as fishermen. An Icelandic merchant navy, in the traditional meaning of that term, was not born until the early twentieth century. Until then Icelanders who wanted to be sailors all sailed in vessels operating out of foreign ports and flying foreign colours.

The present paper is divided into three sections. The first starts with a brief survey of the few ocean-going Icelandic vessels in the Middle Ages and the country's commercial links with Europe before 1800. Then the diaries of two seventeenth- and eighteenth-century Icelandic sailors will be discussed as well as the fragmentary evidence of Icelanders sailing in Dutch vessels between 1600 and 1800. The second section deals with Icelandic fishermen from the thirteenth through the eighteenth century, while the third section covers the nineteenth century, where it will be argued that the period up to 1870 was transitional in that a "new" class of Icelandic fishermen and sailors emerged.

## Icelandic Sailors, 900-1800

Scanty – and often unclear – sources describe merchant vessels owned by Icelanders between the late ninth century and about 1100. From 1100 to 1170, we know with certainty of five ocean-going vessels owned by Icelanders, but from about 1200 until the nineteenth century Iceland's population was entirely dependent on foreigners for all trade and communication with other lands.[1] The importance of the link with Europe can be seen from the fact that when Iceland recognized the supremacy of the king of Norway in 1262, he promised to ensure that six vessels would sail from Norway to Iceland in the next two years. After

[1] Jón Jóhannesson, *Saga Íslendinga* (Reykjavík, 1956), I, 117-121.

that the king and the "best Icelanders" would come to an agreement on the annual number of vessels to ply the seas between the two countries.[2]

For the next 350 years the commercial link between Iceland and Europe was served by Norwegian/Danish merchants as well as by English and Hanseatic fishermen/merchants. During this era we know of ocean-going vessels owned by bishops of Iceland but the continuity of their operation is unclear and nothing is known of their crews. In 1602 trade with Iceland was monopolized by a royal decree which gave Danish merchants in Copenhagen, Malmö and Helsingør sole rights to trade with Iceland. The monopoly lasted until 1788, and Icelanders were virtually forbidden to trade with foreigners or to sail their own merchant vessels.

These circumstances were hardly suited to the creation of a class of professional Icelandic sailors. Nevertheless, a number went abroad in the seventeenth and eighteenth centuries to work as sailors in foreign bottoms. Some returned home after relatively short periods, while others seem to have made the sailor's profession a lifetime occupation. The best known of these sailors are Jón Ólafsson (1593-1679) and Árni Magnússon (1726-1810?), both of whom wrote their memoirs, which have been published in Icelandic as well as Danish.[3] The careers and recruitment of these two sailors differed in important aspects. Jón Ólafsson might be considered a soldier rather than a sailor. He left Iceland in 1615 in an English fishing smack and sailed for England, where he planned to settle until he got into trouble. Most of his property was stolen, so he took the first available boat to Denmark, where he joined the king's regiment as a gunner on Danish warships in the Baltic, White Sea and on a voyage escorting whalers to Greenland. In 1622 Ólafsson joined the second Danish expedition to Tranquebar in India as a gunner in the *Christianshavn*; he spent a year in the fortress at Tranquebar.[4] When leaving India

---

[2]*Ibid.*, I, 333.

[3]Jón Ólafsson, *Reisubók Jóns Ólafssonar Indíafara* (Copenhagen, 1908-1909; Reykjavík, 1946 and 1992); and Árni Magnússon, *Ferðasaga Árna Magnússonar frä Geitastekk 1753-1797* (Reykjavík, 1945). Magnússon's memoirs were translated into Danish and published in J. Clausen and P. Fr. Rist (eds.), *Memoirer og Breve*, XXVIII (1918), while Ólafsson's work was published in Danish in *Memoirer og Breve*, I (1905-1907).

[4]Ólafsson, *Reisubók*, also mentions another Icelander bound for India in 1622. He sailed in the *Christian* but died off the Moroccan coast on the way out (155).

Ólafsson was badly injured by a cannon explosion and he was unable to work again at sea. On his return to Denmark he decided to go back to Iceland, where the king gave him two farms as a reward for his services.

The other sailor, Árni Magnússon, left Iceland in a Danish vessel in October 1753 for Copenhagen. The circumstances of his departure are a bit mysterious, but after a year as a labourer he entered the service of the Grønlandske Kompagni and spent the next three years in Greenland. Upon his return to Copenhagen, he sailed for the two years in Danish merchantmen between Copenhagen and St. Petersburg and Königsberg, as well as to Bordeaux. In early 1760 he left Copenhagen on a Danish Chinaman, returning about a year and a half later. After that he sailed on Danish merchant vessels and the warship *Dronning Louise*, before going to the Mediterranean to fight for Catherine the Great. He returned in 1772 to start a new career as a teacher in Thy in Jutland.[5]

The lives of these two sailors have become known because they returned home, told their stories and wrote them down. While they were probably exceptional, they were in no way unique. Although our knowledge of Icelanders sailing abroad during the seventeenth and eighteenth centuries is indeed limited, one source indicates that at least one Icelander sailed in Dutch vessels in the late seventeenth century.[6] The source is a medical diary of an Icelandic pastor/doctor who studied and practised in Copenhagen and Amsterdam in the mid-seventeenth century. He was in Amsterdam in 1652 where he apparently served as a doctor to what appears to have been a small "colony" of Icelanders living in the city. Among his patients was "*Nauta qvidam, nomine Boge Finnesšn*," a seaman named Boge Finneson, obviously an Icelander.[7]

This source leads us onto a new path. During the seventeenth and eighteenth centuries Dutch fishing vessels were frequently seen off Iceland and strong cultural ties seem to have developed between the two countries. Folklore, which can hardly be deemed a reliable historical source but is seldom totally unfounded, tells of several Icelanders who went aboard Dutch vessels and sailed away with them. A few of these men were reported to be convicts who escaped justice; needless to say,

---

[5]Magnússon, *Ferðasaga*.

[6]Th. A. Vídalín, *Lækningar-Curationes* (Reykjavík, 1949).

[7]*Ibid.*, 398.

nothing was heard of them again. We do not know how many there were or what happened to them, but it seems likely that at least some of them probably became sailors or fishermen in their new homes. A careful study of Dutch, English and French crew lists may reveal the fate of some of these men, but it seems clear that Icelandic sailors abroad were never numerous during the period under discussion here.

Tracing Icelandic sailors on foreign vessels between the sixteenth and the eighteenth century is not easy. So far, this author has found information on five persons who sailed in Dutch vessels during the seventeenth and eighteenth century who *may* have been Icelanders. The nationality of four of them, however, is uncertain, while one was most likely born on the Westman Islands off Iceland's south coast. Four join their ships under Dutch names, which makes it impossible to trace them in Icelandic sources. And while it is difficult to deny the sailor reportedly born on the Westman Islands Icelandic nationality, this is equally difficult to confirm. In 1660 the man signed on the Dutch East Indiaman *Hilversum* under the name Cornelis Jansz, which could be a Dutch version of the Icelandic name Kornelíus Jónsson. This is, however, impossible to confirm. No person bearing this name can be found in Icelandic sources from the period, and as no personal registers or lists of people born on the Westman Islands have survived, it is impossible to confirm whether Cornelis Jansz was Icelandic.

Two more sailors, Wouter Jansz and Simon Goverts, were recorded as born in Iceland and sailed for the East Indies in 1601 and 1670, respectively. Neither of the names is Icelandic and neither can easily be translated into Icelandic. As no further information about them is available, it is impossible to say whether they were Icelanders or not.

The fourth person was mentioned in the records of the Icelandic parliament in 1669. His name was Pétur Jakobsson, an Icelandic name, but in the records he was referred to as "a Dutch East-India sailor."[8] Whether this sailor was an Icelander is difficult to know; his name may have been Icelandicized in the records. He was, however, obviously a member of the crew of a Dutch East Indiaman which ran aground on the south coast in 1667; the reason he was mentioned in Icelandic records was that a woman declared him to be the father of her child, born in

---

[8]*Alþingisbækur Íslands* (Reykjavík, 1944-1948), VII, 161.

1668. When the case came before parliament, Jakobsson had left the country.[9]

Finally, there was Johan Adam Dedeleijn van IJsland, who was enlisted as a coxswain on the ship *Blitterswijk* from Hoorn in 1790-1791. Once again, it is impossible to deny that this person may have been an Icelander. His two surnames could be Icelandic, albeit in a slightly different form (Jóhann Adam), but the family name is definitely not. The fact that Johan Adam Dedeleijn was called "van IJsland" does not prove he was an Icelander by birth. Nicknames referring to countries or places were not uncommon in this period and Dedeleijn might have been a Dutch sailor who had sailed for Iceland and even stayed there for some time.[10]

It is thus impossible to say whether the persons discussed above were Icelanders. They may have been among those who left Iceland to start a new life in a strange land, but the available sources do not allow us to confirm this.

## Icelandic Fishermen, 1300-1800

Fishing has always been important in Iceland and since the late thirteenth century fish and other marine products have been the country's most valuable exports. Until the late nineteenth century, the number of full-time fishermen, however, was small. This was due to two main factors: the character of Icelandic society and the small size of the nation.

For more than one thousand years Iceland was predominantly agricultural. Livestock raising was the most important occupation and fishing was done on the side. It was only in the northwestern part of the country, and in certain areas of the southwest, that fishing was the dominant industry. But the whole population depended to a considerable degree on fish for food.

Accurate figures on the size of Iceland's population before 1700 are lacking. Scholars have estimated that the populace numbered about 70,000 by 1400, then decreased sharply due to the plague before increasing again to about 55,000 by the mid-seventeenth century. When

[9] *Ibid.*, VII, 161.

[10] I am grateful to Jaap R. Bruijn and Trausti Einarsson for information on the persons discussed above.

the first general census was taken in 1703, the total was 50,358, which decreased because of epidemics and natural disasters to a nadir of 40,623 in 1785. Thereafter, the population increased continuously to 70,000 by 1870. While these figures may appear somewhat out of place in the context of the subject under discussion, they are necessary to explain the absence of a class of full-time, professional fishermen or sailors in Iceland before the nineteenth century. The numbers were small, and the occupational structure largely pluralistic, with farming at the apex.

The most important fishery was from early February until mid-May. At this time of the year shoals of cod spawn on the banks off the south and west coasts. Fishing stations were scattered all along the coast, but the most important stretched from the Westman Islands in the south to the Western fjords in the north-west. The winter fishery was most intensive in this area and attracted fishermen from all parts of the country. By mid-January groups travelled on foot from their homes to their fishing stations. Those who had farthest to go trekked for about two weeks, often in the most perilous conditions through the highlands.

The seasonal character of the fisheries probably can be traced to the early thirteenth century, when farmers and landowners began to send their workers and tenants to the fishing stations during the winter, a practice that continued into the twentieth century. It has a certain resemblance to the Finnish peasant shipping discussed in Yrjö Kaukiainen's contribution to this volume in that it led to the seasonal migration of a considerable part of the Icelandic work force. Farm workers and peasants left their homes in northern and eastern Iceland by early January for the fishing stations on the south and west coasts and at the Westman Islands, where they spent the winter. Then most returned home, where spring and summer work on the farms awaited. The short but demanding haymaking season traditionally began in northern and eastern Iceland by mid-July. Extra hands were needed and many farmers in the south sent whatever workers they could spare (women as well as men) up north during mid-summer.

We can thus speak of four fairly regular annual migrations in the Icelandic workforce. The first began in January, when the fishermen set out for the winter fishery. The second came in May when they returned home. The third was in June, when farm workers from the south went to the north and east to help in haymaking. The fourth took place in late August or September when these people returned, often accompanied by fishermen going for the autumn season, which began in late September and lasted until Christmas.

The fishermen's life was devoid of comforts. At the fishing stations they commonly lived in huts of turf and stone. These were uncomfortable, cold and drafty. Normally, each hut housed one crew, with two men sharing a bunk of turf and stone. Work in the winter fisheries was both hard and dangerous. The men were up early and normally went to sea before daybreak. All fishing was done using hand lines and rowing boats, which had to be drawn ashore every night and down to the seafront again in the morning. This was strenuous and added to the fishermen's hardships. As soon as the boat was afloat the crew jumped aboard and, after a short prayer, rowed through the surf and out to the fishing grounds, sometimes for an hour or two without a break. They generally stayed at the grounds for four hours or more before rowing ashore again. Then came the landing – often the most hazardous part of the trip – and after that the boat was drawn ashore again, sometimes over difficult terrain. Finally, the fishermen had to gut the day's catch and prepare it for curing. A normal working day was twelve to fourteen hours, much of it at sea. The men sweated while rowing to the grounds, then had to sit over their fishing gear, often in cold weather and heavy seas. Normally, they took no food with them, though some had bottles of whey to drink. Once ashore, the men got a warm meal before withdrawing into their cold huts.

The fishing boats varied in size. The smallest were twin-oared, with room for one or two men, while the biggest were twelve-oared and normally carried a crew of thirteen (the skipper or helmsman plus twelve oarsmen). In some places skippers preferred an extra hand or two, especially if fishing was good. During the winter, eight-, ten- and twelve-oared boats were most common in southern Iceland, while six-oared craft were typical in the Western fjords. Smaller craft were used more in the spring and autumn when fewer hands could be spared from farm work.[11]

The recruitment of fishermen was most often done individually. Most fishermen in the winter fishery were farm workers, smallholders or "dry-house peasants," who lived with their families in huts or cottages at or near the main fishing stations.[12] Most boats were owned by

---

[11]This description is mostly based on L. Kristjánsson, *Íslenzkir sjávarhættir* (Reykjavík, 1982-1985), II-IV.

[12]Dry-house peasants were those who had few or no livestock and depended for their living solely on fishing and other work for the landowner.

farmers or institutions like the church or the crown. The owners normally hired experienced fishermen to command their boats, but the rest of the crew usually consisted of men employed by the owner or his subordinates. Thus, farmers tended to send their workers to sea in their own boats while the church and the crown demanded that their tenants provide men. The fishing station of Grindavík on the south coast is a good example of this practice. Of eight farms in the district, seven belonged to the church and one to the crown. All were leased to tenants who had the duty to provide at least one fisherman each for boats operated by the landowner.[13] By 1690 the crown could demand the services of about 690 fishermen, while the bishop of Skálholt had about 350 at his disposal.[14] To these figures can be added those fishermen going to sea for the bishop of Hólar in northern Iceland. Although their numbers are unknown, an educated guess would be about 200 about 1700. In total, some 1200 fishermen were employed by church and crown at this time.

To this can be added the fishermen who went to sea in boats owned and operated by farmers. Unfortunately, no statistics are available for this activity either before 1770, when we know that there were 1869 fishing boats. Only two were twelve-oared, twenty were ten-oared, 386 were eight-oared and 310 were six-oared.[15] If we calculate that the crew of each of these boats equalled the number of oars plus the skipper, the result is that 5896 fishermen were employed in the winter fisheries. Because of the extra hands in many boats, this figure is probably too low. In 1840, there were 3017 boats and in 1869, 3119.[16] Smacks, which became more numerous during the nineteenth century, are not included in these totals, and since the sources do not give a breakdown on boat size, it is impossible to know the numbers employed in the rowing boat fisheries. The numbers most probably increased between 1770 and 1840, but seem to have fallen thereafter because the proportion of small craft increased by mid-century.

---

[13]J. Th. Thór, *Saga Grindvíkur* (Grindavík, 1994), I.

[14]Kristjánsson, *Íslenzkir*, III, 123.

[15]*Ibid.*, II, 101.

[16]*Ibid.*, II.

Remuneration was usually small and by the share. Normally the owner of a twelve-oared boat received four or five shares for the boat and fishing gear and the rest was divided among the crew. The division could vary from one area to another, and since the fishermen were formally employed by farmers or tenants, their shares went to their employers. Good fishermen and skippers could most often secure bonuses, since they were recruited personally.[17]

A class of full-time fishermen did not develop in Iceland until the mid-nineteenth century, mainly because the only harbours were natural and towns and fishing villages did not come into being until the late eighteenth or early nineteenth century. The only exceptions were the so-called *hverfi*, small clusters of dry-house peasants' huts which began to emerge in some of the main fishing stations in southern and southwestern Iceland in the Middle Ages. Most inhabitants of these places were poor. They flourished in good years but in others starvation often struck.[18]

**Icelandic Fishermen, 1800-1900**

The nineteenth century was characterized by profound shifts in Icelandic fishing and seafaring. The traditional rowing boat fishery continued, but changes began to occur elsewhere soon after 1800.

The monopoly trade was abolished by a royal decree at the start of 1788. Six towns were to be established in various parts of Iceland. While Danish merchants retained the right to trade freely, the biggest advantage with this new system was that it permitted Icelanders could now enter trade, and many did so. They settled in the new towns and some soon acquired decked sailing vessels ("smacks") which they operated in the shark and cod fisheries. This greatly contributed to the rapid growth of some of the trading places, which in a few decades grew into sizeable towns. One of the best examples is Ísafjörður in the northwest.[19]

---

[17]*Ibid.*, IV, 187-194.

[18]Little research has so far been done on those old fishermen's "villages." A recent survey is J. Th. Thór, "Hverfabyggðir," *Árbók Suðurnesja* (Keflavík, 1994).

[19]*Lovsamling for Island* (Copenhagen, 1858), V, 304 ff. On Ísafjörður in the nineteenth century, see J. Th. Thór, "From Shark-Fishing to Salt-Fish Production: The Growth of the Town of Ísafjörður, 1830-1900," *Northern Seas Yearbook 1994* (Esbjerg,

More relevant for this paper was that the decked sailing vessels gradually led to the emergence of a class of full-time fishermen. The smacks added to the traditional rowing boats fisheries. At first they fished mostly for shark off the north and northwest coasts, but by mid-century they had entered the cod fishery. By 1870 the rapidly growing fleet of decked vessels was almost entirely fishing for cod and other demersal species.

The fishing season for the smacks was from late March or early April until late August, the time of year when the traditional rowing boat fishery was idle. This meant that the smacks could to a considerable degree be manned by experienced men, who thus came close to being employed as fishermen all year. Initially, many men were still registered farm workers, but gradually more chose to reside in the growing towns, where they established families and supported themselves mainly by fishing.

The recruitment of smack fishermen was similar to the rowing boats. Most smacks were owned and operated by merchants, sometimes with skippers as co-owners. During autumn or early winter the merchants or skippers wrote to individual fishermen or their masters to offer work. Sometimes the procedure was the other way around, but recruitment always took place on an individual, personal basis. Over time, it became more common for skippers to try to keep good fishermen or to ask them for recommendations to fill vacancies. As a result, crews changed little from one year to the next, and often whole crews came from the same district.[20]

These practices were facilitated by the fact that smack fishing berths were coveted by most fishermen. While the work was hard, it was relatively well paid, and fishermen sailing with good skippers could make more money than in most occupations. How well they did depended mostly on their own energy and luck.

Fishing for demersal species was done with hand lines, and remuneration was by shares. Fishermen kept half of their catch, which they sold to the shipowner for a price that was fixed for each season and

---

1994), 103-112.

[20] J. Th. Thór, *Saga Ísafjarðar* (Ísafjörður, 1988), III, 25.

depended mostly on last year's levels. The skipper usually received monthly wages plus a bonus based on the catch.[21]

No statistics are available on the number of nineteenth-century smack fishermen in Iceland. At Ísafjörður, the main smack port, most vessels carried crews of eight to ten: skipper, mate, cook and five to seven ordinary fishermen. The number of smacks operating from this port peaked at thirty in 1898, which means that then the number of men employed would have been between 240 and 300.[22] Ísafjörður, however, was only one of many similar ports, and it is probably not far wrong to estimate the number of smack fishermen at about 1000 during the 1890s, the heyday of this type of fishing. But soon many British smack operators began to replace their craft with steam trawlers, and a number of old British smacks were sold to Iceland, where they were used until the first decades of the new century, when Icelanders began to build up their own trawler fleet. Many smacks were then sold to Faroe Islanders, while others were either laid-up or scrapped.

The emergence of Icelandic merchants also contributed to the creation of an "Icelandic" merchant navy. Several merchants acquired their own vessels and some loaded fishing smacks with saltfish and other Icelandic exports in the autumn and sent them abroad. Most sailed for Copenhagen, but some went as far as Spain. Little is known about the crews. The smacks that sailed abroad were apparently manned mostly by Icelanders, but bigger vessels, like those owned by the firm Á. Ásgeirsson of Ísafjörður, seem to have used Danish crews.[23] But most crews included some Icelanders and many young Icelandic sailors acquired valuable experience aboard these vessels.

Two late-nineteenth century Icelandic sailors wrote their memoirs, which contain interesting information on the life and work of sailors in international shipping. Sveinbjörn Egilson left Iceland in 1885 to become an international sailor. The son of an Icelandic merchant,

---

[21]*Ibid.*, III, 24-29.

[22]*Ibid.*, III, 21.

[23]On the operation of the firm Á. Ásgeirsson, the biggest of Icelandic shipping and merchant firms during the latter half of the nineteenth century, see *ibid.*, III, 86-119. It is debatable whether the vessels operated by Ásgeirsson and other nineteenth-century Icelandic merchants should be considered Icelandic; while they were owned by Icelanders, they were registered in Denmark and flew the Danish flag.

Egilson spent the summers of 1880-1883 on small Danish merchantmen sailing along the Icelandic coast. During the winter of 1883-1884 he read theology in Reykjavík but decided to give it up and go to sea. In 1885 he left Iceland on a Danish vessel bound for Spain. He was put ashore in Ireland and went to Liverpool, where he found lodgings in a seamen's home until he found work on an English vessel bound for Calcutta.

At the Liverpool seamen's home Egilson paid seventeen shillings a week for food and lodgings. As soon as he arrived the landlord took his chest as a pawn, common practice to ensure that seamen did not run away from unpaid bills. The landlord then undertook to find a ship for his client and enlisted him as an able seaman, although he had never been aboard a big sailing vessel before. He was paid a month's salary in advance, which went to the landlord. Although Egilson did not owe the landlord a penny, this gentleman produced a list of items which he had purchased for the young sailor without consultation. When these were deducted from the advance, Egilson only had enough money to buy himself a quarter-pound of pipe tobacco and stamps for a letter to Iceland!

On his return from India, Egilson found employment on a Danish vessel headed for Denmark. Until the end of his career as a sailor, he sailed on Danish, English, Swedish and Norwegian ships, most frequently out of Copenhagen. Often he was recruited through agencies or shipbrokers, but sometimes through landlords or simply through fellow sailors who happened to know about vacancies.

Egilson's account is vivid and informative, showing clearly that there were frequent fluctuations in the maritime labour market, at least at Copenhagen. Sometimes demand was so great that sailors only had a few days ashore between trips, while at other times they had to wait for weeks and even months before finding a ship.[24]

The other nineteenth century Icelandic sailor to write his memoirs was Tryggvi Jóakimsson, who left Iceland in 1899 for Copenhagen, where he found work as a sailor with the help of an agency. After nine months his ship was sold to a Greek company and the crew was dismissed in a Scottish port. According to Danish law, everyone was given a free passage to Denmark and paid an extra month's salary. After sailing for some time on a second ship out of Copenhagen, Jóakimsson travelled to Hamburg with a Dane. They lodged at a

---

[24] S. Egilson, *Ferðaminningar* (2 vols., 2nd ed., Reykjavík, 1949).

seamen's home, where Jóakimsson experienced something similar to what Egilson had in Liverpool. His advance had to be promised to the landlord, who was entitled to take all the money, even if the sailor had stayed only one night in his house. All the sailor got was a mattress, two or three pounds of tobacco, several packets of matches and a piece of soap.

Jóakimsson spent seven weeks in Hamburg looking for a ship, although his more experienced colleague found employment after three weeks on a German steamer bound for Australia. The Dane was given a two-month advance (130 German marks), which barely sufficed to settle the bill at the seamen's home; the landlord took the cheque, which was payable two days after the ship left port. When that day came, however, Jóakimsson's colleague had deserted in Newcastle and the company refused to honour the cheque, leaving the landlord with a sizeable loss. Jóakimsson sailed for many years out of Hamburg, Antwerp and Copenhagen, and his experiences were much the same as those of Egilson.[25]

Egilson and Jóakimsson are only two examples of late nineteenth-century Icelandic sailors. During the last two or three decades of the century it became common for Icelanders to go abroad and to sail in Danish and English vessels. Many returned to form the core of the Icelandic seafaring profession that came into being in the early twentieth century.

## Conclusion

On the basis of existing sources, we can hardly speak of Icelandic sailors prior to 1850. Fragmentary sources show that some Icelanders went abroad during the seventeenth and eighteenth centuries and sailed in foreign bottoms, mostly Danish. The exact numbers are unknown, but they were probably not large. Icelanders were therefore evidently not a force as sailors at the time.

On the other hand, fishermen were numerous in Iceland during the same period. Because of the character of Icelandic society, a distinct class of full-time fishermen did not develop until the nineteenth century, but the number of men who earned their living mostly by fishing during

---

[25]Tryggvi Jóakimsson, "Endurminningar frá siglinga- og Ameríkuárum," *Ársrit Sögufélags Ísfirðinga*, XXXV (1994).

the late eighteenth century appears to have been somewhere around 6000, or about fifteen percent of the population. Many, however, must be considered migratory labour, much like the peasant seamen described by Kaukiainen.

The nineteenth century was a period of transition. An Icelandic merchant class began to emerge, and many of the first merchants acquired decked smacks for use in the fishery and sometimes to sail abroad with Icelandic exports. Others managed to buy ocean-going merchant vessels, which they operated successfully for longer periods of time. The fishing smacks were mostly manned by Icelanders, while the merchant vessels had predominantly Danish crews. Both types, however, served as "training grounds" for Icelandic seamen who in the process acquired experience which proved indispensable when an Icelandic merchant navy came into being in the early twentieth century.

# The International Labour Market for Seamen, 1600-1900: Norway and Norwegian Participation

Gustav Sætra

## Seamen on Norwegian Ships: Norway and Shipping

Because of Norway's lengthy coastline, ships were a common means of transport and communication. During the Norwegian North Sea empire (*vesterhavsriket*) in the Middle Ages, the country was important for shipping, but by the beginning of the sixteenth century Norwegian shipping was insignificant compared to its competitors. The majority of freight to and from Norway was carried by foreign ships. Due to the Hanse's dominant position in Bergen, Germans had a strong grip on the trade of western Norway and on the supplies of fish from the north. But Bergen still showed signs of being a westward-oriented town, maintaining contacts with Iceland, the Orkney and Shetland Islands, and Scotland, partly because western Norway at that time could supply these barren lands with timber. In the districts of Rogaland and Vest-Agder, timber was the most important export; here the Scots were dominant. From Aust-Agder eastwards, the timber trade was especially important, and it was at first dominated by the Dutch. Of course, no nation had total control over any district. For example, in Trondheim the economy depended on fishing as well as timber, and vessels from various nations called at the port.[1]

---

[1]Anders Bjarne Fossen, *Norsk økonomisk historie 1500-1850* (Oslo, 1979), 101; Yngve Nedrebø, "Frå Skandinavias største by til strilane sin hovudstad. Om folketalsutvikling og folkegrupper i Bergen 1600-1900," in *Frå Fjon til Fusa* (Bergen, 1992); Arnvid Lillehammer, *The Scottish-Norwegian Timber Trade in the Stavanger Area in the Sixteenth and the Seventeenth Centuries. In Scotland and Europe 1200-1850* (Edinburgh, 1986), 97-111; Lillehammer, "Boards, Beams and Barrel-Hoops. Contact between Scotland and the Stavanger Area in the Seventeenth Century," in *Scotland and Scandinavia 800-1800* (Edinburgh, 1990), 100-106; Oddleif Hodne, "Handel på Agder 1600-1620" (Unpublished manuscript); Henry Berg, "Trondhjems sjøfart under eneveldet 1660-1814," *Trondhjem Sjøfartsmuseums årsskrift* (Trondheim, 1938), 82-86; and Knut Sprauten, "The Family Hornemann in Trondheim" (Unpublished manuscript).

It was crucial to Norwegian shipping to carry a growing share of exports, because the new industries, timber and mining (*bergverk*), grew rapidly. Timber was especially important, since the bulk of mining output was consumed domestically. As the Hanse's power declined, Norwegian vessels engrossed a large part of the fish trade as well. Thus, the growth of Norwegian shipping resulted mainly from heightened demand for the country's exports. This was buttressed by the Dano-Norwegian policy of encouraging shipping, especially through an armed merchant ship agreement (*defensjonsskipsordninga*) which gave domestic craft certain advantages as long as the state could use them in time of war. As the fleet developed, the role of outside shipping was reduced. Growth also resulted from a shift in the locus of world trade from Holland to England. Timber exports, as well as the volume of shipping, increased when the British Navigation Act of 1651 excluded third-party shipping from trading between Norway and England. Another reason a small country like Norway could obtain a foothold was that the great shipping states were constantly at war. The majority of the Norwegian fleet exported fish and timber to western and southern Europe. The craft usually sailed in the summer and were laid-up during the winter. After 1750 the tramp sector grew, and when in the mid-nineteenth century Britain moved to free trade, other nations followed. Then the Norwegians developed their fleet by "cross-trading." As a result, Norway went from an insignificant shipping nation to a world leader. In the period 1850-1880, Norway advanced in rank from eighth to third, behind only Great Britain and the US. During this period, the country increased its share of world tonnage from 3.6% in 1851 to 6.8% in 1878.[2]

In the mid-sixteenth century, Bergen was the only shipping town of importance: its fleet surpassed those of all the other towns combined. But as the timber trade grew from the late seventeenth century, eastern and southern Norway rapidly increased their shares.[3]

---

[2]M. Braun Tvethe, *Norges Statistik* (Christiania, 1848), 80; Ludvig Daae, *Nordmænds Udvandringer til Holland og England i nyere tid. Et Bidrag til vor Søfarts Historie* (Christiania, 1880), 21-22; Ståle Dyrvik, *Grunntrekk i norsk historie* (Oslo, 1991), 134; and Fritz Hodne, *Norges økonomiske historie 1815-1970* (Oslo, 1981), 134-136.

[3]Tvethe, *Norges Statistik*, 105-107 and 152; Fossen, *Norsk økonomisk historie*, 101; Stein Tveite, "Framgangen for norsk skipsfart etter 1690," *Sjøfartshistorisk årbok 1965* (Bergen, 1966), 59; and Jorgen H.P. Barfod, *Danmark-Norges Handelsflåde 1650-1700*

**The Merchant Fleet**

The labour force that manned the merchant fleet increased as a result of the growth of shipping from the end of the seventeenth century. From 1710 there was stagnation and at times recession; not until the 1780s was there continuous growth, which lasted almost until the beginning of the nineteenth century. Blockades during the Napoleonic wars led to another recession and the immediate postwar era was similar. Better times came in the 1830s, and the labour force increased gradually until mid-century, when it experienced explosive growth through the end of the 1870s.[4]

There is no doubt that around 1600 many foreigners were recruited. During the period when Norway depended on others to transport its goods, the Netherlands were the leading nation, and the Dutch became Norway's teachers. Captains with Dutch names were common on Norwegian vessels, but there were a large number of Germans as well. The Danes were in a unique position; because Denmark was part of the same state, they came from a common labour market. But from the late eighteenth century, there have been native officers. Not until the era of tremendous growth in the late nineteenth century did foreigners again become numerous, among both officers and crew. Many were Swedes, a logical outcome of the union after 1814.[5]

Even if there were a large number of foreign officers during the development stage, it is not likely that the percentage of foreigners among seamen was equally high. The country needed the expertise which foreign officers could contribute, but there was no shortage of men to

(Elsinore, 1967), 184-197.

[4]Fossen, *Norsk økonomisk historie*, 102-103, 106; Tveite, "Framgangen;" *Den Norske Rigstidende*, IX (Christiania, 1815); Harald Hamre, "Unge menn under seil. Sjøfolk i Arendalsflåten og Stavangerflåten i seilskipsfartens storhetstid," *Agder Distrikthøgskoles skrifter*, XIV (1989), 7-32; *Historical Statistics* (1968), tables 46 and 56; Ole Gjølberg, "Økonomi, teknologi og historie. Analyser av skipsfart og økonomi 1866-1913" (Unpublished PhD thesis, Norwegian School of Economics and Business Administration, 1979), 369; Hodne, *Norges økonomiske historie*, 136; and Tvethe, *Norges Statistik*, 105-107 and 152.

[5]Tveite, "Framgangen," 73-75 and 90; Daae, *Nordmænds Udvandringer*, 6-7 and 67; Tvethe, *Norges Statistik*, 107; Sprauten, "Family Hornemann," 80-81; Gustav Sætra, "Skutehandelen i Nedenes," *Skog och brännvin* (Oslo, 1984); Anders Monrad Møller, *Fra galeoth til galease* (Esbjerg, 1991); and Fossen, *Norsk økonomisk historie*, 57-60.

man the ships. This did not imply that foreigners were non-existent among ordinary seamen on Norwegian ships. They were there, but they usually signed on for short periods in foreign ports or followed the ship when it was bought from abroad. Nevertheless, it is likely that during the early years, foreign captains recruited some of their countrymen.[6]

## Bergen

A survey from Bergen shows from where the town's bourgeoisie were recruited between the mid-seventeenth and the mid-eighteenth centuries. At the beginning of the seventeenth century only every fifth member of Bergen's bourgeoisie was born there, compared to half by 1740. The emerging Norwegian bourgeoisie was a product of the decreasing flow of people from Denmark, Holland, Scotland and the Orkney Islands rather than a decline in the German population of this Hanseatic town. While between 1613 and 1740 every fifth member of the bourgeoisie was German, the proportion must have declined in the second half of the eighteenth century after the Hanse closed its office. With regard to merchant marine officers, the survey only covers 1661-1740. For technical reasons, the figures can only indicate tendencies, but it suggests that the number of officers born in the town was higher than the number of citizens as a whole and was increasing. More than sixty-four percent of the officers were born in Bergen during that period. In addition, four percent were born elsewhere in western Norway and eight percent in the rest of the country. Still, the number of foreign merchant marine officers in Norway's largest shipping town constituted about one-fourth of the bourgeoisie. The Germans averaged about ten percent, but their share dropped at the end of the period. During the Great Northern War the share had been well over twenty percent. The Danish percentage was about half the German. Dutch captains were declining by the turn of the century and they were replaced by Englishmen and Scots. The literature about Bergen reveals that the number of Norwegian captains was relatively stable until about 1800, while the number of Danish captains rose to above twelve percent. Due to this, only thirteen percent were from abroad. But if the percentage of Danes increased just before the Dano-Norwegian state was dissolved, it fell again during the nineteenth century. By 1875 virtually all captains in Bergen were born in Norway.

---

[6]Sprauten, "Family Hornemann," 168.

It is difficult to say for certain how large a percentage of the crew on Bergen ships were foreigners. Random registrations show that there were some, but a thorough investigation is needed to disclose the levels.[7]

## Immigration and Seamen

In the local history literature, there are several indications that Dutch seamen settled in the Agder area during the seventeenth century. This was of course due to substantial Dutch shipping activity in the area. Because of the policy of self-sufficiency, Norwegian authorities wanted to reduce dependence on the Dutch, but the connection was essential for the exchange of goods. Even when Arendal and Risør were granted charters in the first half of the eighteenth century, the right to this two-way trade with the Netherlands was maintained.[8] Nevertheless, the Agder area increasingly recruited its own officers. In the seventeenth century they were usually trained by the Dutch, either in Norway or in the Netherlands. During the eighteenth century most of the migrant seamen came from Denmark. Several studies reveal clearly that emigration from Agder decreased throughout the nineteenth century, while in-migration from northern Jutland increased. The rapidly growing shipping was undoubtedly the main reason for eighteenth-century immigration, because the majority of the migrants were merchants, shipowners and captains. They came mainly from the rural, sandy west coast of Denmark, where large-scale shipping was impossible. But on the other side of the Skagerrak conditions in towns like Arendal and Kristiansand were perfect. The short distance and established trade connections made it easy to move to the relatively large towns in Agder, where they could get jobs as captains on large deep-sea ships, which offered a higher level of income than the small ships in their home region. Their position was strengthened by intermarriage and relations with Norwegian families. Apart from Danes, a few Germans arrived during the eighteenth century. Many of these were part of the Dano-Norwegian state, as they came from Schleswig-Holstein. Many of the Germans became merchants and captains, members of the town's upper classes.

---

[7]Nedrebø, "Frå Skandinavias;" Yngve Nedrebø, "Kildesituasjonen og forskning på sjøfolk" (Unpublished article, 1992).

[8]Hodne, "Handel." Cf. town privileges 1723 and 1735; Sætra, "Skutehandelen."

side of the Skagerrak conditions in towns like Arendal and Kristiansand were perfect. The short distance and established trade connections made it easy to move to the relatively large towns in Agder, where they could get jobs as captains on large deep-sea ships, which offered a higher level of income than the small ships in their home region. Their position was strengthened by intermarriage and relations with Norwegian families. Apart from Danes, a few Germans arrived during the eighteenth century. Many of these were part of the Dano-Norwegian state, as they came from Schleswig-Holstein. Many of the Germans became merchants and captains, members of the town's upper classes.

At the same time that Danish immigration declined, the number of Swedes rose. This was due to increased shipping between Norway and Sweden after the establishment of the Swedish-Norwegian Union in 1814, which made it easier to sign onto a Norwegian vessel in Swedish ports. Naturally, most Swedes came from the western part of the country. When Denmark-Norway participated in the Napoleonic wars, the number of Swedish immigrants was still relatively small. Most found employment as craftsmen and shipyard workers. Between 1850 and 1910 there was a great upswing in the number of Swedish migrants: approximately 70,000 Swedes came to Norway, with the majority settling in the southeastern part of the country. Almost every fifth Swede who came to Kragerø and Arendal during this era became a sailor. In 1875 Swedes accounted for about sixteen percent of the crew in the Arendal fleet, almost ten percent in Stavanger, and approximately six percent in the Sandefjord fleet. Immigrants continued to arrive from Germany, and some Britons also immigrated, but considering the close shipping relations between Norway and Britain, the numbers were surprisingly small.[9] While many eighteenth-century immigrants were officers, spot

---

[9]Berit Eide Johnsen, "Fra 'Invasjon av jyder' til en hotellvert fra Engeldrup. Dansk innvandring til Lillesand på 17- og 1800-tallet," *Årsskrift for Vestre-Moland og Lillesand historielag 1989-1990* (Lillesand, 1989); Reidar Vollen, "Dansk innvandring til Agder," *Meddelser fra Kattegat-Skagerrak prosjektet*, VII (1984) 14-32; State Archives, Kristiansand (SAK), Klitgaard Collections; Poul Holm, "Forbindelse over Skagerrak. Vendsyssels norske kontakt," *Meddelelser fra Kattegat-Skagerrak prosjektet*, II (1983), 14-30; Holm, *Kystfolk. Kontakter og sammenhænge over Kattegat og Skagerrak ca. 1550-1914* (Esbjerg, 1991), 99-100; Gustav Sætra, "Danmarksfartens vekst 1835-1850," *Meddelelser fra Kattegat-Skagerrak prosjektet*, XVI (1988), 69-98; Sætra, "Danmarksfarten endres – farten mellom Agderkysten og Danmark 1856-1914," *Meddelelser fra Kattegat-Skagerrak prosjektet*, X (1986), 77-126; Sven G. Eliassen, "'Grågjess' og 'lersvensker.' Svensk innvandring til Rolvsø ca. 1860-1900," *Meddelelser fra Kattegat-*

areas. Danes, however, gained a foothold not only in the Norwegian merchant fleet but also in whaling and sealing.

## Whaling and Sealing

Whaling escalated after 1868 with the invention of the high-powered harpoon gun, which overnight made Norway a leading whaling nation.[10] Prior to 1868, the Netherlands dominated the industry, while the Norwegian contribution was said to be of little significance. More recent studies, however, indicate that Norwegians were more important in whaling and sealing east of Greenland than was previously believed. Certainly, fewer Norwegian ships participated, but this kind of activity required a crew two to four times that of an ordinary merchantman. On the other hand, Norwegian ships were considerably smaller than their Dutch and German counterparts. While the Dutch and German catching vessels had carrying capacities of 150-200 commercial "lasts" (one "last" equals approximately 2.1 metric tons), the average capacity of Norwegian vessels was about fifty. Norwegian hunting in the Arctic was relatively insignificant before the second half of the seventeenth century, but from 1672 until 1807 continuous hunting occurred. The year 1672 was important because Bergen was granted a new charter with the right to hunt for whales. Prior to that year, whaling in the Dano-Norwegian state was monopolised by the Danes. Due to the Napoleonic wars, the last Arctic expedition in this early era was equipped in 1807. Bergen was the only Norwegian town to continue the Arctic hunt after this period.

Government support, in the form of duty exemptions, tax reductions and premiums, was important for the Arctic fleet. From 1763 a premium of five Norwegian *riksdaler* per commercial last was given, rising to fifteen in the 1780s. The support measures became indispensable for profitability. It has been estimated that it would not have been possible to make a profit without it, especially in poor seasons. In an unpredictable industry subject to severe fluctuations, government support was essential. In the 1780s, the premiums varied from sixty percent of income in a bad season to just over twenty-five percent in a good one.

---

[10]The account of whaling and sealing is largely based on Thor B. Arlov, "Norsk ishavsfangst ca. 1670-1800," *Forskning om mennesker på Svalbard* (Oslo, 1990), 147-166; and Arlov, "Sjøfolk på Ishavet ca. 1670-1800" (Unpublished paper, Trondheim, 1992), 1-17. Where the term hunting fleet is used, the Arctic fleet is meant rather than the near-shore fishing fleet. See also Hodne, *Norges økonomiske historie*, 128.

Another reason the premiums were so important was that many other countries, like Britain and the Netherlands, had similar systems. Hamburg, on the other hand, provided no such support.

In the hunting industry, a distinction was made early between a ship's crew and a hunting and production crew. Until the 1620s, the Basques monopolised the jobs as hunting leaders because of their experience, but later Northern Europeans acquired the skills needed. As for the Arctic vessels, a late eighteenth-century study on sea captains reveals that many came from the islands of Sylt, Føhr and Rømø. One particular statement on a Greenland expedition reveals that the hunting crew came from Føhr, whereas the greater part of the ship's crew came from Bergen.[11] The Jutes joined Bergen vessels year after year. They could be registered with South Jutland as their home for a number of years, and with Bergen as their home for a single year. This may indicate that they also lived in Bergen. It is not strange that there were so many South Jutes, since they early specialised in Arctic hunting, and because the ancient monopoly policy enabled Danes to acquire longer traditions than the Norwegians. Moreover, they had been supplying the German and the Dutch Arctic fleets with officers and hunters. Besides, they came from the Dano-Norwegian state. Of course, government was interested in retaining the sea captains and the hunters. Based on this policy, a number of regulations in the late eighteenth century made it possible for captains throughout the union to sign on in another town.[12]

The crew of the Arctic fleet does not appear to have remained in the industry for long. Even the captains stayed only to a limited extent; more than two-thirds had an aggregate service time in Arctic hunting of less than twelve months. A contributing factor was probably that the sailing season normally lasted for only four months. Because the season was so short, major replacements were to be expected, unless the individuals engaged in occupational pluralism. Although there was a limited number of permanent sailors, the overall number was large due to the constant turnover of crew. In the Norwegian hunting fleet there were at least 320 men. Still, compared to the Dutch fleet, this was totally

---

[11]State Archives, Bergen (SAB), Head of Enlistment of Bergen Crew Lists, 1789-1846, folder of 1790.

[12]Sætra, "Skutehandelen;" and Møller, *Fra galeoth*.

insignificant. Sometimes the Dutch fleet would have 5000-10,000 men from the late seventeenth century to the late eighteenth century.[13]

**The Navy**

Foreigners in the navy are a bit of a problem, because before 1814 the "navy" implies the common Dano-Norwegian fleet based in Copenhagen. For the navy, there are reports from the second half of the seventeenth and the first half of the eighteenth century. According to Cornelius de Jong, most of the common fleet was manned by Dutchmen. The Norwegian historian Olav Bergersen also holds that the Dutch were strongly represented, particularly among the officers. But according to Bergersen's estimations, the Dutch presence was considerably less than what De Jong suggested. Besides, from the mid-seventeenth to the mid-eighteenth century, the Dutch percentage showed a distinct decrease, although there were rises in wartime. Bergersen claims that the greater part of the common fleet's crew were Danes and, especially, Norwegians. As well, there was a considerable number of Germans. Bergersen's studies reveal that in wartime, the percentage of foreigners increased through overseas recruitment, especially in Holland. But he also shows that many who signed on in Holland were actually Norwegians. The explanation is that there was a substantial emigration of sailors from Norway to Holland. The Dano-Norwegian fleet was manned partly through conscription and partly through recruitment.[14] When Norway developed its own navy after 1814, it was manned by drafted crew only. Consequently, it was no longer possible for foreigners to sign on.

It was of crucial importance that the common fleet was situated in Copenhagen. The fact that most sailors had to leave the country, made Norwegian sailors mobile. They came from the many settlements in Norway to one of the big ports, where many were recruited to foreign ships. This became a convenient stepping stone to service abroad.[15]

---

[13]C. de Jong, *Geschiedenis van de oude Nederlandse walvisvaart*, vol. 2 (Johannesburg, 1978), 18; and vol. 3 (Johannesburg, 1979), 145-149.

[14]Olav Bergersen, *Fra Henrik Bielke til Iver Huidtfeldt. Utsyn over den dansk-norske fellesflåtes historie i perioden 1630-1710* (4 vols., Trondheim, 1953-1956), II, 328 and 409; and Daae, *Nordmænds Udvandringer*, 11-12 and 44.

[15]Bergersen, *Fra Henrik Bielke*, II, 328-409.

## The Trading Companies

The trading companies were also part of the merchant fleet. Since the vessels were owned in Copenhagen, they represented the same thing to Norwegian sailors as did the navy, from which the companies recruited many of their crews. The carrying trade became a constituent part of the Union's colonial policy. The companies controlled a narrow coastline in Guinea, while in the Caribbean the common monarchy owned the three Virgin Islands: St. Thomas (a colony since 1672); St. Jan (1718) and St. Croix (1733). Until 1807, the colonies were important pawns in the state's economic policy. Europe supplied the islands with foodstuffs and in return imported sugar, tobacco and rum. European consumer goods and East Indian textiles were shipped to Guinea, where they were traded for slaves, which in turn were sold in the Virgin Islands before the ships returned to Europe. In other words, Denmark-Norway was involved in the same colonial policy as the great powers. The position of the ships and the sailors in all this has never been analyzed adequately. But studies have been carried out on trade and shipping to Asia. On the Danish-Asian Company's China vessels around 1780, the number of Norwegians varied from five to 118 from one year to the next. As no studies have been done on the other companies' vessels, we can only guess that there were approximately 200 Norwegians in total. There are examples of foreigners among the crews, but they were hardly numerous.[16]

## Crews

During the last quarter of the seventeenth century, the crew in the Norwegian merchant marine comprised approximately 5000 men. In addition, it is probable that there were around 1500 Norwegians in the

---

[16]Erik Gøbel, "Asiatisk Kompagnis kinafarere 1732-1833. Besejling og bemanding" (unpublished PhD thesis, University of Copenhagen, 1978), 106, provides the following numbers of Norwegians (with the percentages of the total in parentheses): 1778-1779, 5 (3%); 1779-1780, 57 (32%); 1781-1782, 118 (41%); and 1782-1783, 23 (14%). See also Erik Gøbel, "Dansk sejlads på Vestindien og Guinea 1747-1807. En brugers erfaringer med elektronisk databehandling af de algierske søpasprotokoller" (unpublished manuscript, 1982). For references to the sugar refineries, see Inger Dübeck, "Industri-privilegier i Danmark 1735-1760 og Sukkerraffinaderiernes stilling," *Industri og bjergværksdrift. Privilegering i Norden i det 18.århundre* (Oslo, 1985); and Gustav Sætra, "Privilegiene til sukkerraffineriet i Bergen 1749-1751," *ibid.*

common Dano-Norwegian fleet in peacetime. In wartime, this number could be doubled many times, but it is important to note that a great part of the men recruited during conflicts came from the merchant marine. In this period, it is unlikely that more than 100 men were involved in whaling and sealing at any time. Therefore, it is possible that the merchant marine, the hunting fleet and the navy employed almost 7000 men at the end of the seventeenth century. At the beginning of the nineteenth century, the number might have reached 14,000.[17] This constituted less than two percent of Norway's total population over

[17]The census of 1801 does not give a good estimate of the total number of seamen, but it does give a picture of their geographic spread and their secondary occupation.

| | Akershus | Kr.sand | Bergen | Trondheim | total |
|---|---|---|---|---|---|
| main occupation | 1,870 | 2,337 | 1,024 | 604 | 5,835 |
| second occupation | 414 | 267 | 11 | 175 | 867 |
| total | 2,284 | 2,604 | 1,035 | 779 | 6,702 |
| main occupation | | | | | |
| captains | 844 | | | | |
| mates and skiffmasters | 1,266 | | | | |
| able seamen | 3,725 | | | | |
| total | 5,835 | | | | |
| second occupation | | | | | |
| farmers | 468 | | | | |
| tenant farmers with land | 134 | | | | |
| tenant farmers without land | 130 | | | | |
| fishermen | 25 | | | | |
| farmers and fishermen | 28 | | | | |
| tenant farmers with land and fishermen | 5 | | | | |
| tenants | 77 | | | | |
| total | 867 | | | | |

*Note*: Based on adapted data files from the 1801 project by Jan Oldervoll, Department of History, University of Bergen.

fifteen years. But the share is higher if we take into account all the men who participated in Norwegian coastal traffic and who sailed without being registered.[18] Furthermore, seamen were "occupationally mobile," and a considerable number of people were occasionally in the profession. It was not unusual for a person to be registered as seaman one year and as a day labourer, carpenter or cooper the next. Working as a seaman was for many a stage in life. A survey of the average age of sailors shows the predominance of young men. Mobility was not only occupational but also geographic. When seamen left town, new boys and men from the countryside came to replace them. Hence, this movement took place in stages. Moreover, seamen could not expect year-round employment, but had the opportunity for other jobs between sailings.[19] Until mid-century, the merchant fleet enjoyed a modest expansion. In 1850 it employed 19,000 men, but explosive growth meant that in 1878 the fleet employed as many as 62,000.[20] The strong growth also resulted in an increase in the share of foreigners compared to earlier in the century. Nevertheless, the proportion of foreigners on Norwegian ships was lower in the nineteenth century than in the two previous centuries. This was undoubtedly related to the wage rates.

## Wages

At the end of the seventeenth century, wages in the Dano-Norwegian navy were on the same level as for seamen in the merchant marine. With wages this low it was virtually impossible to attract foreigners. In order to obtain the necessary expertise from abroad, foreign non-commissioned

---

[18]Knut Sprauten, *Norsk sjøfart 1720-1760* (Oslo, 1989), 243. The rough estimate of 4000 men results from the following figures: in 1802 there were 8700 men in the overseas fleet, while in 1806 the number was 12,300. Adding the number of Norwegians conscripted into the navy in 1790, 1791 and 1794-1801, and working out the average, gives 2046, with 905 as the lowest figure and 3536 as the highest. As for the hunting fleet, the number of conscripts was somewhere between 200 and 400. For notes on the navy, see Hans Jeppesen, "Matroser til den dansk-norske flåte 1770-1802," *Norsk sjøfartsmuseums årsskrift* (1981), 165-211, esp. 210.

[19]Yngve Nedrebø of the SAB has run the "Undersøkelseskommisjonens register for Bergen 1803-1805" through a computer and analysed the mobility of seamen both occupationally, socially and geographically.

[20]Hodne, *Norges økonomiske historie*, 136.

officers and even able seamen were signed on as officers. Hence, it became tempting for foreigners to join the Dano-Norwegian fleet, even though it normally paid lower wages than other leading shipping nations.[21] There might have been a similar situation in the merchant marine, because foreigners on Norwegian craft usually were captains. Research from Bergen shows that many settled as merchant marine officers. A superficial survey of other towns shows a parallel development, and foreigners often settled down as shipowners and merchants.

Even if Norwegian wages were low compared to leading shipping nations, it is reasonable to assume that conflicts and prosperity affected them. Late in the seventeenth century, wages were high compared to the general levels in Norway, and they continued to rise until the end of the Great Northern War in 1720. From that point until the end of the eighteenth century, wages stayed at the same level. Norway was not the only country to show this trend. In Holland, wages were comparatively high at the end of the seventeenth century but dropped at the beginning of the eighteenth. Both Dutch and Norwegian wages stabilised at a lower level at the beginning of the eighteenth century. Later in that century, Norwegian maritime wages seem to have been on a level not too different from those on shore. A comparison with wage scales at the ironworks in Næs proves this point. Correspondence between wages on land and at sea was not a phenomenon particular to Norway but also was the case in Holland.[22] The monthly wages listed above were paid in the merchant marine on sailings in the North Sea and the Baltic, but longer voyages paid slightly higher wages. There are only isolated accounts of wages in the Norwegian whaling and sealing fleets in the eighteenth century. The limited source material which exists suggests that the

---

[21]Bergersen, *Fra Henrik Bielke*, II, 328.

[22]This is according to Tore Nilsen at the Bergen Maritime Museum, who has consulted the "Skipperlaugets protokoll i Bergen" in the University of Bergen Library; and Byfogdarkivet in Stavanger. I have consulted the enlistment officer's crew lists of 1790 in the SAB. See also Sprauten, "Family Hornemann," 144-150; and Sprauten, *Norsk sjøfart*, 247. For the comparison with the workers at the Næs iron works, see Ingeborg Fløystad, *Arbeidsmandens Lod. Det nødtørftige Brød. Arbeiderlevekår ved Baaseland/Næs jernverk 1725-1807* (Bergen, 1979), 541-542, 595 and 598. For the comparison with Holland, see P.C. van Royen, "Recruitment Patterns of the Dutch Merchant Marine in the Seventeenth to Nineteenth Centuries," in Lewis R. Fischer, *et al.* (eds.), *The North Sea. Twelve Essays on Social History of Maritime Labour* (Stavanger, 1992), 16-17.

ordinary monthly wage did not differ noticeably from that in the merchant marine.[23] The whaling and sealing fleets are not the only ones with limited evidence on wages; this is true for the entire maritime sector prior to 1800. When talking about "Norwegian" wages, it is important to be aware that source material is scarce. Surveys of Norwegian wages from 1859 to 1914 prove that there was no national labour market for seamen until 1914, although regional labour markets did develop.[24]

A true picture of monthly wages requires an investigation of trends in real income, but this can be a complicated task. Board on board Hornemann's ships from Trondheim increased by more than fifty percent from the 1720s to the 1750s. This might suggest a decline in real income in this period. However, a survey of miners' (*bergverksarbeidere*) living conditions indicates an increase in real income despite the fact that nominal wages stayed at the same level. This suggests that sailors also had an increase in their real income. Towards the end of the century, sailors' wages increased steadily. Wages at the mining companies (*bergverkene*) also rose; nevertheless, price increases on goods in this area caused a decline in real income towards the end of the century. Thus, it is reasonable to deduce that seamen also had a reduction in their real income. But even if sailors who had to support a family experienced a drop in their real income, the single sailor's purchasing power must be seen in relation to the country in which he spent his money. These factors, together with increments in monthly wages, make it difficult to estimate total income. The increments were sometimes substantial and would change the general picture if taken into account. Nevertheless, the monthly wages were important, because the increment *probably* followed a development parallel to that of the basic wages. But there could be deductions as well as increments. Quite often, captains signing on

---

[23]Arlov, "Norsk ishavsfangst," 157-158; Arlov, "Sjøfolk på Ishavet," 9-10; P.R. Sollied and O. Solberg, "Haabets koloni. Anlegg og beseiling 1721-1726," *Bergensere på Gronland i det 18. århundre* (Oslo, 1932), I, 217-218; and Carl J. Pontoppidan, *Hval- og Kobbefangsten udi Strat-Davis, ved Spitsbergen, og under Eylandet Jan Mayn* (Copenhagen, 1785), 25-26. See also SAB, Crew Lists, 1789-1746.

[24]Lewis R. Fischer and Helge Nordvik, "From Namsos to Halden. Myths and Realities in the History of Norwegian Seamen's Wages, 1850-1914," *Scandinavian Economic History Review*, XXXV (1987), 41-64.

Norwegian sailors at foreign ports kept a share of the wages.[25] There is reason to believe that this also happened to foreigners who signed on in Norway. It is important to note that reliable conclusions about the eighteenth century cannot be reached without a survey of the total payment of sailors' wages.

During the Napoleonic wars, nominal wages reached unexpectedly high levels, but despite high inflation, evidence suggests a growth in real income. Unfortunately, because of the blockade very few seamen were able to sign on to enjoy this wage increase, but those who did sail seem to have benefited financially. This confirms a general tendency: wages increase in wartime. Figures from Arendal and Bergen indicate that nominal wages stabilised towards the mid-nineteenth century.[26]

Norwegian wages in the latter half of the nineteenth century have been the subject of debate. There are two main interpretations. Ole Gjolberg and Fritz Hodne maintain that the nominal wages fluctuated from 1845 to 1880, but that real income was stable or grew marginally in this period. Thus, Norwegian wages were considerably lower than those in competing shipping nations. For the period 1840-1910, Norwegian wages were, on average, fifty percent lower than British wages. American wages were fifty to 100 percent higher than British, and even German wages gradually surpassed the Norwegian level. These low wage rates have been used to explain why Norway enjoyed considerable success in international competition during the latter part of the nineteenth century.[27] In contradiction, Lewis Fischer and Helge Nordvik have argued that wages showed considerable gains in this period. And even if they agree that the real income of crews who signed

---

[25]Daae, *Nordmænds Udvandringer*, 48-54, deals with the problem in Dutch ports. Barmann's account, "Den norske Sjømannsmisjon, gruppe VII Rømning og dens årsager 1870-1908," in the SAB discusses the difficulties in foreign ports around 1900 brought on by employers who usurped a large portion of the seaman's wages.

[26]Gustav Sætra, "Skuteregister for Skagerrak," *Meddelelser fra Kattegat-Skagerrak prosjektet*; XVII (1991); Sprauten, "Family Hornemann," 154-156; Fløystad, *Arbeidsmandens Lod*, 541-542, 595 and 598; Nedrebø, "Kildesituasjonen;" SAB, Crew Lists, 1789-1846; and Aust-Agder-Archive, Arendal (AAA), Ship Records for Shipowners Conrad Fürst, P. Ugland, Jens Sørensen Revesand, Stephansen-Eyde, Jens Lassen, P.B. Lassen, and Thommesen.

[27]Hodne, *Norges økonomiske historie*, 136-138.

on in Norwegian harbours may have been considerably lower than international wages, Fischer and Nordvik point out that the real income on Norwegian ships employing seamen in foreign harbours was only slightly lower than that on foreign ships. Indeed, in the 1860s wages on Norwegian ships were about eighty-five percent of Canadian/British wages in Antwerp, London and New York. But this evened out during the following decades, and by 1900 the levels were almost equal. Fischer and Nordvik believe the reason for this was that Norwegian ships had to adapt to a higher international wage level. This was both a result of an increased demand for maritime labour and the situation in the international labour market during the last half of the eighteenth century. As wages represented only about twenty percent of the total operating costs of a ship, Fischer and Nordvik point out that there had to be another explanation why Norwegians did so well on the international market. They mention briefly that desertion from Norwegian ships was quite common and that this could be an indication of low wages.[28] Desertion was thoroughly discussed by the seamen's padre in London, Gustav Barman, who for many years worked on a report that dealt with social misery following in the wake of desertion. In Great Britain, where the problems were especially acute, Norwegians looking for a berth had to live in inhumane conditions. In America, on the other hand, the problems were less severe due to a brisk demand for labour. From extensive source material he concluded that the main reason why many people escaped from Norwegian ships, mainly in British or American harbours, was largely due to low Norwegian wages. Barman's conclusion was not reached on the basis of the years from 1850 to 1860 but on the period from 1870 to 1900. He based his report on wages paid in Norwegian as well as foreign harbours.[29] The same conclusion was

---

[28]Lewis R. Fischer and Helge Nordvik, "The Norwegian Maritime Sector 1850-1914. A Reinterpretation," in Fischer, *et al.* (eds.), *Shipping and Trade in the Northern Seas* (Bergen, 1988) 21. In addition, see A.N. Kiær, *Statistiske Oplysninger vedkommende den norske Skibsfarts Økonomi* (Kristiania, 1871), 24-27.

[29]Department for Domestic Affairs, Maritime Law Commission, "Angående Rømningssagen 1885;" SAB, "Den norske Sjømannsmisjon, gruppe VII Rømning og dens årsager 1870-1908;" and Yngve Nedrebø, "En Kræftskade på vor Sjømandsstand og en Ulykke for Landet," *Arkivposten* (1989), 75. See also Gustav Barmann, "Om sjømænds rømning," *Aarbog for Norges Handelsmarine 1906* (Kristiania, 1907), 501-517, who is also referred to by Fischer and Nordvik, "Norwegian Maritime Sector." Barmann used enrolment lists from Drammen and Kristiania, consulate reports and engagement reports

reached in an 1899 report from the United States' Department on Commerce.[30] Letters from captains to ship owners reveal that the wage level in American harbours was considerably higher than in Norwegian harbours. No wonder a youngster would desert from a Norwegian ship if he could obtain wages several times higher in America, a captain from Arendal wrote in 1873.[31] Although there is some disagreement regarding Norwegian real income and how much lower they were compared to those of leading maritime nations, there seems to be agreement on at least one thing: Norwegian real incomes were lower. This situation hardly provided a basis for recruiting foreign labour to the Norwegian fleet. Indeed, there did not seem to have been many foreigners on Norwegian ships. Workers from other countries signed on Norwegian ships in foreign harbours, but their nationalities seem almost arbitrary. The main exception were the Swedes.

Wages on Norwegian ships in the eighteenth century did not seem to deviate much from the monthly wages in Norwegian mines. Until the 1780s wages on ships and in Norwegian mines were stable. Later, they increased. Miners were often paid piecework rates in addition to monthly wages. Seamen were also paid extra sums of money in addition to their monthly wages. The board was probably the most important item and represented thirty to forty percent of wages.[32] A corresponding calculation for the hunting fleet in 1785 showed that board

---

from the United States' shipping offices on engagements in 1894.

[30]United States, Department of Commerce, Report of the Commissioner of shipping (Washington, DC, 1899). Fischer and Nordvik, "The Norwegian Maritime Sector," 30-32, state that the report has limited value as a source as it is only based on a few single cases which were not comparable.

[31]Department of Domestic Affairs, Maritime Law Commission, "Angående Rømningssagen 1885" – registrations from the consulate districts, case appendix in file; and SAB, "Den norske Sjømannsmisjon, gruppe VII Rømning og dens årsager 1870-1908."

[32]Fløystad, *Arbeidsmandens Lod*, 125, 134; Bergersen, *Fra Henrik Bielke*, II, 334-335, 344; Sprauten, "Family Hornemann," 144-150; Sprauten, *Norsk sjøfart*, 247; AAA, *Resolutionen*, owner Hans Herlofson, ships records no. 306, and *Providentia*, ships records no. 278; and Kiær, *Statistiske Oplysninger*, 25, 27 and 33.

represented approximately forty percent of wages.[33] Besides, both officers and seamen in the merchant marine received an additional remuneration called *føring*, which allowed them to carry a limited amount of goods for themselves. Sometime during the nineteenth century this arrangement was abolished for seamen, and subsequently applied only to officers. The captain had additional sources of income, such as primage and *landgangspenger*. The former was a remuneration received for taking care of chartering, while the latter was probably the amount of money he had to manage with on shore. As well, the captain was often a part-owner and received a dividend if the enterprise was profitable. In the hunting fleet in 1785, it was estimated that the total income of seamen, including share of profit, a reward and the *føring*, represented almost the same amount as the wages.[34]

## Foreign Seamen on Norwegian Ships

In the sixteenth century the Norwegian merchant fleet was generally not attractive to foreigners in search of work. This was mainly due to the fact that Norwegian foreign trade was dependent on foreign shipping. In short, there were not many Norwegian vessels to join. Norway had no major port towns where it would be natural to look for a berth. This changed towards the end of the seventeenth century, when the merchant fleet expanded and the Arctic fleet was built up. As well, the common navy and the trading companies in Copenhagen provided opportunities. In this era most foreigners joined Norwegian merchant and hunting vessels in Norway, probably as a result of regular visits from foreign ships. It seems that mainly officers were recruited and that this was related to the nationality of the ships calling at various ports throughout the country. Until 1600 many Scots were in western Norway, but immigration to that region decreased during the first decades of the seventeenth century. The majority of immigrants on the southeast coast were Dutch. Foreigners in the Dano-Norwegian navy were also mostly officers. The reason for a strong foreign component was a carefully

---

[33]Pontoppidan, *Hval- og Kobbefangsten*, 39.

[34]Sprauten, "Family Hornemann," 144-150; Sprauten, *Norsk sjøfart*, 247; and Pontoppidan, *Hval- og Kobbefangsten*, 39.

planned recruiting policy in the major ports of Europe. Most foreign naval recruits came from Holland, Germany and Great Britain.

But Norway was mostly able to recruit its own seamen. The policy in this developing stage was to attract officers in particular. To make Norway a shipping nation, the authorities drew up a number of regulations and sent a number of expeditions abroad to promote the country.[35] By giving foreigners better jobs, Dano-Norwegian productivity, and hence wages, rose. This applied mainly to the navy. But these activities also gave Norwegian merchantmen a chance to obtain foreigners. Making use of the possibilities Copenhagen offered, Norway established contacts with seamen from all over the world.

At the same time that Norway received a number of officers and able seamen, it also regained a large number of "lost" seamen. As the fleet developed, Norwegians serving on foreign ships got an incentive to come home. Indeed, the authorities counted on this after the Great Northern War in 1720. When the stream was not as large as hoped, unsuccessful attempts were made to prevent emigration.[36] One opponent of this kind of restriction was Generalprokurør Stampe, a senior government official, who argued that seamen had to be tempted to come by being given special privileges. It was Stampe's policy which set the tone at the end of the eighteenth century.[37]

## Norwegians in Foreign Fleets: Holland and Emigration from the Southwest

In 1723, the Norwegian Governor General issued a survey of seamen from Akershus and Kristiansand dioceses who had left the country. Because this included only two of the four dioceses in Norway – and even this was incomplete – it does not satisfactorily reflect the actual

---

[35]This applied above all to the earliest period, but an act giving foreigners the right to a certificate of citizenship as bosuns was passed as late as in 1786. Wessel-Berg, *Kongelige Rescripter...1660-1813* (Christiania, 1841-1845), 16 September 1786.

[36]Daae, *Nordmænds Udvandringer*, 80.

[37]Henrik Stampe, *Erklæringer, Breve og Forestillinger. General-Procureur-Embedet vedkommende 1753-1782* (6 vols., Copenhagen, 1793-1807), V, 131-136.

situation.[38] A 1755 survey was in many ways a supplement to the 1723 edition. This one was not about seamen specifically, but rather about emigration in general. Taken together, the surveys show that approximately three-quarters of the men who went abroad came from Kristiansand diocese. The remaining quarter were almost solely from Akershus diocese, and less than two percent came from Trondheim diocese (there were no reports at all from Bergen). Surveys from Bergen reveal that for three years around 1780 there were about ninety emigrants. The number is considerable, although hardly as large as in the two southern dioceses.[39] The Governor General stressed that the 1755 figures were likely inaccurate or incomplete. Several uncertainties were present, and enlisted men were excluded. Kristiansand diocese had the following distribution: twenty-eight percent came from the west (Stavanger), five percent from the east (Nedenes), and sixty-seven percent from the intermediate area (Lister and Mandal). An overwhelming share came from the latter; indeed, it comprised nearly half the nation's total.[40]

The substantial numbers from Lister and Mandal is no surprise. Population there increased by only twenty-eight percent between 1660 and 1801, whereas national population doubled over the same period.[41] Indeed, there was no population increase in the core area of emigration in Lister and Mandal, despite the fact that many people from the inland

---

[38]Of 435 registered outward voyages, 341 (78.4%) were from the diocese of Akershus, while ninety-four (21.6%) came from the diocese of Kristiansand, of which eighty (18.4%) were from Nedenes and fourteen (3.2%) from Stavanger. The figures for Kristiansand were incomplete, since the most significant county, Lister and Mandal, was omitted. Norway, National Archives (NA), Governor General's Collection (GGC), file DX 62.

[39]SAB, Enlistment Supervisor, Copybook, 1780-1784.

[40]NA, Governor General's Collection, CVI2, files 56-57. While in the material forwarded to the Danish Ministry of Commerce (*Kommersekollegiet*) it should be possible to locate the ports of departure, it seems that this material has not been preserved; see Denmark, National Archives, Ministry of Commerce, F 6/7-1755, no. 769.

[41]O. Hodne, "Med Nederland som mål," *Agder Distrikthøgskoles skrifter*, XX (1990), 7; and Dyrvik, *Grunntrekk*, 124.

districts moved to the coast.[42] Thus, the population surplus was to a large extent counterbalanced by emigration, especially to Holland.

A Dutch survey of people who gave notice of the banns for first marriage in Amsterdam between 1601 and 1800 reveals that about half came from Amsterdam, one-fourth from elsewhere in the Netherlands, and another quarter from abroad. Most of the foreigners were German, but the second largest group came from Scandinavia. Of the foreigners, 6.5% (almost 12,000 people) were Norwegian. A Norwegian study of the Amsterdam banns for 1626-1800 shows that about half the Norwegians came from Kristiansand, mainly from Lister and Mandal counties, nearly a quarter came from Akershus, and about the same amount from Bergen and Trondheim dioceses.[43]

It has been assumed that Norwegian immigration to Amsterdam comprised two-thirds of total Norwegian immigration to the country. This implies that about 18,000 immigrated to the Netherlands between 1601 and 1800, but this is too low. While the Governor General's report claiming that 15,000 Norwegians were in the Dutch navy in the 1660s, and C.J. Pontoppidan's estimates of 8000-9000 Dano-Norwegian seamen in Amsterdam in 1753, cannot be accepted, there were probably more than 18,000 Norwegians in Holland in the seventeenth and eighteenth centuries. Dutch material confirms that there is every indication that emigration was mainly from southwestern Norway.[44]

There is reason to believe that most of the emigrants were seamen. In the 1660s, the Governor General made this perfectly clear, claiming that there were 15,000 Norwegians serving in the Dutch navy. When a list naming all who had left was made in 1723, the emigrants were mainly from this profession. Pontoppidan's 1753 figures, and the

---

[42]Lyngdal had 3370 inhabitants in 1665 and 3364 in 1801. Oddleif Lian, "Utvandringen fra Lyngdal til Holland ca. 1650-1800," *Agder Distrikthøgskoles skrifter*, XX (1990), 50. See also S. Dyrvik, *Norsk økonomisk historie 1500-1850* (Oslo, 1979), 130; O. Hodne, "Fra Agder til Amsterdam. En studie av norsk emigrasjon til Nederland i tiden ca. 1625-1800" (Unpublished thesis, University of Oslo, 1976), 7; and Anne-Tonne Aanby, "Befolkningsvekst og næringsforhold i Øyestad sogn på Agder 1660-1800" (Unpublished thesis, University of Bergen, 1976).

[43]S. Hart, *Geschrift en getal* (Dordrecht, 1976), 170; and Hodne, "Fra Agder til Amsterdam," 45.

[44]Hodne, "Med Nederland," 20; Hodne, "Fra Agder til Amsterdam," 20, 45 and 52; and Lian, "Utvandringen," 39.

Governor's 1755 numbers, are further evidence. The need for seamen was substantial in Norway, so it was important for the authorities to pay attention, which was probably why the Governor published his survey. According to this survey, eighty-four percent of Norwegian emigrants were males, which also supports the argument about seamen. Even though both studies of the Amsterdam banns from 1600 to 1800 report "only" sixty percent men, the majority of these were seamen.[45]

Despite the incompleteness of the Governor General's 1723 survey, it indicates to which countries Norwegian seamen immigrated. About-three fourths fled to Holland, where more than eighty percent ended up in Amsterdam and nine percent in Hoorn. The emigrants came mainly from Agder and Rogaland. A smaller share went to other towns in the north, like Enkhuizen and Zaandam. Quite a few, especially from Bergen and western Norway, moved to towns in the south.[46]

In the seventeenth century, Holland was the centre of trade and shipping, handling goods from all over the world. Moreover many raw materials were processed and exported as manufactured products. The East and West India companies played an important part in transport to and from the colonies, while the Northern Company had a monopoly on Arctic whaling. To be able to protect the country's overseas interests, a respectable navy had been established. Amsterdam was the most important trading town in Northern Europe until London became a serious equal competitor in the mid-1700s. The spread of the immigrants was also determined by where in Holland they were allowed to settle. Amsterdam was free for all to inhabit, as well as being the largest town. The East and West India companies were based there and it was the leading centre for the European grain trade. Moreover, its timber trade was substantial; most of the wood came from Norway. In short, Amsterdam was a logical place for Norwegians to settle. To a slightly lesser extent, so too were Hoorn, Enkhuizen, Rotterdam and Middelburg.[47]

---

[45]Bergersen, *Fra Henrik Bielke*, II, 409; Daae, *Nordmænds Udvandringer*, 45-46; NA, GGC, file DX62; Hodne, "Med Nederland," 19; Hodne, "Fra Agder til Amsterdam," 60 and 83; and Hart, *Geschrift en getal*, 170.

[46]See Sølvi Sogner's data processing of the material from NA, GGC, file DX62; Hodne, "Fra Agder til Amsterdam," 29; and Hodne, "Med Nederland," 17.

[47]Hodne, "Med Nederland," 13-14 and 18; Hodne, "Fra Agder til Amsterdam," 45-49; and Van Royen, "Recruitment Patterns," 13.

Bearing in mind the large number of Norwegian seamen, variations over time can be explained by altered conditions in both Norway and the recipient countries. People started emigrating to Holland in the late 1500s, but this did not accelerate until the early 1600s, peaking around 1675. Thereafter, it decreased before finally ending in the 1790s.[48] It is justifiable to regard this as related to the development of Norwegian shipping, which was totally insignificant prior to the end of the seventeenth century. But when shipping grew, Norwegian seamen had the opportunity to join their own ships.

According to surveys carried out for the merchant marine and the navy, there were more foreigners in Holland in the 1600s than in the 1700s. Nevertheless, every fourth seaman in the 1700s came from abroad, and one in five was Norwegian. At the beginning of the 1600s, every third man on a Dutch whaler was a foreigner, a number that decreased considerably during the century. It is not known how many Norwegians sailed on Dutch whalers, but based on Norwegian participation in the Dutch merchant marine, it seems reasonable to assume that there were quite a few. If this were the case, a possible explanation for the sinking number during the 1600s could be the occurrence of new opportunities for whaling with Norwegian ships.[49]

It seems likely that the economic considerations were important in the merchant marine as well as the navy. In general terms, it has been asserted that the most important reason why Holland became the target for Norwegian seamen was higher wages than in Norway. As for the navy, it has also been added that the problem was exacerbated because the government did not always pay promptly. While there is reason to believe that Dutch wages were well above Norwegian levels in the 1600s, this does not necessarily mean that seamen had a better standard

---

[48]Hodne, "Med Nederland," 11; and Daae, *Nordmænds Udvandringer*, 10 and 44.

[49]Sølvi Sogner, "Young in Europe around 1700. Norwegian Sailors and Servant-Girls Seeking Employment in Amsterdam," in 1993 Jean-Pierre Bardet, *et al.* (eds.), *Mesurer et comprendre. Mélanges offerts à Jacques Dupâquier* (Paris, 1993), 515-532; Sølvi Sogner, "Ung i Europa. Norsk ungdom over Nordsjøen til Nederland i tidlig nytid" (Unpublished manuscript, Oslo, 1993), 57-58; P.C. van Royen, "Foreigners Aboard the Dutch Merchant Marine Around 1700," in W.G. Heeresm *et al.* (eds.), *From Dunkirk to Dantzig. Shipping and Trade in the North Sea and the Baltic, 1350-1850* (Hilversum, 1988), 391-404; Jaap R. Bruijn and Jan Lucassen, *Op de schepen der Oostindische Compagnie* (Groningen, 1980), 50-52; and SAK, 1769 census for Lister.

of living in the former. Nonetheless, there are several examples of Norwegian seamen who prospered financially in Holland in this period. The great number of Norwegian seamen who emigrated to Holland is a clear sign that real income must have been higher. The fact that Dutch navy officers had to be promoted to reach acceptable pay levels in the Dano-Norwegian navy indicates that Dutch wages were higher, but it does not necessarily imply that this was the case with the real income. It seems that the nominal wages on Dutch and Norwegian ships at the end of the 1700s levelled out. It seems likely that this was the case with real income too, as it was in this period that mass emigration declined. This is probably related to the fact that Norway was advancing as a shipping nation while Holland was weakening.[50]

## Old Contacts

Emigration flows from Norway ended in Dutch towns with close shipping connects to the north. And Norwegian emigrants came from coastal districts with ports visited by the Dutch. At first, contact was established along the coast, but the Dutch also traded with foresters and farmers in non-coastal districts. This could be a possible explanation for the fact that people from both coastal and inland districts migrated to the Netherlands. Because of its location, the Agder coast became very important to the Dutch. Indeed, its coastal forests provided the first timber, although large quantities came from all over southern Norway. "Amsterdam is piled on Norway," a traveller wrote in 1671. The timber trade with Holland lasted a long time. Even in 1770, the bulk of timber from Drammen was still transported in Dutch ships. In the 1600s, the export of lobster from Agder to Holland began, centred on the Dutch town of Zierikzee. Granite came from Lister and Mandal counties, while boats came from Søgne. Because of this close relationship, boys and girls from Agder always had an opportunity to sign on a Dutch ship.[51]

---

[50]Daae, *Nordmænds Udvandringer*, 12; J.R. Bruijn, "Zeevarenden," *Maritieme Geschiedenis der Nederlanden*, III (1977), 170-171; Van Royen, "Recruitment Patterns," 16-17; and Astrid Friis and Kristof Glamann, *A History of Prices and Wages in Denmark 1660-1800* (2 vols., Copenhagen, 1958), I, 72-96.

[51]Hodne, "Med Nederland," 17; Hodne, "Fra Agder til Amsterdam," 45-49; and Daae, *Nordmænds Udvandringer*, 9-10, 43 and 67.

In the early period, emigrants went to large Dutch towns, which was quite natural. Until Kristiansand was founded in 1641, there were no towns on the Agder coast. Some people left for eastern Norway or Stavanger, but Holland was a more obvious choice. In the period 1650-1800, as many as ninety-five percent of the emigrants from Lyngdal settled in Amsterdam. The reason was probably that it was more likely for people from country districts to meet relatives and friends in Amsterdam than in their coastal towns. There was an entire community of Norwegians in Amsterdam, most from Agder. The greater part of the Norwegians settled near the shipyards on the east side of the town, including large numbers of seamen. The main argument for building the Lutheran Church in Amsterdam in 1671 was the overwhelming number of Norwegians who had settled here.[52]

**Return to Norway**

Because such a large Norwegian colony had been established in Amsterdam, integration into the Dutch community was limited. For most people, emigration was only a temporary part of their life-cycles. Young people apprenticed in Holland for one to three years. Boys left Norway shortly after their confirmations, and girls entered into service in Dutch homes. The urge to travel, along with tales from relatives and neighbours about the "promised land," drove the process.[53]

According to some sources, more men than women emigrated to Holland, but the opposite contention has also been advanced. Female emigration, however, was largely confined to Agder and Rogaland. Despite the uneven sex distribution, the possibilities of finding a partner from one's home district were quite good. A survey from Lyngdal shows that twelve percent of the male emigrants married in Holland, mostly to women from their native land. According to the banns registers in Amsterdam, forty-five percent of male emigrants from Mandal found a spouse from their home district, and seventeen percent married women from other parts of Agder. As many as sixty-eight percent married a Norwegian. The men from Bergen did not to the same extent find a bride

---

[52]Hodne, "Med Nederland," 17 and 32; Lian, "Utvandringen," 47 and 48; and Daae, *Nordmænds Udvandringer*, 16-17 and 71-80.

[53]Lian, "Utvandringen," 46.

from their home district: "only" thirty-six percent married Norwegian women, and seventeen percent found a spouse from Bergen. Because both spouses came from Norway, and often from the same district, reverse migration was quite extensive. As well, males who were already married before they emigrated did not usually settle down in their new country. Many were employed on Dutch ships for a season or two, while wife and children stayed home to look after the farm. Some spent several years on Dutch ships as long-term commuters, returning home for only short periods. Few brought their families to Holland. The fact that most of the male emigrants were seamen led to a comparatively high flow of reverse migration – more than twelve percent – whereas for women, the percentage was less than half that for men.[54]

Quite often, the returned migrant had obligations in Norway, often linked to marriage or a small farm. When he was away, his farm duties were probably carried out by substitutes, including women, older men and people who had moved in from non-coastal districts. There were many tasks to do, because farming on the Agder coast generally included forestry and fishing. The custom among freeholders was that the eldest son was entitled to take possession of the farm. And there were more incidents of freehold in Agder than elsewhere in the country. Thus, in places like Lyngdal it was natural for the eldest son to farm while the younger went abroad. But the eldest son also had the opportunity to migrate in order to build some capital. As coastal farming was seasonal, it was possible for Agder farmers to sign on a Dutch ship during off-peak periods. In other areas, however, there were more tenant farms, where younger sons had an equal chance of taking over.[55] So even if the structure of ownership was significant in deciding which sons could leave for Holland, it did not always have to be the youngest.

## Labour Migration

Thus far the term "emigrant" has been used to describe most of those who left Norway. It is necessary, however, to distinguish between

---

[54]Lian, "Utvandringen," 45, 51; and Hodne, "Med Nederland," 23.

[55]Fie Skaar Trysnes, "Kvinner og skipsfart," *Agder Distrikthøgskoles skrifter*, XIV (1989); Gustav Sætra, "Med beina i vannet. Skipsfart og gårdsdrift i Nedenes krets i 1875," *ibid.*, XIV (1989); Lian, "Utvandringen," 49; Sogner, "Young in Europe;" and Sogner, "Ung i Europa," 30.

emigration and labour migration. Migrant workers are those who earn the better part of their income in seasonal work so far away from home that they cannot commute daily. Labour migration can last from a few months to two or three years. A migrant worker leaves home with the intention of returning. The job is temporary and is normally a supplement to the income he can earn in his home district. Emigration, on the other hand, describes people who go abroad permanently. Labour migration is thus an alternative to permanent settlement elsewhere. This type of migration has been particularly widespread in Lister and Mandal, the core area of emigration to Holland. It has also contributed to the division of large farms in Agder.[56]

For centuries, going to sea has been the most typical way of migrating from Agder. In the seventeenth and eighteenth centuries people from Lister and Mandal emigrated to Holland; in the eighteenth, Denmark became a target; and in the nineteenth and twentieth centuries America was the preferred destination. During the past few decades, oil work in the North Sea has become a new alternative for migrants, largely replacing seafaring. In addition, there have been internal migrations, from the inland to the coastal, and from Lister and Mandal to the prosperous shipping areas in Nedenes toward the end of 1800.[57] Although it was the poor economy that primarily triggered emigration from Lister and Mandal, it is likely that an area with such highly-mobile manpower would adapt to migration fairly quickly. Mobility became part of their character.

## Motives

In the first half of the seventeenth century Norwegian sailors undoubtedly welcomed a berth on any vessel, since there were few domestic jobs for seamen. As Norway's shipping expanded, the domestic fleet became an alternative. Nevertheless, there are several examples of Norwegians who continued to go to Holland because wages were higher. In 1739 "Amtmann" Resen, the chief administrative officer in Lister and Mandal, maintained that many people emigrated to Holland because the county

---

[56]Hans Try, "Noen samlande merknader (om arbeidsvandring og utvandring)," *Agder Distrikthøgskoles skrifter*, XX (1990), 137-139.

[57]Hodne, "Handel;" and Try, "Noen samlande merknader," 136.

was too impoverished. Some sent money home to their parents, while others brought money when they returned – sums as large as 1000 *riksdaler*. His successor, "Amtmann" Holm, was not equally optimistic. In 1790 he wrote that some brought small amounts of money, others nothing at all – except a Dutch jacket – while still others remained in Holland, either voluntarily or because they had sold themselves to bondsmen for debt. The principal reason for the discrepancy between the accounts was undoubtedly the temporal difference. In 1739, Holland was still a tempting destination with its high wages, but by 1790, wages in Norway had started to rise. "Amtmann" Resen's description of Dutch prosperity is not unique: this impression was part of the popular consciousness. A story about the sailor Brynjulv Kvaas illustrates this. When he met his sister on the street in Holland, he simply grasped a handful of silver coins from his pocket and ladled them into her hands. Written sources confirm that Norwegian sailors accumulated fortunes in Holland. When the sailor Knud Tollaksen Udland from Lyngdal died in Amsterdam in 1750, his heirs in Norway received 2050 guilders, or 854 *riksdaler*. In 1790, August Stenersen from Austad in Lyngdal left an estate of 350 guilders (160 *riksdaler*). The price of a large farm in Norway was approximately 200 *riksdaler*, while a cow cost four or five *riksdaler*. But it is not only reports from Agder that suggest that in the second half of the 1700s Holland was becoming a less attractive destination: spot checks in Bergen reveal that Nordland in Norway was replacing Holland as a destination for migration.[58]

Population growth and lack of income are popular explanations of emigration. Emigration occurs because sources of income must be sought elsewhere. This is particularly valid for Lister and Mandal. Emigration and migration from Agder predominately took place among "ordinary people;" it was neither the wealthiest nor the most deprived who left. A survey shows a clear connection between available resources and emigration. In the parish of Vanse, the trend was that after a division of inheritance, the number of emigrants from a farm increased inversely with the productivity. Another survey, however, gives quite a different impression. In Lyngdal there were more emigrants from the fairly prosperous shipping districts than from the more impoverished upland farms. Other factors must have been decisive here. It was, for instance,

---

[58]Daae, *Nordmænds Udvandringer*, 12, 82 and 84; Lian, "Utvandringen," 52-53; and Nedrebø, "Kildesituasjonen."

easy for people living on the coast to board a Dutch ship. But Lyngdal was poor compared with the country as a whole.[59]

Although Holland became less attractive over time, skilful people were still required. As it became less favoured by working people, the Netherlands remained an alternative for the bourgeoisie. Nonetheless, ordinary people always constituted the largest group of emigrants. On that account, it seems plausible to presume that there were a number of factors which led to emigration or migration. Its large extent in Lister and Mandal can probably be ascribed to this area's close relations with Holland. The distance was reasonably short; the Dutch had sailed in these waters for a long time; and they traded directly with the Lister and Mandal population. The coastal people had better chances of getting a legal berth on foreign ships than those inland, since they were drafted as seamen for the fleet, whereas the inland population was enlisted in the militia. The overwhelming predominance of men from the coast indicates that men went to sea to escape a static society where everyone had his or her pigeonhole ordained at birth.[60]

Desertion also played a crucial part in the process. Fear of military service impelled many to emigrate, particularly during the Great Northern War. The Governor General's 1723 list reflected a desire to get the sailors back into the registers. While it did not improve matters that other nations recruited soldiers in Norway, the authorities had divided views on the situation. During wars they tried to prohibit such recruitment and threatened harsh punishment to those who left. But once peace was restored, the young boys were enticed to return to Norway and were promised that everything would be forgiven. This was done by sending recruiters to Holland and by posting notices of pardon there. It was also in the interest of the authorities that the crew acquired seagoing experience. For this reason, it was not uncommon that men from the coast were allowed to sail abroad for a few years before doing their military service. Hence, it could be to the advantage of the authorities for overseas ships to train Norwegian sailors during times of peace, provided that they returned when there was a threat of war.

---

[59]Hodne, "Med Nederland," 24-25; Lian, "Utvandringen," 44-45; and Try, "Noen samlande merknader," 140.

[60]Hodne, "Fra Agder til Amsterdam," 71; and Lian, "Utvandringen," 44-45.

During the long period of peace in the mid-eighteenth century, it was realised that shipping was an international industry and that the coast of Norway was so difficult to control that it was impossible to bind Norwegian seamen. Instead, they had to be enticed to stay in the country by providing a number of privileges. Moreover, the population had differing opinions on the alleged advantage of emigration. Whereas military authorities tried to prevent it, the "Amtmen" of Lister and Mandal sometimes defended those who had left.[61]

It was not only those who evaded military service who had reason to flee. Criminals escaped from their punishment, and many lads even ran away from their confirmation tuition and compulsory schooling, which was established around 1740.[62] The level of Dutch wages tempted all those who struggled to maintain an acceptable standard of living in a poor area. Besides, going to Holland did not imply that one had to start a completely new life: in towns like Amsterdam there were many people from the same region in Norway, including women. Many married a Norwegian woman and moved back to Norway at some point. In fact, for many migration was only a stage in their life-cycle designed to bring prosperity, experience and education in seamanship. Despite all this, only a fragment of the Norwegians who obtained a berth on Dutch ships became officers, most of whom were Dutch. This was of course a natural outgrowth of Holland's long tradition of shipping and education.

## Education and Cultural Influence

Navigational education was well-known in Holland, and the Dutch rate of literacy was far higher than abroad. This was a main reason why the Dutch preferred to recruit officers domestically. By the mid-1600s, the share of those who were able to write among the men from Bergen and Mandal in Amsterdam was only five percent. For the men from Bergen, however, progress was evident. By the end of the century, nearly fifty percent could write, while the Mandal men remained at the lower level.

---

[61]Daae, *Nordmænds Udvandringer*, 11, 12, 44-47, 68-69, 80-81 and 83; Wessel-Berg, *Kongelige Rescripter*, 11 January 1692, 1 December 1701, 10 June 1702, 2 December 1702, 16 February 1759, 31 July 1779, 8 April 1780, 18 November 1780, 7 September 1799, 23 April 1802 and 15 May 1802; Lian, "Utvandringen," 45-54; and Stampe, *Erklæringer*, V, 131-136.

[62]Daae, *Nordmænds Udvandringer*, 69.

This is probably a reflection of the higher proportion of bourgeoisie among the emigrants from Bergen. There is reason to believe that this was caused by a greater need for more educated captains in the maritime town of Bergen than in the rural areas surrounding Mandal.[63]

The many elements of Dutch in Norwegian seamen's language reflects the close contact between the two countries. The Dutch influence in Agder was so strong that natives returned with "somewhat foreign manners of speaking," as well as with a number of trousers on top of each other and with gold buttoned arms and collars. They often used Dutch names and were said to have been influenced by the more liberal Dutch moral. A man from Vanse, admonished by his minister for adultery, could not understand the commotion "because in Holland it was not paid attention to." In homes in coastal Agder, the Dutch influence was even said to have manifested itself in concern about cleanliness.[64]

## Denmark and Sweden

The connection with Holland has been given special attention because it was most important from the 1500s to the beginning of the 1700s. The Governor General's 1723 report, for instance, stated that nearly three-quarters of escaped seamen still went to Holland. Nevertheless, many emigrants also went to Denmark in the 1700s and Sweden in the 1800s. In 1723, the Governor General never mentioned Denmark because it was not considered a foreign country; this was also the case with Schleswig-Holstein. The 1755 report was not of much help either, although it did report that more than twelve percent of migrants left for domestic places, including Denmark and Schleswig-Holstein, but we do not know how many were seamen. Most likely few were, because even in 1670 the Norwegian merchant marine was larger and the gap increased in the first half of the next century, before large-scale investment in Copenhagen brought the ratio back to the level of the 1690s by 1800. But even though the Danish fleet was not as large as the Norwegian, it still represented an alternative for Norwegian seamen.

---

[63]Hodne, "Med Nederland," 26-27.

[64]Daae, *Nordmænds Udvandringer*, 63, 85 and 92-94; and Lian, "Utvandringen," 52-54. Dutch Christian names in Agder included Arian, Bernt, Cornelius, Claus, Evert, Jan, Reinert and Theis.

In the 1700s, the flow of emigrants from Agder to Denmark was modest. It seems that some moved to northern Jutland, where they became shipbrokers and captains. During the Napoleonic wars the numbers increased, but in general the flow to Norway was greater, since Agder during "normal times" was wealthier than northern Jutland.[65] On the other hand, there was a stable flow of Norwegians to Copenhagen to join the navy. And it is likely that many joined foreign ships after finishing their service.

In 1814, Norway severed its ties with Denmark and joined Sweden. This led to an increase in shipping and in commerce with Sweden, while Denmark became a foreign country. In the growing timber trade, the Norwegian fleet could now start sailing between Sweden and Great Britain, because after the union Norway was no longer "a third country" to be excluded by the Navigation Acts. The expanded trade with Sweden also led Norwegians to join Swedish ships. The extent of this is unclear, but it is reasonable to assume that there was a gradual rise, which peaked during the shipping prosperity in the 1870s.

**Russia**

In a story from 1715, it is said that most Russian naval officers were Dutch, Norwegians and Danes. Most were probably Dutch, but there is reason to believe that the Norwegian share was significant, especially in the lower ranks. Many Norwegians joined the Russian navy, some of which were recruited in Holland. In both the 1600s and 1700s, a significant number found their way to the Russian navy via Norwegian recruiters, although we have no figures. Most likely, the numbers decreased during peacetime. The Governor General's 1723 report characterizes the numbers as totally insignificant, but especially along the northern border, there were ancient connections of trade and fishing. From the 1700s and until 1914, the "Pomor" trade was quite extensive, and likely drew increasing numbers of Norwegians, including seamen.[66]

---

[65]Holm, *Kystfolk*, 85-86, 100 and 122-123.

[66]Ludvig Daae, "Nordmænd og Danske i Rusland i det attende Aarhundret," *Historisk Tidsskrift*, II (1884), 4; NA, GGC, "Report" (1723); and Einar Niemi, *Pomor, Nord-Norge og Nord-Russland gjennom tusen år* (Oslo, 1992).

## France

During the Napoleonic wars seamen also joined the French navy. In 1809-1810 approximately 2000 Dano-Norwegian seamen were handed over to French authorities in Hamburg; most of them were Norwegians. In 1811 Norwegian crews were again sent to French ships-of-the-line, where they remained until 1813. It is well-known that Norwegian seamen were on board French ships both before and after the war, but their numbers seem to have been modest. According to the Governor General's 1723 report, only three percent of escaped Norwegian seamen went to France. On the other hand, a number of Norwegian shipowning families and tradesmen sent their children to France to learn about trade and culture. Moreover, there were several Norwegian traders in France. The number of Norwegian seamen in the French fleet did not increase later, despite a flourishing trade, although in 1900 Marseilles was one of the most popular desertion ports for Norwegian seamen.[67]

## Great Britain

In trade with Norway, the Dutch had long taken the leading role in shipping. This was not to be the case, however, with Great Britain. The London fire in 1666 produced a demand for timber. When Norway began to export it, growth in Norwegian shipping soon followed. This was done in the context of the introduction of the Navigation Act in 1651, which excluded third-country vessels from trade. Because the Dutch did not export timber, Norway entered a growing market. The Napoleonic blockade clearly demonstrated the degree to which Norway had become dependent on its timber exports to Britain. Even though Britain contributed to the development of Norwegian shipping, the British connections did not give rise to an immigration of Norwegian seamen to the British Isles at levels comparable with the flow to Holland.

Nonetheless, it became customary for Norwegians to have agents in Great Britain and to send their children there for schooling in trade and culture. For this reason, six of the Anker children were in London and Norwich in about 1760. A number of Norwegian tradespeople were also resident in Britain, where they had their own trading society in

---

[67] Daae, *Nordmænds Udvandringer*, 124. Wessel-Berg, *Kongelige Rescripter*, 20 March 1744; and SAB, Barmann Collection.

London and their own church. Among the parishioners of this church were also teachers from Norway. In Ireland there was also a Lutheran parish of which the Norwegians were members. The Norwegians often returned home with fashionable English clothes and with difficulties in expressing themselves in their native tongue. Nonetheless, fewer Norwegian seamen emigrated to Britain than to Holland. According to the Governor General, in 1723 Britain was second to Holland, attracting thirteen percent of escaped seamen. That more went to Holland was no doubt due to the fact that Britain was large and populous and did not need as many seamen from abroad.[68] Furthermore, Norway's commercial relations with Great Britain developed after it had put together a fleet of its own and there was work available on Norwegian ships.

Strangely, it was not until the 1807 blockade ended peaceful trading that Norwegian seamen really came in touch with British society, albeit as prisoners. The entire Dano-Norwegian navy was seized by the British, and many Norwegians trying to run the blockade were put in British prison hulks (officers were given somewhat more liberal treatment). About 5000 of the 7000 Dano-Norwegian prisoners were Norwegian. Roughly thirty-six percent of these came from Agder, twenty-four percent from western Norway, and forty percent from elsewhere. That most came from southwestern Norway likely resulted from the close contact these areas had with Jutland; the need for grain led them to try to evade the Royal Navy. About thirty percent of Norwegian captives eventually joined British ships, chiefly merchantmen; only five percent chose the navy. Of 2100 seamen, 1750 were in the merchant marine and 350 in the navy. Most who joined the merchant marine went into the East India service. It is hardly surprising that such a large number of captives entered British service, since it was a way of escaping captivity. Although it could also be regarded as treason, Norwegian seamen had learned that the authorities tended to forget such matters, particularly if there was great demand for seamen. Further, the navigational training they received in captivity made it possible for many to be promoted to officers. Indeed, quite a few taught navigation on their return. Prison thus had some positive effects on Norwegian seamen.[69]

---

[68]NA, GGC, "Report" (1723); and Daae, *Nordmænds Udvandringer*, 98-122 and 126.

[69]*Lillesandsposten*, 12 January 1982; and Berit Eide Johnsen, *Han sad i prisonen ... Sjofolk i engelsk fangenskap 1807-1814* (Oslo, 1993), 7-10 and 129-144.

It is difficult to estimate how many Norwegians remained in British service after the peace. But there is little to indicate that the Norwegian element was significant until the last half of the nineteenth century. At this point, however, seamen frequently deserted from Norwegian ships in British ports. A survey from the enlisting districts of Drammen and Kristiania for the years 1870-1900 reveals that forty-one percent of those who deserted did so in Great Britain and thirty-five percent in America. The British percentage is artificially high, for many who left in British ports later deserted in America. Half who deserted British ships in America were foreigners, mostly Scandinavians. The large number of Norwegians leaving in British harbours was due to the fact that the British fleet was in need of crew: in about 1900, it employed one-third of the world's crew, of which about fifteen percent were foreigners. Scandinavians, more than 4000 of whom were Norwegians, comprised thirty-five percent of the foreigners. Scandinavians were a much larger element in sail than in steam, mostly in subordinate positions. The proximity of the British Isles, higher rates of pay, and the ease with which one could make it from Britain to America were also factors in Norwegians joining British vessels.[70]

**North America**

No shipping nation used as many foreign seamen as the US. In about 1900 it was estimated that eighty percent of the crew in coastal navigation in the US were Scandinavians. Thirty-one percent of those signing on in 1894 were Scandinavians, the same proportion as Americans. Moreover, the bulk of the Americans were allegedly Americanized Scandinavians, many of them former deserters. The most important desertion ports were New York, Philadelphia, Mobile, Pensacola, San Francisco, and Portland, Oregon. Desertion in American ports peaked in the 1880s, precisely when desertion was at its highest on Norwegian ships: at that time, a staggering twenty-three percent of seamen in the Bergen fleet deserted. Certainly, some of those who escaped in Britain to get to America, or who deserted in American harbours, did so not to become seamen but to emigrate to America. Notwithstanding, there were many Norwegian seamen on American ships: by 1900, more than 12,000. Despite the fact that considerably more Norwegian seamen

---

[70]SAB. Barmann Collection.

deserted in British ports, far more ended up in the American than the British fleet. The main reasons must have been emigration and higher pay. The 1880 US census indicates that a number of seamen born in Norway settled on both the east and west coasts, as well as in states around the Great Lakes like Illinois, Wisconsin and Michigan. In Canada, Montréal and Québec were the most frequent locations of desertion, a fact that brought almost 11,000 Norwegians into the Canadian merchant marine between 1863 and 1913. In the 1870s, Norwegians comprised almost six percent of Canadian crews. Most Norwegians were young men in their twenties serving in subordinate positions. The greater part came to the Canadian fleet via ships from the US and Britain; since few Canadian ships called at Norwegian ports, Norwegians more often signed on Canadian ships in other European countries or in North America. The work force was transient, as is evidenced by the high percentage of deserters. More than 4000 (thirty-nine percent) of the almost 11,000 Norwegians also deserted from the Canadian fleet.[71]

**Other Countries**

Occasionally it is mentioned that Norwegians joined Hanseatic or later German craft, but this was probably rare. While the Governor General's 1723 report notes that approximately seven percent of Norwegian seamen escaped to Spain, there is not much else to indicate that the Spanish fleet particularly attracted Norwegian seamen.[72]

The most striking feature thus seems to be the substantial Norwegian element on Dutch ships, while other nations were less significant, except during wars. The comparatively large Norwegian element on Dutch ships was closely related to emigration. There were no other similar phenomena until the lure of America beginning in the second half of the nineteenth century, which also resulted in many Norwegians joining the American fleet. Typically, Norwegians also signed on ships in countries to which their countrymen emigrated, like

---

[71] *Ibid.*; and Lewis R. Fischer and Helge Nordvik, "A Crucial Six Percent. Norwegian Sailors in the Canadian Merchant Marine 1863-1913," *Sjøfartshistoriskårbok 1984* (Bergen, 1985), 140.

[72] Daae, *Nordmænds Udvandringer*, does not mention Spain as a particular target for Norwegian seamen.

Argentina, Australia and South Africa. In South Africa, Norwegians primarily signed on in Cape Town; in Australia, Melbourne, Newcastle and Sydney; and in Argentina, Buenos Aires. The general pattern seems to have been that the great migrations spurred Norwegian participation in foreign fleets. Still, many Norwegians joined foreign ships in Europe, especially in Antwerp, Rotterdam and Hamburg.[73]

**Conclusion: The Labour Market, 1570-1870**

Only in the late 1600s did the Norwegian fleet become significant. Before then, Norway attracted few foreign seamen. In the late 1600s and early 1700s, the Norwegian fleet attracted foreigners, mainly officers, although rapid population growth meant that there were seldom problems finding domestic recruits. The navy in Copenhagen, however, received both officers and recruits from other countries, but more of the former. Most of the foreigners were Dutch. The modest Norwegian Arctic fleet was manned with seamen from the Dano-Norwegian state, but a considerable number of the officers were Danish. In the eighteenth century, Norwegian vessels were increasingly manned with natives due in large part to policies that discourage foreigners and, like the provision of navigational education, encouraged Norwegians. In the late 1800s, some foreigners, mainly Swedes, served on Norwegian craft.

Norwegian seamen have also played roles in foreign fleets. The Dutch fleet was most important, and it was there that large numbers of Norwegians learned to be seamen. Norwegians generally signed on as raw recruits. For many, their service was only a brief part of their life cycles, since a large share later returned home. The flow to Holland gradually decreased until the end of the 1700s, when it virtually ceased. When Norway participated in the Napoleonic wars, a number of seamen served in both the British and French fleets. Ironically, Norwegian seamen had often left the country to escape active service, as during the Great Northern War. During the first half of the 1800s, most Norwegian seamen served on domestic ships. But despite explosive shipping growth in the second half of the century, wages in foreign fleets increased considerably relative to domestic wages, leading many Norwegian seamen to join foreign ships, mostly American or British.

---

[73]SAB, Barmann Collection.

In many ways Norway from the end of the seventeenth to the middle of the eighteenth century was a peripheral country, at least as far as seamen were concerned, while Holland represented the centre. Towards the end of the seventeenth century the number of seamen in the Dutch fleet was about ten times that in the Norwegian, and it was still five times greater at the end of the eighteenth century. In this period the Netherlands received seamen while educated Dutch officers were sent abroad. By the 1870s, however, the situation had reversed: there were twice as many seamen in the Norwegian as in the Dutch fleet.[74]

The period from 1570 to 1870 can be divided into three periods. The Dutch period, 1570-1750, and was characterised by strong dependence on Holland. As the leading shipping nation, the Netherlands found it useful to have an open labour market. The second era (the "national" period) spanned the years from 1750 to 1850 and was a century in which the Norwegian fleet was manned mostly by Norwegians. Until the dissolution of the Dano-Norwegian, there was a strong Danish element within what was, after all, a common domestic labour market. The third period covered the years after 1850 and was distinguished by an international labour market for seamen, although the Norwegian fleet was largely manned by natives, with a Swedish component as the only other significant component. Although Norway was increasingly developed, it still had many of the features of a periphery nation even in 1870, including extensive desertions due to low wages.

---

[74]Bruijn and Lucassen, *Op de schepen*, 24; Jaap R. Bruijn and Els van Eyck van Heslinga, "Seamen's Employment in the Netherlands 1600-1800," *Mariner's Mirror*, LXX (1984), 10.

# Finnish Sailors, 1750-1870

Yrjö Kaukiainen

## Introduction

In this contribution I will focus mainly on the period 1750-1870. This is due to two factors. First, Finnish vessels engaged in little besides coastal and Baltic navigation before the mid-eighteenth century. Second, there is little data on the manning of other than naval vessels before the 1780s. These features are also clearly reflected in the existing literature. While there are a fair number of articles – including ethnological studies – on sailors and maritime labour in the nineteenth century, little has been written about earlier periods. Some scattered data can be found in histories of coastal towns, but the bulk is far from impressive.[1]

## Finnish Shipping and the Demand for Maritime Labour before 1700

In the Middle Ages, Finnish shipping was confined to the Baltic. Although the Hanseatic League dominated trade, there were some active Finnish shipowners. When the League declined, Finnish coastal towns began to increase their maritime trade during the reign of Gustav Vasa. Still, by 1560 there were only about thirty vessels large enough to sail across the Baltic to North German and Danish ports, while the number of small coasters, used on voyages to Sweden and Estonia, may have amounted to seventy or eighty. Even in the former category, the vessels were small, carrying only about fifty tons on average, and the latter group obviously included many craft only marginally larger than fishing boats. It is thus quite clear that manning such a fleet did not require large numbers of sailors – a fair guess might be close to five hundred.[2]

---

[1]A good overview of the literature can be gained from *Historisk Tidskrift för Finland*, III (1988), on "sjöfolk," in which all essays are on the nineteenth or early twentieth centuries. See also Yrjö Kaukiainen, *A History of Finnish Shipping* (London, 1993).

[2]The section is based primarily on Kaukiainen, *History of Finnish Shipping*.

In addition, peasants and other coastal dwellers carried on shipping across the Gulfs of Finland and Bothnia. According to customs records, the number of Finnish "peasant vessels" visiting Tallinn and other Estonian ports, Stockholm and ports on Lake Mälaren, may have amounted to 350-400. Their trade, however, consisted mainly of the simple barter of dried or salted fish for grain for local consumption. This was a trade using small boats that did not involve large numbers of real sailors. Still, as a "nursery" for sailors for foreign-going vessels, "peasant shipping" had an interesting, if little known, role.

During the first decades of the seventeenth century, Finland developed into an important producer of tar: by 1640, it had become the leading producer in the Baltic. Although most production was shipped to Western Europe, there was no upsurge in foreign shipping. The initial expansion of the trade was organized by Dutch merchants, whose vessels carried most of the tar beyond the Sound. Later, Sweden tried to displace the Dutch by creating a monopoly company to handle exports. Since this was controlled by important Stockholm burghers, and the trade was controlled in and directed to Stockholm, Finnish traders gained little. From 1648 (when the first tar company was started) to the beginning of the nineteenth century, Stockholm dominated the trade to such an extent that even the product itself was known as Stockholm, not Finnish, tar.[3]

**Table 1**
**Finnish Shipping, 1670-1680**

| Locale | Number | Capacity |
|---|---|---|
| Staple towns | 12-15 ships | c. 800 lasts |
| Ostrobothnian towns | 70-80 ships | c. 2000 lasts |
| Other non-staple towns | c. 70 ships | c. 600 lasts |
| Coastal parishes | 370-400 ships | 3500-4500 |

*Note*: The last was a unit of weight, corresponding with fifteen barrels of tar or eighteen *skeppund* of iron (2448 kg.). In the 1870s, the ratio between last and the net register ton was fixed at 1.85:1. In practice, it corresponded to almost three tons of deadweight capacity.

*Source*: Yrjö Kaukiainen, *A History of Finnish Shipping* (London, 1993), table 7.

[3]See Yrjö Kaukiainen, "Finland and the Core: Stages of Integration (c. 1600-1850)," *Review*, II (1993).

The result was that shipping remained much as it had been in the sixteenth century. The staple towns, which had the right to engage in foreign trade, owned only a few craft capable of sailing beyond the Sound. On the other hand, tar transports from Ostrobothnia to Stockholm required additional tonnage. Even traditional "peasant shipping" seems to have expanded, if only because Stockholm's growth increased demand for grain, fish, firewood and other primary products. Around 1670-1680 the tonnages of different kinds of vessels can be estimated (see table 1).

According to seventeenth-century sources, a ship of thirty to fifty lasts, sailing within the Baltic, required a master and three men, while a vessel of fifty to 100 lasts normally carried one or two more men. Only the very largest long-distance vessels over 100 lasts may have hired more than ten or fifteen men, while small peasant craft still sailed with only two or three.[4] A rough estimation of the total demand for labour, including masters, in the late seventeenth century suggests about 1600 men: 150 from staple towns; 300 from Ostrobothnia; between 150 and 200 from other coastal towns; and more than 1000 on peasant vessels.

In addition to the merchant and coastal fleets, some men were required by the Swedish navy. During the reign of Gustav II Adolf (1611-1632), Sweden emerged as a military power and expanded its possessions around the Baltic. Such an aggressive policy required a strong navy and a reliable supply of sailors. While warships earlier were manned using various *ad hoc* recruitment measures, a permanent system, covering all coastal provinces, was created in 1634. Normally, four farms comprised a *rote*, which was responsible for providing one sailor; towns also had quotas. In Finland, the total number of *båtsmen*, as they were called, was about 1200. Normally, men were engaged during the sailing season and went home in late autumn. During wars, however, the number doubled, so that in the 1670s the number of Finnish *båtsmän* rose to about 2000. When the main Swedish naval base was moved from the Stockholm archipelago to Karlskrona in the 1680s, Finland was too distant for recruitment and the numbers dropped to about 600.[5]

---

[4]Armas Luukko, *Vaasan historia* (2 vols., Vaasa, 1971), I, 166; Carl-Erik Olin, *Åbo sjöfarts historia* (2 vols., Åbo, 1927), I, 209-10; and Yrjö Kaukiainen, *Koiviston merenkulun historia* (Lahti, 1975), 115.

[5]Armas Luukko, *Suomen historia 1617-1721* (Porvoo, 1967), 147, 153 and 645; Nils-Erik Villstrand, "Från det avlägsna Finland till orter nära flottan," in Villstrand (ed.), *Kustbygd och centralmarkt 1560-1721* (Stockholm, 1987), 387-417.

## Expansion in the Eighteenth and Nineteenth Centuries

In the 1720s, Sweden promulgated its own Navigation Act, *produktplakat* (decree on imported products), which closely followed the principles of the English Navigation Acts (1651 and 1660) and their European counterparts. Above all, it aimed at displacing Dutch and British vessels from carrying imports of salt from southern Europe. It was used not only to prohibit the use of foreign shipping but also to raise funds: since 1726, substantial and increasing fees were charged for foreign vessels loaded with Swedish iron or sawn goods. For a shipload of deals, for example, such extra fees increased total dues and other charges four-fold compared with domestic vessels.[6]

All this meant that Swedish (and Finnish) owners were materially favoured in all shipping between Sweden and other countries. This gradually boosted shipping even in the small Finnish staple towns. In the 1730s bigger vessels were either built or bought from abroad, and direct contacts with the Netherlands, Britain and Spain established. In the 1760s, even the Ostrobothnian towns were given the privileged "staple" status allowing them to export their tar and timber abroad directly. Although Stockholm still retained some importance as a middleman in the tar trade, many Bothnian burghers began real "blue water" shipping.

A good indicator of the increasing shipping activity is furnished by Sound toll statistics. While the annual number of outward passages by Finnish ships averaged only ten as late as the 1750s, the figure rose to almost sixty in the 1780s.[7] At the same time, longer voyages to Spain and the Mediterranean became more common than voyages to North Sea ports. Moreover, an increasing number of vessels did not return directly with a cargo of salt but spent a winter – sometimes even a few years – carrying cargo in the Mediterranean, the Atlantic and sometimes even South America and East Asia. In the 1780s, fifty to seventy percent of the tonnage of Finnish staple towns spent the winter outside the Baltic.

In 1809, Finland was severed from Sweden and made an autonomous Grand Duchy in the Russian Empire. The political change did not at first affect economic legislation; the old Swedish Navigation Act, for example, remained valid (in principle, until World War I). Gradual-

---

[6]Staffan Högberg, *Utrikeshandel och sjöfart på 1700-talet* (Lund, 1969), 28-30.

[7]Kaukiainen, *History*, table 10.

ly, however, these privileges were undermined as Russia concluded reciprocal commercial treaties with most major European powers guaranteeing equal rights of navigation to both parties. The competitive position of Finnish sailing vessels nonetheless remained fairly strong; low wages combined with the availability of inexpensive timber was enough to offset any loss of privileges. Moreover, since increasing income was earned in "cross-trading," the old *produktplakat* lost its former importance. It was only in the 1870s and 1880s that the tide turned; steam was adopted slowly in the Finnish merchant navy and this lag robbed Finnish shipping of most of its traditional competitive advantages.

During the latter half of the eighteenth century Finnish foreign-going tonnage grew about five-fold, but even in 1800 it amounted to a mere 14,000 lasts. Much more important was growth in the nineteenth century, mainly between 1825 and 1865. During these four decades – in spite of a huge drop during the Crimean War – urban-owned foreign-going tonnage increased from about 15,000 to 80,000 lasts. In addition, the technical quality of vessels improved, and the role of long-distance voyages and cross-trading increased so much that in the 1860s about sixty percent of all national shipping income came from such trades. A crude illustration of this development is the proportion of tonnage sailing outside the Baltic during the winter.[8] From forty-six percent of total urban tonnage in 1825, this jumped to sixty-seven percent in 1840 and to seventy-nine percent in 1853 and 1861.

In addition to long-distance trading, some tonnage always sailed only in coastal waters. In particular, traditional peasant shipping was still flourishing. Such non-urban traders gradually gained the right to sail to Germany and Denmark from 1830 and in 1868 were granted the same right to sail abroad as urban owners (at the same time, the old distinction between staple and other towns was abolished). This ushered in a new heyday of sail in coastal districts: in the 1860s and 1870s "peasant" tonnage grew faster than urban. The result was that total Finnish tonnage grew to over 160,000 lasts (300,000 net register tons) in the latter half of the 1870s. This placed Finland in the same category as Sweden,

---

[8]Figures for "absent" tonnage may include a few vessels caught by winter within the Baltic, but such cases are rare. For 1825, 1840 and 1853, see the original ship lists compiled by magistrates of the Finnish towns, the archives of the Finnish Senate, Economic Department (*ekonomidepartementet*) or the Office of Finance (*finansexpeditionen*). For 1861, see Kustaa Hautala, "Merimiesten karkaaminen suomalaisilta laivoilta," *Näkökulmia menneisyyteen. Eino Jutikkalan juhlakirja* (Porvoo, 1967), 105.

Denmark or Spain, and compared with population, merchant tonnage was among the top five or six.[9] This, of course, meant that the demand for sailors was high, even by international standards.

## Demand for Sailors in the Finnish Merchant Navy

In principle, there are many sources concerning sailors in Finnish ports. This is because the maritime labour market was controlled by a public institution, the *sjömanshus* ("seamen's house"). The system was created in Sweden in the mid-eighteenth century, obviously following Dutch and French models. The prime motive was to register sailors and thus to make it easier for the navy to enrol men in wartime. In practice, however, military interest gave way to market functions; the *sjömanshus* developed into an institution which, above all, hired men and registered their working and wage agreements. Of course, they also fulfilled the original task by listing sailors who lived within their districts. In the late nineteenth century, every major seaport in Finland had a *sjömanshus*, and every Finnish sailor going abroad should have been enrolled in one.

From the 1780s, the reports of these institutions to the central government have been preserved.[10] They provide excellent material on sailors, including name, age and even the years of practical sailing. But if one wants to determine the total number of sailors, they are not quite as excellent since they also recorded seamen who had left the sea: in most reports, it is difficult to distinguish them from the active sailors. Thus, if one is not just interested in the number of *potential* but of *actual* sailors, the totals tend to be too high. Although for a few years (1863-

---

[9]See Yrjö Kaukiainen, *Sailing into Twilight* (Jyväskylä, 1991), table 1.1.

[10]Before 1808, they are to be found in the Swedish National Archives and the archives of the Foreign Trade Office (*Kommerskollegium*), *Årsberättelser, Handelsflottan*, Stockholm. Data concerning Finland has been published in summary form in Aulis J. Alanen, *Der Aussenhandel und die Schiffahrt Finnlands im 18. Jahrhundert* (Helsinki, 1957). Data for 1787-1794 seems to be missing. After Finland was incorporated in Russia, annual reports, together with lists of merchant vessels, were sent to provincial governments (*länstyrelse*) and to the new Finnish central government, the Senate. They are normally found in the department of finance (*finansexpedition*) among the letters from provincial governments (for 1848 and 1872-1887 in series Ef).

1870) the reports were even published in Finnish shipping statistics, it is only from 1918 that we have reliable published statistics on seamen.[11]

The data from the *sjömanshus* is also less than perfect in another respect: they do not list men aboard "peasant" vessels. It was only in the late 1870s that coastal districts were included. From 1841, however, there are special lists of "peasant" vessels which give the number of crew aboard each one.[12]

**Table 2**
**Finnish Merchant Tonnage and Sailors, 1783-1784**
(Swedish lasts)

| Town | No. of Ships | No. of Masters | Tonnage of Ships | Average Tonnage | No. of Sailors | Sailors per 54 Lasts |
|---|---|---|---|---|---|---|
| Turku | 16.0 | 21.5 | 2161 | 135.0 | 476 | 11.9 |
| Helsinki | 11.0 | 11.0 | 1583 | 143.9 | 258 | 8.7 |
| Loviisa (1783) | 7.0 | 6.0 | 1120 | 160.0 | 121 | 5.8 |
| Oulu | 22.5 | 20.5 | 2995 | 133.1 | 250 | 4.5 |
| Kokkola | 10.5 | 14.0 | 1550 | 147.6 | 172 | 5.9 |
| Vaasa | 4.5 | 8.0 | 588 | 130.7 | 97 | 8.8 |
| Pori | 25.5 | 11.0 | 1128 | 44.2 | 98 | 4.6 |
| Kristiinankaup | 6.5 | 7.5 | 569 | 87.5 | 72 | 6.8 |
| Pietarsaari | 7.0 | 10.0 | 900 | 128.6 | 132 | 7.9 |
| Raahe | 6.5 | 6.0 | 786 | 120.9 | 66 | 4.5 |
| Tornio | 1.5 | 1.5 | 236 | 157.3 | 23 | 5.3 |
| Total | 118.5 | 117.0 | 13616 | 114.9 | 1765 | 7.0 |

*Source:* Aulis J. Alanen, *Der Aussenhandel und die Schiffahrt Finnlands im 18. Jahrhundert* (Helsinki, 1957), I, 2.

The problems inherent in the *sjömanshus* data are clearly seen in table 2. The last column, showing the relationship between the number of sailors and tonnages (fifty-four lasts was chosen as divider since it equals 100 register tons), shows a wide variance from almost twelve (Turku) to four and a half (Oulu and Raahe). If masters are included, the

[11]See, for example, the Finnish shipping statistics, 1866-1870, in *Bidrag till Finlands Officiela Statistik*, ser. I, vol. II (1866-1870), 8-9.

[12]Such lists can be found in the archives of the Finnish Senate as well as in the archives of the provincial governments. For more information, see Yrjö Kaukiainen, *Suomen talonpoikaispurjehdus 1800-luvun alkupuoliskolla* (Loviisa, 1970).

lower ratios would have been close to five, which is roughly the same man-ton ratio that was found on ships of 200-250 lasts in mid-century.[13] It is clear that sometimes the lists only observed men actually sailing, but more often retired sailors and others were also included. This was certainly the case for Turku, where the high number may be explained by the fact that the town had a relatively big shipyard which employed many former sailors. In addition there is another factor which may explain the differences: how long the local *sjömanshus* had been in existence, since it is quite clear that over a longer time more inactive or former sailors were included. The ratios reflect the fact that a "house" was founded in Turku in 1753 and in Helsinki in 1760, but not until 1778 in Oulu.[14]

It is clear that a more realistic picture of the number of sailors requires estimating normal manning ratios. Unfortunately, systematic data on crews aboard different-sized vessels have not been collected for the period before 1860; there are only individual examples in the literature. Still, it seems that the lowest man-ton rations in table 1 represent typical crews for ships of 100-200 lasts; on the other hand, a ratio as low as three was found on a 300-last vessel and a *galea* of less than fifty lasts may have required more than ten men per 100 tons.[15]

Given the average size of vessels in 1783-1784, it seems that a realistic global man-ton ratio would be around five, including masters. The total number of sailors would then be somewhere between 1350 and 1400. But this figure only comprises men sailing on foreign-going ships, which means that vessels carrying tar from Ostrobothnia to Stockholm are not included, and table 1 lacks data on a few small towns (Rauma, Porvoo) which normally traded within the Baltic. A qualified guess would be that vessels in these categories would have required about 500 sailors. Finally, there is the fairly large peasant fleet, which at the end of the eighteenth century included 250-300 vessels. While their average

---

[13]In 1732-1748, the largest Turku vessels had man-ton ratios ranging between 4.6 and 5.7, with a declining trend. See Olin, *Åbo sjöfarts historia*, I, 209-215.

[14]*Ibid.*, I, 227; Eirik Hornborg, *Helsingin kaupungin historia* (2 vols., Helsinki, 1950), II, 341; and Aimo Halila, *Oulun kaupungin historia* (2 vols., Oulu, 1953), II, 337.

[15]Olin, *Åbo sjöfarts historia*, I, 227; Halila, *Oulun kaupungin historia*, II, 264 and 333; and Ilkka Mäntylä, *Tornion kaupungin historia* (2 vols., Tampere, 1971), I, 345.

size was only about thirty lasts, requiring normally only three men, it may be estimated that this fleet would have needed 900-1000 men.[16] Since many vessels only made three or four trips to Stockholm during a sailing season, and sometimes were manned by ordinary farm hands, it may be debated whether they were proper seamen at all.

From the early 1780s to 1800, the Finnish merchant fleet seems to have increased slightly. Total numbers of seamen as reported by the *sjömanshus* grew by ten percent, which suggests about 1500 active sailors. Such a favourable development is, in fact, what might have been expected, since Sweden (along with Denmark) remained neutral during the French Revolution. On the other hand, it is doubtful whether domestic shipping grew at all. After 1805, when Sweden joined the third alliance, the situation was reversed, even in foreign shipping.[17]

A new period of growth started in the late 1820s and early 1830s. Along with merchant tonnage, the number of seamen grew substantially, according to the *sjömanshus* reports (see table 3). While the totals are as inflated as in the 1780s, they show one remarkable thing. Although the increase was substantial, it was much slower than the rise of tonnage. Accordingly, man-ton ratios improved. This was caused partly by the rise in average vessel size: around 1826, it was well below 100 lasts and in 1852 close to 120. Yet it seems that even on similar-sized craft, crew size fell. A small sample of 270-320-last vessels shows that in the 1830s the man-ton ratio was 4.5, but in 1853 the same ships recorded a ratio of only 3.1, a drop of almost fifty percent in two decades. The former ratio is remarkably close to that found by David Williams for Liverpool ships in 1832 (his figures show an average of slightly below 4.5). In the beginning of the 1850s, however, the Finnish ratio was already smaller than in Liverpool (which was over 3.5).[18] Finnish trends clearly paralleled those elsewhere.

---

[16]Kaukiainen, *Suomen talonpoikaispurjehdus*, 51.

[17]This was mainly because shipping was increasingly directed to Britain and traditional contacts with the Mediterranean were severed. When Finland was conquered by Russia, it was also forced to join the continental blockade and sailing outside the Sound became very risky.

[18]Arne Engström, *Åbo sjöfarts historia* (2 vols., Åbo, 1930), II, 167-171; and David M. Williams, "Crew Size in Trans-Atlantic Trades in the Mid Nineteenth Century," in R. Ommer and G. Panting (eds.), *Working Men Who Got Wet* (St. John's, 1980), 111.

**Table 3**
**Total Number of Registered Sailors in Finnish Seaports, 1826-1866**( Masters Included)

| Year | Number of Sailors | Sailors/54 Lasts |
|---|---|---|
| 1826 | 2306 | 7.3 |
| 1841 | 5204 | 5.7 |
| 1852 | 5861 | 6.0 |

*Source*: Figures for seamen from Arne Engström, *Åbo sjöfarts historia* (Åbo, 1930), II, 168. Tonnages are from Jorma Pohjanpalo, *Suomen kauppamerenkulku ja erityisesti linjaliikenteen osuus siinä* (Helsinki, 1949), appendix 1.

It must be pointed out that while the figures above only concern urban seamen, they include towns with very little foreign trade and almost no long-distance shipping – in other words, the data are more comprehensive than for the 1780s. To present a realistic estimate of the number of seamen around 1850, it seems useful to divide the sector into three categories: long-distance shipping, with a total tonnage of around 43,000 lasts and average size of ships about 330 lasts, it may be assumed that they required an average of 4.5 men per 100 tons, including masters; smaller urban vessels, sailing in Baltic and domestic waters, with a total of about 11,000 lasts and average size about thirty-five lasts, requiring seven men per 100 tons; and peasant vessels, sailing within the Baltic and in domestic waters, with a total tonnage of 25,500 lasts and a total manning requirement of 2600 men, including masters, of 5.5 men per 100 tons.[19]

Starting with the man-ton ratios and other data presented above, the number of sailors in different categories around 1850 may be estimated as follows: 3440 men in long-distance shipping; 1420 men on smaller urban vessels; and 2600 men on peasant vessels, totalling 7560 men. Only for the period 1860-1913 has a proper study of the number of Finnish sailors been done.[20] It was based on the ship lists of the *sjömanshus*, most of which by that time even tell us the number of men

[19]Kaukiainen, *Suomen talonpoikaispurjehdus*, 237, appendix 1. Of these vessels, about ninety-five sailed to Germany and Denmark, averaged about fifty lasts and required a total manning of around 500 men.

[20]The most recent was Kaukiainen, *Sailing into Twilight*, 104-111.

on each vessel. Although the data are incomplete, it is possible to compute representative man-ton ratios (see table 4). Since the ratios include peasant and coastal vessels, no special estimates are needed for them. The only distinction made was between sail and steam.

**Table 4**
**Man-Ton Ratios in the Finnish Merchant Marine, 1865-1913**
(Men per 100 net tons, masters included)

| | Size - Class | | | | | | |
|---|---|---|---|---|---|---|---|
| Year | 19<100 | 100<200 | 200<300 | 300<500 | 500<700 | 700<1000 | 1000- |
| A. Sailing vessels | | | | | | | |
| 1865 | 7.1 | 4.8 | 5.1 | 3.7 | 2.8 | 2.4 | -- |
| 1875 | 7.4 | 5.0 | 4.0 | 3.2 | 2.6 | 2.1 | -- |
| 1885 | 7.4 | 4.6 | 3.8 | 2.9 | 2.3 | 2.0 | 1.8 |
| 1895 | 7.8 | 4.7 | 3.7 | 2.8 | 2.1 | 1.7 | 1.5 |
| 1905 | 7.5 | 4.7 | 3.7 | 2.9 | 2.2 | 1.8 | 1.4 |
| 1913 | 7.8 | 5.3 | 3.8 | 2.9 | 2.1 | 1.7 | 1.3 |
| B. Steamships (excl. restaurant personnel on passenger ships) | | | | | | | |
| 1865 | -- | 8.3 | 7.0 | -- | -- | -- | -- |
| 1875 | 13.5 | 8.6 | 6.1 | 4.6 | -- | -- | -- |
| 1885 | 12.9 | 8.5 | 6.1 | 4.9 | 2.7 | -- | -- |
| 1895 | 13.3 | 6.8 | 6.9 | 4.4 | 2.8 | -- | -- |
| 1905 | 11.3 | 6.5 | 6.0 | 4.3 | 2.8 | 2.0 | 1.9 |
| 1913 | 12.3 | 7.2 | 5.7 | 4.5 | 2.9 | 2.5 | 1.8 |

*Note*: Only three observations for the smallest class of steamers in 1875.

*Source*: Yrjö Kaukiainen, *Sailing into Twilight* (Jyväskylä, 1991), table 2.25.

Corresponding totals are presented in table 5. They have been computed by examining the structure of merchant tonnage at different times. It can be seen that the number of sailors peaked in the 1870s, which also was the apex of Finnish sailing tonnage. After that, the merchant fleet actually declined, and it was only after the turn of the century that earlier tonnage totals were again attained.

The shipping categories in table 5 are not exactly the same as those in earlier estimates. Coastal vessels do not include ships in the Baltic, but these can be found in group B ("other sailing vessels"). In the 1860s this category was dominated by true long-distance craft (vessels in year-round occupation): their total tonnage exceeded 100,000 and the corresponding total labour must have been close to 3700 men. During the next decade, the relative importance of wood exports to Britain and Germany increased, while the tonnage of long-distance ships declined to about 95,000 (1875).[21] Since average vessel size continued to rise, the total number of sailors fell even more than tonnage, to 2500-2600 men.

**Table 5**
**Estimated Numbers of Crew and Officers in the Finnish Merchant Marine, 1865-1913**

| | 1865 | 1875 | 1895 | 1913 |
|---|---|---|---|---|
| A. Coastal Sailing Vessels | | | | |
| Masters | 814 | 666 | 694 | 912 |
| Other Crew | 1,830 | 1,590 | 1,630 | 2,000 |
| Total | 2,650 | 2,250 | 2,300 | 2,900 |
| B. Other Sailing Vessels | | | | |
| Masters | 481 | 655 | 398 | 248 |
| Mates | 780 | 1070 | 540 | 360 |
| Crew | 4,320 | 5,230 | 3,130 | 2,270 |
| Total | 5,600 | 6,950 | 4,050 | 2,900 |
| C. Steamships | | | | |
| Masters | 26 | 46 | 117 | 203 |
| Mates | 30 | 50 | 140 | 260 |
| Machine Officers | 35 | 75 | 160 | 280 |
| Crew | 140 | 360 | 760 | 1,410 |
| Total | 230 | 530 | 1,180 | 2,150 |
| D. Restaurant Personnel on Passenger Steamers | | | | |
| Total | 40 | 80 | 140 | 250 |
| Grand Total | 8,500 | 9,800 | 7,700 | 8,200 |

*Source*: Kaukiainen, *Sailing into Twilight*, table 2.26. The number of restaurant personnel has been estimated on the basis of *påmönstringsrullor* of the Helsinki *sjömanshus* and the data of steamship officers and crews, 1914-1915, in the archives of *sjöfartsinspektören*.

From the end of the seventeenth century, the requirements of the navy were quite modest, at least as far as Finnish sailors were concerned. In the 1750s, when Sveaborg was being built outside Helsinki, a special coastal fleet was established, with many of its vessels based there. In peacetime, the squadrons in Finland amounted to about 2000 men. But all remaining Finnish *båtsmen*, and even some Swedish men, were now ordered into it and the gunners came from the army, which means that the increase in demand for sailors from Finnish coastal areas

[21]Kaukiainen, *Sailing into Twilight*, 155.

was quite modest. During the war with Russia (1788-1790), the coastal navy was almost doubled, and coastal towns had to send a number of merchant seamen to man the ships.[22] This was an exception, however, and in normal years the role of the navy remained modest – at least its demand for sailors did not affect the supply of merchant seamen.

After Finland was ceded to Russia, old regiments and the coastal fleet were dissolved. After that, there was no proper Finnish navy, with the exception of a marine corps of four companies (1100 men). It was founded in 1830, when Russia started fortifying the Aaland Islands, and was dissolved in the 1860s.[23]

## Finnish Sailors and the International Labour Market

It is quite possible that some Finnish sailors served on Dutch ships in the seventeenth century; it may be assumed that foreign vessels that visited Finnish staple towns sometimes needed replacements. But it was during the next century that recruitment for foreign merchant fleets became more common. When Finnish ships started to sail on longer voyages, they also started to lose men in foreign ports, because desertion quickly became common. For example, in 1744-1764, nine different ships from Turku lost no fewer than fifty men, including two mates. So far, no estimates for overall desertion exist for the eighteenth or early nineteenth centuries. It is illustrative, however, that in the 1810s it was usually possible to find enough Swedish or Finnish sailors in Liverpool to replace sick men and deserters.[24]

Although desertion carried a heavy penalty, the possibilities for entering foreign service lawfully were almost nonexistent. Still, because sailors' wages in Western Europe were much higher, many men took the risk. On the other hand, because of the potential punishment, quite a few never returned home. Accordingly, desertion remained the main means of international recruitment for Finnish sailors until the end of the nine-

---

[22] Oscar Nikula, *Svenska skärgårdsflottan 1756-1791* (Helsingfors, 1933); Aulis J. Alanen, *Suomen historia vapaudenajalla* (Porvoo, 1963), 388; and Alanen, *Suomen historia kustavilaisella ajalla* (Porvoo, 1964), 458-459 and 466.

[23] Erkki K. Osmonsalo, "Itsevaltiuden kausi," in A. Korhonen (ed.), *Suomen historian käsikirja* (2 vols., Porvoo, 1949), II, 102-103.

[24] Olin, *Åbo sjöfarts historia*, 212-214.

teenth century, and the numbers of deserters suggest, however roughly, the "pull" of foreign markets for maritime labour.

Around the middle of the nineteenth century, most Finnish *sjömanshus* compiled special lists of deserters. Although the material is far from complete, it seems that in 1856-1860 about 500 men, or 100 per year, jumped ship. In 1872-1875 the corresponding figure was over 800, or 200 per annum.[25] The latter figure amounts to an *annual* desertion rate of about ten percent of the men serving in the Finnish blue water fleet, and since Finnish tonnage was very low after the Crimean War, the figure for the late 1850s was in fact of the same order. In the well-known Canadian sample *decadal* desertion rates ranged between sixteen and twenty two percent of all seamen entering into service in the 1860s, 1870s and 1880s. It seems probable that Finnish comparative rates would have exceeded twenty percent in the 1860s and 1870s.[26]

Some Finnish sailors who deserted in North America may have aimed at finding new opportunities as immigrants on dry land, but most must have continued their seafaring careers aboard foreign vessels. In fact, the low level of Finnish maritime wages remained a prime factor for desertion. According to one qualified estimate, about 6000 Finnish sailors were to be found abroad in the early 1880s. In the Canadian sample which comprised the best part of that country's merchant tonnage in 1863-1913, about 5600 men, or three percent of the total labour force, were Finns by birth.[27]

---

[25]Hautala, "Merimiesten karkaaminen," 105-108. The figures for 1872-1875 lack data for a few towns, and by extrapolation a total of between 800 and 900 seems probable.

[26]Canadian desertion rates are from Lewis R. Fischer, "A Dereliction of Duty: The Problem of Desertion on Nineteenth Century Sailing Vessels" in R. Ommer and G. Panting (eds.), *Working Men Who Got Wet* (St. John's, 1980), 56. If thirty percent of non-deserters only remained for one voyage, the total number of entrances in the Finnish deep-sea merchant fleet in 1871-1875 was close to 4500 men, of which about 1000 deserted.

[27]Yrjö Kaukiainen, "Från jungman Jansson till Kalle Aaltonen. Sjömän i Finlands handelsflotta 1860-1914 – en kvantitativ översikt," *Historisk Tidskrift för Finland*, III (1988), 364; and Lewis R. Fischer and Helge W. Nordvik, "Finländare i den kanadensiska handelsflottan 1863-1913," *ibid.*, 377.

Desertion figures diminished already during the late 1870s, and they were only a third of the early-1870s levels during the next decade.[28] This undoubtedly reflects a radical worsening of shipping cycles: not only was demand for seamen, and thus opportunities for desertion, lower than before, but even Finnish deep-sea tonnage started to diminish. On the other hand, it is evident that lawful emigration to foreign services increased at the same time.

In addition to the all-important western direction, there was even a modest eastern element in the movement of maritime labour. From 1809, Finnish sailors could lawfully be engaged by the Russian merchant marine. Since there was quite a substantial demand for foreign sailors, it might be thought that St. Petersburg in particular offered plentiful opportunities for Finns. The available data suggest that to some extent this was the case – in particular from the 1840s. But even by 1820, about 200 Finnish sailors were in St. Petersburg. Between 1852 and 1867, over 800 were recorded on Russian deep-sea ships, about three-quarters of whom were engaged in St. Petersburg and the rest in Riga.[29]

In addition to normal foreign trade, there were two special markets where Finnish seamen were to be found. The local traffic emanating from St. Petersburg used many small river steamers, and this business was dominated by a Finnish company founded in 1873. In the early 1880s, it already owned fifty vessels and fifteen years later the number was about eighty. Not surprisingly, the company employed many Finns, not just common sailors but also masters and engineers. But since these were small river vessels, the numbers were not large: in 1915, about 300 Finns were reportedly engaged during the sailing season.[30]

Another special case was the transport of oil on the Caspian Sea and River Volga. From the 1870s, the Swedish Nobel brothers dominated the new oil business in Baku and they imported an important proportion of skilled labour from Sweden and the other Nordic countries.

---

[28]Hautala, "Merimiesten karkaaminen," 106. In the comparison only ports with continuous data have been used.

[29]Max Engman, "Sjömän från Finland i Ryssland," *Historisk Tidskrift för Finland*, III (1988), 427-437, especially table 1. In 1820, about half these men were from the easternmost province and three-quarters from the south coast east of Hangö; in 1852-1867, the corresponding proportions were one-third and three-quarters.

[30]*Ibid.*, 422-423.

Even a number of Finns, mainly masters and engineers, made their living on these distant waters. Reliable estimates are unavailable, but it seems that the number of Finns (including even common sailors) increased in the 1890s, when the Finnish merchant fleet was rapidly declining.[31]

It is probable that the estimate of some 6000 Finns sailing abroad around 1880 did not include those on Russian river and coastal services. Compared to this figure, even the proportion of Russian foreign trades would have been fairly modest. On the other hand, it is possible that the figures increased after the 1880s. As vague as the quantitative data are, it seems clear that the eastward "pull" was rather smaller than might have been expected. Whether this depended on practical preferences or national prejudices is difficult to determine. It must, however, be remembered that since desertion was for long the main channel to foreign service, the strong westward "pull" was logically connected with the equally strong westward orientation of Finnish shipping.

## Social and Age Structure of Sailors

There are only a couple of detailed local studies of Finnish seamen. If they do not produce any surprises, they do corroborate what already has been regarded as general truths. First, they show that being a seaman was a young man's profession. In Rauma at the end of the 1850s, sixty-two percent of all seamen were between fifteen and twenty-four years of age; boys below fifteen amounted to over ten percent. In Helsinki between 1819 and 1849, roughly one-half of seamen were in the twenty-one to thirty-year age class, while the proportion of sailors older than thirty normally fluctuated between one-third and one-quarter.[32]

The low median age also tells us that this was a lifetime occupation for relatively few men. Instead, it was a profession with great mobility and a high proportion of short-term workers. This may sound unexpected, because it is generally accepted that sailing required great skills, which only could be gained by experience. But there was always lots of work aboard which did not require much skill, and many ships

[31] *Ibid.*, 418-421.

[32] Jari Lybeck, "Sjöfolket i Raumo under sjöfartens expansionsår 1840-1870," *Historisk Tidskrift för Finland*, III (1988), 543; and Christian Ahlström, "Sjömän i Helsingfors 1819-1849," *ibid.*, 521.

sailed with crews comprising only a small number of able-bodied seamen. In fact, I am inclined to think that the market for maritime labour was not as separated from local landward labour markets as has sometimes been supposed. This view is further corroborated by the simple fact that in the 1860s and 1870s most sailors in the smaller Finnish coastal towns were drawn from home port or its vicinity.[33] Instead of belonging to a special national maritime pool of labour, they were part of a local labour market. Moreover, sailors normally originated from and belonged to the working class, that is, their career did not produce any social advancement. The separation between forecastlemen and officers was quite distinct. The latter were normally members of the local middle or upper class by birth and, typically, only served the minimum number of years in lower ranks to gain the expertise required of officers. The other side of the coin is that few ordinary sailors became mates or masters. In addition to social determinants, one additional hinderance was the fact that navigation schools required elementary school education, which working-class children seldom received.

## Working Conditions

Since the 1840s, when Richard Henry Dana published his *Two Years before the Mast*, much attention has been paid to the harsh discipline and difficult working conditions aboard sailing vessels. While some descriptions have greatly exaggerated the cruelty of maritime life, it is clear that a "naval" system of discipline prevailed on European and American ships in the nineteenth century. This was the case on Finland vessels: despite the peripheral situation of the country, the traditions of shipboard management and discipline closely resembled British and American patterns. Thus, for example, the new Finnish maritime code of 1873 allowed public flogging as a punishment for more serious offences.

In many countries this "naval" type of management, with the master as an absolute supreme authority, seems to have been a sixteenth-, seventeenth- or eighteenth-century innovation, replacing an older, more egalitarian system of decision-making. In Sweden, the maritime code of

---

[33]Lybeck, "Sjöfolket," 542. I have made similar observations concerning Oulu and Hannu Kujala has presented comparative material from Turku in a manuscript which he kindly copied for me. Helsinki was an exception, but this is no surprise because there was substantial immigration.

1667 reflected different traditions. Fr example, corporal punishment was practically unknown and most offences were punished by fines. The master, however, was allowed to hit ("fillip") a man "by hand or by cane" without being fined, but only once: if hit again, the man in question was entitled to defend himself.[34] Although the code reflected legislative ideals rather than sailors' realities, it seems reasonable to expect that corporal punishments and the use of rope and cane in everyday labour management were rare before the 1660s. It may also be that the change was brought about by naval and European examples.

It seems that such a change took place fairly late in Finland. Turku, which was then the leading seaport, began to make the shift in the 1730s, when the crews of three long-distance traders – three of only five owned in the town – mutinied against their masters, claiming that they were being treated harshly and despotically. This seems to indicate that the men were still used to a different working environment. On the other hand, it is unclear that there was a total transformation. As late as the 1750s, two Turku masters had to change their plans because their crews refused to sail in conditions they regarded as too risky.[35] But such cases of sailors clinging to traditional rights were few, and they became practically nonexistent in the nineteenth century.

Since Finnish long-distance shipping was modest during the seventeenth century, there were few experienced and competent masters. Shipowners thus had to hire foreign masters and even mates to command their vessels. In the beginning, there were Dutch and Danish masters and a few former Swedish naval officers, but later men from Stockholm were more common. It was the foreign masters who introduced the new "naval" systems to Turku merchantmen. The same thing probably happened in the easternmost staple town, Hamina (Fredrikshamn), where practically all deep-sea vessels in the 1730s were Dutch-owned "ships of convenience." Even in Helsinki long-distance shipping started under the command of German and Swedish ex-naval masters. It is even probable that some direct Dutch and Low German influence reached the Ostro-

---

[34]And. Anton Stiernman, *Samling utaf Kongl. Bref, Stadgar och Förordningar...* (4 vols., Stockholm, 1747-), 12 June 1667.

[35]Olin, *Åbo sjöfarts historia*, 211-225.

bothnian seaports, but since they in effect were the hinterlands of Stockholm, this must have been the prime origin of the innovations.[36]

In yet another respect – the division of the day into watches – the working conditions of Finnish sailors closely followed Western European examples. The name of the afternoon watch, *plattfoten*, suggests that even here the Dutch were of primary influence. Still, in the 1830s and 1840s Finnish deep-sea sailors did not enjoy free watches during the daytime: with the exception of Sundays, all the crew was kept at work at least from noon to eight p.m. (or to the "first watch," according to Dutch terms), and sometimes for even longer. A similar system was described by Dana, who sailed on the brig *Pilgrim* in the 1840s. In the 1860s it was more common for crews to work together for only two hours, the watches having a six-hour "long watch" on alternating days. Such a system also took care of the "dogging" of watches. It was only around 1900 that the "modern" standard system with five four-hour and two two-hour dog watches became the rule.[37]

When discussing the watch system, it is important to understand that the work did not consist solely of "sailing;" men were kept busy as well at routine maintenance, which was carried on all through the voyage. A ship was indeed, as Dana wrote, like "a lady's watch," requiring constant repair. This kind of work was normally done during the day only, while during the night the men on watch were only expected to "sail" the ship. As late as in the 1930s, the common practice aboard Finnish ships was that the watches "worked" – that is, did maintenance – from six a.m. to six p.m.[38]

The development of watches directly affected the total working time. According to the late nineteenth-century system, one watch remained on deck for sixteen hours every other day, and average working time amounted to twenty-eight hours every two days. Earlier,

---

[36]Yrjö Kaukiainen, "Five Years before the Mast: Observations on the Conditions of Maritime Labour in Finland and Elsewhere," in Lewis R. Fischer and Walter Minchinton (eds.), *People of the Northern Seas* (St. John's, 1992).

[37]Engström, *Åbo sjöfarts historia*, 186-187; R.H. Dana, *Two Years before the Mast* (Harmondsworth, 1981), 52-53; Albin Stjerncreutz, *Suomalainen Meri-sanakirja* (1863; reprint, Uusikaupunki, 1982), 407-408; and Lauri Pyy, "Merimieselämää Raahessa ja raahelaisella laivalla vv. 1855-1875," *Kyläkirjaston Kuvalehti*, VIII (1914).

[38]See Eric Newby, *The Last Grain Race* (London, 1990), 76.

working time may have been even longer, and it was only around the turn of the century – weather permitting – that men were allowed to stay below for twelve hours a day.

In ports, the working system was different because no sea-watches were needed (although a few men normally had to stand night-watches). All the men started work at six a.m. and continued until supper, or six p.m. – on Saturdays, working times were shorter. At the end of the nineteenth century, this resulted in a longer working day than what was common among stevedores in big European ports.[39] Even after six o'clock, the men were not necessarily free to do what they wanted – at least they were not allowed to go ashore unless they were given explicit permission. In this respect practices seem to have varied in different times and across different nationalities – unfortunately, this is a fairly little known aspect of maritime life.[40] As an example, it seems that in the 1870s and 1880s Finnish sailors were normally given shore leave only every second or third Sunday, depending on the time the vessel stayed in port.[41] This feature closely resembles the working conditions of American sailors in the 1830s, as recorded by Dana.

In terms of wages, working conditions of Finnish sailors differed remarkably from general standards. Not surprisingly, considering the peripheral position of the country and its relative abundance of labour, Finnish shipowners were able to hire crews for much less than their West European colleagues. In the late nineteenth century, wages of able-bodied seamen in Finland were on average only about two-thirds of British and one-half of North American levels (see table 6).

---

[39]In a newspaper article in 1864, an old Finnish sailor described the work day as follows: "Both before and after the hours of loading or unloading, as long as there is any daylight, are we required to do ship's maintenance work, which never occurs on foreign vessels." Oscar Nikula, *Åbo sjöfarts historia* (Åbo, 1930), II, 176.

[40]Compare, for example, the descriptions of Dana, *Two Years before the Mast*, and Herman Melville, in *Redburn* (1849).

[41]The conclusion has been drawn from a fairly limited number of logs and crew accounts. Such sources only seldom tell anything about shore liberties but some idea can be formed by seeing how often men were given "pocket-money" to spend ashore (normally, the balance of the wage was only paid at home when the voyage was completed).

**Table 6**
**Average Wages for Able-Bodied Seamen (*Matroser*) in Finland and Selected Other Countries (Pounds Sterling per Month)**

| | 1860s | 1870s | 1880s |
|---|---|---|---|
| Finland | 1.7 | 2.3 | 2.2 |
| Norway | 1.8 | 1.9 | 2.3 |
| England | 3.1 | 3.2 | 2.9 |
| British North America | 6.0 | 5.4 | 5.2 |
| Europe, average | 2.8 | 3.1 | 2.9 |

*Source*: Kaukiainen, *Sailing into Twilight*, table 2.30.

Unfortunately, there are no comparable data for earlier periods, but the basic pattern must have been similar. Neither is it possible to present a reliable picture of the development of wages in the long run. The scanty material which can be found in the existing literature suggests a substantial increase – about one-quarter – in real wages between the middle of the eighteenth century and the second quarter of the nineteenth, and a new and relatively rapid growth – at least forty percent in two decades – from 1850 to the mid-1870s. These changes, however, were roughly similar to general "landward" developments in Finland.[42]

## Conclusion

It can be said that at least during the nineteenth century, the Finnish maritime labour market was integrated with the international, or North Atlantic, maritime world. The integration did not imply similar wage-levels; in this respect the labour markets were still more local. Even in terms of mobility, the integration was far from complete, but it must be remembered that the integration of labour markets has never been comparable to that of commodity markets.

---

[42]See, for example, Engström, *Åbo sjöfarts historia*, 171; Olin, *Åbo sjöfarts historia*, 209-210; Kaukiainen, *Sailing into Twilight*, 111-113; Sakari Heikkinen, *et al.*, "Förändringar i levnadstandarden i Finland 1750-1913," in G. Karlsson (ed.), *Levestandarden i Norden 1750-1914* (Reykjavík, 1987), 68-71.

On the other hand, as far as labour conditions and shipboard management were concerned, Finnish ships closely followed Western European examples, sharing the main components of a common maritime culture. This was not surprising, since there were practically no older traditions of blue water navigation before the eighteenth century; instead, they were imported by foreign shipmasters. But this only concerns long-distance shipping. The traditions of management and labour control were quite different aboard small coastal craft, the crews of which often consisted of family members or neighbours. On such craft, labour and wage conditions resembled more closely those of traditional agriculture than modern wage labour.

# Danish Sailors, 1570-1870

Hans Chr. Johansen

Over the 300 years covered by this survey, the Danish realm went from being a major power in the northern Europe to a new status as one of the smallest countries in Europe. In the late sixteenth century the Danish king ruled present-day Denmark, Norway, southern and western Sweden, Germany north of Hamburg and Lübeck, and the islands in the northern Atlantic – Greenland, Iceland, and the Faroes. A series of political disasters led to the loss of the Swedish provinces in the mid-seventeenth century, Norway in 1814, and the German provinces in 1864.

These changes had a deep impact on Danish maritime history and in some cases make it difficult to analyze long-run tendencies, especially when dealing with the navy, which always has had its main base in Copenhagen despite having to protect the whole realm; its tasks in the early period obviously differed decisively from those of the nineteenth century. Moreover, the maritime traditions of the various provinces have been very different: some have a coastal population, while others have almost no connection to the sea.

To get as homogeneous an area as possible for the entire period, we will deal only with Denmark proper, i.e., the area north of the Kongeå, which was Danish after 1864. This gives a natural delimitation as far as the merchant marine and the fishing fleet are concerned, whereas there is a break regarding the navy in 1813, because the loss of Norway meant that it was reduced to a much smaller size.

## Danish Maritime History: A Research Review

The only comprehensive Danish maritime history which also covers deep-sea fishing and whaling was published in 1919.[1] It was rather heterogeneous with regard to topics treated: while some chapters were based on new research, others were more popular and impressionistic.

[1]Bering Liisberg (ed.), *Danmarks søfart og søhandel fra de ældste tider til vore dage* (2 vols., Copenhagen, 1919).

The main emphasis was on maritime trades, but some chapters dealt with ship construction, navigation, lights and buoys services, and marine insurance. The labour market for sailors, their lives at sea, and their careers were on the other hand only treated cursorily.

Later books dealing with longer periods of Danish maritime history are mainly short surveys and do not add much to our understanding of shipping, trades, or recruitment of crews.[2] At present, however, funding has been secured to write a seven-volume Danish maritime history based on new research. Publication is planned for 1996-1998. The project covers both ships, trades, maritime economics, and the lives of the sailors, but so far no results are available for the sixteenth to nineteenth centuries.

The literature on shorter periods is much more valuable, especially for the eighteenth century. The merchant navies of the provincial maritime communities from 1700 to 1864 have been analyzed by Anders Monrad Møller. The chartered companies – primarily the Asiatic Company – have been studied by Aage Rasch, P.P. Sveistrup and Erik Gøbel. The importance of the merchant marine for Danish neutrality during the great European wars has been stressed by Ole Feldbæk, and there are also biographies of the most important eighteenth-century shipowners. For earlier periods, the sources for late seventeenth-century maritime history have been examined by Jørgen Barfod and the early years of whaling have been analyzed by Sune Dalgård.[3]

In general the central themes in these contributions, and in a large number of shorter articles, are routes and cargoes, types of ships, and political aspects of Danish participation in international shipping; the sailors and their lives have been allotted little room. Danish naval history

---

[2]C. Rise Hansen (ed.), *Den danske skibsfart gennem tiderne* (Copenhagen, 1941); Knud Klem, *De danskes vej, rids af dansk søhistorie* (Copenhagen, 1941); and L.E. Grandjean and Ernst Mentze (eds.), *Danmark og havet* (2 vols., Copenhagen, 1946).

[3]Anders Monrad Møller, *Fra galeoth til galease* (Esbjerg, 1981); Møller, *Jagt og skonnert* (Copenhagen, 1988); Aage Rasch and P.P. Sveistrup, *Asiatisk Kompagni 1772-92* (Copenhagen, 1948); Rasch, *Niels Ryberg 1725-1804* (Århus, 1964); Erik Gøbel, "Danske oversøiske handelskompagnier i det 17. og 18. århundrede," *Fortid og Nutid* (1980), 533-569; Ole Feldbæk, *India Trade under the Danish Flag 1772-1808* (Odense, 1969); Feldbæk, *Dansk neutralitetspolitik under krigen 1778-1783* (Copenhagen, 1971); J. Werner, *En dansk storkøbmand* (Copenhagen, 1927); Jørgen H.P. Barfod, *Danmark-Norges handelsflåde 1650-1700* (Elsinore, 1967); and Sune Dalgård, *Dansk-Norsk Hvalfangst 1615-1660* (Copenhagen, 1962).

has mainly concentrated on strategic aspects and naval campaigns, but some of the major histories of the navy also provide lists of ships, their armour and officers, size of the crews, and enlistment systems for conscripted personnel.[4]

**Ships and Crew Sizes**

The number of vessels in the merchant marine, deep-sea fishery and whaling is not known until sometime in the seventeenth century, but the number of Danish ships registered in the Sound when passing Elsinore increased sharply from the late 1560s. Although this mainly reflects voyages from Copenhagen and Elsinore, there are also other indicators, such as the number of Danish ships calling at Amsterdam, which seem to point at an increase. Most of the vessels, however, were rather small, and the majority seem to have been coasters.

From the mid-seventeenth century we have more detailed data about the number of ships and their tonnage, although the earlier figures most likely have some deficiencies due to missing ports in some years. There were also varying practices with regard to the lower limit of sizes included in the statistics. A sample of these figures is shown in table 1, which underscores the position of Copenhagen as the largest seafaring community from at least the mid-seventeenth century.

The general picture is of long-term growth, but there were some serious setbacks, mainly due to wars. The first occurred in 1657-1660, when Denmark suffered a decisive defeat in two consecutive wars with Sweden and only secured its future existence through assistance from the Dutch navy when Copenhagen was under siege. A second, equally serious conflict, was the Great Northern War (1700-1721). During the remainder of the eighteenth century Denmark was neutral in the great European wars; this fact, combined with an active maritime policy and the general expansion of the world economy, provided the context for the growth of the merchant marine, especially in the second half of the century.

[4]H.G. Garde, *Efterretninger om den danske og norske sømagt* (4 vols., Copenhagen, 1832); R. Steen Steensen (ed.), *Flåden gennem 450 år* (Copenhagen, 1970); and Halfdan Barfoed, *Vor flåde i fortid og nutid* (2 vols., Copenhagen, 1941).

**Table 1**
**Danish Merchant Marine, 1639-1871**

| Year | Copenhagen | | Provincial Towns | | Denmark | |
|---|---|---|---|---|---|---|
| | No. of ships | 1000 kml. | No. of ships | 1000 kml. | No. of ships | 1000 kml. |
| 1639 | 135 | 6 | 484 | 15 | 619 | 21 |
| 1656 | | 8 | | 7 | | 15 |
| 1670 | | | | | 772 | 8 |
| 1680 | | 3 | | 5 | 615 | 8 |
| 1688 | | | | | 828 | 12 |
| 1696 | | | | | 1249 | 24 |
| 1699 | | 10 | | 7 | 1005 | 17 |
| 1746 | 116 | 5 | 469 | 6 | 585 | 11 |
| 1777 | 182 | 10 | 623 | 7 | 805 | 17 |
| 1787 | 331 | 26 | 681 | 9 | 1012 | 35 |
| 1807 | | 29 | | 16 | | 45 |
| 1832 | 302 | 16 | 1324 | 16 | 1626 | 32 |
| 1847 | 280 | 15 | 1636 | 27 | 1916 | 42 |
| 1860 | 336 | 21 | 2434 | 48 | 2770 | 69 |
| 1871 | 370 | 49 | 2735 | 182 | 3105 | 231 |

*Note*: Until 1867 Danish ships were measured in commercial lasts (kml.), in principle equal to Dutch lasts, although there were frequent changes in the method of computation, which means that tonnages are not completely compatible. From 1868 tonnage was measured in net register tons; one last was equal to about two tons. See Anders Monrad Møller, "Skibsmålingen i Danmark 1632-1867," *Handels- og Søfartsmuseets Årbog* (1974), 16-47. The 1871 data are thus in net register tonnages.

*Sources*: Ole Degn, unpublished material; Jørgen H.P. Barfod, *Danmark-Norges handelsflåde 1650-1700* (Elsinore, 1967); Anders Monrad Møller, *Fra galeoth til galease* (Esbjerg, 1981); Møller, *Jagt og skonnert* (Copenhagen, 1988); and Danish official statistics.

It was not until 1807 that the kingdom became embroiled in the Revolutionary and Napoleonic wars – on the French side – and had many ships seized by the British navy. The nineteenth century – after 1814 – was characterized at first by slow growth, but after the mid-1820s it became rather steady.

In order to get a more detailed impression of the merchant marine and the size of the seafaring population, three years have been selected for a more thorough examination. The first is 1676, chosen because there are registration lists for all customs districts for this or a proximate year.[5] Total Danish tonnage in that year was close to 10,000 lasts, half of which used Copenhagen as a home port. The second largest district was Aarhus, but its tonnage was only about one-tenth that of Copenhagen. In most provincial ports there were only boats and small craft for coastal traffic, local fisheries, or ferries between the numerous islands and to and from Jutland. Only nineteen districts out of forty-nine had any vessels of twenty lasts or above, and the ten of 100 lasts or more were all from Copenhagen. Several of the largest vessels had been built as so-called "defence ships," constructed so that they could easily be converted into naval vessels; shipowners were obliged to place them at the navy's disposal in case of war. The types of rig are not known for all craft, but among the larger ones were *galiots*, *caryers* and *skibe*.

The men in the merchant service totalled about 6500 in 1696, when the tonnage was 24,000 lasts, or on average 3.7 lasts per man.[6] The smallest craft had crews of two to four men and the largest six to twelve, which means that there were economies of scale, but the information is too scattered to allow more detailed calculations.

From the late eighteenth century, 1787 has been selected for an analysis in order to exploit the database created at the University of Odense which contains for all Danish ships information about size and crew, type of ship, and the voyages in 1787 – as far as the several sources used provide this information.

The size and geographic distribution are shown in table 2. Total tonnage was now 46,000 lasts, of which almost three-fourths was owned by Copenhagen shipowners, among them several chartered companies, the largest being the Baltic and Guinean Company, with thirty-eight ships and a tonnage of 4300 lasts. But the most famous was the East Asiatic Company (Asiatisk Kompagni) established in 1732. It owned ten ships with a total tonnage of 3400 lasts, including the Danish fleet's largest vessels. The total tonnage of the various companies was about 13,000 lasts, or nearly one-third of the entire merchant marine. Moreover, nearly all the other large vessels were owned in the capital. The only craft with a tonnage above 100 lasts in the provinces was a 109-last frigate from Svendborg.

---

[5]See the appendix tables in Barfod, *Danmark-Norges handelsflade*.

[6]*Ibid.*, 139.

Close to twenty different types of vessels were mentioned in the registration lists. Among those of 100 lasts or more the dominant type was the frigate, but there was also a significant group called "ships." From fifty to 100 lasts most were brigs, but there were also many snows and brigantines. Among the smaller vessels from twenty to fifty lasts the *galeas* (ketch) was most common, followed by hookers and brigs, and in the smallest category there were many sloops (*jagter*) and some barges (*chalupper*).

The registration lists and some other sources also mention the size of the crew, but the practice differed dramatically from one source to another. In some cases, for example, masters and mates were excluded, and general muster rolls, such as those used in a later section, suggest that crews were slightly larger than would be judged from the registration lists. According to the latter, the total number of seamen, which includes those in whaling and the deep-sea fishery, was close to 7000; when masters and mates are included, there were probably between 7500 and 8000. This is about six lasts per man, which is a significant decline in crew size compared to the late seventeenth century. This average, however, masks some substantial differences between various voyage patterns. For ordinary merchantmen in European waters and in direct traffic with the West Indian colonies, the average was about nine lasts per man, slightly higher for the smallest craft and down to seven to eight lasts per man for ships above about 140 lasts. Surprisingly, there were no economies of scale in this type of manning.

**Table 2**
**Danish Merchant Navy, 1787 (Ships of 5 lasts or more)**

| Home Port | 5-19 Lasts | | 20-49 Lasts | | 50-99 Lasts | | 100 Lasts and Over | |
|---|---|---|---|---|---|---|---|---|
| | No. of ships | 1000 kml. | No. of ships | 1000 kml. | No. of ships | 1000 kml. | No. of ships | 1000 kml. |
| Copenhagen | 34 | 0.4 | 161 | 5.8 | 115 | 8.2 | 128 | 19.3 |
| Provinces, | 552 | 6.5 | 182 | 5.0 | 14 | 0.9 | 1 | 0.1 |
| Of which: | | | | | | | | |
| Dragør | 17 | 0.3 | 67 | 1.8 | 1 | 0.1 | - | - |
| Aalborg | 33 | 0.4 | 23 | 0.6 | 3 | 0.2 | - | - |

*Sources*: University of Odense, Database. See also Hans Chr. Johansen, "Scandinavian Shipping in the Late Eighteenth Century in a European Perspective," *Economic History Review*, XLV (1992), 479-493.

But there were some important deviations from this general pattern. The vessels used for whaling, seal hunting and fishing in Arctic waters had much larger crews: on average, they were about 100 lasts and carried about thirty-nine men, which gives 2.6 lasts per man. Many of the sailors were probably used not seafarers but fishermen or hunters. Ships in the East Indian, Chinese and West African/West Indian trades also had larger crews than normal: two to four lasts per man. The larger crews were most likely due to defence requirements.

The third year selected is 1871, the earliest year for which detailed lists of all ships exist in printed form. Table 3 shows that Copenhagen still was the dominant home for the merchant marine, with more than one-fourth of total tonnage. As well, most of the biggest shipowners lived in the capital, among them the first steamship companies, which over the next few decades would dominate Danish shipping in most trades.

**Table 3**
**The Danish Merchant Navy 1871 (Ships of 4 net register tons or more)**

| Home port | 4-49 nrt. | | 50-99 nrt. | | 102-299 nrt. | | 300 nrt. and Over | |
|---|---|---|---|---|---|---|---|---|
| | No. of ships | 1000 nrt. | No. of ships | 1000 nrt. | No. of ships | 1000 nrt. | No. of ships | 1000 nrt. |
| Copenhagen | 133 | 2.2 | 68 | 5.0 | 143 | 26.4 | 36 | 15.9 |
| Provinces of which | 1513 | 26.4 | 384 | 29.0 | 427 | 63.2 | 31 | 13.4 |
| Svendborg | 103 | 2.0 | 43 | 3.2 | 62 | 9.3 | 4 | 1.4 |
| Marstal | 176 | 4.3 | 57 | 4.2 | 18 | 2.7 | - | - |
| Fanø | 44 | 0.7 | 48 | 3.7 | 66 | 9.6 | 1 | 0.3 |

*Source*: Denmark, *Statistisk Tabelværk*.

The first Danish steamer was bought in Scotland in 1819, but for a long time such vessels were used only for coastal passenger traffic. In 1871 there were still only ninety-one steamships in the merchant marine, comprising less ten percent of total tonnage. The largest steamship owner was the United Steamship Company (DFDS), established in 1866 through a merger of several smaller firms. DFDS took over most of the regular shipping routes in the coastal traffic and on routes to and from other north European countries. Many of these steamers were combined passenger and freight vessels. Most sailing vessels were under 200 tons.

There were more than twenty different types, but most over two hundred tons were barques, while under that threshold brigs, schooners, and sloops predominated.

While the published registration lists from 1871 give no indication of the size of crews, an estimate of total manning of the 2735 vessels in table 3 can be made from samples in the *mønstringsruller* used later in this essay. If they are representative of the total merchant marine, the crew requirement must have been about 10,000 men or about nine lasts per man, which is almost the same as 100 years earlier in the general freight trade. But there probably was a small decline in crews per last for sailing vessels, since steamers carried larger than average crews because of the engineers and stokers needed for the engines.

By 1871 the fishery was in many places an independent trade, but only fishermen in larger vessels are included in the figures above. The 1870 census had a group called "living from the sea;" in this category were 14,140 persons, probably including a few thousand fishermen, some pilots and other minor groups.

In order to evaluate the importance of the sea for the Danish population over the three hundred years covered in this survey, we must also include the personnel on warships. The navy is normally regarded as having its origin in 1509, when the first ships exclusively for naval purposes were built. By the late sixteenth century there were twenty-two ships equipped with 624 guns, but a major expansion occurred under King Christian IV (1588-1648), when the navy reached a strength of nearly sixty ships and 4000-5000 men. In 1615 the *Holmens faste stok*, a permanent corps used as sailors on naval ships and workers in the naval shipyard in Copenhagen, was established. In the beginning the corps comprised about 1500 men, but grew gradually. The rest of the crews were conscripted from various regions of the realm, probably from among sailors in the merchant marine.

From 1648 to 1807 the most important naval vessels were ships-of-the-line and frigates. Table 4 shows for some sample years the size of the navy and its crew. The figures, however, seldom depict the effective force at sea. Even in wartime only part of the navy was fitted out for operations, and in the long peace between 1720 and 1807, the larger vessels would sail at periodic intervals as guard ships in coastal waters, to convoy the merchant marine in European wars, or to train young cadets. The ship-of-the-line *Delmenhorst*, for example, which belonged to the navy from 1735 to 1777, sailed in only nine years, and even then the sailing season spanned only a few months. There were only two longer voyages: to Algiers in 1746 and Lisbon in 1759-1760. The result of this practice was that the *Holmens faste stok*, which grew to about 7000 men in the late eighteenth century, was able to man most ships. Conscription took place solely in a few special years and only involved 1000 or perhaps 2000 men out of the 17,000 which in principle could be drafted. About 6000 were from Denmark proper, a significant proportion of the total manning of the merchant marine.

**Table 4**
**The Larger Ships of the Danish Navy, 1674-1807**

| Year | Ships-of-the-Line | Frigates | Guns | Total Crew Size (000 men) |
|---|---|---|---|---|
| 1674 | 21 | 12 | 1662 | 9 |
| 1700 | 33 | 9 | 2778 | 17 |
| 1709 | 41 | 11 | 3008 | 21 |
| 1720 | 24 | 12 | 2172 | 15 |
| 1746 | 29 | 13 | 2580 | 19 |
| 1780 | 33 | 18 | 2602 | 23 |
| 1807 | 20 | 17 | 1972 | 19 |

*Sources*: Anders Monrad Møller, "Måneden drejer – om søfolk til den københavnske handelsflåde 1777-87," in *Oderint, dum metuant* (Copenhagen, 1992), 21-26; and Erik Gøbel, "Asiatisk Kompagnis kinafart 1732-1833" (Unpublished monograph, 1978), 105-107.

After the British attack on Copenhagen in 1807, most of the navy was conquered and incorporated into the Royal Navy, and with the loss of Norway there was no need for a naval force of the same size. The plans for reconstruction therefore included only six ships-of-the-line, eight frigates and eight corvettes with a force of about 7000 men. At the same time the permanent *stok* was reduced to about 3000. Even this more modest goal was not achieved until about 1840 and there was little active sailing in the interim. In the 1840s the first naval steamships were built. By 1871 the navy had thirty-three ships, including eight armoured vessels, one ship-of-the-line, four frigates and three corvettes, all propelled by steam.

Based on the information in this section it is possible to make a rough estimate of the total number of Danes who earned their living from the sea. In order to avoid double-counting we must take into consideration that most naval conscripts came from the merchant marine. Bearing this in mind, it seems most likely that about 10,000 Danes derived their livelihoods directly from the sea in the seventeenth century, increasing to about 15,000 in the late eighteenth century, and perhaps to a few more in the nineteenth century. Compared to the number of males between fifteen and sixty-four, this represents between two and four percent of the labour force. While the direct effect on employment has been marginal, there have been important linkages to commerce, shipbuilding, and other branches of manufacturing.

## Voyage Patterns of the Merchant Marine

Most late sixteenth-century Danish merchant ships were small and used in coastal traffic. According to the Sound Toll lists, however, there were also voyages to northern Germany and Norway, and the larger towns had some connections with the Netherlands. Seldom were more distant places visited, and most voyages to the North Atlantic islands seem in this early period to have been made by Norwegians, especially from Bergen.

By the late seventeenth century this pattern had changed, but the shift almost exclusively involved Copenhagen. Most voyages by provincial craft were limited to the Baltic, Norway and the North Sea close to Denmark. Only on rare occasions did a Danish vessel visit more remote ports. But for Copenhagen the situation was different. There was now a significant traffic to and from the North Atlantic Islands. Some Copenhagen vessels annually called at French and Portuguese ports, and there were occasional overseas voyages to the first Danish colonies and trading posts in Asia, the Guinea coast, and the West Indian island of St. Thomas, which was acquired in 1672.

This difference became even more marked in the second half of the eighteenth century, by which time there are better sources for voyage patterns. The relatively small provincial ships were still engaged in coastal voyages, the important Danish-Norwegian trade, and trips to the nearest Baltic ports. As well, the maritime communities along the North Sea coast continued an earlier tradition of regular connections to Hamburg and Amsterdam. Most local traffic was engaged in supplying the capital with foodstuffs and firewood. In the Danish-Norwegian trade, Denmark exported rye, barley, malt and meat, and imported timber, iron and fish. Between 1733 and 1788 there were special privileges that discriminated against foreign imports. From the Baltic came flax and hemp, and in years of poor domestic harvests, rye and wheat as well.

The smallest Copenhagen vessels followed the same pattern as the provincial craft, but from the 1740s an active policy to promote the construction of larger ships and to gain access to new markets began to cause change. Among the measures adopted were a 1742 ordinance which required imports to be shipped directly from the country of origin; treaties with the North African states to curb the actions of corsairs; the founding of new colonies; the establishment of a net of consuls in southern European ports; and the paying of premiums for whaling and deep-sea fishing off the coasts of Iceland and Greenland. The neutrality policy between 1720 and 1807 also conferred a number of benefits. These opportunities were exploited by Copenhagen merchants and state-subsidized chartered companies (see table 5).

**Table 5**
**Destination of Voyages for Copenhagen Ships, 1787**

| Destination of Voyages | 5-49 lasts | | 50+ lasts | |
|---|---|---|---|---|
| | No. of Ships | 1000 Lasts | No. of Ships | 1000 Lasts |
| Denmark and the Duchies | 55 | 1.4 | 5 | 0.4 |
| Norway | 23 | 0.7 | 4 | 0.3 |
| Baltic Ports | 37 | 1.1 | 10 | 2.0 |
| North Sea Ports | 12 | 0.4 | 1 | 0.1 |
| France and the Mediterranean | 22 | 0.8 | 43 | 4.0 |
| North Atlantic | 49 | 1.9 | 46 | 3.8 |
| West Indies | 3 | 0.1 | 62 | 7.4 |
| Far East | - | - | 26 | 6.3 |
| Laid-up | 19 | 0.7 | 57 | 5.7 |

*Note*: Ships used on more than one route are included on the route on which it sailed the most during the year.

*Source*: University of Odense, Database.

Most important was the navigation to the three Danish islands in the West Indies, which sent sugar to refineries in the mother country that was partly re-exported to the Baltic. The Asiatic Company had a monopoly on Danish trade with China, but from 1772 the India trade was open to other Danish shipowners. Voyages to the Mediterranean were part of a larger pattern: vessels would normally go to a port in the Baltic in late summer for cargoes of flax, timber or grain, which were carried to France, Portugal or Spain, where the ships would spend the winter sailing between Lisbon and the Mediterranean, returning to Denmark in the spring with salt, fruit or wine.[7] During European wars the pattern was dominated by long-distance voyages.

But North Atlantic and Arctic waters were also important. There were supplies to be sent to the Faroes, Iceland and Greenland, and return cargoes from these areas, but there were also fishing, sealing and whaling. The first expedition to Spitsbergen for whales was made in 1615, but for most of the seventeenth century the annual number of ships averaged fewer than five. In the late eighteenth century this trade grew in importance. Twenty-nine vessels returned to Copenhagen in 1787 with blubber, but only seventeen had sufficient crews to have caught the whales themselves; the remainder probably picked up cargoes at a shore-based whaling station in Greenland. For Copenhagen whalers the normal pattern was to leave Denmark in March and return in August.

During the nineteenth century, provincial craft extended their activities and the differences between provincial and Copenhagen sailing vessels narrowed. While grain transports to Britain and trade with northern Europe remained its backbone, consular reports also mention many calls in South America, primarily at Rio de Janeiro and Buenos Aires, and East Asia, where Hong Kong was the most visited port. The West Indies, on the other hand, were of lesser importance, although Denmark retained the Virgin Islands until 1917.

## Who Were the Sailors?

Lists with personal details about crews in the merchant navy do not exist for large numbers of vessels until the eighteenth century, but the scattered evidence from earlier periods indicates that the small craft in the Baltic and North Sea used men recruited mainly from areas near their home ports. Only Copenhagen vessels needed a somewhat larger recruitment area, and in the seventeenth century several Dutch masters gained burghership in the capital. This pattern continued into the eighteenth century. Most shipowners lived in towns and the seamen were

---

[7]Hans Chr. Johansen, "Danish Shipping Services as a Link between the Mediterranean and the Baltic 1750-1850," in Lewis R. Fischer and Helge W. Nordvik (eds.), *Shipping and Trade 1750-1950: Essays in International Maritime Economic History* (Pontefract, 1990), 15-24.

drawn from the town itself and the neighbouring rural parishes. In some cases they were related to the shipowner or master.

But in those areas where there were many vessels, the local population was often too small and recruitment took place over a wider zone. In 1798 some ships from Dragør, close to Copenhagen, recruited more than half their sailors from nearby southern Sweden, and a few other foreigners can also be found on these vessels. In Elsinore there were examples of larger ships with sailors from Memel and other Baltic ports. The masters and mates on provincial craft, on the other hand, nearly always came from the home port.[8] It should be noted, however, that 1798 was a year of European wars and the neutral Danish fleet was in particular demand. In peacetime, the need for foreigners was almost certainly smaller.

For Copenhagen ships we have lists with information on crews in the late eighteenth century. When a ship cleared the capital it had to be registered by the *waterschout*, an officer of the conscription system. His ledgers contain the name, position on board, and normally also the birthplace, age, and wage for each crew member.

**Table 6**
**Birthplaces of Crew on a Sample of Copenhagen Ships, 1787**

| Birthplace | Masters | Mates | Others | Total |
|---|---|---|---|---|
| Copenhagen | 19 | 16 | 37 | 72 |
| Rest of Denmark | 1 | 6 | 65 | 72 |
| Norway | 1 | - | 30 | 31 |
| Duchies | - | 2 | 20 | 22 |
| From the navy | - | 1 | 7 | 8 |
| Abroad | - | - | 4 b) | 4 |

*Notes*: Sailors belonging to the navy could, especially in peacetime, get special permission to join the merchant marine to obtain practical training. Two of the "others" from abroad were from Sweden and one from Danzig; there was also "a negro."

*Source*: Provincial Archives, Copenhagen, *Waterschoutens* Arkiv, 1787.

For 1787 a ten-percent sample of these lists has been analyzed. The distribution of birthplaces is shown in table 6. Danes dominated,

[8]Møller, *Fra galeoth*, 166-167.

with about one-third from Copenhagen and another third from the provinces – a large proportion came from the island of Bornholm in the Baltic. Only a few were foreigners. The same is true if we look at ships going to the West Indies or Asia. Only in war years, when such voyages increased dramatically, was there a need to recruit foreigners, most of whom came from Sweden and various German ports.[9]

The names of the seamen might be another indication of nationality. There is a significant proportion with Dutch names, such as Jacob Roelofs, Dreves Jansen, Adrian Dirks and Jan Jansen Theis, but it is most likely that they were descendants of earlier immigrants. In 1521 a group of Dutch farmers from Marken moved to Store Magleby, about five miles southeast of Copenhagen, to grow vegetables. Population growth was rapid and several families later settled in nearby Dragør, which in 1787 was the largest shipping community outside Copenhagen (see table 2). Nearly all the sailors with Dutch names seem to come from this community or Copenhagen, which also had a group of second- or third-generation Dutch immigrants. An analysis of all Danish masters in 1787 also reveals a few with British names – Thomas Price, James Wemyss, Joseph Greenway, and Alexander MacIntosh. They commanded ships going to India and may have been recruited because of specific knowledge of routes or places in that region.

The age distribution of the sailors is very special. About three-fourths were under thirty and nearly none, expect a few masters, were over forty. Even if there was a significant mortality rate, this must have meant that life at sea in a Copenhagen vessel was not a lifetime job. It must have been normal for sailors to switch to a land-based occupation some time in their thirties, unless they continued to serve on foreign or provincial ships. No investigations, however, have been conducted into the types of jobs to which they turned. It is also unknown whether the same pattern characterized the men on provincial ships.

The information in the *waterschout*'s lists about wages is rather heterogeneous. For longer voyages it is given as wages per three months, whereas for shorter ones it may have been for one or two months, but also in several cases for "half of the wages for the voyage." In those

[9]Anders Monrad Møller, "Måneden drejer – om søfolk til den københavnske handelsflåde 1777-87," in *Oderint, dum metuant* (Copenhagen, 1992), 21-26; and Erik Gøbel, "Asiatisk Kompagnis kinafart 1732-1833" (Unpublished monograph, 1978), 105-107.

cases where the wages can be converted into yearly amounts, a master received from 240 to 288 *rixdollars* – higher on ships to East India – a mate 120 to 192 *rixdollars*, an ordinary sailor sixty and a boy twenty-four to forty-eight *rixdollars*.[10] To this should be added the value of food and accommodation on board. But it must also be remembered that the sailing season for many seamen was only from March until November or December, which means that yearly income should perhaps be reduced by one-fourth. As a comparison, an unskilled worker in the towns at the time earned about fifty *rixdollars* per year and a small handicraft master perhaps 100 to 150 *rixdollars*.

In 1871 crew lists (*mønstringsruller*), containing the same type of information as the *waterschout*'s lists, were completed for all vessels leaving Danish ports, and most have survived. A sample has been selected from Copenhagen and the provincial district of Svendborg. In Svendborg local sailors dominated: about eighty-eight percent were born in the town, neighbouring parishes on the island of Funen, or on the many smaller islands south of Funen, especially Thurø and Tåsinge. Another eleven percent were from other places in Denmark, and only two sailors were foreigners, one from Halmstad in Sweden, and one from Stavanger in Norway.[11]

**Table 7**
**Birthplaces of Crew on a Sample of Copenhagen Vessels, 1871**

| Birthplace | No. of Sailors |
|---|---|
| Copenhagen | 22 |
| Rest of Denmark | 104 |
| Norway | 5 |
| Sweden | 7 |
| Schleswig | 20 |
| Other Foreign Places | 1 |

*Source*: Provincial Archives, Copenhagen, mønstringskontoret i København, skibsbemandingslister, 1871.

[10]The Danish *rixdollar* courant of the late eighteenth century had a value of approximately 0.17 British pounds.

[11]Provincial Archives, Odense, 5. udskrivningskreds arkiv, *mønstringsrulle* for Svendborg, 1871.

The Copenhagen pattern (see table 7) shows a wider recruitment area, but Danes were still by far the largest group. Most foreigners were from Schleswig, which after 1864 was Prussian, but it is most likely that they were recruited from the large Danish-speaking minority in the former duchy.

The age distribution for sailors in 1871 does not include data on masters. For other crew members it again shows a very young population. This was especially true for Svendborg, where eighty percent were below thirty years of age and only two percent were forty or above. Many in this region began a career at sea immediately after their confirmation, normally when they were fourteen or fifteen. Some seem to have switched to Copenhagen or foreign ships later in their lives, but many who survived the first ten or fifteen years at sea must have found jobs ashore. It is perhaps also significant that the few older sailors on Svendborg craft all served on the small steam ferries that connected the town with the nearby islands. Copenhagen sailors were on average older. While the twenty to twenty-nine-year age group still provided forty percent of the crew, excluding masters, about twenty percent were forty years or older. The latter group was concentrated on the few steamers in the sample.

In 1871 there was almost no difference in wages paid to Copenhagen or provincial sailors. The *mønstringsruller* normally reported weekly amounts. Converted into annual figures, this showed that mates earned 300-360 *rixdollars*; able seamen were paid 216-252 *rixdollars*; and younger crew were given 144-216 *rixdollars*.[12] For comparison, workers in Copenhagen earned about 400 *rixdollars* a year, but they of course had to pay for their own food and accommodation, which consumed a substantial part of their budget. On the larger vessels, the sailing season was now longer than a century earlier.

When the first whalers were fitted out in the sixteenth century, the lack of experienced Danes led to the employment of both Dutch and Basque specialists. Their numbers decreased over time, but even in the eighteenth century there were crew whose surnames may have been Dutch. There was also a trend toward hiring Danes, especially from the North Sea island of Rømø, which geographically was south of the 1864 border but was formerly a Danish enclave in the Duchies. In the eighteenth century some whalers were fitted out on this island, and many

---

[12]The convertible *bankrixdollar*, used until 1874, had a value of 0.11 British pounds.

local seamen were recruited as "commanders" of Dutch and Hamburg whalers.

As far as the navy is concerned, there was a permanent group of officers, as well as sailors and conscripts. The latter were especially prominent in wartime and were recruited principally from the coastal regions of Denmark, Schleswig and Norway, or from those who were merchant mariners in peacetime. The ordinary sailors among ***Holmens faste stok*** were predominantly of Danish or Norwegian origin, and since it was common for sons to follow in their fathers' footsteps, an increasing number of this segment of the crew was born in Copenhagen, even if the earlier generation had migrated to the capital from Norway. In an early period, primarily during the Great Northern War, there were also examples of recruitment abroad, mainly in Germany, but the exact number of foreigners among the naval seamen is unknown.

**Table 8**
**Birthplaces of a Ten-Percent Sample of Danish Naval Officers (Percent)**

| Birthplace | Before 1680 | Birth Year 1680-1780 | 1781-1850 |
|---|---|---|---|
| Denmark | 19 | 82 | 92 |
| Norway | 19 | 8 | - |
| Schleswig-Holstein | 6 | 8 | 5 |
| Netherlands | 3 | 1 | - |
| Other Foreign Places | 8 | 1 | 3 |
| Unknown, but Danish-Norwegian Name | 31 | - | - |
| Other Unknown | 14 | - | - |
| Total | 100 | 100 | 100 |

*Source*: Th. A. Topsøe-Jensen and Emil Marquard, *Officerer i den dansk-norske søetat 1660-1814 og den danske søetat 1814-1932* (2 vols., Copenhagen, 1935).

We have better knowledge of the origins of the officers because of published biographies. Based on a ten-percent sample from these (see table 8), we can see that in the early period of Danish naval history there was some recruitment abroad, especially in the Netherlands. But by the eighteenth century it was a national navy, a fact also stressed by contemporaries. One symptom of this was that while the langauge of command in the army remained German for quite a long time, the navy always used Danish.

## Danish Sailors on Foreign Vessels

There are no sources that allow us to estimate at any time the total number of Danes sailing on foreign craft. Instead, we must limit ourselves to fragmentary evidence which on occasion can provide some hints about tendencies, about the foreign merchant marines which used Danish manpower, and about the destinies of these migrants.

As long as the large Danish realm existed, and despite the existence of local recruitment districts, there were always some seamen who joined vessels belonging to other parts of the kingdom. Danes in this way became sailors on Norwegian and Schleswig-Holstein ships. There were close relations between Odense in Denmark and Bergen in Norway in the late eighteenth century, characterized both by common ownership of vessels and sailors who moved from one town to the other.[13] Over shorter distances there were also close ties between northern Jutland and southern Norway; between the island of Ærø in the Duchies and neighbouring south Funen; and between south Jutland and some of the important shipping communities in the northern part of Schleswig. In this way even before 1814 there was a common labour market for the three main parts of the kingdom, with Bergen and Flensburg the most attractive places for Danish sailors.

Migration over longer distances was mainly to the most important seafaring nations. In an early phase the Netherlands was most attractive. While it is not known when this exodus began, by the mid-seventeenth century there were significant Danish communities in Amsterdam and other Dutch maritime towns. The majority of these Danes were sailors and women who worked as servants. Around 1700 it has been estimated that more than half the foreign sailors on Dutch ships who signed protests in Dutch ports came from the Danish realm

[13]Hans Chr. Johansen, *Næring og Bystyre, Odense 1700-1789* (Odense, 1983), 170.

and that eleven percent were Danish.[14] In 1725 the total number of Danish and Norwegian sailors in the Dutch merchant, whaling and VOC fleets was between 8000 and 9000.[15] Many were probably from western Jutland, where parish registers often contained nicknames such as "Hollander" or "Eastindiaman." In the early eighteenth century there were many examples in the conscription lists of "living in Holland" or "has gone to Holland to earn his bread and living."[16] The main reason for this migration was probably the lure of higher wages on Dutch ships and a higher standard of living in Dutch towns. There are examples of Danes returning with substantial savings compared to their more sedentary contemporaries.

In the nineteenth century it was increasingly the US merchant marine which became the main foreign employer for Danish sailors who left home. Among shipowners there were complaints about young sailors who deserted in American ports, and the conscription rolls in Danish ports regularly mentioned that the conscript had joined an American ship. Again, higher wages may have been an incentive, but at least after 1865 desertion could also be an inexpensive means of permanent emigration.

Naval personnel were also allowed to join foreign warships in peacetime to get practical training. Many of the first-generation admirals and other high-ranking officers received part of their training in the Dutch navy, and there were also Danish sailors on both British and French ships during the Napoleonic wars. On the other hand, there have also been periods when Danish naval officers served as advisers to foreign navies. This was the case in Russia in the early eighteenth century and in the Siamese navy more than 100 years later.

## Conclusion: Danes At Sea

Seafaring has normally been considered an important occupation in Danish history. Although the number of sailors never reached large

---

[14] P.C. van Royen, "Foreigners Aboard the Dutch Merchant Marine Around 1700," in W.G. Heeres, *et al.* (eds.), *From Dunkirk to Danzig. Shipping and Trade in the North Sea and the Baltic 1350-1850* (Hilversum, 1988), 396.

[15] *Holland Danmark* (Copenhagen, 1945), II, 441; and Carl Steenstrup, "Scandinavians in Asian Waters in the 17th Century," *Acta Orientalia*, XLIII (1982), 69-83.

[16] *Holland Danmark*, 221 ff.

dimensions compared to agriculture or later to secondary trades, there is no doubt that this generalization is true. The long coastline and many islands made ships necessary to connect and defend the various parts of the kingdom at a time when land transport was difficult and bridges had yet to be constructed.

The examples in this article demonstrate that Danish ships and Danish sailors not only sailed in domestic waters but took part in a larger international division of work. Indeed, in certain periods they played a role in wider European and overseas trades, and in various maritime labour markets.

# German Sailors, 1650-1900

Michael North

## Introduction

Shipping in the Holy Roman Empire and later in the German states was largely regional. Up to 1871 there was no such thing as a German merchant marine – and only recently was there a German navy.[1] But Hamburg, Bremen, Lübeck, and a number of small cities, such as Emden, Papenburg, Husum and Tönning had merchant fleets.[2] That is why national statistics and research on the social history of sailors before

[1]German naval history from the seventeenth to the mid-nineteenth century comprises only a few short episodes. Friedrich Wilhelm of Brandenburg not only had a navy between 1675 and 1707 but also acquired some colonial possessions. From 1847 Prussia – and between 1848 and 1852 the Frankfurt parliament – started to build up navies. In 1867 the Prussian navy was transformed into the North German navy, which in turn became the Imperial navy in 1870. Naval history from the second half of the nineteenth century belongs for the greater part to the age of steam. See A. von Crousaz, *Kurze Geschichte der deutschen Kriegsmarine, nach ihrem Ursprunge, ihrer organischen Entwicklung, und ihren seitherigen Leistungen* (Berlin, 1873); and Walter Ried, *Deutsche Segelschiffahrt seit 1470* (München, 1974). On the state of German naval history, see: Werner Rahn, "Germany," in John B. Hattendorf (ed.), *Ubi Sumus? The State of Naval and Maritime History* (Newport, 1994), 137-158.

[2]Cities like Stettin or Danzig, which for all or most of the period were Polish, are excluded. For research on Danzig sailors, see Maria Bogucka, "Recruitment of seamen for Gdansk Ships in the 16th-18th Centuries," *Northern Seas Yearbook 1994*; Bogucka, "Conditions of Life on Board the Fleet of Gdansk in Early Modern Times," *Northern Seas Yearbook 1996*; and Ried, *Deutsche Segelschiffahrt*. For certain periods, such as the Napoleonic era, small ports were very important. See J.F. van Dulm and A.N. baron de Vos van Steenwijk, "De vlag van Kniphausen," *Marineblad*, LXXXII, No. 1 (1972), 17-32; E.S. van Eyck van Heslinga, "De vlag dekt de lading. De Nederlandse koopvaardij in de Vierde Engelse oorlog," *Tijdschrift voor zeegeschiedenis*, I, No. 2 (1982), 102-113; and van Eyck, *Van Compagnie naar koopvaardij. De scheepvaartverbindingen van de Bataafse Republiek met de koloniën in Azië, 1795-1806* (Amsterdam, 1988), 26-30. For German coastal shipping in the nineteenth century, see Karl-Heinz Wiechers, ... *und fuhren weit übers Meer* (3 vols., Norden, 1988-1995).

1870 has to focus on regional developments. Indeed, before unification we are forced to use mainly data on Hamburg ships and sailors. Although this represents only a segment of the history of German sailors, it was an important one due to Hamburg's role as the most important German harbour, a position it gained after the Thirty Years' War when, unlike most of the Holy Roman Empire, it managed to stay at peace by making frequent loans to the neighbouring states.[3] Hamburg's rise as a port was bolstered by two factors: first by its location on the Elbe, which gave it access to the interior of Germany and central Europe; and second by its consistent neutrality during the wars of the seventeenth and eighteenth centuries, when it became an alternative to Amsterdam.

**Table 1**
**Hamburg Sailing Ships and Sailors, 1672-1901**

| Year | Merchant Vessels | Tonnage (Lasts) | Sailors | Whaling Vessels | Tonnage (Lasts) | Sailors |
|---|---|---|---|---|---|---|
| 1672 | 267 | 20193 | 2670 | 10 | 1065 | 430* |
| 1674 | 309 | 23822 | (including c. 45 whaling ships) | | | |
| 1765 | 85 | 8890 | 850* | 49 | 5190 | 1854 |
| 1800 | 278 | 30040 | 2780* | 15 | 1780 | 694 |
| 1830 | 152 | 13253 | 1520* | | | |
| 1850 | 288 | 32333 | 2880* | (+11 steamers = 1560 1.) | | |
| 1871 | 390 | 86853 | 3900* | (+36 steamers = 17093 1.) | | |
| 1901 | 205 | 207958** | 3144 | (+526 steamers = 843635 1.) | | |

*Notes:* * estimated; ** register tons.

*Sources:* Ernst Baasch, "Ein Verzeichnis der hamburgischen Kauffahrteiflotte vom Jahre 1672," *Zeitschrift des Vereins für Hamburgische Geschichte*, XV (1910), 39-52; Pierre Jeannin, "Zur Geschichte der Hamburger Handelsflotte am Ende des 17. Jahrhunderts: Eine Schiffsliste von 1674," *Zeitschrift des Vereins für Hamburgische Geschichte*, LVII (1971), 67-82; Walter Kresse, *Materialien zur Entwicklungsgeschichte der Hamburger Handelsflotte 1765-1823* (Hamburg, 1966); Kresse, *Die Fahrtgebiete der hamburger Handelsflotte 1824-1888* (Hamburg, 1972); and Siegfrid Heckscher, "Die Lage der in der Seeschiffahrt Hamburgs beschäftigten Arbeiter," *Schriften des Vereins zur Socialpolitik*, CIV (1903), 135. As regards the Hamburg whaling fleet, Wanda Oesau, *Hamburgs Grönlandfahrt auf Walfischfang und Robbenschlag vom 17.-19. Jahrhundert* (Glückstadt, 1955), 303-314, mentions forty-seven whalers clearing from the port in 1772 and seventy-four in 1774, but only two-thirds appear on a 1774 manuscript list and far fewer on a 1772 list. I assume that Oesau included whalers registered in Altona and other ports.

[3]There is not much literature available on sailors from ports like Bremen and Lübeck. See the articles of Klaus Friedland, Hermann Kellenbenz and Jürgen Brocksted in: Paul Adam, *Seamen in Society* (3 vols., Paris, 1980).

**Table 2**
**German Ships and Sailors, 1851-1901**

| Year | Sailing Ships | Tonnage (rt.) | Sailors | Steam Ships | Tonnage (rt.) | Sailors |
|---|---|---|---|---|---|---|
| 1851 | 3655 | 516410 | 26746 | 22 | 4830 | 316 |
| 1871 | 4589 | 906902 | 35456 | 132 | 82224 | 4760 |
| 1901 | 2492 | 593723 | 13689 | 1390 | 1347875 | 36861 |

*Source*: Max Peters, *Die Entwicklung der deutschen Rhederei seit Beginn dieses Jahrhunderts bis zur Begründung des Deutschen Reichs* (2 vols., Jena, 1905), II, tables 43-45.

The data on Hamburg shipping in the seventeenth and eighteenth centuries suggests limited maritime development (tables 1 and 2). And the trends were negative: there was a 40.9% decline in tonnage between 1674 and 1765, although average tonnage did rise from 77.1 to 104 lasts. Not until the 1790s did Hamburg's tonnage reach 1674 levels and again provide sufficient capacity for the buoyant grain trade. This growth in the last third of the eighteenth century was stimulated by a decline in whaling, as Hamburg's Greenland whale fishery ceased to be profitable due to a decline in stocks. Hamburg shipowners thus had an incentive to concentrate on the carrying trades. Although the city's merchant fleet was expanding, it could handle no more than twenty percent of Hamburg's total trade.

Hamburg's merchant fleet declined again from 1806 due to the continental blockade and the consequent British blockade of the Elbe. After 1815 it stagnated; recovered somewhat in the 1830s and 1840s; and grew rapidly between 1850 and the end of the century. Before 1800 Hamburg merchantmen were mainly confined to European waters; only a few crossed the Atlantic. Transoceanic traffic to the West Indies, Brazil, Africa and East Asia grew after the end of the Napoleonic wars. The 1850s and 1860s were marked by a remarkable boom, due largely to the growing numbers of emigrants bound for North America and by increasing East Asian and China traffic. In the last decades of the century sailing vessels were increasingly replaced by steamers, and regular steamer lines were established on major routes and with the German colonies to ensure a regular mail service (*postdampfer*).[4]

[4]Kresse, *Die Fahrgebiete*, parts 2 and 3.

Evidence on the crews aboard Hamburg vessels exists from 1761 in the lists of enrolment (*Anmusterungprotokolle*) of the Hamburg *Wasserschout*. Although they show different crew sizes in whaling, sailing vessels and steam shipping, they also depict long-term stability on each type of vessel. While Hamburg whalers had average crews of forty-three during the whole period, merchantmen carried comparatively small compliments of ten to eleven. The smaller crews of six to eight sailors documented in the German statistics are the result of the inclusion of coastal vessels, while the Hamburg statistics include only seagoing ships. The emergence of steamers from the 1860s changed the picture, leading to larger crews and a variety of new jobs. Steamer crews around 1900 ranged between twenty-six and thirty-six crew members on average.

## Origin of Sailors

On the recruitment of sailors in Hamburg the *Wasserschout*'s lists have been examined with special respect to whaling and to the participation of North Frisian sailors. Between 1761 and 1821 North Frisians, especially from Röm and Föhr, provided between twenty and twenty-five percent of Hamburg whalemen. Other crew were recruited from Hamburg (fifteen percent), Lower Saxony along the Lower Elbe (twenty percent), and Holstein, Scandinavia and inland regions of the Holy Roman Empire, such as Thuringia and Frankonia.

The more qualified and better paid positions were even more dominated by North Frisians, who comprised sixty-three percent of captains (*kommandeure*), sixty-seven percent of helmsmen (*steuerleute*), forty-two percent of blubber cutters (*speckschneider*), forty percent of harpooners (*harpuniers*), forty-two percent of bosuns (*bootsleute*), thirty-eight percent of cooks (*köche*), twenty-three percent of carpenters (*zimmerleute*), twenty percent of *schiemänner* (in charge of storage), fifteen percent of ordinary seamen (*matrosen*), and fifty-two percent of apprentices (*kochsmaate* and *schiffjungen*). Hamburg, on the other hand, contributed a majority of coopers (*kuipers*), carpenters, bosuns and barbers (*meister*). Ordinary seamen came from everywhere.[5]

[5]Harald Voigt, *Die Nordfriesen auf den Hamburger Wal- und Robbenfängern 1669-1839* (Neumünster, 1987), 112 ff., 159 ff. and 189. For Dutchmen on Hamburg whalers, see K. Davids, *this volume*.

The phenomenon of North Frisians in the higher ranks of Hamburg whalers was not confined to the second half of the eighteenth century. Between 1669 and 1712 there were fifty-one captains from Föhr, eighty-eight from Röm, thirty from Sylt, and twenty from Amrum.[6] But the majority of North Frisians joined Dutch whalers. In the 1760s the number of Föhr sailors on Dutch whalers was estimated in the range of 1100-1200, while about 100 served on Hamburg whalers. Every year on St. Peters Day (22 February) *schmacken* sailed from the North Frisian Islands to Holland and Hamburg, where the sailors enroled in the whaling fleet. They usually returned to their wives and families in October (captains and helmsmen were often married). Often captains took their young sons (aged ten to thirteen) with them to Holland or Hamburg and enroled them as apprentices. The wives ran the small peasant farm, and retired sailors also took up agriculture. Some captains opened nautical schools, teaching navigation and astronomy and thus contributing to the rise of North Frisian sailors into the highest ranks of Dutch, Hamburg, and even Danish whaling fleets.[7]

**Table 3**
**Origin of Sailors, Enroled in Hamburg, 1872-1912**

| **Sailors** | 1872 | 1882 | 1892 | 1902 | 1912 |
|---|---|---|---|---|---|
| Hamburg | 364 | 205 | 578 | 494 | 845 |
| Inland | 1888 | 3782 | 5582 | 8745 | 8563 |
| Abroad | 490 | 916 | 887 | 817 | 872 |
| Together | 2742 | 4903 | 7037 | 10056 | 10280 |
| **Firemen** | | | | | |
| Hamburg | 316 | 545 | 2505 | 1100 | 1001 |
| Inland | 3070 | 4535 | 6617 | 12800 | 16701 |
| Abroad | 152 | 195 | 482 | 861 | 2538 |
| Together | 3538 | 5275 | 9604 | 14861 | 20240 |

*Source*: Ursula Winkens, "Soziale Lage, rechtliche Rahmenbedingungen und Interessenartikulation der Seeleute im Deutschen Kaiserreich 1872-1914. Ein Beitrag zur seemännischen Sozialgeschichte" (Unpublished Phd thesis, University of Hamburg, 1987), 18 ff.

---

[6]Kresse, *Die Fahrgebiete*, 38.

[7]On the nautical schools, see Wanda Oesau, *Schleswig-Holsteins Grönlandfahrt auf Walfischfang und Robbenschlag vom 17.-19. Jahrhundert* (Glückstadt, 1937), 271 ff.

On the origins of sailors in Hamburg's merchant fleet we have only casual evidence for the eighteenth and nineteenth centuries; statistical data began only in the 1870s. What we have shows that sailors came from the *Waterkant*, the coastal areas of northern Germany. The evidence for 1872-1912 (table 3) differentiates only between Hamburg, inland, and abroad, but it shows the growing proportions of inlanders, especially as firemen on steamers. As well, the material on age structure reveals something about their life cycles. By the end of the nineteenth century the majority in Hamburg were between twenty and thirty years of age (53.8%), with 16.4% below twenty and 20.8% between thirty and forty. Life as a sailor was often a transition between youth and marriage.

**Table 4**
**Wages on the Whaler *Anna Maria*, 1791**

| | mark courant | *quardeel* |
|---|---|---|
| **Partfahrer** | | |
| mate | 60 | 24 |
| blubber cutter | 60 | 22 |
| blubber cutter | 45 | 21 |
| harpooner | 45 | 21 |
| 2 harpooners | 42 | 20 |
| **Monatsfahrer** | | |
| carpenter | 42 | 4 |
| carpenter | 21 | - |
| bosun | 33 | 11 |
| cook | 33 | 11 |
| cooper | 33 | 11 |
| cooper | 15 | - |
| surgeon | 54 | - |
| seaman | 26 | 5 |
| 2 seamen | 25 | 6 |
| 3 seamen | 25 | 5 |
| 8 seamen | 21 | 3 |
| 3 seamen | 21 | 2 |
| 2 seamen | 20 | 1 |
| 1 seaman | 18 | 2 |
| 3 seamen | 18 | 1 |
| 1 seaman | 15 | - |
| 4 seamen | 13 | - |
| cook's mate | 12 | - |
| boy | 12 | - |

*Note*: *quardeel* = 232.8 litres blubber.

*Source*: Walter Kresse, "Die Heuern Hamburger Seeleute 1760-1860," *Zeitschrift des Vereins für Hamburgische Geschichte*, LXX (1984), 169.

## Wages

The wages paid to Hamburg sailors were different in whaling and merchant shipping. Aboard Hamburg whalers the wages of the better paid *partfahrer* (mate, harpooner and blubber cutter) consisted of monthly stipend (*Heuer*) and a considerable part of the whales' blubber, to be boiled into whale oil. The majority of the crew were *monatsfahrer*, who received their main pay in money and only a small part in blubber (see table 4).

In the merchant marine seamen received their monthly pay in money. Wages in the Hamburg merchant fleet show great stability throughout the latter half of the eighteenth and the first half of the nineteenth century. Normally the first mate and the carpenter received the same pay, while the cook and ordinary seamen received half and the apprentices about one-quarter (see table 5).

**Table 5**
**Monthly Wages of Hamburg Sailors, 1796-1860**
**(in marks courant)**

| | 1796 | 1803 | 1810 | 1820 | 1830 | 1840 | 1850 | 1860 |
|---|---|---|---|---|---|---|---|---|
| first mate | 54 | 48 | 72 | 48 | 48 | 54 | 60 | 60 |
| second mate | | | | | 36 | 36 | | 45 |
| carpenter | | 48 | 72 | 48 | 48 | 51 | 36 | 42 |
| bosun | 40.8 | 36 | 54 | 36 | | | | |
| cook | 27 | 36 | 54 | 36 | 36 | 36 | 36 | 48 |
| cooper | | | | 24 | | | | |
| sailmaker | | | | 27 | | | | |
| seaman | 5x27 | 6x24 | 5x36 | 6x24 | 2x24 | 3x27 | 2x30 | 4x36 |
| apprentice | | | | 1x21 | 2x18 | 1x24 | 1x21 | |
| cook's mate | | 12 | | | | | | |
| boy | 12 | 12 | 30 | 2x12 | 12 | 12 | 9 | 1x15 |

*Source*: Kresse, "Die Heuern," 172.

Still, there were some fluctuations in the wages, which rose during wars and declined in depressions, as after the Hamburg fire of 1842 or during the crisis of 1857. The period 1870 to 1900 was marked by a slight increase in wages, a fall in the 1890s, and a recovery by the end of the century.[8] Taking the two- and sometimes three-year voyages of Hamburg sailing vessels into consideration, mates and carpenters often accumulated as much as 1000 and ordinary seamen up to 500 marks courant. They might invest this in the purchase of a *ewer*, thus starting a career in coastal shipping. Comparative figures on sailors' annual wages are only available for the end of our period. Table 6 shows that the ports with the highest demand for labour, such as Hamburg and Bremen, paid the highest wages and attracted sailors from a national or even an international "hinterland," while the Baltic ports in general paid much lower wages. For "push" areas like North Friesland wages can not be reconstructed, and I doubt that there existed any transparent maritime labour market, because one-man coastal shipping dominated.

**Table 6**
**Annual Wages of Seamen and Firemen 1902 (Marks)**

| Region/Port | Seamen/Firemen |
|---|---|
| East and West Prussia | 800-900 |
| Rostock-Wismar | 800-900 |
| Schleswig-Holstein | 1000 |
| Hamburg | 1100-1165 |
| Bremen | 1100-1225 |

*Source*: Winkens, "Soziale Lage," 57.

## Recruitment Policies

The most efficient recruitment "policies" were practised by North Frisian whaling captains, who recruited mates, harpooners, blubber cutters, and apprentices in their own region and enroled them either on their own or other whalers. Government policies varied, but since they were preventive in Denmark and "promotive" in Hamburg, relations between Hamburg and Denmark were often strained. From 1754 Danish subjects, including the North Frisians, who wanted to enrol on Hamburg ships had to show a letter of permission from the Danish ambassador in Hamburg. This required registration on his lists, which today are a valuable source

[8]Kresse, "Die Heuern," 173; and Heckscher, "Die Lage," 154.

for historians.[9] More important were the restrictions with respect to the military service of North Frisians in the Danish navy. In 1780, during the Fourth Anglo-Dutch War, the Danish king forbade his subjects to enrol abroad, as they were needed in the navy and the Danish merchant marine. Supplications by Hamburg shipowners like Beerend Roosen and the efforts of the Hamburg *rat* and the *Deutsche Kanzlei* in Copenhagen for a suspension of the decree were ignored by the Danish admiralty, and the decree remained in force until the fall of 1783. From 1784 the license system was reactivated. But even while the decree was in force North Frisian sailors – albeit in small numbers – managed to enrol on Hamburg whalers by changing their area of origin to Lower Saxony or Holland. Others enroled on the whalers of the Danish Greenland Company, which tried from 1776 to attract North Frisians by promising higher wages than in Hamburg or Altona and reimbursing travel costs.[10]

## Mobility between Sailing and Agriculture

When examining the careers of sailors, the mobility of North Frisians between seafaring and rural occupations is apparent. Evidence may be gleaned from the census of the island population in 1769 and by data on the population of sailors' villages in the Föhr parish of St. Laurentii. Table 7 shows that a stable quarter of North Frisians were employed at sea, a field in which Föhrites outnumbered other islanders by far. If we include their dependents, nearly two-thirds of families in the second half of the eighteenth century earned their living from the sea.

**Table 7**
**Census, 1769**

| | Röm | Föhr | Sylt | Amrum |
|---|---|---|---|---|
| Inhabitants | 1386 | 6146 | 2814 | 600 |
| Sailors | 278 | 1600 | 700 | 150 |
| % | 20 | 26 | 25 | 25 |

*Source*: Voigt, *Nordfriesen*, table 5.7.

[9]Voigt, *Die Nordfriesen*, 54 ff.

[10]*Ibid.*, 122-145; and Erich Riewerts, *et al.*, *Föhringer als Grönlandfahrer von Kopenhagen* (Neumünster, 1991), 60.

**Table 8**
**Sailors in the Parish of St. Laurentii, 1757-1860**

| | 1757 | 1787 | 1801 | 1834 | 1860 |
|---|---|---|---|---|---|
| Inhabitants | 1480 | 1544 | 1487 | 1244 | 1280 |
| Sailors | 437 | 367 | 205 | 146 | 138 |
| % | 30 | 24 | 14 | 12 | 11 |

*Source*: Brar C. Roeloffs, *Von der Seefahrt zur landwirtschaft. Ein Beitrag zur Geschichte der Insel Föhr* (Neumünster, 1984), 23 and 38.

The proportion of sailors in St. Laurentii was similar to the North Frisian islands, but it declined from the late eighteenth century (see table 8). The decline is even more impressive if we consider that among the 138 persons counted as sailors in 1860, forty-one emigrated, which reduced the sailors' share to eight percent. This decrease in maritime employment was caused by the decline of Greenland whaling, which was replaced only partially by merchant shipping, and a shift to the rural sector made more attractive by Danish agrarian reforms. As in Schleswig and Holstein, the royal decree of 1798 aimed to eliminate the open-field economy and to partition common lands. This in turn contributed to the intensification of agriculture on Föhr and increased the number of people who made their living from the land. As a result, agriculture replaced shipping as the major source of income in the first half of the nineteenth century; those who did not find employment in agriculture or shipping emigrated.[11] In the late nineteenth century the occupational shift away from shipping was stimulated further by an emerging seaside tourism sector. While manufacturing did not exist in North Frisia, along the North Sea coast, such as the Weser region, textiles presented a further alternative from the 1870s.[12]

[11]Brar C. Roeloffs, *Von der Seefahrt zur landwirtschaft. Ein Beitrag zur Geschichte der Insel Föhr* (Neumünster, 1984), 129-170. For the agrarian reforms in general, see Wolfgang Prange, *Die Anfänge der großen Agrarreformen in Schleswig-Holstein bis um 1771* (Neumünster, 1971).

[12]E. Fitger, "Die wirtschaftliche und technische Entwick lung der Seeschiffahrt von der Mitte des 19. Jahrhunderts bis auf die Gegenwart," *Schriften des Vereins für Socialpolitik*, CIII (1902), 114 ff.

## Mobility between Whaling and Merchant Shipping

The Föhr census of 1769 and the parish registers of St. Laurentii also tell us a good deal about mobility between whaling, merchant shipping and the navy (see table 9). The Föhr census counts 1600 sailors, of whom 1100-1200 sailed on Dutch whalers, and another 100 on Hamburg whalers. About 300-400 earned their daily bread in the merchant marine or in coastal shipping. We know that sailors from Föhr sailed on Hamburg merchantmen as well as with Dutch and Danish trading companies, although we cannot quantify their numbers. We know also that in the early nineteenth century the Danish navy served as outlet for North Frisian sailors who could not find employment in the whaling or merchant fleets due to Napoleon's continental blockade. All professions in whaling eventually declined, while only the number of captains – and between 1787 and 1801 the number of coastal skippers – increased.

**Table 9**
**Sailors in the Föhr Parish St. Laurentii, 1787-1860**

| | 1787 | 1801 | 1860 |
|---|---|---|---|
| Whaling captains | 12 | 6 | - |
| Captains | 7 | 7 | 12 |
| Shipper | 5 | 23 | - |
| Helmsmen | 29 | 35 | 8 |
| Blubber cutters | 27 | 15 | - |
| Harpooners | 62 | 17 | - |
| Others | 223 | 119 | 118* |

*Note*: * including 41 emigrants.

*Source*: Roeloffs, *Von der Seefahrt*, 26.

## Individual Careers

We lack any systematic data on sailors' vertical mobility. From a few individual examples, however, we know that North Frisian captains started with an apprenticeship (from about ten to sixteen years of age), continued as ordinary seamen (from about fifteen to twenty), and, having attended the local nautical schools, worked for a longer period as mates (between about eighteen and thirty). In their thirties they normally received command of a whaler, sailing as captain for twenty years or more.[13] Their crews were remarkably stable: harpooners, blubber cutters and mates were recruited locally by captains and hence had inducements to remain, while apprentices and ordinary seamen were more transitory.

## Group Formation

The first strike to be recorded in German shipping involved a partially-successful work stoppage by Altona and Hamburg seamen and firemen for higher wages in 1872.[14] Problems with discipline were obvious on two- and three-year voyages, which led shipowners to demand steeper fines and even imprisonment for rebellious sailors. A growing problem from the mid-nineteenth century was desertion, an individual form of resistance. With the 1849 California gold rush, most Hamburg ships that called in North America had to face the problem. Often sailors deserted from Hamburg ships only to enrol on American or British ships that offered higher wages.[15]

## Sailing in Another Country: North Frisian Sailors in Holland

While we know that North Frisians served on Dutch vessels, this phenomenon has not been systematically examined. What we know derives largely from the publications of Pieter Dekker on Föhr sailors on Dutch whalers and in the Dutch merchant marine. From the seventeenth century Föhr sailors joined whalers and merchantmen, the majority serving as ordinary seamen in the merchant marine.[16] Only seldom did Föhr sailors rise to the rank of captain on a Dutch whaler in the seventeenth and early eighteenth centuries, although one commander of a VOC vessel, Broer Hofman, was of Föhr origin.

---

[13] Oesau, *Schleswig-Holsteins Grönlandfahrt*, 213-231.

[14] Winkens, "Soziale Lage," 146 ff.

[15] Walter Kresse, "Die Diskussion über das Hamburger Seemannsrecht um 1850 – nebst Vorgeschichte," *Zeitschrift des Vereins für Hamburgische Geschichte*, LXVII (1981), 115-125; and Heckscher, *Die Lage*, 198 ff.

[16] Pieter Dekker, "Föhrer Seeleute bei der niederlandischen Walfangfahrt besonders im 18. Jahrhundert," *Nordfriesisches Jahrbuch*, XIV (1978), 132-136.

The numbers of Föhr sailors in Dutch service rose from the 1720s, when Hamburg's whaling declined for two decades, and peaked between 1758 and 1762, when annually 1100-1200 (1186 in 1762) Föhr sailors joined Dutch whalers. With this "invasion," the number of Föhr whaling captains rose from eight (1722) and twenty-three (1746) to thirty-four (1762), Föhr captains being outnumbered only by men from Den Helder/Huisduinen. At the same time, the proportion of Föhr sailors in the ranks of mates, harpooners and blubber cutters also increased.[17]

In the 1770s and 1780s the number of Föhr sailors in Dutch whaling decreased, and by 1789 only five Föhr captains and about 300 sailors could be found on Dutch ships. The North Frisians were replaced by sailors from Lower Saxony (Oldenburg and the Weser area) and Westfalia, the majority serving as ordinary seamen, but increasingly entering the higher ranks, although captains remained overwhelmingly Dutch.[18] What did Föhr seamen then do? Several captains enroled on merchant ships, while others joined the Danish Greenland Company, which recruited North Frisian sailors and sent out whalers from 1776. In this period twenty Föhr captains ran the company's whalers. Due to shrinking yields, the numbers declined to fifteen and fewer in the 1780s. The remaining captains commanded company ships, which supplied the Greenland settlements or sailed in the West Indian trade.[19]

## Careers in Holland

Career patterns for North Frisian sailors in Holland were similar to those in Hamburg, although there were greater opportunities in Dutch merchant shipping. Examples of Föhr sailors in Holland lead to the conclusion that shipowners preferred to hire former harpooners, mates, bosuns and even ordinary seamen from successful whaling crews.

The careers of North Frisians who reached the top ranks of the Dutch East India Company (VOC) are also illuminating. Nickels Petersen (Dutch name Cornelis Pietersz) from Sylt began as an apprentice and ended as commander of the VOC return fleet. Even more successful was

---

[17]*Ibid.*, 123 ff.

[18]*Ibid.*, 143.

[19]Riewerts, *et al.*, *Föhringer*, 55-77.

Nis de Bombell (Dutch name Nicolaas de Beer), who started with the Amsterdam shipping company Vermeeren, but after five years (in 1732) became a cadet in the Amsterdam admiralty. In 1746 he switched again, this time to the VOC. After several voyages in the East Indies between Batavia and Manila he was appointed commander of the return fleet in 1753. Back in Amsterdam, he again entered the navy, becoming an *ordinares Kapitein* in 1759, seven years before his retirement.[20]

## Conclusion

Despite a medieval Hanseatic tradition Hamburg and northern Germany were late entrants into early modern shipping. Only a small part of Hamburg's growing trade was carried on local ships, mostly in European coastal waters between Archangel and Cadiz, before the late eighteenth century. By the mid-eighteenth century, Greenland whaling absorbed a considerable amount of Hamburg's maritime resources. American and Latin American independence in the nineteenth century opened the door for transoceanic shipping. Hamburg seized these opportunities, especially from the 1830s, when the city's shipping had recovered from the Napoleonic wars and the postwar depression.

The years 1790-1860 were essentially a single period for sailors' opportunities. Whaling declined, but despite cyclical fluctuations there was long-term stability, although changes occurred in the "push" regions due to agrarian reforms. Industrialization and steam shipping induced more substantial shifts from the 1870s. The period up to 1900 was marked by a further concentration of shipping in Hamburg and Bremen. Potential sailors in the former push regions adapted to these structural changes by entering into agriculture and – if possible – industry, or tried to gain a foothold in the growing branch of sea tourism.[21]

---

[20]Pieter Dekker, "Zwischen Amsterdam and Batavia. Der Aufstieg des gebürtigen Sylters Nickels Petersen vom Schiffsjungen zum Kommandeur in niederlandischen Seediensten," *Nordfriesisches Jahrbuch*, X (1974), 133-142; and Dekker, "Der 'Admiral' Nis de Bombell (1706-1772). Ein Nordfriese in niederlandischen Seediensten," *Nordfriesisches Jahrbuch*, XIII (1977), 107-133.

[21]For an overview of the structural changes, especially between 1870 and 1914, see Jürgen Brocksted, "Seefahrende an deutschen Küsten im Zeitalter der Industrialisierung (1815-1914)," in Brockstedt (ed.), *Seefahrt an deutschen Küsten im Wandel, 1815-1914* (Neumünster, 1993), 29 ff.

# Sailors in the Southern Netherlands and Belgium (16th-19th Centuries)

**Roland Baetens**

To understand the labour market for seamen in the Southern Netherlands (Belgium from 1830) from the sixteenth through the nineteenth centuries, we should ask about government's attitude toward maritime affairs, as well as about the size of the merchant fleet and the navy, the area of recruitment, working conditions, wages and opportunities for promotion.

## Size of the Mercantile Marine and Navy

By and large maritime affairs have not been one of government's priorities for the past 500 years for various reasons. Primarily, the extension of a maritime tradition depends on geopolitics. The reduced coastal strip along the North Sea from Dunkirk to Heist, and the fact that only artificial harbours were possible – vessels could only make port at high tide – are two obvious explanations.[1] A second aspect involves the international balance of power. Spanish military strategy required that Dunkirk and Ostend, which were only significant as fishing harbours, be used for naval fleets as well. War and trade, however, do not always coexist well, and the merchant marine became the first victim. There was also Antwerp, which had only become a true port in the fifteenth century. In the last quarter of the sixteenth century direct access to the sea was severed by the Dutch, and the Eighty Years' War further disturbed the growth of the harbour.

Antwerp then slumbered until the Napoleonic era. When Napoleon wanted Antwerp to become a military bulwark, a British

[1]R. Baetens, "Het uitzicht en de infrastructuur van een kleine Noordzeehaven tijdens het Ancien Régime: het voorbeeld van Oostende," *Mededelingen van de Marine Academie van België*, XXIII (1973-1974), 47-62; and A. Cabantous, *Histoire de Dunkerque* (Toulouse, 1983).

blockade ended this brief commercial expansion.[2] While during the Dutch period shipowners from the Netherlands dominated, it is notable that Antwerp still developed a merchant fleet.

In Belgium, industry and trade were given absolute priority by 1830. The success of the industrial revolution was vital to the young nation. Since many shipowners moved to the North with ships and crew, the merchant fleet had declined. To stimulate the investment in the fleet, government offered some modest subsidies, but indifference, lack of insight and limited expertise led to poor results.[3] Shipowning remained of minor concern to firms in the Southern Netherlands. The famous Della Faille concern in Antwerp was typical in the sixteenth century: it owned only two vessels, and only for a brief period. Otherwise, it was content with just one share in a ship. Profits on commercial and financial transactions appeared preferable and less risky. A net profit of three or four percent was a windfall. Merchants invested only in shipping when all other possibilities were exhausted.[4] Moreover, during Antwerp's golden age shipping in the Scheldt delta was determined mainly by internal supply and demand in the Netherlands rather than by any exchange between northern and southern Europe.

The politics of the time caused strong fluctuations in both the merchant fleet and the navy. As well, in uncertain times Flemish shipowners preferred to disguise their nationality: flags changed and vessel names could be altered.[5] The lack of governmental concern also means that we are now left with only fragmentary archival evidence.

---

[2]R. Baetens, "Le rôle de Dunkerque dans l'histoire maritime et commerciale des Pays-Bas méridionaux (XVIe-XVIIIe siècles)," *Les Amis du Vieux Dunkerque*, VI (1977), 35-44; S.T. Bindoff, *The Scheldt Question to 1839* (London, 1945), 82-107; and K. Veraghtert, "De havenbeweging te Antwerpen tijdens de negentiende eeuw. Een kwantitatieve benadering" (Unpublished PhD thesis, University of Leuven, 1977), II, 22-26.

[3]Veraghtert, "Havenbeweging," II, 28-48; and Veraghtert, "From Inland Port to International Port," in F. Suykens, *et al.*, *Antwerp: A Port for All Seasons* (Antwerp, 1986), 351.

[4]W. Brulez, "La navigation flamande vers la Méditerranée à la fin du XVIe siècle," *Revue belge de Philologie et d'Histoire*, XXXVI (1958), 1229; and Brulez, "De scheepvaartwinst in de nieuwe tijden," *Tijdschrift voor Geschiedenis*, XCII (1979), 17-18.

[5]Brulez, "La navigation," 1235.

## The Sixteenth Century

The only way to calculate the number of seamen is to estimate the size of the merchant and naval fleets. In the twelve months from April 1563 we know that sixty Antwerp vessels were engaged in trade with France. How many individual masters were involved is uncertain. The London port books mention forty-nine Antwerp ships between Easter and 29 September 1565. Other investigations have revealed that between 1555 and 1558 at least seventeen Antwerp masters traded with France; on average, their ships were about sixty tons. On the route to the Iberian Peninsula and the Mediterranean, there were at least twelve Antwerp skippers. Some vessels went to the Canary Islands or North Africa; these were slightly larger (100-120 tons). Perhaps twenty Antwerp vessels were in this trade.[6]

Antwerp merchants, such as de Haro, Affaitadi and Schetz, initiated new maritime connections with the Canaries and North Africa. Between 1549 and 1555, about sixty voyages per year went to the former and thirty-four to Morocco, requiring about twenty-five craft for the sugar islands and another ten for Africa. Many were Spanish or came from Holland or Zeeland. Likewise, Antwerp masters remained a minority. The London port books recorded thirty-three Antwerp vessels (1567-1568). Forty tons was a maximum on this route. About five ships were in the Baltic trade. Altogether we know about roughly eighty vessels in the Antwerp merchant fleet with a total capacity of at least 3000 or 4000 tons.[7]

There is another approach. Gustaf Asaert determined that at the end of the fifteenth century, there were sixty to seventy masters. About seventeen, or one-quarter of the total, were active at sea. They were in charge of vessels with a total tonnage of 2400 to 2800. For the period 1555-1559 a minimum of 485 masters existed. It is not unrealistic to

---

[6]G. Asaert, "From Wharf to Commercial Metropolis," in Suykens, *et al.*, *Antwerp*, 135 and 161.

[7]M. Cassiers, "Bijdrage tot de geschiedenis van de Antwerpse scheepvaart en scheepvaartbeweging in het midden van de 16e eeuw (1555-1558)" (Unpublished PhD thesis, University of Ghent, 1978); J. Denucé, *Afrika in de XVIe eeuw en de handel van Antwerpen* (Antwerp, 1937), 12-13, 28 and 93-94; and W. Brulez, "Scheepvaart in de Zuidelijke Nederlanden," *Nieuwe Algemene Geschiedenis der Nederlanden*, VI (1979), 124.

suppose that the Antwerp merchant fleet – based on the same one to four ratio – comprised about 120 ships. According to a 1551 ordinance, vessels bound for Spain, Portugal and the Canaries required a minimum tonnage of eighty and a crew of sixteen men over the age of eighteen. If one-sixth of the fleet averaged eighty tons, one-sixth sixty tons, and the remainder forty tons, then there would have been about 6000 tons of shipping and approximately 1200-1500 men.[8] This was hardly impressive considering Antwerp's commercial and financial capacity at the time.

The Zeeland and Holland masters were much more numerous. For the period 1565-1567 we know the masters who imported wine into Walcheren. There were 609, including fourteen South Netherlanders, 104 Zeelanders and ninety-three "Hollanders." We also know that in 1557-1560 only two percent of the total traffic came from the Southern Netherlands. In 1550 the Antwerp guild of bargemen protested that five-sixths of the important goods arriving in the Scheldt were transported by these "Northerners." Of course, a comparison can only be made with other ports and not with a national fleet. The South had far fewer than the 38,000 tons owned in Holland and Zeeland at the beginning of the sixteenth century or the eight hundred vessels in the same fleet mentioned by L. Guicciardini in 1567.[9]

Less is known about Bruges or the North Sea ports. The London port books mention eight craft from Bruges in 1552, and in the same year five were chartered to Spain.[10] At the same time, a merchant fleet of forty vessels protected by warships left the coast of Walcheren for the South and in 1553 twenty-four merchantmen did. Most belonged to Zeeland and Holland. At any rate, we can conclude that in Antwerp's

---

[8]G. Asaert, *De Antwerpse scheepvaart in de XVe eeuw (1394-1480). Bijdrage tot de ekonomische geschiedenis van de stad Antwerpen* (Brussels, 1973), 396-397; Cassiers, "Bijdrage tot de geschiedenis," 54; and *Recueil des ordonnances des Pays-Bas, II: 1506-1700* (Brussels, 1921), 163-177.

[9]Brulez, "Scheepvaart," 124; J. Craeybeckx, "De organisatie en de konvooiering van de koopvaardijvloot op het eind van de regering van Karel V," *Bijdragen voor de Geschiedenis der Nederlanden*, III (1948), 206; and H.P.H. Jansen, "Handelsvaart van de Noordnederlanden," *Maritieme Geschiedenis der Nederlanden*, I (1976), 2.

[10]Brulez, "Scheepvaart," 125.

golden age, the size of the Southern Netherlands' merchant fleet was modest compared to its commercial or industrial significance.

Concerning the war fleet we know about four ships in 1537 and a convoy of eight vessels and 125 seamen in the next decade. In 1554 the Netherlands had twenty warships at their disposal. Jan Craeybecx has reported that Walcheren took most of the profits. It is too much to assert that the Southern Netherlands was extending its naval power.[11]

## Seventeenth and Eighteenth Centuries

The Eighty Years' War cut off Antwerp's route to the open sea. It was only North Sea ports like Dunkirk and Ostend which then had the option of investing in merchant shipping. Estimates of the size of the merchant fleet in the seventeenth century are always thwarted by the existence of raiders and convoy vessels. Especially during the Twelve Years' Truce, when privateering was unremunerative, and later in periods of peace, Ostend convoy vessels carried freight.[12]

Merchants knew the risks but sometimes had little choice. The political situation exacerbated things. The merchants of the Southern Netherlands preferred a neutral flag like Hamburg and well-armed English vessels to carry goods in a regular service between Dunkirk or Ostend to Dover. During the Truce, ten or twenty ships from Dunkirk maintained the connection with Iberia. These data are fragmentary. There was also a coastal trade as far as the Baltic. The Dunkirk shipowner Van

---

[11]J. De Smet, "De krijgsvloot van de Staten van Vlaanderen in de zestiende en zeventiende eeuwen," *Handelingen van het Genootschap voor Geschiedenis. Société d'Emulation te Brugge*, LXXXI (1938), 2; C. Koninckx, "Convoyeurs et Convoyés au XVIe siècle aux Pays-Bas espagnols. Quelques aspects de la vie à bord en mer," *Atti del V convegno internazionale di studi colombiani* (Genova, 1990), 74-75 and 86; and Craeybeckx, "De organisatie," 201-203.

[12]E. Stols, *De Spaanse Brabanders of de handelsbetrekkingen der Zuidelijke Nederlanden met de Iberische Wereld 1598-1648* (2 vols., Brussels, 1971), I, 297-299; and J. Everaert, *De internationale en koloniale handel der Vlaamse firma's te Cádiz 1670-1700* (Brugge, 1973), 99 and 102.

de Walle sent three ships to Brazil.[13] A conservative estimate suggests fifty ships (6000-7000 tons) during the best years of the Truce.

For the second half of the seventeenth century only sporadic data are known. In 1674 eight ships sailed to Spain; in 1689, fourteen; and in 1694, seventeen, including convoy ships. Estimates of the frequency of sailings and the size of the fleet are precarious. Moreover, the number of seamen is unknown. The fact that merchants sometimes had to ship their goods to Spain via the United Provinces tells an important story.[14]

Since the navy also transported freight, it is worthwhile to examine its size because surviving information is more complete. The war fleet of the South Netherlands had two cornerstones: the "Armada of Flanders" and the private raiders. In the 1630s, when the fleet was at its peak, there were twenty or thirty vessels with 2500 to 3700 men, soldiers included. Admiral Jacques Colaert reported in 1637 that he had fewer than 2500 sailors at his disposal. On a warship of 250 lasts (about 500 tons) 150 sailors and 100 soldiers were needed.[15] If we apply this ratio on 3700, then we have 2200 sailors for the Armada, which is identical with Colaert's statement.

There were also the private raiders. During the peak years about sixty were afloat, some of which operated with the Armada. There were also about ten Ostend inhabitants active in the 1630s. We can estimate that about forty percent of the total were frigates of between fifty and 300 tons, with the remainder comprised of smaller craft of twenty to forty tons. According to a 1628 decree, the admiralty advised carrying

---

[13]R. Baetens, *De nazomer van Antwerpen's welvaart. De diaspora en het handelshuis De Groote tijdens de eerste helft der 17de eeuw* (Brussels, 1976), I, 71-72 and 81-83; Baetens, "De Zuidelijke Nederlanden en de handel op de Baltische ruimte (17de eeuw)," in *The Interactions of Amsterdam and Antwerp with the Baltic Region 1400-1800* (Leiden, 1983), 59-71; Everaert, *De internationale en koloniale handel*, 91-92; and Stols, *De Spaanse Brabanders*, 298 and 304.

[14]Everaert, *De internationale en koloniale handel*, 103, 110-111 and 789-791.

[15]R.A. Stradling, *The Armada of Flanders* (Cambridge, 1992), 252; J. Dams, "Un mémoire de l'amiral Jacques Colaert au gouvernement espagnol," *Revue de la Société dunkerquoise d'histoire et d'archéologie*, XVI (1983), 87; and E. Hambye, *L'aumônerie de la flotte de Flandre au XVIIe siècle* (Louvain, 1967), 151.

fifty sailors on a 100-ton vessel and sixty on a 140-ton ship.[16] If we assume an average of 100 tons for forty frigates, that would require 2000 sailors. The other twenty ships of twenty tons with ten sailors adds another 1000, or 3000 in all. If we add this to the sailors in the Armada, we end up with 5000, excluding soldiers. Is this a realistic number?

We know that the admiralty had great difficulty with recruitment. Seamen preferred service on private craft since it was much more lucrative. Hence foreigners were regularly used. Archduchess Isabella recruited 200 Genoese in 1627. Dunkirk, Ostend and Newport could not provide similar numbers. Dunkirk had 5100 inhabitants in 1659, of which 1061 were adult men; in 1676, there were about 7000, of whom 13.6% were seafarers. Taking into account emigration, Dunkirk must have had a population of about 7000 during the Spanish era. If we apply the same ratio, it suggests 1000 sailors. Ostend had 4388 inhabitants in 1645 and 6728 in 1698. Using the same ratio there must have been 600 sailors among the 1500 adult males. Still, it is difficult to estimate the population of a port, since the "floating population" – the seamen – were difficult to register.[17]

About thirty percent of the sailors were supplied by the two most important Flemish seaports. The rest came from the interior of the Southern Netherlands or from Normandy, Brittany, England, Scandinavia, neutral areas of Germany or even Holland and Zeeland. In 1634 C. Penninck of the admiralty declared that the most skilled seamen came from Holland, attracted by the hope of a rich booty.[18]

In the second half of the seventeenth century the number of Ostend privateers usually varied from fifteen and thirty. The tonnage also decreased and hence fewer seamen were required. Even adding the

---

[16]R. Baetens, "The Organization and Effects of Flemish Privateering in the Seventeenth Century," *Acta Historiae Neerlandicae*, IX (1976), 54 and 57-58.

[17]Hambye, *L'aumônerie*, 151; C. Pfister, "Dunkerque, de Cromwell à Charles II (1658-1662)," *Guerres et Paix 1660-1815* (1987), 43; A. Cabantous, *La mer et les hommes. Pêcheurs et matelots dunkerquois de Louis XIV à la Révolution* (Dunkerque, 1980), 41-43 and 52; and R. Baetens, "La population maritime de la Flandre: une religiosité en question (XVe-XVIIIe siècles)," *Foi chrétienne et milieux maritimes (XVe-XXe siècles)* (Paris, 1989), 90.

[18]Hambye, *L'aumônerie*, 152-153.

convoy vessels – six in 1696, with about 700 men – the admiralty had great difficulties in recruiting the necessary crew.[19]

The next peak came between 1715 and 1732, when private persons and later the Ostend Company started shipping to Bengal, China and sporadically to Africa. There were fifty-five ships of about 15,000 tons. The average tonnage of vessels trading to China increased from 379 to 447 tons. The ratio between the number of seamen and tonnage was 21.8 per 100 tons for company ships to China and 23.7 for those to India. In 1725-1726 seven ships, with a total of about 625 seamen, departed.[20]

It is obvious that Ostend and its hinterland could not provide enough sailors. Besides, there was also the merchant fleet (of unknown size). If we take into account the turnover in crew on Asian routes due to illness, mortality and desertion, about 1500 sailors were needed. In the second half of the eighteenth century the Bruges Chamber of Commerce noted that the merchant fleet numbered about thirty.[21]

The establishment of the Company of Trieste and Fiume (1750) and the Asian Company of Trieste (1775, renamed the Imperial Asian Company of Trieste in 1781) had only a slight impact on the domestic labour market, since their vessels sailed from foreign ports (Leghorn, Lorient, Nantes and Trieste). The 1200-ton *Prince of Kaunitz* had a crew of 287 men, among whom the Flemish and French seamen were continuously in conflict. The only vessels sailing from Ostend were at least three owned by the Bruges House of Commerce, established under

[19]Baetens, "Organization," 55 and 57; L. Gilliodts-Van Severen, *Cartulaire de l'ancienne Estaple de Bruges* (4 vols., Bruges, 1906), IV, 500; De Smet, "De krijgsvloot," 496-497; and De Smet, "La flotte de guerre flamande au XVIIe siècle," *Les amis du vieux Dunkerque*, XI-XII (1980), 43-55.

[20]R. Baetens, "Investering en rendement bij de Generale Indische Compagnie: de handel op Bengalen vergeleken met de China handel," in *Album aangeboden aan Charles Verlinden* (Wetteren, 1976), 33; and K. Degryse, "De Oostendse Chinahandel (1718-1735)" (Unpublished PhD thesis, University of Ghendt, 1971-1972).

[21]R. Baetens, "Le comportement des marins sur les navires ostendais vers l'Orient," *Revue du Nord* (1986), 394; and J. Lefèvre, *Etude sur le commerce de la Belgique avec l'Espagne au XVIIIe siècle* (Brussels, 1921), 85.

the aegis of the Asian Company. In the prosperous years of Ostend's neutrality (1778-1785) these craft also went to America.[22]

Many foreign shipowners preferred the neutral Austrian flag. In 1782 the merchant and fishing fleet consisted of 2539 vessels (455,804 tons) and at the end of 1783 there were still 1530 (248,803 tons). According to contemporaries at least two-thirds were foreigners. The camouflage techniques, however, obscure a clearer view on this short rise of the maritime activities of Ostend. No doubt Flemish shipowners made use of the circumstances. The Ostend population – 7077 souls in 1784 – could not meet the temporary rise in demand for labour. As before, seamen had to be recruited from abroad. The short periods of prosperity prevented immigration of the type that might result in permanent residence in Ostend.[23]

## Nineteenth Century

The Belgian fleet developed greatly under Dutch rule. In 1829 the Southern merchant marine had grown to 182 ships of 26,962 Moorsom tons. The home ports were Antwerp, Ghent and Ostend. After independence the fleet diminished briefly, but by 1850 there were again 154 vessels of 27,914 tons, including five steamers. In 1846 the man-ton ratio averaged 5.4 men per 100 tons for sailing vessels. Supposing all were at sea, about 1100 seamen would have been required. We still have to add the crew of the five steamers, but that was but a small number. According to the contemporary A. Lecointe, the Belgian merchant

[22] L. Michielsen, "De handel," in *Antwerpen in de XVIIIde eeuw* (Antwerp, 1952), 105-110; L. Dermigny, *La Chine et l'Occident: le commerce de Canton au 18e siècle (1719-1833)* (Paris, 1964), III, 965-967; Antwerp Municipal Archives, Insolvente Boedelskamer, Archief de Proli, 1920, letter of 20 October 1780; and H. Houtman-De Smedt, *Charles Proli, Antwerps zakenman en bankier, 1723-1786. Een biografische en bedrijfshistorische studie* (Brussels, 1983), 91.

[23] Houtman-De Smedt, *Charles Proli*, 92; J. Everaert, "Le pavillon impérial aux Indes occidentales. Contrebande de guerre et trafic neutre depuis les ports Flamands (1778-1785)," *Collectanea Maritima*, IV (1988), 47; and J. Walgrave, "De bevolking van Oostende en haar betrekkingen met de zee in de Franse tijd 1797-1814," *Mededelingen van de Marine Academie van België*, XIV (1962), 18.

service numbered 2100 seamen in 1898.[24] In 1900 the fleet totalled seventy-three steamers and nine windjammers for a total of 105,917 tons. Ranked by tonnage, the Belgian fleet was the 171st largest in the world.

In 1834 the Belgian navy comprised fourteen ships and 645 seamen. Shortly thereafter it had to help the merchant fleet, which after the departure in 1830 of many shipowners to Holland faced a severe lack of experienced seamen. In 1862 the navy virtually no longer existed: there were only eighteen officers and 250 petty officers and sailors. At the outbreak of World War I Belgium lacked its own naval force.[25]

**Social Status of the Crew**

As employment increased, the crew became more international due to the limited supply of manpower. For the seventeenth century there are enough indications to make some observations. In years of great demand the crews of the Armada and the private raiders must have been at least forty-eight percent foreign, a situation that continued in Dunkirk even after its attachment to France. Flemish sailors preferred to serve only under their own masters. While the Armada used mostly Spanish officers, the privateer captains were Flemish.[26]

At the time of the Ostend Compagnie the crews sailing to Bengal were thirty-four percent foreign, while on the ships to China half were non-Belgian; this works out in total to about forty percent foreign. On the private expeditions the average proportion of foreigners was 41.4%. The private shipowners (1715-1722) of Ghent and Bruges preferred Flemish seamen, but their lack of experience had consequences. Antwerp shareholders, on the other hand, preferred well-qualified seamen. For the private expeditions, British seamen were dominant among the foreigners,

---

[24]R. Baetens, "A Survey of Maritime Relations between Belgium and the United States of America (1830-1939)," *Collectanea Maritima*, V (1991), 229 and 248; National Maritime Museum (Antwerp), Muster Rolls; and A. Lecointe, *Developpement de la marine marchande en Belgique* (Ostend, 1898), 39.

[25]*De Zeemacht. Van de Admiraliteit van Vlaanderen tot de Belgische Zeemacht* (Tielt, 1992), 107 and 113; and *Moniteur Belge*, 30 November 1834.

[26]H. Malo, *Les corsaires dunkerquois* (Paris, 1912), 433-449; and J.S. Bromley, "Les équipages des corsaires sous Louis XIV (1688-1713)," in *Les Hommes et la Mer dans l'Europe du Nord-Ouest*, 306-307.

especially the officers. At the time of the Ostend Company, their number decreased due to rigorous measures undertaken by British authorities. As a result, they were replaced by people from Dunkirk. In the meantime Flemish officers, with traditions of privateering and merchant service, became familiar with sailing to Asia.[27]

For the nineteenth century we have only some fragmentary numbers, especially since the muster rolls at the Public Record Office in Beveren survive only for 1815-1840, 1842-1844, fragments of 1892-1903 and from 1919 onwards. There are also lists for the relief fund for seamen, but these only include pensioners. Still, we know that of about ten vessels on the Atlantic route departing from Antwerp between 1844 and 1847, at best sixty percent of the seamen were Belgian.[28] In 1898 two-thirds of the crew on Belgian craft were foreign. Ten years later the Belgian share had increased to about fifty percent.

In *Vlaanderen's economische ontwikkeling* (1905), Lodewijk de Raet noted that among the 2201 seamen in the fleet only 721 were Belgian. This picture is confirmed when we analyze the officer corps. An inquiry in 1900 of sixty-six Antwerp-based vessels showed only forty-three percent of the 223 officers were Belgian. The same report noted a shortage of qualified individuals. Moreover, it showed that only ninety-four of 172 qualified Belgian merchant officers actually occupied relevant positions. The result was a clear propensity for the greater incidence of shipwrecks. An 1899 report concluded that Belgian ships were up to nine times more likely to be wrecked than were British ships; seven times more likely than German; six times more likely than French; and three times more likely than Norwegian. In 1888 only twenty percent of first machinists on domestic steam vessels were Belgian.[29]

---

[27]Baetens, "Le comportement," 394-395; K. Degryse and J. Parmentier, "Maritime Aspects of the Ostend Trade to Mocha, India and China (1715-1732)," in J.R. Bruijn and F.S. Gaastra (eds.), *Ships, Sailors and Spices. East India Companies and their Shipping in the 16th, 17th and 18th Centuries* (Amsterdam, 1993), 144.

[28]C. Lis, *Social Changes and the Labouring Poor. Antwerpen, 1770-1860* (New Haven, 1986), 57, notes that "As might be expected, more than half of the sailors were foreigners."

[29]Lecointe, *Developpement*, 13-14; *Recrutement de nos officiers de marine marchande* (Brussels, 1900), 5-7, 33; P. Vandensteen, "De Belgische koopvaardij van 1900 tot nu," *Vijftig jaar Koninklijke Marine Academie* (Antwerpen, 1986), 37; and S. Raats, "Een profiel van de zeeman op de Belgische koopvaardij tussen 1895 en 1930," *Mededelingen*

A second constant in the maritime history of the South Netherlands is the alliance of the coastal population from Dunkirk to Flushing. In this area, even beyond the political borders, there were regular migrations, either temporary or permanent. After the capture of Ostend in 1604, there was a migration to Sluis, Flushing and Veere. After Dunkirk was taken by the English and later by the French, many inhabitants left for Ostend "où il semble que la ville de Dunkerque ait emigré." About one-third of privateering captains left, for example.[30] During the eighteenth century the same phenomenon recurred.

Despite French prohibitions, the Ostend Company recruited fifteen to seventeen percent of its crews from Dunkirk. The officers were half foreign, and fifty percent of the foreigners came from Dunkirk. Even after this period relations between Dunkirk, Newport and Ostend remained close and migrations continued. In twenty-four percent of the marriages contracted at Dunkirk between 1737 and 1791, one of the partners came from Flanders, while no fewer than sixty percent of the foreign spouses were from the South Netherlands. In 1804 fifteen percent of the "not-from-Dunkirk-families" came from Flanders. For the sake of completeness, it is notable that during the last quarter of the sixteenth century there was also a migration of Antwerp seamen to the North.[31]

The sea had only a small influence on the agrarian hinterland. An examination of the crew lists of the Ostend Company shows that even Bruges and Ghent provided only a small number of seamen (one to two percent). It is striking that skilled workmen, like carpenters, blacksmiths, cooks and surgeons, came from abroad. The mentality and lifestyle of deep-sea sailors was completely different from those of farmers. The

---

*Koninklijke Marine Academie*, XXVII (1983-1985), 71-73.

[30]W. Debrock, "Toen Duinkerke nog Vlaams was. Mensen van Oostende en Duinkerke in oorlog en vrede," *Neptunus*, XXVII (1979-1980), 2-8; Malo, *Les corsaires dunkerquois*, I, 413 ff.; and Baetens, "Organisation," 54.

[31]Baetens, "Le comportement," 394-395; C. Pfister, "Dunkerque-Ostende: quelques jalons sur l'évolution de leurs rapports au XVIIIe siècle," *Actes du 101e congrès national des sociétés savantes* (Lille, 1976), I, 39-59; Cabantous, *La mer et les hommes*, 87 and 91; and J. Van Roey, "De eerste reis van Middelburg naar West-Indië. De tocht van de Antwerpse schipper Gillis van Dornhoven naar San Domingo, La Margarita en Cumana," *Mededelingen van de Marine Academie van België*, XXI (1969-1970), 37-49.

authorities, the church included, emphasized the difference in every possible way to the detriment of seafaring.[32]

Wages throw a special light on the social status of the seamen. These are examined here in three ways. First, we examine the differences between pay for the most important kinds of labour on a single ship. Then we compare rates of pay in the navy, merchant marine and foreign vessels. Finally, we look at landward versus seafaring wages.

For the sixteenth century, J. Van Roey found that in 1584 and 1585, eighty-seven percent of Antwerp sailors were too poor to pay taxes.[33] This at least in part resulted from wide discrepancies in pay between captains and others, a trend that continued in all branches of the maritime sector (see table 1).

**Table 1**
**Wage Index of Mates and Seamen Compared to Masters, 1626-1771**

| | Armada (1626) | Armada (1633-1646) | Warship (1691) | Merchantman (1771) |
|---|---|---|---|---|
| Master | 100 | 100 | 100 | 100 |
| First Mate | 43 | 60 | - | 60 |
| Seaman | 14 | 16 | 18 | 15 |

*Notes:* Masters' wages equal 100 in all years. Index numbers are rounded where necessary to the nearest whole integer.

*Sources:* E. Hambye, *L'aumônerie de la flotte de Flandre au XVIIe siècle* (Louvain, 1967), 147; R.A. Stradling, *The Armada of Flanders* (Cambridge, 1992), 242; L. Gilliodts-Van Severen, *Cartulaire de l'ancienne Estaple de Bruges* (Bruges, 1906), IV, 499; and C. Vandenbroecke, "Bijdrage tot de studie van de voeding en de lonen van de zeelui tijdens de tweede helft van de achttiende eeuw," *Tijdschrift voor sociale wetenschappen*, XVI (1971), 414.

[32]De Smet, "De krijgsvloot," 12; Municipal Archives of Antwerp, Generale Indische Compagnie, no. 2008; Baetens, "La population maritime," 88-93; and A. Cabantous, *Les citoyens du large. Les identités maritimes en France (XVIIe-XIXe siècle)* (Paris, 1995), especially 42-68 and 95-118.

[33]J. Van Roey, "De Antwerpse schippers als sociaal-professionele groep en hun houding inzake godsdienst in het laatste kwart van de XVIe eeuw," *Mededelingen van de Marine Academie*, XIX (1967), 4-5.

The figures in table 1 do not include the share in prizes, which was higher for men serving on privateers than for those in the Armada. Privateers were entitled to one-twelfth of profits after deducting one-tenth for the sovereign and two percent for the health insurance fund; officers got an even larger share. For the navy of the United Provinces, the proportions during the seventeenth century were 100:36:11.[34] The gap between the different categories was thus significantly greater.

On the merchantmen the situation in general was even worse (see table 2), a generalization that is true both within the Ostend Company and when the Belgian company is compared to similar mercantile enterprises throughout northern Europe. Indeed, profits from the *pacotilles* only worsened the gaps among categories. A captain of the Ostend Company earned on one journey between 20,000 and 30,000 guilders. His colleagues of the Swedish Company did even better. Before 1748 twenty-five to twenty-nine percent of their cargoes on average consisted *pacotilles*, while for the Ostenders this figure was seven to nineteen percent.[35]

**Table 2**
**Wage Index of Mates and Seamen Compared to Masters in Various Long-Distance Trading Companies**

| | Ostend | VOC | EIC | Swedish Cy |
|---|---|---|---|---|
| Master | 100 | 100 | 100 | 100 |
| First Mate | 39 | 62 | 50 | 80 |
| Seaman | 9 | 13 | 11 | 15 |

*Notes*: Masters' wages equal 100 in all years. Index numbers are rounded where necessary to the nearest whole integer.

*Sources*: R. Baetens, "Le comportement des marins sur les navires ostendais vers l'Orient," *Revue du Nord* (1986), 391-392; Dermigny, *La Chine et l'Occident*, 233; and C. Koninckx, *The First and Second Charters of the Swedish East India Company (1731-1766)* (Kortrijk, 1980), 322-323.

[34]Baetens, "Organisation," 53. According to Gilliodt-Van Severen, *Cartulaire*, IV, 499, in 1718 Ostend seamen received only one-sixth of profits. On the United Provinces, see Lucassen, "Zeevarenden;" and G. Asaert, *Maritieme Geschiedenis der Nederlanden* (Bussum, 1977), II, 141.

[35]Koninckx, *First and Second Charters*, 326.

For the nineteenth century we know the wages on a variety of vessels (see table 3). This suggests that the differences among ranks appear to have become smaller. The wages also show a greater diversity. Seamen on sailing vessels have higher wages than their colleagues on steamers. But there are differences between vessels and during the second half of the nineteenth century there was a slow upward trend in wages, as L.R. Fischer has shown.[36]

**Table 3**
**Wage Index of Mates and Seamen Compared to Masters on Various Belgian Merchantmen, 1846-1882**

| | Sailing Vessels | | Steamer | Cutter |
|---|---|---|---|---|
| | (1846) | (1855) | (1881) | (1882) |
| Master | 100 | 100 | 100 | 100 |
| First Mate | 70 | 91 | 69 | 90 |
| Seaman | 33 | 50 | 23 | 70 |

*Notes:* Masters' wages equal 100 in all years. Index numbers are rounded where necessary to the nearest whole integer.

*Source:* National Maritime Museum of Antwerp, D 16.309, II-IV.

Let us now compare the wages in the merchant fleet and the navy with the situation abroad (see table 4). It is clear that service on company ships was better paid than on naval ships. Moreover, the duration of the voyage of a company ship – an average of 504 days for a China journey and 579 for India – was much longer than for the precarious trips of a warship or a privateer. Moreover, on both privateers and Company ships there were extra earnings, although these are difficult to sort out. As well, injury, captivity and death have to be considered when calculating the final balance. The Spanish government paid poorly: in the Armada a sailor earned only nine pennies a day and twelve on privateers. Families with a father at sea had to do with a small advance and lived in great poverty. Often six to seven families lived together in very small houses. To ease the need of ordinary seamen there was a deduction from the profits: in 1657 a health insurance fund was founded for those who went privateering. Even privateering captains were poor. Records show

[36]L.R. Fischer, "Seamen in the Industrial Revolution: Maritime Wages in Antwerp during the Shipping Transition, 1863-1900," *Collectanea Maritima*, V (1991), 338.

that their property varied only from 1000 to 30,000 florins. Premature death also made it difficult to accumulate capital. Jan Bart, one of the most successful captains in privateering, left only 125,000 Tournois Pounds (68,052 florins) when he died, hardly a great amount.[37]

**Table 4**

**A. Monthly wages (guilders Brabants courant) in the Southern Netherlands**

| | Armada (1626) | Marine (1691) | Marine (1718) | Marine (Holl.) |
|---|---|---|---|---|
| Master | 55 | 60 | 100 | 110 |
| First Mate | 24 | - | 32 | 40.5 |
| Seaman | 8 | 15 | 15-18 | 11.2 |

| | Ostend | VOC | Swedish Co. | French Co. | Asiatic Co. (1771) |
|---|---|---|---|---|---|
| Master | 150.10 | 89 | 92.10 | 108.10 | 97.10 |
| First Mate | 59.10 | 55.16 | 73.10 | 32.12 | 58.10 |
| Seaman | 14 | 12.5 | 14 | 10 | 15 |

**B. Monthly Wages (Belgian francs)**

| | Barque (1844) | (1846) | Cutter (1882) | Steamer (1881) |
|---|---|---|---|---|
| Master | - | 126.93 | 100 | 325 |
| First Mate | 84.65 | 88.89 | 90 | 225 |
| Seaman | 42.32 | 42.33 | 70 | 75 |

*Notes*: Wages for the VOC were calculated on a maximum wage of eighty guilders for the master, fifty for the first mate and eleven for a seaman.

*Sources*: See text.

---

[37]Malo, *Les corsaires dunkerquois*, I, 272-274; Baetens, "Organisation," 53; and W. Debrock, "Een mutualiteitskas van de Oostendse reders ter kaapvaart 1657-1716," *Handelingen Société d'Emulation Brugge*, XLVII (1960), 74-103; Baetens, "An Essay on Dunkirk Merchants and Capital Growth during the Spanish Period," W.G. Heeres, *et al.* (eds.), *From Dunkirk to Danzig. Shipping and Trade in the North Sea and the Baltic 1350-1850* (Hilversum, 1988), 133-137; A. Cabantous, "Héros et mentalités collectives: Jean Bart et la naissance d'un mythe 1700-1870," in *Actes du XVIIIe congrès de la Fédération des sociétés savantes du Nord de la France* (Lille, 1979), 83-100; and A. Lesmaries, "Jean Bart et sa fortune," *Mémoire de la Société dunkerquoise pour l'encouragement des lettres, des sciences et des arts*, LXIII (1926), 5-88 and LXIV (1927), 57-91.

When we compare the wages of crew on the company ships, the earnings of the Ostend Company were remarkably high. The scarcity of experienced workers forced the directors to adopt a wage policy that was, at least in relative terms, somewhat attractive. For the same reason the other companies around 1730 were confronted with demands for higher wages.[38]

The way in which the monthly salary was paid was the same for masters as for sailors. Every crewman received two months' salary in advance. During the journey another three months wages were paid. The rest was distributed when the vessel returned. There was a debenture system for families ashore. Relatives of a crew member were entitled to three months wages after respectively six, twelve and eighteen months. Nevertheless complaints to the "poor masters" were continuous.[39]

An average day's wage for a sailor in the South Netherlands varied in the seventeenth and eighteenth centuries from nine to ten pennies. A skilled labourer, on the other hand, earned on average ten to thirteen pennies, and a foreman was paid fourteen to sixteen pennies. Because the sailor received his food free of charge, we need to add another seven to eight pennies to his stipend, which means that seamen actually were paid about eighteen pennies. But his family still had to be taken care of and temporary unemployment was inherent in the job. Perhaps, therefore, he would in fact have been better off working ashore. Craftsmen aboard were better off, though: a carpenter earned twenty-four pennies a day ashore, but he got thirty-two pennies plus food at sea.[40]

In the nineteenth century the picture is more diversified but the conclusions are broadly the same. Seamen's earnings were subject to

---

[38]K. Glamann, *Dutch-Asiatic Trade (1620-1740)* (Copenhagen, 1958), 238.

[39]A decree of 22 October 1515 prescribed that one-half of the wage had to be paid before departure and the other half after return. Many seamen did not fulfil their contract (C. Laurent and J. Lameere, *Ordonnances des Pays-Bas. Règne de Charles Quint (1506-1555)* (Brussels, 1893), I, 424; Municipal Archives of Antwerp, Generale Indische Compagnie, 5539, registers van rekeningen en facturen; 5818, request from the Chamber of the poor; Library of the University of Ghent, manuscript 1880, examples of printed obligations. This was also the case for the Dutch East India Company; see J. De Hullu, "Matrozen en soldaten op schepen der Oostindische Compagnie," *Bijdragen tot de Taal-, Land- en Volkenkunde van Nederlandsch-Indië*, LXIX (1914), 361 ff.

[40]Vandenbroecke, "Bijdrage tot de studie," 405, 415-419; and C. Verlinden, *Documenten voor prijzen en lonen in Vlaanderen en Brabant* (Gent, 1965), VI, 354-461.

strong fluctuations related to the type of vessel and his employers. Before 1850 a seaman on a sailing vessel earned 1.30 to 1.50 BEF per day. In the second half of the century the wages on a sailing vessel increased from 2.18 to 2.52 BEF. Sailors on steamers earned the same. Wages in Antwerp until 1870 were only eighty-five percent of British wages. Later they increased very quickly but decreased again after 1875.[41] Because of better wages and labour conditions, sailors on Belgian ships deserted in American ports to enlist on North American vessels. We still know little about the factors which influenced this market mechanism. The intensity of the traffic may have been beneficial for international labour in Antwerp, but scarcity and oversupply certainly influenced wages. It is worth mentioning that in the 1880s the chief engineer earned wages that were as high or higher than those paid to a master. This was, for instance, the case on the steamer *Alex Smyers*, where the chief engineer had 350 BEF and the captain only 325 BEF per month.

Between 1845 and 1850 a day labourer in a Ghent textile mill earned about 1.33 BEF for five and one-half days work, while textile workers in Antwerp in 1855 earned only 1.15 BEF. Seamen had to work longer for wages that were barely higher. But industrial wages increased earlier and faster than in the merchant marine – by an average of fifty-four percent to only fifteen percent between 1860 and 1900. The Belgian seamen could, however, rely after 1845 on a relief fund in case of illness, disability, and old age.[42]

What career patterns can be discerned? In privateering, the chances for a real career were poor because of the risks. Nevertheless, a few captains received official recognition by the Spanish Authorities.[43] During the second half of the seventeenth century there was a rather

---

[41]National Maritime Museum of Antwerp, D 16.309, II, III, IV; Muster Rolls 1844-1846; and Fischer, "Seamen," 336-339. "Mean wages:" £2.6-3 between 1863-1900. 1 £ = 25,2215 BEF (V. Janssens, *De Belgische Frank. Anderhalve eeuw geldgeschiedenis* [Brussels, 1975]).

[42]Lis, *Social Changes*, 176; G. Avondts, *et al.*, *De Gentse textielarbeiders in de 19e en 20e eeuw* (Brussels, 1976), 100-102; Fischer, "Seamen," 336; and G. Teitler, "Zeevarenden;" and Asaert, *Maritieme Geschiedenis der Nederlanden*, IV (1978), 125.

[43]J. Dams, "Michel Jacobsen et la Flotte de Flandre 1621-1632," *Revue des amis du vieux Dunkerque*, V (1976), 43-49; XIII (1981), 7-20; Dams, "Un mémoire;" and N. Pasquini, *Histoire de la ville d'Ostende* (Brussels, 1842).

select group of privateering captains who alternately served in the navy and the merchant fleet. They provided the first group of officers for the Ostend ships sailing to Asia between 1715 and 1732. Some of them made a fortune. They or their progeny went into commerce or governmer service. Others continued their seafaring activities with the Swedis Company. A few were later admitted into the nobility.

In general, however, there was not enough continuity in tl South Netherlands navy and merchant fleet to build up a seafarir career. In the nineteenth century the education and experience of Belgia officers were insufficient and they could not compete with foreigners. was only in the twentieth century that the government and shipowne took measures to correct this.[44]

## Conclusion

Belgium, regardless of what it has been called, has never been able to build a maritime tradition. There were two short prosperous periods. The first had to do with privateering, but war is never rewarding in the long run. Second, there was the growth stimulated by the Ostend Company, which proved that it was possible for commercial seafaring to flourish. The maritime powers, however, crippled its development. Later, the industrial sector enjoyed preference over maritime activities.

---

[44]Baetens, "Le comportement," 396, 403; C. Koninckx, "La compagnie suédoise des Indes orientales et les Pays-Bas autrichiens. Esquisse succincte d'une participation 'belge' à l'étranger au XVIIIe siècle," *Mededelingen van de Koninklijke Academie voor Overzeese wetenschappen*, XXIV (1978), 295-329; and Raats, "Een profiel," 71. In 1898 there were thirty-seven percent Belgian officers and sixty-three percent foreigners; *Recrutement de nos officiers de marine marchande*, 7-21.

# The Labour Market for Sailors in France

T.J.A. Le Goff

## State of the Art and Sources

In maritime history, as in so much French historical writing, there is a great divide around the beginning of Louis XIV's personal reign in 1661. That regime marked the emergence of the Caribbean and Indian trades and the development of a large navy, manned by sailors conscripted, rather than impressed, from the maritime labour force. At the same time, the French state developed civilian-managed administrative services which not only ran the recruitment and logistical services of the navy but also came eventually to oversee many of the relations between maritime capital and its labour force. This new bureaucracy, which left an abundant and centralised documentation, has in turn had a massive impact on historical writing on French shipping and sailors. Such works on the period before the 1660s usually take the form of the port-based monograph, grounded in research in often recalcitrant regional sources, such as local port records, notarial archives and registers of baptisms, marriages and burials. After this date, centralised and uniform administrative documentation is more abundant, which makes it easier to write about the situation in each port as a part of a whole.[1]

If 1661 forms one boundary in maritime history, 1789 forms another. Maritime historians follow the convention of their colleagues in

[1]The pre-1661 literature is summarised briefly in F. Braudel and C-E. Labrousse (eds.), *Histoire Économique et sociale de la France* (3 vols., Paris, 1977), I, 474-476, while the post-1789 works are covered in the same series, x-xxi. Up-to-date bibliographies for the maritime history of individual ports, from the earliest times down to the present are given in the different volumes of the series *Pays et Villes de France*, edited by P. Wolff and F. Lebrun (Toulouse, 1973 - ); for current production, see the annual volumes of the *Bibliographie annuelle de l'Histoire de France* (Paris, 1953/1954-) and the handy *Chronique d'histoire maritime* (1979-), published by the Commission française d'histoire maritime. See also the special number of the *Bulletin de la Société d'Histoire Moderne et Contemporaine* (1997), Nos. 1-2, on "Européens et espaces maritimes au XVIIIe siècle," which contains useful overviews and a bibliography of recent work.

other branches of French history by dividing into experts on "modern" and "contemporary" France on either side of that fateful watershed. French trade as it had developed during the eighteenth century was seriously disrupted by warfare and blockade during the French Revolutionary and Napoleonic Wars, and whole sectors of activity were eradicated permanently, so that the student of the eighteenth century who looks at the situation under the Bourbon Restoration finds the familiar landmarks of French maritime history much displaced. Although there is a much greater continuity of sources, particularly administrative, between 1780 and 1820 than from, say, 1640 to 1720, and although it would quite feasible to write about themes over a *longue durée* from the late seventeenth to the late nineteenth century, in fact it is rarely done, and nineteenth-century French maritime history is still relatively unexplored territory.[2]

All these observations are true, *a fortiori*, of the maritime labour force. On these grounds, and also in order to avoid superficiality, I have chosen to write about the period between 1661 and 1789. This central period is the one which is best covered in the secondary literature at the present, though more from the perspective of the history of commerce than of its labour force. Weighty monographs have been written since World War II on all the great French ports, but many have little or nothing to say about the labour supply for merchant shipping. Those that do are the studies of Butel and Huetz de Lemps on Bordeaux, Meyer on Nantes, Haudrère on Lorient, Lespagnol on Saint-Malo and Rambert on Marseille.[3] The cod fisheries are well served in the works of J-F. Brière

---

[2]One exception to this is the collective work on fisheries in M. Mollat (ed.), *Histoire des pêches maritimes en France* (Toulouse, 1987).

[3]On Dunkerque, see C. Pfister-Langanay, *Ports, navires et négociants à Dunkerque (1662-1792)* (Dunkerque, 1985); For Rouen and Le Havre, see P. Dardel, *Navires et marchandises dans les ports de Rouen et du Havre au XVIIIe siècle* (Paris, 1963); and *Commerce industrie et navigation à Rouen et au Havre au XVIIIème siècle* (Rouen, 1966). On Saint-Malo, see J. Delumeau, *et al.*, *Le mouvement du port de Saint-Malo 1681-1720. Bilan statistique* (Paris, 1966); and A. Lespagnol, *Messieurs de Saint-Malo. Une élite négociante au temps de Louis XIV* (Saint-Malo, 1990). On Lorient, see P. Haudrère, *La Compagnie française des Indes au XVIIIe siècle (1719-1795)* (4 vols., Paris, 1989), notably 539-600 and 1255-1269. On Nantes, see J. Meyer, *L'armement nantais dans la deuxième moitié du XVIIIe siècle* (Paris, 1969); "L'armement nantais au XVIIIe siècle d'après les registres des classes," *Actes du quatre-vingt-onzième congrès des sociétés savantes* (2 vols., Paris, 1969), I, 143-151; and "Le commerce nantais du

on Saint-Malo and Granville.[4] There is a large corpus by Alain Cabantous on the seafaring populations of Dunkerque and the ports of the Channel coast down as far as Le Havre with much useful information on seafarers' migrations, but his main concern is with the demographic history of seafarers and the history of religious mentalities rather than seafarers as a labour force.[5] There are a number of local studies of seamen's migrations in periodicals, in the form of unpublished *mémoires de maîtrise* and other research projects. The bibliography in Cabantous' *Dix mille marins* provides a fair guide to all of these. Concerning the

---

XVIe au XVIIIe siècle," in P. Bois (ed.), *Histoire de Nantes* (Toulouse, 1977), 117-154. On La Rochelle, see H. Robert, "Les trafics coloniaux du port de La Rochelle au XVIIIe siècle," *Mémoires de la Société des antiquaires de l'Ouest*, 4e sér., IV (1960); and J.G. Clark, *La Rochelle and the Atlantic Economy during the Eighteenth Century* (Baltimore, 1981). On Bordeaux, see C. Huetz de Lemps, *Géographie du commerce de Bordeaux à la fin du règne de Louis XIV* (Paris-La Haye, 1975), 578-593; P. Butel, *Les négociants bordelais l'Europe et les Iles au XVIIIe siècle* (Paris, 1974); and especially, the full version of Butel's thesis: P. Butel, *La croissance commerciale bordelaise dans la seconde moitié du XVIIIème siècle* (Lille, 1973), I, 737-755; see also the chapters by F. Crouzet in G. Pariset (ed.), *Bordeaux au XVIIIe siècle* (Bordeaux, 1968), 191-286. On Bayonne, see F. Jaupart, "L'activité commerciale et maritime de Bayonne au XVIIIe siècle," *Société des sciences, lettres et arts de Bayonne*, n. sér, No. 110 (1996), 3-231; and No. 111, 233-469. On Marseille, see C. Carrière, *Négociants marseillais au XVIIIe siècle Contribution à l'étude des économies maritimes* (Marseille, 1973); and G. Rambert (ed.), *Histoire du Commerce de Marseille* (Paris, 1949-), esp. II, 887-890; III, 316-317; IV, 430-457; and VI, 250-255.

[4]J-F. Brière, *La pêche française en Amérique du Nord au XVIIIe siècle* (Montréal, 1990); and "L'armement français pour la pêche à Terre-Neuve au XVIIIe siècle" (Unpublished PhD thesis, York University, Toronto, 1980). See also M-T. Gueguen, "La main-d'oeuvre maritime à Saint-Malo: présentation et évolution de son bassin de recrutement fin XVIIème – fin XVIIIème" (Mémoire de maîtrise, Faculté de Lettres, Université de Rennes-II, 1985); and the pioneering work of C. de La Morandière, *Histoire de la pêche française de la morue dans l'Amérique septentrionale (des origines à 1789)* (3 vols., Paris, 1962-1966).

[5]See particularly Alain Cabantous, *La mer et les hommes Pêcheurs et matelots dunkerquois de Louis XIV à la Révolution* (n.p., 1980), the published version of his *thèse de troisième cycle* "Les gens de mer de Dunkerque à l'époque moderne 1662-1791. Etude sociale" (Thèse de troisième cycle, Université de Lille III, 1978); and *Dix mille marins face à l'Océan les populations maritimes de Dunkerque au Havre aux XVIIe et XVIIIe siècles (vers 1660-1794). Etude sociale* (Paris, 1991), which is taken from his *thèse d'Etat*, "Les populations maritimes du littoral français de la mer du Nord et de la Manche orientale (vers 1660-1793): essai d'histoire sociale comparative" (Lille, 1987).

demand and supply of seamen for the navy, a good deal has been written about the *système des classes*, the regime of naval conscription and the ancestor of the present-day *inscription maritime*, dealing mostly with its difficult beginnings under Colbert and Seignelay.[6] By the 1730s, it had come to manage many aspects of the labour supply in the civilian maritime economy, but not much appears in these works about the interaction between voluntary employment in the private sector and compulsory employment in the King's service. Nor has much been said about the effect on the structure and operation of the labour market of the various regulations which the King imposed in order to enhance naval recruitment. There is a large and uneven literature on privateering.[7] Finally, there are some works on galleys, which in France were used almost exclusively for military purposes before the demise of the royal galley corps in 1749, and which were a Mediterranean specialty, except

---

[6]The main studies are J-G. de Crisenoy, *Le personnel de la marine militaire et les classes maritimes sous Colbert et Seignelay* (Paris, 1864); J. Captier, *Etude historique et économique sur l'inscription maritime* (Paris, 1907); R. Mémain, *Matelots et soldats des vaisseaux du Roi. Levées d'hommes au département de Rochefort* (Paris, 1937); E. L. Asher, *The Resistance to the Maritime Classes* (Berkeley, 1960); G.R. Symcox, *The Crisis of French Naval Power 1688-97*; M-T. de Martel, *Etude sur le recrutement des matelots et soldats des vaisseaux du Roi dans le ressort de l'intendance du port de Rochefort (1691-1697)* (Vincennes, 1982); M. Perrichet, "L'administration des classes de la Marine et ses archives dans les ports bretons," *Revue d'Histoire économique et sociale*, XXXVII (1959), 89-112; J. Dull, *The French Navy and American Independence* (Princeton, 1975); M. Acerra, *Rochefort et la Construction navale française 1661-1815* (Paris, 1993); Acerra, "Le matériel de la marine de guerre française : effectifs, arsenaux et approvisionnements au XVIIIe siècle," *Bulletin de la Société d'Histoire Moderne et Contemporaine*, Nos. 1-2 (1997), 64-79; M. Vergé-Franceschi, *Les officiers généraux de la Marine royale (1715-1774). Origines conditions services* (Paris, 1990); Vergé-Franceschi, *La Marine française au XVIIIe siècle. Guerres-Administration-Exploration* (Paris, 1996); W.S. Cormack, *Revolution and Political Conflict in the French Navy 1789-1794* (Cambridge, 1995); and M. Acerra and J. Meyer, *Marines en Révolution* (Rennes, 1988), provide useful and recent bibliographies on the navy. Other recent works on the navy include E.H. Jenkins, *A History of the French Navy from its Beginnings to the Present Day* (London, 1973); J. Pritchard, *Louis XV's Navy 1748-1762: A Study of Organization and Administration* (Montréal, 1987); and Pritchard, *Anatomy of a Naval Disaster: The 1746 French Expedition to North America* (Montréal, 1995).

[7]A full bibliography can be found in P. Villiers, *Marine royale, corsaires et trafic dans l'Atlantique de Louis XIV à Louis XVI* (Dunkerque, 1991), which brings together much of the existing quantitative data.

for a few that saw action as support vessels in the Channel and on the Atlantic during Louis XIV's wars.[8]

This is a large literature, much of it of high quality. Yet it seldom engages directly the questions which this conference was called to address, and which have been the main focus of my own research on the seafaring population. So although I shall to refer to these various works in passing, most of my conclusions here are based on my own research on the French seafaring population and the role of the naval conscription administration, the *classes*, which I have carried out over the past twenty years.[9] I shall deal with the period 1661-1789, the years

---

[8]P. Masson, "Les galères de France, 1481-1781: Marseille, port de guerre," *Annales de la Faculté de Lettres d'Aix*, XX (1937-38), 1-4, and 7-479; P.W. Bamford, *Fighting Ships and Prisons The Mediterranean Galleys of France in the Age of Louis XIV* (Minneapolis, 1973); and A. Zysberg, *Les galériens Vies et destins de 60 000 forçats sur les galères de France 1680-1748* (Paris, 1987).

[9]"Offre et productivité de la main-d'oeuvre dans les armements français au XVIIIème siècle," *Histoire, économie et société*, II (1983), 457-474 (an earlier version appeared without notes in Paul Adam [ed.], *Seamen in Society* [3 vols., Paris, 1980], II, 95-108); "Les origines sociales des gens de mer français au XVIIIe siècle," in A. Croix and F. Lebrun (eds.), *La France d'Ancien Régime Etudes réunies en l'honneur de Pierre Goubert* (Toulouse, 1985), 367-380; "L'impact des prises effectuées par les Anglais sur la capacité en hommes de la marine française pendant les guerres de 1744-1748, 1755-1763, 1778-1783," in M. Acerra, *et al.* (eds.), *Les Marines de guerre européennes XVII-XVIIIe siècles* (Paris, 1985), 103-122; "Les gens de mer devant le système des classes 1755-1763: résistance ou passivité?" *Revue du Nord* (1986), 463-479; "Le recrutement géographique et social des gens de mer bretons à la fin de l'Ancien Régime (résultats préliminaires)," in *La Bretagne, une province à l'aube de la Révolution. Colloque, Brest, 28-30 septembre* (Brest-Quimper, 1989), 207-224; "Problèmes de recrutement de la marine française pendant la guerre de Sept Ans," *Revue Historique*, CCLXXXIII (1990), 205-233; "De la paix à la guerre, les origines des équipages de commerce français en Méditerrannée pendant les guerres du XVIIIe siècle," in M. Vergé-Franceschi (ed.), *Guerre et commerce en Méditerranée IXe-XXe siècles* (Paris, 1991), 279-308; and "Les gens de mer des années 1780," in U. Bonnel (ed.), *Fleurieu et la Marine de son temps* (Paris, 1992), 139-160. See also the following conference papers: "L'augmentation du nombre de gens de mer au XVIIIe siècle: projets et réalités" (Unpublished paper presented to the Séminaire d'histoire maritime, Ecole Pratique des Hautes Etudes [IVe Section], Paris, 1977); "The Making of a Pre-Industrial Labour Force: Government Control and Management of French Seamen in the Eighteenth Century" (Unpublished paper presented to the "Popular Protest and Popular Ideology: The George Rude Colloquium," Concordia University, October 1982); "Seamen as Prisoners" (Unpublished paper presented to the Seminar on Modern French History, Institute of Historical Research, University of London, June 1984); "Manning the French Navy in the

covered by the archives of the administration of the *classes*, and more particularly from about 1720, when the whole system began to be substantially reorganised.

I have used four main types of source. First, I have used the correspondence of the naval administration, principally of the administration of the *classes*.[10] These provide the figures from periodic censuses and administrative estimates of the total number of seafarers, of ships and shipping patterns. Second, there are the conscription registers (*matricules*) of the *classes*, which, in the regions where they survive, contain more or less standardised information on resident qualified sailors (*matelots*) and petty officers (*officiers mariniers*), as well as less complete documentation on other classes of seafarer.[11] I have a data file of about 45,000 seafarers from these sources – about 33,000 of whom are *officiers mariniers* and *matelots* from around the time of the 1784 review – which permits conclusions about permanent migration patterns, social origins of seafarers, marriage patterns and so forth.[12] Third, there

---

Eighteenth Century" (Paper presented to the Research Group, Department of History, York University, May 1985); "Wages of Seamen in Eighteenth-Century French Shipping" (Unpublished paper presented to the Annual Conference of the Society for French Historical Studies, Columbia, SC, March, 1988); "The Civilian Impact of a Military Institution: The French System of Maritime Conscription, 1715-1789" (Unpublished paper presented to the Annual Conference of the Society for the Study of French History, University of Warwick, March 1993, and to the conference on "Unfree Labour in the Development of the Atlantic World," York University, April 1993).

[10]Mainly Archives National (AN), Archives de la Marine (AM), series C4, and its counterpart in the provincial ports.

[11]Copies of the registers for *matelots* and *officiers mariniers* and for sedentary workers were made for the central administration and survive from the review conducted in 1784-1785 for ports from Dunkerque to the Loire estuary, providing a more-or-less uniform group of documents. The originals survive in many port archives; some have also been consulted for northern France and the Mediterranean ports. On these sources, see E. Le Maresquier, "Les Archives de l'inscription maritime," *La Gazette des Archives*, C (1978), 30-50; and Ph. Henwood, "La Bretagne maritime aux XVIIIe et XIXe siècles. Administration et archives," *Mémoires de la Société d'Histoire et d'Archéologie de Bretagne*, LXIV (1987), 65-114.

[12]The collection of data from the conscription registers was done using the FORCOD programmes developed by Marcel Couturier of the Ecole des Hautes Etudes en Sciences Sociales, Paris; I wish also to thank Mr. Daniel Bloom of the Department of Computing

are the series of ships' muster rolls drawn up at the beginning and end of voyages from the major French ports, which complement the conscription registers by indicating patterns of temporary migration, wage rates, ages, and the fates of crewmen. The collections in the relevant French departmental and port archives have been complemented for wartime years with rolls and related documents from captured ships in the Prize Papers at the Public Record Office in London.[13] Finally, there are the archives of the *Amirauté* (maritime courts), kept in the *Archives Départementales* (AD) of the *département* in which each port is situated. These, together with gleanings from administrative correspondence, allow some conclusions about the nature of labour relations.

This paper takes up the problems of the nature and total demand for labour during this period; the sources of labour supply, dealing with the social and geographical origins of the seafarers; changes in wage rates and their relation to demand for seamen's services; factors affecting the labour supply; links between wages and migrations; and the question of the outward migration of sailors from France.

Maritime France presented many diversities in the eighteenth century: one can speak of distinct though sometimes interdependent labour markets in the cod-fishing economy, centred on the coasts from the Cotentin to Poitou; the Atlantic; the transoceanic economy, which existed in all the major ports from Dunkerque to Marseille and touched many of the minor ones as well; the East India trade, focused on Lorient; the omnipresent (but not very well known) coastal shipping and coastal and short-range fishing sectors; and even a sort of market, or anti-market, for labour created by the needs of the French navy and privateering in wartime. There were also spatial diversities, the principal one being the distinction between the Mediterranean, where a large supply of immigrant labour had a big impact on wages and the labour supply, and the rest of France; though even within the latter, at either

---

Services, York University, for his valuable technical advice.

[13]A[rchives] D[épartementales] Gironde (ADG), Rôles d'armement, 6B, 372-375, 384-387, 400-401, 428-439 and 495-503; rôles de désarmement in AD Seine-Maritime (ADSM), Archives de l'Inscription Marine du Havre (AIMH): 6P6, 1, 5-6, 9-10, 13-14; AD L[oire] A[tlantique] (ADLA), fonds "Marine," 1737-1738, 1751-1752, 1764-1765, 1774-1775 and 1785-1786; and Archives du Port de Toulon (APT), 13P9, 1-2, 1Q, 15. On the Public Record Office (PRO) sources, see Le Goff, "Offre et productivité;" "L'impact des prises;" and "De la paix à la guerre."

end of the Atlantic and Channel coastlines, places like Dunkerque and Bayonne replicated in some ways the "Mediterranean" situation, with more mobile and international workforces than elsewhere. All this diversity, however, was diminishing with the increasing importance of transatlantic shipping in the maritime economy. In dealing with the interaction of wages and migrations, I have chosen to focus on changes in that sector, principally in the two Atlantic ports with the best available data, Nantes and Bordeaux.

**Demand for Labour: Increased Shipping Capacity and Concentration**

Total national capacity (excluding naval forces) rose from about 2500 vessels of at least 125,000 *tonneaux* (tx) in 1664 to 5254 ships with about 724,000 tx after the War of American Independence. This tonnage can be considered in three sectors: the mercantile marine, deep-sea fishing, and coasting and coastal fishing.

National tonnage in colonial and foreign shipping rose from about 125,000 tx in the 1720s to around 300,000-350,000 tx at the end of the 1780s. The rate of growth was slightly higher than in the comparable English sector, though starting from a lower base. As table 1 shows, clearances to virtually all overseas and colonial destinations increased, but the order of importance of the various sectors had changed. In the 1720s, shipping to the Mediterranean and the Iberian peninsula required fifty-four percent of French colonial and foreign shipping, while voyages to the French Americas – the Caribbean and, as an accessory, the Gulf of Mexico, New France and, later, the United States – plus the East Indies and West Africa, only accounted for thirty-seven percent of tonnage cleared. But by the eve of the French Revolution shipping to North America and the Caribbean, Africa and the East Indies accounted for over half of all clearances, and the Iberian and Mediterranean had fallen into second place with only thirty-three percent. This differing pattern of dynamic growth in colonial shipping, set against the stagnation of the Mediterranean trade, is important for understanding the different patterns of demand for maritime labour in northern and southern France.

A second element within this framework is the rise of the large ports. Table 2 shows how, from mid-century onwards, French shipping to colonial North America was dominated by outfittings in the great ports of Nantes, Bordeaux and Le Havre.

**Table 1**
**Annual Clearances of French Ships,**
**Exclusive of National Coasting (*tonneaux*)**

| | 1726-34 | 1742-43 | c.1751 | c.1779 | 1787-89 | 1792 |
|---|---|---|---|---|---|---|
| French America | 44,141 | 60,943 | 71,880 | 89,000 | 167,208 | 139,229 |
| Iberia | 19,400 | 19,354 | 21,565 | 42,600 | 41,614 | 23,901 |
| Mediterra-nean | 51,729 | 38,558 | 62,582 | 73,800 | 87,940 | 70,108 |
| West Africa | 4,143 | 9,463 | 2,800 | 6,600 | 38,596 | 15,641 |
| East India | 4,368 | 5,440 | 6,010 | 7,000 | 26,267 | 33,563 |
| Northern Europe | 7,772 | 11,275 | 9,439 | 19,600 | 33,759 | 29,842 |
| All Colonial and Foreign | 131,553 | 145,032 | 174,276 | 238,600 | 395,384 | 312,294 |
| N. American Codfishing | 29,405 | 36,359 | 59,625 | 80,000 | 45,227 | 19,497 |
| Whaling | 5,952 | 1,095 | 5,815 | 7,500 | 3,696 | 11,675 |
| Herring | 4,606 | 8,251 | 4,824 | 7,800 | -- | 5,880 |
| Mackerel | -- | 4,310 | -- | -- | -- | 12,219 |
| Total | 171,516 | 195,046 | 244,540 | 333,900 | 444,307 | 361,565 |

*Sources*: BN, nouv. acq. fr. 2550-2; Archives National (AN), Archives de la Marine (AM), C4/64, 117-119; C4/144; and F12/252, 1834B; and W. Mildmay, *An Account of the Southern Maritime Provinces of France* (1764), 133.

Colonial and overseas shipping, however, was only one employer of the overseas labour force. National figures on demand, or potential demand, in other sectors are less abundant, but suggest less dynamic overall growth. The most important single sector here was the deep-sea fishery, particularly to Newfoundland, the much-vaunted *pépinière des matelots*. National tonnage in use in the cod fisheries, as indicated by annual departures, showed a slow upward trend from 33,700 tx in 1726-1734 to 38,000 tx in the 1790s. These not dissimilar totals at each end of the period mask the industry's varied fortunes in the intervening years. Codfishing tonnage increased in volume until mid-century but fell substantially after 1763. Subsequently, in the 1780s, it enjoyed a renewed boom, but the levels then reached were only a return to mid-century levels. Table 3 shows what is known on the national level of fishing tonnage fitted out in the two principal codfishing ports, Granville and St-Malo. Just as in transatlantic shipping, there was a tendency for the bigger ports to monopolise tonnage. In the 1720s and 1730s, St-Malo and Granville had less than two-fifths of national tonnage in use, but took nearly half on the eve of the War of the Austrian Succession. In the extraordinary expansion of fishing activity in the early 1750s, their share appears to have fallen, but it increased again after 1763, reaching fifty-eight percent of national tonnage in the period 1784-1789.

**Table 2**
**Concentration of French American Colonial Shipping**
***(tonneaux)***

| Origins: | 1742-43 | 1751 | 1779 | 1787-89 | 1792 | 1792 |
|---|---|---|---|---|---|---|
| 1) Nantes | 14,437 | 14,785 | 18,263 | 34,181 | 37,461 | 29,656 |
| 2) Bordeaux | 12,088 | 30,875 | 35,512 | 75,558 | 63,287 | 50,937 |
| 3) Le Havre | 9,531 | 12,980+ | 8,000? | 26,565 | ? | 11,030 |
| Three major ports | 36,056 | 58,640+ | 61,775 | 136,304 | 100,748+ | 91,623 |
| 4) All France | 60,943 | 71,880 | 96,000 | 167,208 | 139,229 | 131,784 |
| 1) to 3) as % of 4) | 59.2 | 81.6 | 64.3 | 81.5 | 72.4+ | 69.5 |

*Notes*: Dardel does not furnish figures for 1792; second 1792 column is from AN, F12 1834.

*Sources*: As in table 1, plus AN F12, 1834B, Département des Affaires étrangères, Douanes de la république, Extraits des Résultats du Commerce extérieur...pendant l'année 1792; J. Meyer, *L'Armement nantais dans la deuxième moitié du XVIIIe siècle* (Paris, 1969), 83-86; Meyer, "L'armement nantais au XVIIIe siècle d'après les registres des classes," *Actes du quatre-vingt-onzième congrès des sociétés savantes* (2 vols., Paris, 1969), I, 143-151; P. Dardel, *Navires et marchandises dans les ports de Rouen et du Havre au XVIIIe siècle* (Paris, 1963), 634-635 and 642-643. The figures for Bordeaux were kindly provided by Professor Paul Butel. As in table 1, the national figures for 1779 are somewhat suspect.

**Table 3**
**Codfishing: Annual Departures for North American Fishing Grounds (*tonneaux*)**

| Years | Ports All France | Granville+ Saint-Malo | % of national tonnage |
|---|---|---|---|
| 1726-34 | 33,654 | 11,866 | 38.1 |
| 1742-43 | 36,359 | 17,999 | 49.5 |
| 1751 | 59,625 | 24,305 | 40.8 |
| 1767-68 | 37,913 | -- | -- |
| 1770 | 29,833 | -- | -- |
| 1773 | 27,539 | -- | -- |
| 1784-89 | 38,807 | 22,542 | 58.1 |

*Sources*: As in table 1, plus AN, AM C4, 156, "Etat général des armemens faits par le Commerce...pendant les années 1774, 1775, 1776 et 1777;" C. de La Morandière, *Histoire de la pêche française de la morue dans l'Amérique septentrionale (des origines à 1789)* (3 vols., Paris, 1962-1966), II, 999; J-F. Brière, "The Port of Granville and the North American Fisheries in the 18th Century," *Acadiensis*, XIV (1985), 96-97; and Brière, "L'armement français pour la pêche à Terre-Neuve au XVIIIe siècle" (Unpublished PhD thesis, York University, Toronto, 1980), graphique 45.

Precise information on change in coastal fishing during the eighteenth century is hard to acquire. Such figures as exist suggest a long-term stagnation in the herring fishery and a tendency for activity to shift to Norman ports away from the Boulogne-Dunkerque region. Sardine fishing on the west coast of Brittany is thought to have increased during the eighteenth century, though the base was very small.[14]

National tonnage used for coasting is more difficult to ascertain (see table 4). The crew rolls and other documents, such as the *congés* delivered by the *Amirauté*, used by administrators at the time and by historians ever since to determine clearances, were issued only annually for many short-range types of coasting, so annual statistics do not reflect the volume of actual departures and voyages but rather tonnage employed in a given year. It would appear that after healthy growth between the 1720s and the early 1740s a plateau was reached, because the figures for

[14] E. Dardel, *La pêche haranguère en France* (Paris, 1941); A. Cabantous, "Le Hareng et son monde. Structures de la pêche haranguière de Boulogne à Blanckenberghe (vers 1650-vers 1830)," *Revue du Nord*, I (1986), 47-72; and T.J.A. Le Goff, *Vannes and its Region A Study of Town and Country in Eighteenth-Century France* (Oxford, 1981), 20-21.

coasting vessels and tonnage in use in 1785 were lower than in the 1730s and 1740s. Of course, the actual volume of coastal shipping may have increased because of more intensive use of vessels.

**Table 4**
**Ships, Tonnage and Crews Employed in Coasting**

| Years | Ships | Tonnage | Men Active | Remarks |
|---|---|---|---|---|
| 1725 | 1,000 | -- | 5,000 | |
| 1726 | 2,200 | -- | 12,000 | "y compris la pesche du Macquereau" |
| 1727 | 3,383 | -- | 19,477 | *ibid.* |
| 1728 | 2,500 | -- | 12,500 | |
| 1729 | 3,707 | -- | 19,472 | "y compris la pesche du Macquereau" |
| 1730 | 3,948 | -- | 20,786 | |
| 1731 | 3,978 | -- | 21,069 | "y compris la pesche du Macquereau" |
| 1732 | 3,842 | -- | 21,997 | *ibid.* |
| 1733 | 3,735 | -- | 20,551 | *ibid.* |
| 1734 | 3,642 | -- | 19,821 | *ibid.* |
| 1742 | 3,482 | 130,616 | 17,450 | |
| 1743 | 3,648 | 138,585 | 18,052 | |
| 1785 | 2,304 | 107,550 | (n.a.) | |

*Sources*: BN nouv. acq fr. 2550-2552; AN, AM, C4/64,117-119; C4/144; the figures for 1785 are from AN, AM, C5/51: "Etat qui fait connoître la situation des Bâtimens du Commerce à l'époque du 1er Janvier 1785;" see also T.J.A. Le Goff, "Économie d'échange et société rurale (XVIe-XVIIe siècle)," in J-P. Leguay (ed.), *Histoire de Vannes et de sa région* (Toulouse, 1988), 123-152; and G. Le Bouëdec, "La Compagnie des Indes et le cabotage atlantique au XVIIIe siècle," *Bulletin de la Société d'Histoire Moderne et Contemporaine*, Nos. 1-2 (1997), 140-167.

On the military side, France's naval capacity rose too, but not linearly. According to a comparison by officials in 1779, while Louis XIV's navy had at its peak in 1692 some ninety-five ships-of-the-line plus thirty-six fifth-rates, thirty-three frigates and assorted other craft for a total of 265 vessels, Louis XVI had only 264 craft, including seventy-eight ships-of-the-line, sixty-seven frigates and twenty-eight corvettes. But though the later Bourbon's fleet was inferior in numbers, it had much more firepower and required larger crews: 72,000 men as against only 48,000 under Louis XIV. In between, there had been a big decline in the size of the French naval fleet at the end of Louis XIV's reign and during the Regency. There followed a naval build-up during the 1730s and 1740s, losses in the War of the Austrian Succession (naval hostilities from 1744 to 1748), and even greater losses in the Seven Years' War (naval phase, 1755-1762). Then came a big naval revival running up to the War of American Independence, in which French arms did much better than in the preceding two conflicts, and a continued increase in the period running up to the French Revolution.[15] In peacetime, the navy required only 2000-3000 skilled men a year for its limited activities, but wartime demands could be overwhelming. Privateering provided a useful and often profitable adjunct. It was mostly a specialty of northern France, where the three main privateering ports were Dunkerque, Saint-Malo and Bayonne. In all of northern France privateering required about 6000 men of all ranks in each year of the two mid-century wars and perhaps 9000 in the last two wars of Louis XIV. It declined seriously in Saint-Malo after 1748 and in Bayonne after 1762, so that Dunkerque dominated this activity during the War of American Independence, but by that time total outfittings in all of France may have needed no more than about 4000 crew annually; large numbers were landsmen and foreigners.[16] Finally, there were the King's galleys, based in Marseille and thoroughly reorganised between 1665 and 1690 under Louis XIV. At the height of his naval power in 1690, Louis had over fifty galleys with crews totalling more than 15,000. With the exception of the officers and petty officers, it is difficult to think of these as a normal part of the maritime labour force. The bulk were of course oarsmen, men convicted

[15]AN, AM, B5/12: "Comparaison de la Marine de l'année 1692 à celle de l'année 1779;" and Acerra, *Rochefort*, 198-261.

[16]Estimates based on data from Villiers, *Marine royale*, 131-135, 145-146, 317-321 and 351-353; and Le Goff, "L'impact des prises," 111.

of serious criminal offences, or Protestant victims of religious persecution; they were brought for this purpose to Marseille from all over France, though among the oarsmen there were also a few paid volunteers (*benevogli*) and slaves obtained from Muslim countries. The galleys ceased to have anything but a ceremonial function after 1715, and the establishment at Marseille was closed completely in 1748; after that date, *galériens* continued to be employed, but as forced labour in the royal dockyards at Brest, Rochefort and Toulon.[17]

Since the time of Colbert, petty officers (*officiers mariniers*) and able seamen (*matelots*) were registered for military service, an institutional arrangement with far-reaching implications, not only for the French Navy but also for the organisation of the labour supply in civilian shipping. Official figures for petty officers and sailors liable to naval service suggest the existence of about 43,000 skilled seafarers in France at the end of the seventeenth century and perhaps 55,000 by 1789. At the height of a conflict, a large proportion would be sent to serve in the navy, thus depriving merchant shipping and fishing of their services and driving up the cost of skilled labour. The navy, merchant shipping and fishing also used large numbers of boys (*mousses*), unskilled and semi-skilled seamen (*novices*), non-navigating tradesmen and officers, even though these were, in varying degrees, exempt from the actual obligation to serve in the king's ships. Overall, the numbers of men going to sea rose, but not in proportion to tonnage increases. The discrepancy is explained by productivity gains in commercial shipping and fishing.[18]

## Origins of the Labour Force within and without France

The social and geographic recruitment of French seafarers can be studied in some detail. When we look at permanent migration, as reflected in the evidence on place of residence and birthplace of petty officers and able seamen recorded in the conscription registers of the navy, we see that the composition of the seafaring population was to some degree bipolar: on the one hand, there was a traditional group, centred on smaller ports,

---

[17]Bamford, *Fighting Ships and Prisons*; and Zysberg, *Les galériens*.

[18]Le Goff, "Problèmes de recrutement;" Le Goff, "De la paix à la guerre;" Le Goff, "Offre et productivité;" and J. Pritchard, "The Sailors of the French Expedi-tionary Force to Acadia, 1746," in C. Howell and R. Twomey (eds.), *Jack Tar in History: Essays in the History of Maritime Life and Labour* (Fredericton, 1991), 203-204.

which accounted for slightly more than half of the maritime population in northern France and about one-third in the Midi; on the other, there was a more-or-less urbanised group, characteristic of greater ports, with more varied recruitment (see figures 1-3). Generally, the bigger and the more commercial the port, the more socially varied its recruitment. Overall, about half of French skilled seamen were the sons of seamen, but the percentage of second-generation sailors was much higher in the smaller localities, and such social mobility as existed toward seafaring in these places tended to be from agriculture. In large centres, like the port complexes of Nantes-Paimbeuf and Le-Havre-Rouen-Honfleur, rural recruitment was supplemented by a sizeable inflow of men from the shopkeeper and artisan classes in those or other towns of similar size. The larger ports were also characterised by a greater range of geographic mobility. With only a few exceptions, ports with the greatest long-distance mobility were the bigger ones: St-Malo (fourteen percent of its skilled seamen from localities more than fifty km away), Honfleur (eighteen percent), Brest and Lorient (twenty percent), Paimbeuf (twenty-three percent), Nantes (seventeen percent), Le Havre (twenty-six percent), Dunkerque (thirty-eight percent, but only counting the less sedentary non-Flemish sailors) and Marseille (eighteen percent, but excluding the numerous foreign-born seamen characteristic of that port).[19]

Crewmen of foreign origin were not a large proportion of the permanent resident seafaring population of northern France and never formed more than three percent of registered seamen at the end of the eighteenth century. In individual ports north of the Loire, the proportion could be a little higher, but not much. The reason why there were so few resident foreign-born seamen in northern France was in part because the officials of the *classes* only registered such men when they gave the most tangible of proofs that they had settled in the country: marriage.[20] Unlike foreigners, a young French *novice* was automatically registered as an able seaman after his second or third voyage and a *mousse* was enrolled on coming of age.

---

[19] Le Goff, "Les origines sociales;" Le Goff, "Le recrutement géographique et social;" Le Goff, "De la paix à la guerre;" and Le Goff, "Les gens de mer des années 1780."

[20] AN, AM, C5/58, Thirat (Marseille) to Minister, 31 October 1788.

Map 1 - Origins of officiers mariniers & matelots c. 1785: Marseille

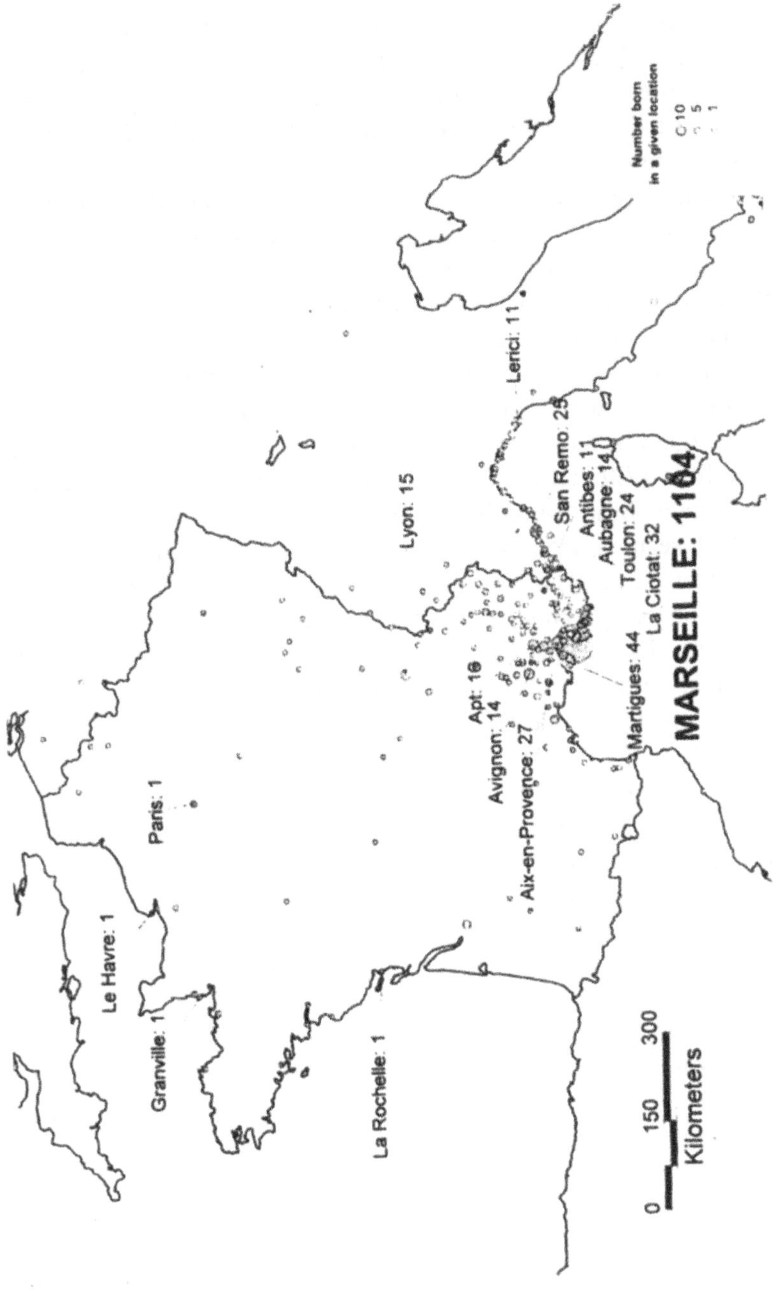

**Map 2 - Origins of officiers mariniers & matelots c. 1785 : selected ports in Northern France**

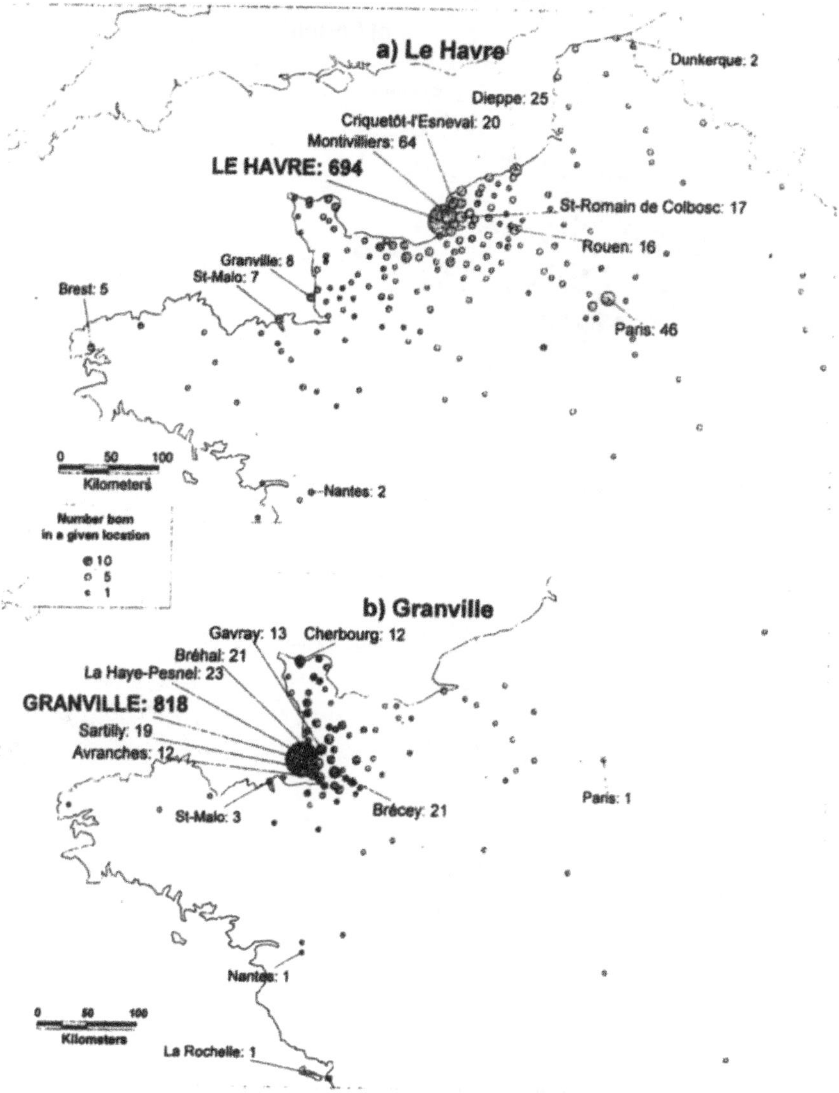

**Map 2 - Origins of officiers mariniers & matelots c. 1785 : selected ports in Northern France (continued)**

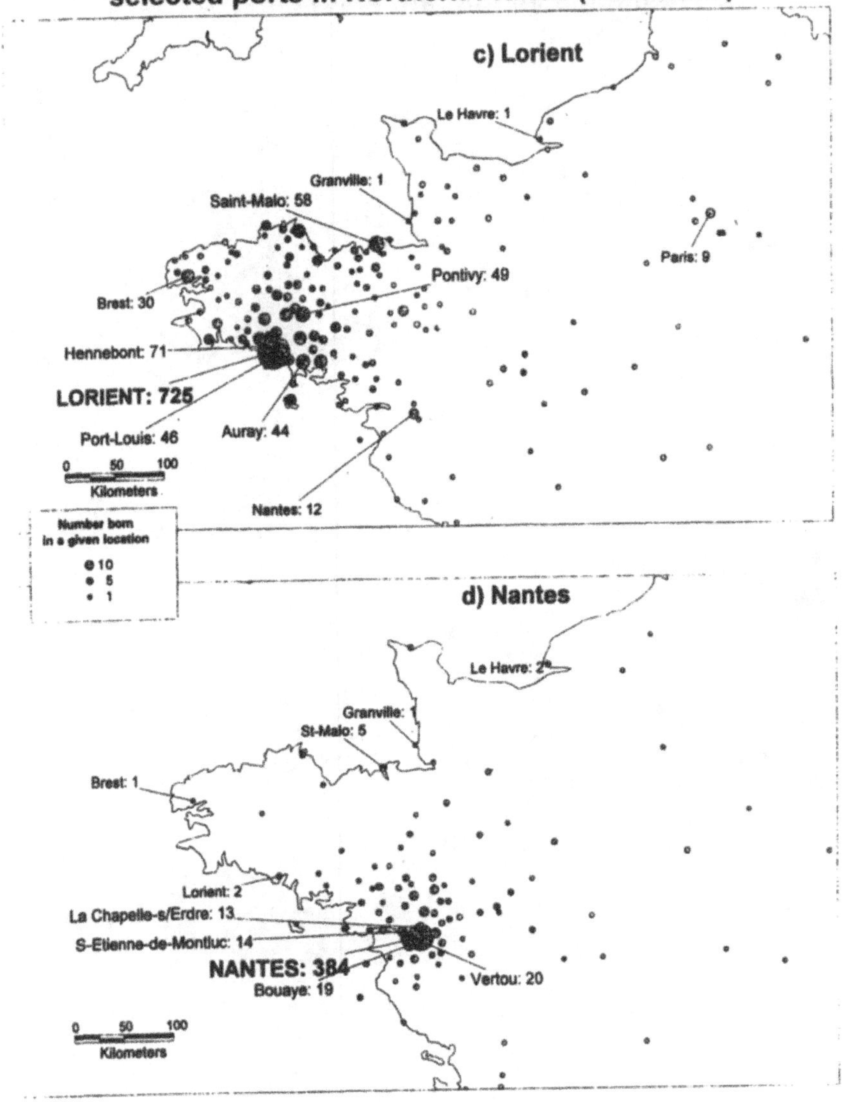

## Map 3 - Officiers mariniers and matelots c. 1785: fathers' occupations

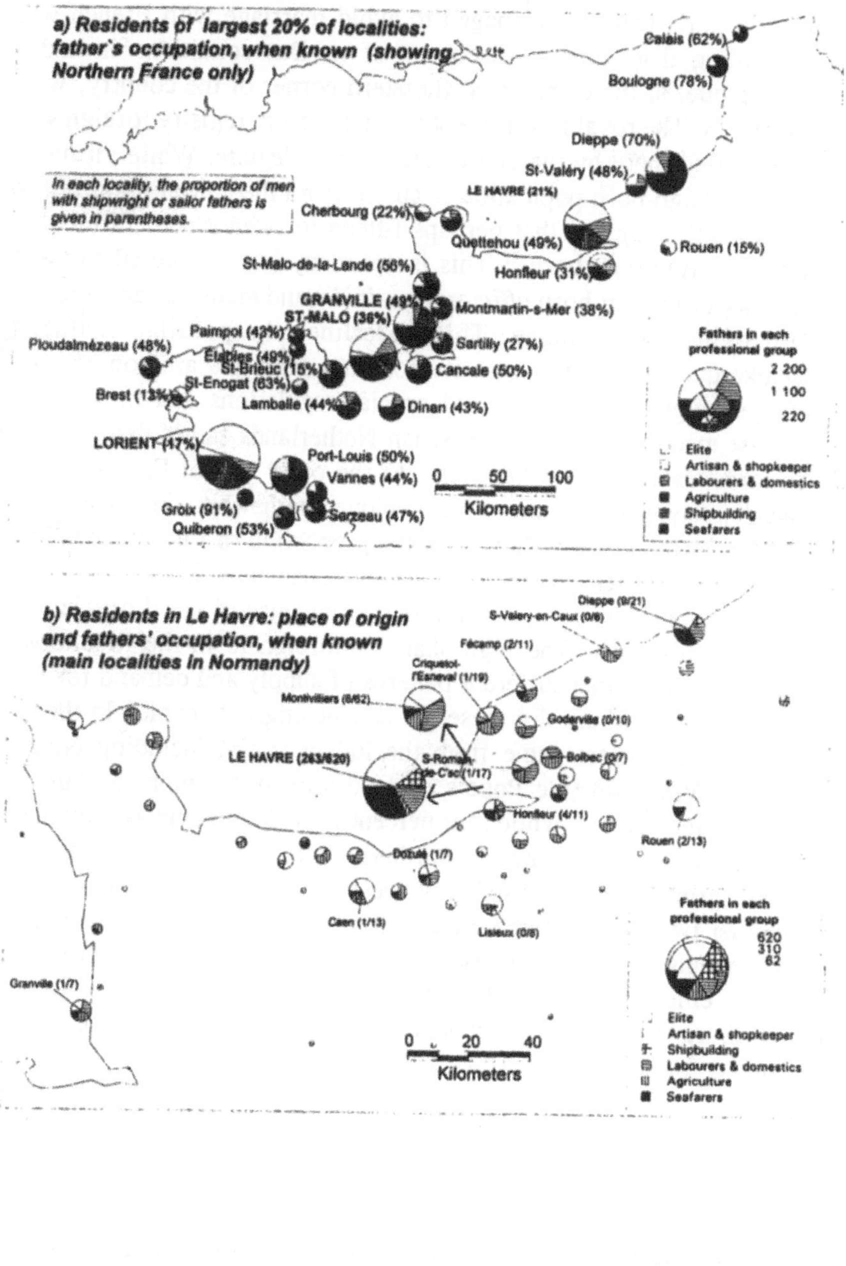

It is conceivable that many of the temporary foreign migrants aboard French ships were in fact more-or-less permanent denizens of French ports who had managed to avoid marriage with French women or, failing that, official discovery of it. But conditions in and near Dunkerque, at the extreme northeastern corner of the country, were an exception. The royal government exempted from registry foreign seamen who settled there by the end of the *Ancien Régime*. While virtually the entire foreign-born population is absent from the conscription registers, local studies suggest that perhaps fifteen to twenty percent (about 120 men) were foreign-born.[21] This is not many but it is equal to the *total* number of foreign-born *officiers*, *mariniers* and *matelots* registered in the rest of northern France. This underlines the peculiar character of Dunkerque which, as far as its port and seafarers are concerned, had unique migration patterns and special regulations and privileges that almost made it part of the Austrian Netherlands rather than the littoral towards Calais and farther west. At the other end of France's Atlantic facade, Bayonne appears to have enjoyed somewhat similar conditions. On the Mediterranean, however, the proportion of foreign-born seamen was much greater: 12.8% of registered seamen in Marseille and 5.9% in St-Tropez were foreign, despite the reticence of naval officials to list them as residents. The high share of foreigners in the Mediterranean resulted from rather different patterns of supply and demand for labour.

From where did these permanent migrants come? In the south, over three-quarters came from the Italian states, including Nice. The *Comtat Venaissin* (the Pope's enclave around Avignon) accounted for nearly nine percent, while four percent were from Spain and another two percent from the Levant. In northern France, Italians were the largest single group, but comprised only twenty-five percent of the foreign-born; another twenty-four percent were from the various French colonies and settlements of North America and seventeen percent from the British Isles, chiefly southern Ireland. Flemish sailors, mainly from the Habsburg Netherlands, accounted for a further eight percent; West Indians for seven and Spaniards for five percent.[22]

---

[21]Cabantous, *La mer et les hommes*, 41-55.

[22]Dunkerque also had a different pattern judging from marriages in the last four decades of the *Ancien Régime*. Italians comprised about a quarter of the immigrants, but another quarter came from the Austrian Netherlands.

These data point up three main features of maritime immigration: a dichotomy between northern France, where permanent in-migration was not great, and southern France, where men from the Italian peninsula made up a large part of the permanent work force; a big proportion of Italians in relation to the total number of permanent migrants: overwhelmingly so in southern France, and even in northern France, over one-quarter of permanent migrants; and the attraction that the larger and expanding ports exerted over the workforce.

Temporary migrants in the seafaring labour force had basically the same characteristics. Statistics gleaned from national surveys throughout the eighteenth century show the same divide between southern France, open to a great deal of migration, and northern France, where it was the exception (see table 5). Generally, temporary foreign migrant labour appeared in trade to the Levant, and to some extent in the Spanish coasting trade. These men were virtually absent from fishing, but played a large role in the relatively small whaling sector – a Basque specialty out of St-Jean-de-Luz in the early part of the century and a Nantucket novelty in Dunkerque after the War of American Independence. Overall, the proportion of foreigners in direct trade to the Americas (principally the West Indies) was not high except on ships out of Marseille, but because this sector employed so many men, there was a recognisable group of temporary foreign migrant sailors in American shipping, even in northern French ports. The same was true of the slave trade.[23]

The role of foreigners in the labour supply increased in wartime. Then, even though the volume of commercial shipping shrank, great strains were put on the labour supply. Captures of French ships in the northern European theatre during the wars of 1744-1748 and 1755-1763 took large numbers of French sailors out of the civilian labour supply precisely at the moment when the French navy was also subtracting thousands of experienced sailors from it. Increased wages in commercial shipping, rising much more in northern France than in the Mediterranean, were a sign of this (see figure 4).[24]

---

[23]Not too much weight should be attached to the fifteen percent foreign crew component for January 1785 in figure 5: most vessels in the Africa trade which returned in that month happened to be Marseille slavers.

[24]Le Goff, "De la paix à la guerre;" and Le Goff, "L'impact des prises."

**Table 5**
**Foreign-Domiciled Crew Members as a Proportion of Total Crew**

| Destination | 1725-1734 (yearly average) | | | 1774-1777 (yearly average) | | | 1785 (January only) | | |
|---|---|---|---|---|---|---|---|---|---|
| | Foreign | Total Crew | % Foreign | Foreign | Total Crew | % Foreign | Foreign | Total Crew | % Foreign |
| Americas | 110 | 8,411 | 1.3 | 223 | 13,543 | 1.6 | 18 | 978 | 1.8 |
| Africa coast | 12 | 1,062 | 1.1 | 32 | 2,041 | 1.6 | 40 | 268 | 14.9 |
| India | 0 | 1,047 | 1.1 | 23 | 2,036 | 1.1 | 0 | 61 | 0 |
| Levant & Italy | 1,115 | 8,492 | 13.1 | 1,824 | 12,065 | 15.1 | 15 | 259 | 5.8 |
| Northern Europe | 31 | 1,248 | 2.5 | -- | -- | -- | -- | -- | -- |
| Iberia | 190 | 2,527 | 7.5 | 147 | 830 | 17.7 | -- | -- | -- |
| Codfishing | 95 | 8,563 | 1.1 | 24 | 9,917 | 0.2 | 9 | 1,515 | 0.6 |
| Whaling | 1,020 | 1,559 | 65.4 | -- | -- | -- | -- | -- | -- |
| Mediterranean coasting | -- | -- | -- | -- | -- | -- | 21 | 319 | 6.6 |
| Other coasting | -- | -- | -- | -- | -- | -- | 9 | 526 | 1.7 |

*Source*: BN, nouv. acq. fr. 2550-2552; AN, AM C4/64, 117-19; C4/156, Etat général des arememens faits par le commerce dans les différents ports de la Provence...pendant les années 1774, 1775, 1776 et 1777; Etat général des armemens faits par le Commerce dans les différents Ports de France et destinés pour les colonies, de l'Inde...pendant les années 1774, 1775, 1776 et 1777...; C4/153 Désarmements [1785]. The latter is a ship-by-ship list of information for ships on arrival in all French ports in January 1785, obviously done for the purposes of a survey.

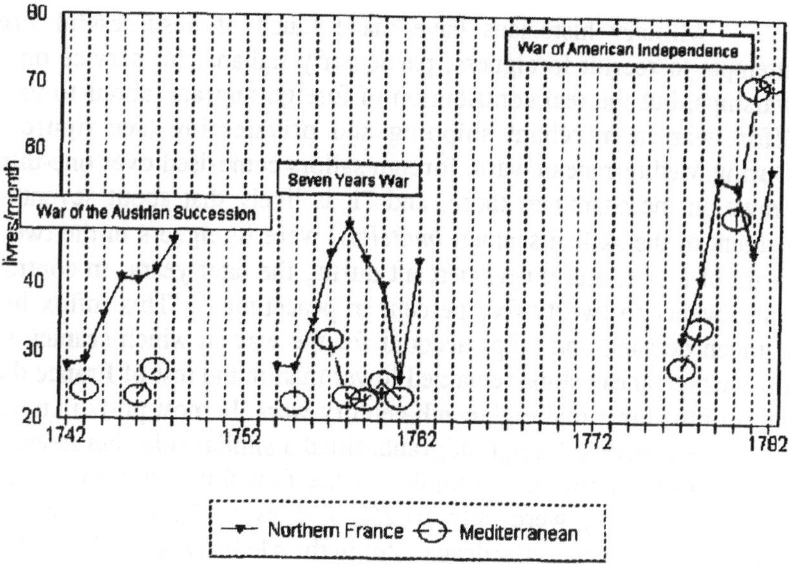


*Figure 4*: *Matelot* Pay in Wartime (commercial shipping).

*Source*: Great Britain, Public Record Office (PRO), High Court of Admiralty (HCA) 32/94-136 (1744-1748); 32/161-185 (1755-1763); 32/260-327 (1778-1783); and (for peacetime years in the Mediterranean) Archives du Port de Toulon (APT), 13P9, 1-2.

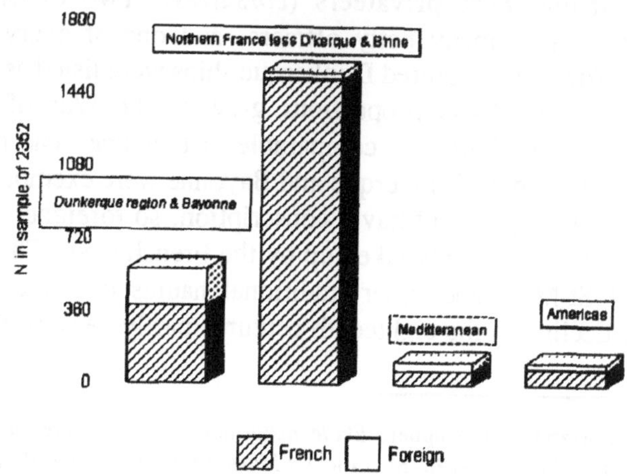


*Figure 5*: Crews on Captured French Ships, 1755-1759.

*Source:* See figure 4.

Military historians have made much of unsuccessful French attempts to recruit foreigners, particularly Italians, for service on their warships, but the real contribution of foreign migrant labour to the war effort was in merchant shipping and privateering (see figure 5).[25] During Mediterranean wars, foreign sailors comprised over one-third of crews on merchantmen there, and "it is likely that about seventy-five percent of the skilled seamen *(matelots)* were foreigners in the two first years of a war, and ninety percent during the later years, in contrast to only twenty to twenty-five percent in peacetime."[26] This influx helped dampen demand and helps account for the way in which seamen's pay on Mediterranean ships remained lower than in the rest of France during most of the three mid-eighteenth-century wars. In most ports in northern France, temporary foreign migrants filled a similar role, but never in as great a proportion. For example, in the first four years of the Seven Years' War, they were only 10.2% of crew in the ports from Saint-Valéry-sur-Somme to Bordeaux. But in the Mediterranean, foreigners on French merchantmen helped compensate for the loss of Frenchmen conscripted into the navy; in any event, most commercial tonnage seized by the British came from northern, not southern, ports.

In the enclaves of Dunkerque-Calais-Boulogne in the extreme northeast and of Bayonne in the southeast, the role of foreign sailors in wartime was both different and similar. Unlike the situation in the Mediterranean, almost all the ships seized by the British from these two ports in wartime were privateers (*corsaires*). Two of every three *matelots,* almost as many petty officers, and one of every two non-navigating officers on captured Dunkerque ships were listed as foreigners in 1755-1759, and these proportions grew in the War of American Independence. The share was comparable in Bayonne. The reasons for this were evident: both Dunkerque and Bayonne were exempt in varying degrees from the system of naval conscription, so foreigners who went there ran little risk of being taken up by the French navy. The privateering role of St-Malo and other traditional haunts of *corsaires* was in permanent decline in the eighteenth century, partly because the govern-

---

[25]See, for example, J. Captier, *Etude historique et économique sur l'inscription maritime* (Paris, 1907), 191-192; M. Loir, *La Marine royale en 1789* (Paris, 1892), 40-41; V-F. Brun, *Guerres maritimes de la France* (Paris, 1861), II, 13, 20-21, 50-51; 382-387, 408 and 452; and Dull, *French Navy*, 144.

[26]Le Goff, "De la paix à la guerre," 300-301.

ment discouraged them in order to claim the services of French sailors from those ports. But it flourished in Dunkerque and Bayonne, and provided an important auxiliary to the French war effort, by allowing privateers to carry on activity which would otherwise have drained sailors away from French commerce and the French navy.[27]

## Wages

Probably forty to forty-five percent of all working seafarers were paid monthly between 1725 and 1743; another quarter received shares in fishing, and about as many were still paid on a share basis in coastal and Levant shipping. With the expansion of transatlantic shipping and the spread of wage labour in other sectors, wage-earners were a majority by the 1780s. But even where they were not, as in cod and coastal fishing, the actual amounts paid tended to follow the trend in the other sectors.[28] Of course sailors' remuneration was supplemented by food and drink and by the custom of allowing them to take small amounts of trade goods (*pacotilles*) on long-distance voyages. It could also vary according to the number of voyages a man might undertake, but assuming that these factors remained more-or-less constant, the movement of money wages can provide some indication of the evolution of total remuneration.

Most historians believe that the eighteenth century was not a good time for wage labour throughout Europe.[29] Seamen's nominal

---

[27]AN, AM C4/136: August 1755; C4/1776, 289-290 (1755); C4/77, 15 and 40: Minister to President of Chamber of Commerce of Dunkerque, 26 January 1756, and 23 February 1756; C4/78, 49-50: Minister to Bégon, 13 February 1757; Captier, *Inscription maritime*, 190; and Ordinance of 16 February 1759. See also AN, AM, C4/13, fol. 260-263v, 28 November 1757; C4/77, 64, Minister to Basle and *jurats* of St-Jean de Luz, 9 March 1756; C4/78, fol. 143, Minister to Darancette; C4/17, fol. 562-563v, 17 December 1766; and Le Goff, "Manning the French Navy."

[28]Brière, "L'armement français pour la pêche," graphs 1-9.

[29]R. Davis, *The Rise of the English Shipping Industry in the Seventeenth and Eighteenth Centuries* (London, 1962), 135-138 and 152; J.R. Bruijn, *De Admiraliteit van Amsterdam in Rustige Jaren 1713-1751. Regenten en financien, schepen en zeevarenden* (Amsterdam, 1970), 146-152; and P. Jansen, "Poverty in Amsterdam at the Close of the Eighteenth Century," *Acta Historica Neerlandica*, X (1978), 98-114. See also J.R. Bruijn and E.S. van Eyck van Heslinga, "Seamen's Employment in the Netherlands (c. 1600-c. 1800)," *Mariner's Mirror*, LXX (1984), 7-20.

wages in most of Europe did not rise much, except in wartime, when competition for labour from navies and privateering pushed them upward. Given the general rise of food prices, such stagnant rates in peacetime must have implied a long-term decline in real wages. What was the situation in France? I have developed two principal long series for salaries in voyages to the West Indies in Bordeaux and Nantes, which offer the only documentation allowing the construction of long wage series. Table 6 and figure 6 show what happened to nominal mean wages of *matelots*. Two features should be noted. The first is the alternation between peacetime years, when nominal wages changed only gradually, and wartime, when naval conscription reduced the labour supply and pushed wage rates to twice or more peacetime levels. Most of the analysis which follows deals with peacetime rates, but wars did have an impact on peacetime trends. And it is worth remembering that those sailors lucky enough in wartime to be able to join merchant vessels and to survive did very well.

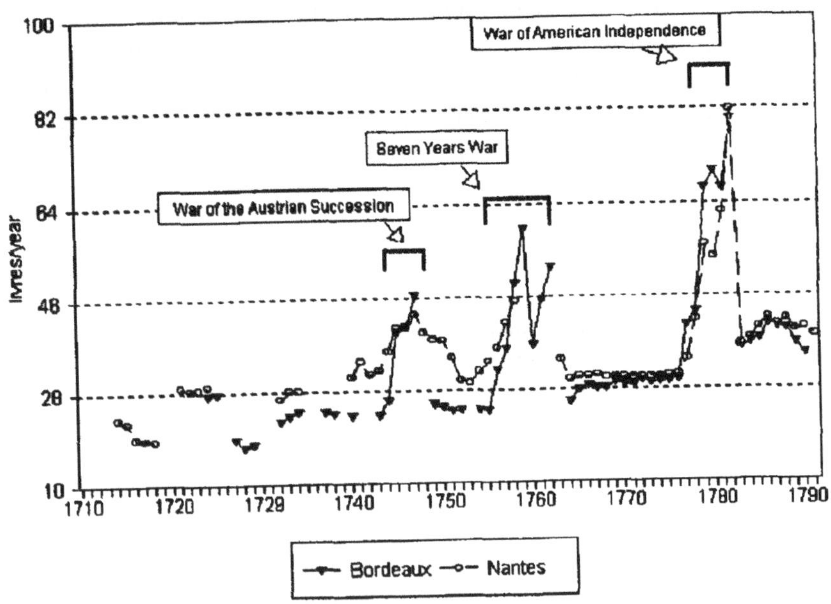


*Figure 6*: *Matelot* Pay in Bordeaux and Nantes.

*Source*: See text.

**Table 6**
**Comparison of Labrousse Wage and Price Indices with Selected Seamen's Pay**

| Period | Labrousse | | *Matelot* Wages | | *Novice* Wages | | Wages, All Ranks |
|---|---|---|---|---|---|---|---|
| | Consumer Price Index | Wages Index | Nantes | Bordeaux | Nantes | Bordeaux | Bordeaux |
| 1726-41 | 100 | 100 | 100 | 100 | 100 | 100 | 100 |
| 1771-89 | 154 | 117-120 | 142 | 197 | 150 | 187 | 170 |
| 1785-89 | 162 | 118-124 | 138 | 179 | 140 | 179 | 167 |

*Sources*: C-E. Labrousse, *Esquisse du mouvement des prix et des revenus en France au XVIIIe siècle* (Paris, 1933), II, 493 and 598-599.

The second feature is the considerable increase in nominal wages across the period. As the eighteenth century is generally thought to have been a bad time for wage-earners, these figures invite comparison with other wages and with the cost of living, particularly with Labrousse's figures. French sailors fared better than might have been expected. Closer analysis, using a cost-of-living index on a year-to-year basis, and breaking down the changes over wartime and peacetime periods, shows wages still surprisingly stable in real terms from the 1720s to the 1780s (table 7). The long-run peacetime trend in real wages was more stable than the nominal wage trend because it incorporated price increases, mainly in the cost of grain. After about 1773-1774 things improved, as agricultural prices fell and French participation in the War of American Independence pushed both real and nominal wages up again. On the whole, the picture is mildly optimistic. By the 1780s, there was also a better chance of a sailor surviving to claim his pay (see table 8). French seamen did not suffer the absolute decline in real wages that was the lot of most wage-earners, especially sailors, elsewhere in Europe.

The explanation of this distinctive pattern is complex. On the demand side, it seems clear that the expansion of French shipping exerted long-term pressure on the labour supply. Closer examination of the evidence confirms the conclusions I reached several years ago: that French shipowners and captains were able to alter the demand schedule for labour by lessening turnaround times on transatlantic voyages; increasing capital productivity through economies of scale by using bigger ships; and raising productivity per crewman, measured in tons carried per man aboard. The latter rose even when tonnage remained constant, probably by incremental technological improvements more than by the decline in the number of cannon, contrary to the suggestion offered by G. Walton and D. North for British shipping.[30]

**Table 7**

**Annual Growth Rates in Seafarers' Nominal and Real Wages, 1726-1789**

| Rank | Nominal Salary | Real Salary I | II |
|---|---|---|---|
| **1) Bordeaux** | | | |
| *a) All years* | | | |
| *Officiers* | 0.9 | -0.4 | -0.1 |
| *Officiers mariniers* | 1.3 | 0 | 0.3 |
| *Officiers non-mariniers* | 1.4 | 0.2 | 0.4 |
| *Matelots* | 1.2 | -0.1 | 0.2 |
| *Novices* | 1.2 | -0.1 | 0.2 |
| *Mousses* | 0.9 | -0.4 | -0.1 |
| *Matelots* and *Novices* | 1 | -0.3 | 0 |
| All ranks | 1 | -0.3 | 0 |
| *b) Peacetime years only* | | | |
| *Officiers* | 0.8 | -0.4 | -0.2 |
| *Officiers mariniers* | 1 | -0.2 | 0 |
| *Officiers non-mariniers* | 1.3 | 0.1 | 0.3 |
| *Matelots* | 1 | -0.2 | 0 |
| *Novices* | 1.1 | -0.2 | 0.1 |
| *Mousses* | 0.7 | -0.5 | -0.3 |
| *Matelots* and *Novices* | 0.9 | -0.4 | -0.1 |
| All ranks | 0.9 | -0.4 | -0.14 |
| **2) Nantes** | | | |
| *a) All years* | | | |
| *Matelots* | 0.5 | -0.4 | -0.2 |
| *Novices* | 0.7 | -0.3 | 0 |
| *b) Peacetime years only* | | | |
| *Matelots* | 0.4 | -0.6 | 0 |
| *Novices* | 0.6 | -0.4 | 0.2 |

*Notes*: I: deflated by indices of Bordeaux and Nantes wheat prices; II: deflated by national CPI derived from Labrousse, as above.

*Source*: See text.

---

[30]Le Goff, "Offre et productivité," 469, n. 29. Tests on 1340 ships sailing during the peacetime years, 1726-1789, from Bordeaux to the Caribbean show that productivity often grew regardless of changes in cannons or size. A partial correlation of ton/man ratios and years of departure, controlling for cannon and tonnage, yields a coefficient of .4760. The coefficient for cannon and year is -.5493 and for tons/man and year +.7067.

**Table 8**
**Mortality, Desertion and Disembarkation Rates**
**(Percentage of crew at start of voyage)**

| Years | Died | Deserted | Disembarked | All losses |
|---|---|---|---|---|
| 1) Nantes - Caribbean | | | | |
| 1714-25 | 6.7 | 6.6 | 1.3 | 14.6 |
| 1726-43 | 5.9 | 3.8 | 1.4 | 11.1 |
| 1744-48* | 12.0 | 10.0 | 6.2 | 28.2 |
| 1749-55 | 5.1 | 6.2 | 1.7 | 13.0 |
| 1756-62* | 7.8 | 13.8 | 27.9 | 49.5 |
| 1763-77 | 3.2 | 5.8 | 2.4 | 11.4 |
| 1778-82* | 4.5 | 15.7 | 19.0 | 39.2 |
| 1783-89 | 3.7 | 6.4 | 3.5 | 13.6 |
| 2) Nantes - West Africa - Caribbean | | | | |
| 1714-25 | 20.2 | 6.2 | 4.5 | 30.9 |
| 1726-43 | 19.6 | 4.5 | 6.5 | 30.6 |
| 1744-48* | 15.7 | 12.3 | 11.4 | 39.4 |
| 1749-55 | 18.9 | 6.0 | 7.7 | 32.6 |
| 1763-77 | 15.2 | 3.6 | 5.6 | 24.4 |
| 1778-82* | 29.0 | 4.4 | 5.8 | 39.2 |
| 1783-89 | 13.2 | 4.2 | 8.4 | 25.8 |

*Note*: * denotes wartime years.

*Sources*: See text.

## Factors Affecting Labour Supply

The principal factors affecting the labour supply were those that influenced the size of the pool of labour (mortality, desertion abroad and migrations) and those that changed its composition. Mortality and desertion among crews sailing to Africa and the West Indies were high in the eighteenth century. This was particularly true on slave ships, where sailors' deaths were roughly proportional to losses among slaves. Many men also died on direct voyages from France to the West Indies, which had lower mortality rates but used many more men. In addition, desertions were particularly high in the first part of the century and in wartime. But desertions on both kinds of voyage matter less than deaths, since in the West Indies one captain's deserter was another's potential replacement. Table 8 shows the results from the crew rolls in Nantes.[31] More fragmentary data from Le Havre suggest parallel rates and trends there. In both ports, there was a marked drop in mortality rates across the century, except for the disastrous conditions of wartime.[32] The result of the decline in peacetime mortality was two-fold. First, it increased the size of the labour pool available in French ports. Second, it would have resulted in more sailors receiving their full wages instead of perishing during the course of their voyage.

The mobility of the labour supply into the large ports and, *a fortiori*, the smaller ones, appears to have been fairly limited. Even in a large and booming port like Nantes, a very high proportion of permanent and temporary migrant labour for shipping came from its immediate environs: as late as 1785, sixty-four percent of *novices* and fifty-one percent of the *officiers mariniers* and *matelots* resided in the surrounding region (the *département* of Loire-Inférieure after 1789), twelve and thirteen percent came from the neighbouring *département* of Morbihan, and another nine and eight percent from the future Vendée.

This brings us to a third variable in labour supply: changes in the different sorts of specialists available to the market and the ability and

---

[31]See the very similar results in the shorter series collected by R. Stein from ADLA B 4583-4584 and 4588-4596. I wish to thank Dr. Stein for allowing me to use his notes on this series. See also H. Klein, *The Middle Passage: Studies in the Atlantic Slave Trade* (Princeton, 1978), 175-208; and S. Engerman and H. Klein, "Facteurs de mortalité dans le trafic français d'esclaves au XVIIIe siècle," *Annales: Economies, Sociétés, Civilisations*, XXXI (1976), 1213-1224.

[32]The following are some selected mortality rates of initial crews, from muster rolls handed in on return:

| *Year* | *Destination* | |
|---|---|---|
| | West Indies | Africa and West Indies |
| *Departing: Le Havre* | | |
| 1751-1752 | 5.5 % | 17.5 % |
| 1765-1766 | 4.6 | 14.3 |
| 1774 | 1.7 | 8.6 |
| 1785-1786 | n.a. | n.a. |
| *Departing: Marseille* | | |
| 1765-1766 | 3.0 | n.a. |
| 1767-1768 | 2.1 | n.a. |
| 1784-1785 | 2.2 | 34.3 |

willingness of those specialists to find work outside seafaring.[33] On civilian vessels, each of the five classes of seafarer had varying degrees of involvement with the non-maritime labour market. *Officiers non mariniers* (cooks, coopers, etc.) and *novices* (the semi-employed of the urban, rural and semi-urban artisan and labouring classes) could also market whatever landward skills they had. Merchant officers, drawn largely from the bourgeoisie, though often with connections to seafaring, could also choose other careers to some extent. Some officers also acquired experience at sea which they could turn to account on land: surgeons, for example, and senior officers who learned something of business methods in handling their ship's affairs and acting as outfitters' agents, particularly in the West Indies. *Mousses* (boys) were supposed to be chosen from among seamen's sons, but an abundant alternate supply was available from the families of landsmen and in orphanages in the big ports. *Matelots* (able seamen), on the other hand, were specialised workers by the time they had earned that qualification, and their way of life and experience made it difficult to move out of their profession.[34] *Officiers mariniers* were even more highly specialised and inbred; they were recruited from among *officiers mariniers'* sons and the offspring of experienced seamen.

Wars acted on the supply of each of these groups differently. Conflicts sped normal advancement through the ranks, particularly for the four inferior ranks of *officiers mariniers*, *matelots*, *novices* and *mousses*. They tended to increase the number of *officiers mariniers* for two reasons. First, this group was not taken on board the King's ships in proportion to their importance in the seafaring community and therefore less of the existing stock of petty officers was exposed to the dangers of war. Second, wars increased the supply of potential *officiers mariniers* for merchantmen, because they gave *matelots* valuable experience on the King's ships and a chance for recognition: at the end of each campaign, commanders awarded *officier marinier* status in the navy to *matelots* who had distinguished themselves. The same thing

---

[33]It is also conceivable that later generations of sailors might become more skilled than their fathers, or give better work in return for better pay.

[34]As R.H. Dana Jr., *Two Years Before the Mast* (reprint, Harmondsworth, 1981), 349, observed on being told that he would have to stay with his ship on the California coast for another two years "two years more in California would have made me a sailor for the rest of my days."

happened in an even more indiscriminate way to *novices*, who automatically gained the status of *matelots* by virtue of having served on the King's ships. When they went back to their home ports to seek civilian employment, it was difficult to give them jobs at pay rates less than those for the other *matelots*. *Novices*, on the other hand, could become rarities if merchant shipowners lost enthusiasm for fitting out their ships during hostilities. When peace returned after each of the wars, these groups were returned *en masse* to the labour market, but their respective abilities to command salaries were altered by the impact of war. In short, the elasticity of the supply curve for each sort of seaman varied within a given period and each could be altered in different ways over time.

The data for growth rates point up these differences and help provide some explanations for the movement of seafarers' wages. Discussion can be best carried out by taking each of the interwar periods separately.

The first two peacetime decades after 1726 were marked by very rapid growth in overseas shipping (see table 9). Tonnage grew at a yearly rate of nearly seven percent in Bordeaux, which rose into the front rank of French shipping, but Nantes, which already had a well-established position as a great port, also enjoyed a tonnage growth rate of well over four percent. These increases in capacity were met mainly by increasing the size of the labour force almost proportionately; it grew by five percent in both ports. The rest of the growth was handled through economies of scale in the form of increased tonnage per ship (three percent in Bordeaux); growth in output per man was small. Despite substitution of cheaper for more expensive labour (decreases in the proportion of *matelots* and officers and increases in the share of *novices*), the expansion put great pressure on wages and, unlike England, where expansion was less dynamic, both nominal and real wages duly rose.

**Table 9**
**Some Growth Rates, 1726-1743**

| | Bordeaux | Nantes |
|---|---|---|
| Total tons | 6.7 | 4.6 |
| Total crew | 5.0 | 4.2 |
| Tons/ship | 3.0 | -0.4 |
| Tons/man | 1.6 | 0.2 |
| Wages/ton (nominal) | -0.6 | n.a. |
| Matelot wage (nominal) | 1.7 | 1.5 |

*Source*: See text.

The 1749-1755 period was characterised by a dramatic decline in tonnage growth and, indeed, an absolute decline in tonnage in Nantes (see table 10). Ship capacity, with its attendant economies of scale, grew, though more slowly than in the previous period. In Nantes, though not in Bordeaux, output per man actually grew faster than the growth in average ship capacity. Demand for labour, in short, was almost stagnant or even declining in Nantes.

**Table 10**
**Some Growth Rates, 1749-1755**

| | Bordeaux | Nantes |
|---|---|---|
| Total tons | 2.5 | -1.4 |
| Total crew | 0.5 | -2.8 |
| Tons/ship | 2.0 | 1.4 |
| Tons/man | 1.1 | 1.7 |
| Wages/ton (nominal) | -1.2 | n.a. |
| Matelot wage (nominal) | -0.8 | -2.6 |

*Source*: See text.

On the supply side, there were also changes. The royal ordinance of 23 July 1745 had enforced the employment of cheaper labour by making it obligatory to take on *novices* in a proportion of one to four other crewmen.[35] More important, the War of the Austrian Succession created a reserve army of the employable skilled, or at least formally qualified, through conscription and promotion. The more expensive grades of "professional" seamen – *officiers mariniers* and *matelots* – were less rare after the war. Nominal wages actually declined, slightly for most, but sharply for *officiers mariniers* and somewhat less sharply for *matelots*. A decline in the cost of living, however, saved their real wages in both ports from erosion.

The third interwar period, 1763-1777, was marked by a repetition of what happened between 1749 and 1755, albeit in a more dramatic form (see table 11). Shipping tonnage grew during this period in Bordeaux at a respectable rate, four percent per year, though only by 1.2% per annum in Nantes. In both ports, economies of scale continued to increase with ship capacity. But the most significant change for seafarers' wages was, once again, the demographic effects of war. The

[35]This was already required in Bordeaux since 23 August 1730.

Seven Years' War had been horrific for the seafaring population, but such horrors were unusual mainly for men from the cod fisheries and from smaller ports, unused to the decimation that occurred on West Indies and African voyages; for men in the larger ports, the chances of death in the King's service or in British prisons were about the same as on distant merchant voyages.[36] Nevertheless, upward mobility again filled the ranks of *officiers mariniers* and *matelots*. Because of the length of this period, it is possible to study the consequences of the war for the composition of crews more fully, comparing the age structures of the various ranks immediately after the peace and just before the next war.

**Table 11**
**Some Growth Rates, 1763-1777**

| | Bordeaux | Nantes |
|---|---|---|
| Total tons | 4.0 | 1.2 |
| Total crew | 1.6 | 1.5 |
| Tons/ship | 2.8 | 4.9 |
| Tons/man | 2.3 | 2.9 |
| Wages/ton (nominal) | -1.6 | n.a. |
| Matelot wage (nominal) | 1.6 | 0.1 |

*Source*: See text.

At the end of the war, the labour force for commercial shipping was in some sense rejuvenated (see table 12). Older sailors – men in their late thirties or forties – were used in wartime shipping but were eliminated by the hazards of wartime navigation or by promotion to the ranks of *officiers mariniers*. Meanwhile, large numbers of younger men had been given the chance to serve on the King's ships and to experience the campaign necessary to qualify as skilled seamen. Comparison of the age structure of the various ranks at the end of the war with that a dozen years later shows a second significant phenomenon. This relatively long period of peace, combined with a more stable pattern of demand expansion, permitted the natural tendencies of this labour force to assert themselves. One was the trend of the established elements in this labour force to age while still retaining their jobs, thus blocking the way for younger men.

---

[36] Le Goff, "Problèmes de recrutement."

**Table 12**
**Percentage of *Matelots* and *Novices* by Age Group for Nantes Colonial Shipping**

| Age Groups | 1727-29 | 1738 | 1742 | 1751 | 1776 | 1786 |
|---|---|---|---|---|---|---|
| < 15 | 0.3 | 0.1 | 0 | 0 | 0 | 0.1 |
| 15-19 | 9.0 | 8.4 | 15.7 | 18.2 | 12.7 | 19.8 |
| 20-24 | 33.8 | 36.5 | 39.1 | 41.0 | 39.6 | 42.0 |
| 25-29 | 29.9 | 24.4 | 26.0 | 24.6 | 22.3 | 24.3 |
| 30-34 | 13.2 | 14.9 | 9.4 | 8.1 | 14.4 | 8.4 |
| 35-39 | 5.1 | 8.8 | 4.9 | 4.9 | 6.0 | 2.9 |
| 40-44 | 4.5 | 3.9 | 3.0 | 1.7 | 3.3 | 1.2 |
| > 44 | 4.1 | 3.2 | 0.9 | 1.3 | 1.7 | 1.3 |
| > 35 | 13.8 | 15.9 | 8.8 | 7.9 | 11.0 | 5.4 |

*Source*: See text.

Besides inertia and the lack of demand for new labour, another factor tended to limit access to the labour force. The key to rising in the merchant service from the rank of *novice* or *mousse* to full-fledged sailor lay through doing a campaign on the King's vessels. A heavy burden in wartime, the King's service in peace was a career necessity. In peacetime, however, the King could usually afford to outfit only tiny fleets, employing perhaps 4000 men a year. Who were the fortunate few called up? Many were permanent denizens of naval ports like Brest and Toulon. Elsewhere, there is considerable indirect evidence to suggest that the naval commissaries in the ports picked the sons of sailors, rather than newcomers, doubtless as part of their traditional strategy of maintaining a hold on the seafaring community by controlling as many aspects of favour and grace as they could. In Nantes during the 1770s, young men were carried as *novices* on merchant crew rolls with not just one, but two and three years' experience at sea, and grew older without promotion to the rank of *matelot*. The result can be seen in the age structure of the *novices* awaiting their turn to go to Brest or Rochefort. Doubtless the same was the case at Le Havre and Bordeaux. The only force acting against this trend was the expansion in shipping volume in the 1760s and 1770s: 1.2% per year in Nantes and some four percent per annum in Bordeaux, almost equal to the boom period of 1726-1743.

It would seem that the normal hazards of peacetime navigation had not been enough in the 1763-1777 period to remove enough of the older sailors who had survived the Seven Years' War. To judge from data from Nantes, mortality rates on transatlantic voyages, after rising between 1726 and 1743, declined dramatically after the peace of 1748, and, after a brief upsurge in the Seven Years' War, reached an all-time low in the period 1763-1777.[37] Less of the more expensive kinds of seamen were being created through promotion and service in the navy, but fewer seafarers of all sorts were dying at work. At the same time, a group of older, cheaper *novices*, with sufficient experience to merit the title of able seamen in other circumstances, was kept waiting for promotion. As the process of substitution of *novices* for able seamen in the workforce continued, shippers had no difficulty meeting their labour requirements. Nominal wages grew a little or stagnated; real wages declined, but the blockage of the promotion mechanism saved the more experienced sailors from the worst consequences, which were borne by the more highly-paid *officiers*, *officiers-mariniers* and the poorly-paid *novices*. The decline of *novice* pay in a period when they were being employed in increasing proportions has to be explained by this blockage and, possibly, by declining real wages and higher unemployment in other sectors of the urban and semi-urban economies.

**Table 13**
**Some Growth Rates, 1783-1789**

| | Bordeaux | Nantes |
|---|---|---|
| Total tons | 1.8 | 4.2 |
| Total crew | -6.5 | 3.5 |
| Tons/ship | 4.7 | 0.1 |
| Tons/man | 8.6 | 4.4 |
| Wages/ton (nominal) | -4 | n.a. |
| Matelot wage (nominal) | 3.1 | 1.1 |

*Source*: See text.

The final peacetime period, 1783-1789, was characterised by a dramatic change in these patterns (see table 13). Total tonnage continued to grow, but only modestly. Yet French shipowners during the war had become used to using much bigger ships on transatlantic voyages in order to take advantage of the convoy system which, in this war, the French

[37]Those in Bordeaux cannot be calculated; those in Le Havre can be reckoned only from 1751, but the pattern there is downward too.

navy finally succeeded in operating on a regular basis. These bigger ships, and others like them, continued to operate after the war. Large savings in manpower were possible and tonnage growth was relatively modest; demand for labour was therefore slacker than before. On the supply side, the usual postwar surplus of skilled crew had accumulated and crew mortality on transatlantic voyages was basically stable. But wages, both nominal and real, continued to rise, except for those paid to the *officiers mariniers*, which stagnated, as might be expected. This overall wage rise was the result of the deregulation which marked so much government economic policy in the latter decades of the *Ancien Régime*: in this case, the removal in 1784 of the requirement that merchant ships take on one-fifth of their crew as inexperienced men (*novices*). In the last seven years of peacetime shipping in the *Ancien Régime*, this change appears to have permitted a different kind of productivity growth from that which took place earlier. Total tonnage grew, albeit modestly, but from a base vastly higher than sixty years before. Ship size increased dramatically in both Bordeaux and Nantes. But the total number of men employed in transatlantic shipping now fell in absolute terms. The reason lay in dramatic increases in productivity measured in tons per man. The American War of Independence had created another generation of trained seamen, and captains and shipowners showed themselves ready to take advantage of deregulation and willing to pay higher wages for its advantages. In short, productivity growth now came more decidedly from an increase in output per man rather than just from economies of scale. But there is also a second reason. A constant theme across the century was the decline of nominal and real wages per ton. By the late 1780s, shipowners were paying about sixty percent less wages in *nominal* terms for each ton, and at no time was the fall in overall cost greater than in the last postwar period of the *Ancien Régime*. For the shipowner, beset by the rising costs of ship construction, gear and merchandise, and increased competition in West Indies and slaving ventures, seamen came relatively cheap, and were getting less expensive all the time. One can understand the willingness in these circumstances to expend their money on more expensive experienced seamen.

## Wages and Migrations

Where do migrations fit into this pattern? The organisers of the conference at The Hague have suggested that differential wage rates in various regions may account for the movement of seamen from one labour market to another. The level of seamen's pay did differ from port to port. A cursory glance at figures 6 and table 7 shows that there was a significant difference between wages in French Mediterranean ports and those in northern France, and a less marked difference among the ports of northern France. The figures also show that the gap between the various wage rates was narrowing. What role did migrations play in this process and how did wage gaps affect migration flows?

As for foreign immigration, it seems clear that the availability of Italian and other migrant labour in the Mediterranean was the main factor that allowed captains and outfitters to keep wages below the rest of France. Elsewhere, migrations seem to have had a more limited effect. The fact that men came from other countries in significant numbers suggests they believed that pay in France was attractive. But there was not an unlimited demand for such men. Nowhere during peacetime, not even on the Mediterranean, did captains take full advantage of the government's permission in the ordinance of 20 October 1723 to allow temporary foreign migrants to comprise up to one-third of the *matelots*.

This suggests that the maritime labour supply within France was, in a general fashion and in the long run, adequate for peacetime shipping. Further evidence of this is the relatively limited long- and short-term migrations of sailors between major centres in France. But it makes more sense to analyse migration movements of seamen in terms of the different sorts of men employed. As the movement of wage rates makes clear, there was usually relatively weak demand in peacetime for older and more skilled seamen, such as the petty officiers, and more for the semi-skilled and younger men. Here was another reason why foreign seamen were not taken on in greater numbers, except in the Mediterranean: when these men migrated, they did so in the prime of life, and they almost invariably were among the better-paid sailors on French ships. But opportunities for such men were limited: the same ordinance which allowed them to ship on French vessels specified that the officers and pilots had to be French natives residing domestically. At most, foreign sailors might hope to become petty officers – but the usual road to that position lay through the French King's service. It was therefore difficult for a foreigner to "fit in" to the world of French sailors, even assuming that he wanted to do so.

Instead, the renewal and increase of the labour force for French seafaring during most of the century was assured by the constant inflow at the bottom of the wage scale of young, unskilled and semi-skilled men. A series of government measures during the 1730s and 1740s requiring captains to take on a proportion of crew as *novices* appear to have encouraged a pattern of hiring which might in the end have been adopted anyway.[38] This, plus the presence of the underemployed young from the countryside; the population of boatmen in the great estuaries of France; and the children of artisans, shopkeepers and labourers in the great ports, seems to have provided a flow of labour to the sea which, if it was not steady enough to prevent some upward pressure on wages, was generally sufficient.

## Outward Migration from France

It is harder to trace out-migration quantitatively than in-migration. My own extensive reading in the administrative correspondence leads me to believe that one must distinguish between short- and long-term movements. Short-term out-migration could be quite large, especially in wartime, when men tried to flee the onerous obligations of service on the King's ships. These migrations took place on the fringes of the kingdom, where it was easy to get away and where local sailors might have friends and family abroad – in places like Dunkerque, Bayonne and particularly on the Mediterranean coast.[39] After each war, and whenever the authorities believed that another conflict was in the offing, amnesties would be issued in the hope of luring these people back.

That there was also a small, permanent flow of migrants abroad seems evident. True, higher wage rates and the extension of control by naval administrators over much of the labour market, and the nature of seafarer's family structures in northern France, seem to have restrained permanent migrations to other northern European ports. The Mediterranean, however, was characterised by lower wages, weaker administrative control, local power structures which counterbalanced to a greater extent the coercive power of the *classes*, and a much more mobile labour

---

[38]The Ordinance of 23 August 1730 (applicable only to Bordeaux) required outfitters to take one-tenth of their crew in the form of *novices*, and another of 23 July 1745 extended the requirement to all ports and raised the proportion to one-fifth. These measures were removed by the reformed general Marine Ordinance of 4 July 1784.

[39]Le Goff, "Les gens de mer devant le système des classes."

force.[40] We see mostly the inflow of migrants in French records, but it seems likely that migration moved in the other direction as well, away from Marseille and back into the ports of the Italian Riviera whence most of these men came. But in all the major French ports the main outflow of labour was overseas to the New World. Men were doubtless left behind in every port on the far side of the Atlantic. In 1744 Québec, the main city of New France, contained 315 *navigateurs*, or about ten percent of its population; many must have been born in France.[41] Another study suggests that French seafarers who did settle permanently in New France may have been mostly youths at the time of migration. *Mousses* and *novices* – but no *officiers mariniers* or *matelots* – from the cod-fishing fleet sometimes remained on the lower St Lawrence.[42] But doubtless older men were also involved in what was probably the biggest destination of seamen's out-migration, the West Indies, where French seamen manned the coasting trade in the islands. The data on desertions and disembarkments in peacetime years in table 8 are consistent with a certain amount of seepage from the labour force in this direction.

## Conclusion

France enjoyed remarkable growth in its shipping and fisheries between the late seventeenth century and the onset of the Revolution in 1789. By the 1780s, France had also successfully challenged British naval hegemony and the increasing size of its navy meant that big demands would be made on its conscripted maritime labour force in wartime. Along with this went an increased concentration of the commercial and fishing economy in the larger ports. These factors put pressure on the supply of seamen and insured that there would have to be an inflow of

---

[40] *Ibid.*

[41] Y. Desloges, *Une ville de locataires Québec au XVIIIe siècle* (Ottawa, 1991), 53-58.

[42] A. Laberge, "Communautés rurales et présence étrangère au Canada au 18ème siècle: les Granvillais sur la Cote-du-Sud (1730-1770)," in G. Bouchard and J. Goy (eds.), *Famille, économie et société rurale en contexte d'urbanisation (17e-20e siècle)* (Chicoutimi, 1990), 359-69; and R. Litalien, "Granville et la pêche à la morue dans le golfe du Saint-Laurent au XVIIIe siècle, d'après les registres de l'inscription maritime," *Etudes canadiennes/Canadian Studies*, XIII (1982), 30-31.

labour to large-scale commercial shipping and to the cod fisheries: young men, whether skilled seamen from abroad or, more often, from smaller ports, country people or the offspring of the urban lower orders.

Because demand for seamen grew quickly, particularly in wartime, the real wages of sailors did not decline markedly between the 1720s and the 1780s, unlike what happened in the rest of Europe. In a general way, this stability or rise of real wages was probably natural, but the forms which wage movements took depended in part on the institutional arrangements of the French navy, specifically the conscription system (*système des classes*), which provided some advantages and protection to French-born seafarers and also discouraged permanent immigration by foreigners. The result was, by and large, an indigenous seafaring labour force. Only in the Mediterranean and on the extreme ends of the Atlantic coastline, where foreigners were exempt from conscription or where escape abroad in wartime was easy, was this different. The lower rates of pay in civilian service in the Mediterranean, where migration was common, compared to those in northern France, where it was not, would suggest that the conscription system was responsible for the rather high wages which prevailed in French shipping. But a factor which there is unfortunately no space to discuss here – the actions of naval recruitment officers in organising the labour market and disciplining the labour force for French seamen in commercial fishing and shipping – may well have compensated civilian employers for these higher wages by reducing their overheads in a way that cannot be determined statistically. This would not have surprised the administrators of the *classes*, whose stated aim was not only to man the navy's ships in wartime and maintain subordination within the labour force but also to further the commercial prosperity of France.[43]

[43]Le Goff, "The Civilian Impact of a Military Institution."

# The Labour Market for Sailors in Spain, 1570-1870

Carla Rahn Phillips

## Introduction

Spain has had a long and distinguished history of seafaring, but its political culture has been shaped largely by its hinterland. Throughout history, inland Castile held most of the country's arable land and the bulk of its people, and most Spaniards did not identify with the sea. In the Habsburg period (sixteenth and seventeenth centuries), though shipping lanes bound Spain's empire together, government neglected the navy when financial exigencies diverted funds to more pressing needs.

The Royal Navy (*Real Armada*) was not founded until 1714, after Spain had lost its dominant position in Europe. The Bourbons streamlined the complex organization that had defined royal maritime affairs and succeeded in defending and even expanding the empire in the eighteenth century. After most of Spain's colonies broke away in the early nineteenth century, there was less need for a navy and less commerce to occupy the merchant marine. When the final remnants of empire were stripped away at the end of the nineteenth century, the days of Spain's maritime prominence were already long past.

Given these circumstances, modern Spain might have neglected its maritime history, yet it has not. The *Revista General de Marina*, founded in 1877, has published nearly 11,000 articles in its long career. Although most have concerned the military history of the sea (naval history), that does not define the full range of topics covered. Articles also deal regularly with the merchant marine and the fishing industry. The *Revista de Historia Naval*, founded in 1983, created a venue for more focused naval history, but there seems to be little antagonism among scholars who study various maritime topics. Instead, they seem to agree with a nineteenth-century merchant marine captain who wrote that "the merchant marine and the navy have identical interests to promote, and instead of divorcing themselves they complement one another. They are like two bodies with a single soul."[1] Such sentiments were undoubtedly more common when multipurpose vessels dominated the world's sea lanes, and that tradition may have lasted longer in Spain than elsewhere. A wide range of books on maritime matters has also appeared in the past century, and the pace of publications in all aspects of maritime history has increased notably in recent years.[2]

Overall, maritime publications have tended to follow the general history of Spain, intertwining several themes within the context of a single historical moment. A given theme, such as the labour market for sailors, however, might be fully covered for one period and almost ignored for another. The discussion that follows will concentrate for the most part on deep-sea voyaging, which related most closely to the international market for labour. Nonetheless, fishing and coastal trading will be mentioned in passing, because those occupations produced most of the sailors involved in deep-sea sailing. Even such a brief overview should demonstrate that much important research has already been done, and that the topic continues to engage the interest of historians interested in Spain's relationship with the sea.

## Number of Sailors

Although foreigners were habitually employed on Spanish ships, the vast majority of seamen were native-born. The size of the population is therefore a key element in examining the labour market. Spain had about 4.7 million people in 1530 and about 6.6 million in 1591.[3] The rising

---

[1]Quoted in José Cervera Pery, "Marina Mercante y Armada: anáisis de una interrelación," *Cuadernos Monográficos del Instituto de Historia y Cultura Naval*, IX (1990), 25. Cervera has also published *La marina mercante española Historia y circunstancia* (Madrid, 1990), as well as a wide variety of studies on both naval and maritime history.

[2]An analysis of nearly 1400 recent books and articles about Spanish maritime history appears in Carla Rahn Phillips, "Spain," in John B. Hattendorf (ed.), *Ubi Sumus? The State of Naval and Maritime History* (Newport, RI, 1994), 325-343.

[3]See Annie Molinié-Bertrand, *Au siècle d'or: L'Espagne et ses La Population du Royaume de Castille au XVIe siècle* (Paris, 1985), 308-309. Reliable household counts do not appear much before the sixteenth century, and the best censuses therein date from 1528-1530 and 1591. See also Jordi Nadal, "La población española durante los siglos XVI, XVII y XVIII. Un balance a escala regional," in Vicente Pérez Moreda and

numbers eased the strain of naval recruitment, even though Spain's Indies trade and merchant marine grew exponentially in the sixteenth century.[4]

The House of Trade in Seville kept voluminous records of ships in the annual trading fleets and the military vessels that accompanied them. Based on those records, by the 1520s nearly 100 ships each year carried merchandise across the Atlantic between Spain and its colonies.[5] Together, the ships represented about 9000 *toneladas* of carrying capacity, each *tonelada* being equivalent to about 1.42 cubic meters.[6] By the late sixteenth century, a yearly average of 150-200 ships was involved in the Indies trade, with a total tonnage of about 30,000-40,000 *toneladas* (an average of 200 toneladas per ship). In other words, the number of ships had doubled since the 1520s, and their average size had also doubled, leading to a four-fold increase in carrying capacity.[7]

---

David-Sven Reher (eds.), *Demografía histórica en España* (Madrid, 1988), 40. The figures for total population use a multiplier of four persons to convert household totals to population totals.

[4]Discussion of ships, tonnages, manning ratios, and crews is taken from three previously published articles of mine: "The Growth and Composition of Trade in the Iberian Empires, 1450-1750," in James D. Tracy (ed.), *The Rise of Merchant Empires. Long-distance Trade in the Early Modern World, 1350-1750* (New York, 1990); "Spain," in Hattendorf (ed.), *Ubi Sumus?*; and "Maritime Labour in Early Modern Spain," in Lewis R. Fischer (ed.), *The Market for Seamen in the Age of Sail* (St. John's, 1994), 1-25.

[5]Pierre and Huguette Chaunu painstakingly analyzed listings of Indies fleets in the *Contratación* section of the Archive of the Indies in Seville; see *Séville et l'Atlantique, 1504-1650* (8 vols. in 12, Paris, 1955-1960). The authors argued that the listed tonnages had to be adjusted downward, but most scholars have rejected their rationale, preferring to use the listed tonnages unaltered.

[6]That was about the same as the old sea ton (*tonneau de mer*) of Bordeaux; see Michel Morineau, *Jauge et méthodes de jauge anciennes et modernes* (Paris, 1966), 31-34, 64 and 115-116. See also José Luis Rubio Serrano, "Las unidades de medida españolas en los siglos XVI y XVII," *Revista de Historia Naval* VI (1988), 77-94; and "Métodos de arqueo en el sigo XVI," *Revista de historia Naval* VI (1989), 29-70.

[7]Fernand Braudel estimated that there were about 350,000 tons of shipping capacity in the Mediterranean in the late sixteenth century and 600,000-700,000 tons in the Atlantic for all maritime activities, including fishing, figures that would seem to overestimate the Mediterranean and underestimate the Atlantic for that period. Fernand

Based on the Chaunus' figures, Indies shipping from 1585 to its peak in 1610 averaged 170 ships and more than 38,000 *toneladas* per year. If the Indies fleets comprised one-tenth to one-eighth of Spain's shipping tonnage, the total would have been 300,000 to 380,000 *toneladas*, probably too high but not inconceivable.[8] Military vessels would raise the total somewhat, perhaps ten percent. The crown maintained a minimum of vessels for escort and defense during peacetime and rented additional private vessels during wars.[9] The manning ratio for Spanish ships varied considerably, depending on the type of vessel and the purpose of the voyage, but even merchantmen had to carry sufficient crews to defend against enemies and pirates. Sixteenth-century manning ratios ranged from one man for every five to ten *toneladas*.[10] If we extrapolate from estimates of the tonnage afloat and the manning ratio, merchant shipping would arguably have required over 36,000 men at the turn of the seventeenth century, when the Indies trade reached a

---

Braudel, *The Mediterranean and the Mediterranean World in the Age of Philip II* (2 vols., New York, 1972), I, 445-448. Richard W. Unger, "The Tonnage of Europe's Merchant Fleets, 1300-1800," *American Neptune*, LII (Fall 1992), provides a more carefully reasoned estimate. Unfortunately, Unger (256) adopts the Chaunus' mistaken notion of the size of the *tonelada* and therefore underestimates the tonnage of the average ship in the Indies trade by about half.

[8]Abbott Payson Usher, "Spanish Ships and Shipping in the Sixteenth and Seventeenth Centuries," *Facts and Factors in Economic History: For Edwin Francis Gay* (Cambridge, 1932), 211-212.

[9]The official Spanish summary of the fleet sent against England in 1588 included 130 vessels of 57,868 *toneladas*. Nine of the twenty largest vessels were Spanish warships, for a total of about 5100 *toneladas*. Many other ships in the Spanish fleet were merchantmen (*naos*), and over half tonnage was foreign built, mostly rented by the crown. Colin Martin and Geoffrey Parker, *La Gran Armada* (Madrid, 1988), 61-62, reproduce the official spreadsheet summarizing the fleet. This work also appeared in English as *The Spanish Armada* (London, 1988). José Luis Casado Soto, *Los barcos españoles del siglo XVI y la Gran Armada de 1588* (Madrid, 1988), 186-226, analyzes the Spanish fleet in detail and adjusts the official figures somewhat.

[10]Pablo Emilio Pérez-Mallaína Bueno, *Los hombres del Océano. Vida cotidiana de los tripulantes de las flotas de Indias. Siglo XVI* (Seville, 1992), 57-59, eschews manning ratios by tonnage in favour of a ratio of men per vessel, based on several lists of important ships in the Indies trade. He estimates a need for 7000-9000 mariners during the peak of the Indies trade, which seems high but may be plausible.

peak. Military needs would have raised the total to over 40,000 men. With the population growing rapidly through most of the sixteenth century, much of that demand could be met with Spanish sailors.[11]

Population growth slowed or ceased nearly everywhere in Spain between about 1570 and 1620.[12] Trade also declined, and the system of Atlantic convoys almost broke down. In the late 1620s, there were still nearly 120 ships per year in the Indies trade, with a capacity of about 37,000 *toneladas*. By the late 1640s, however, an annual average of fewer than seventy-five ships carried the remaining trade, and from the late 1650s to the late 1660s, fewer than thirty-five.[13] As the merchant marine contracted there were more men available for naval recruitment but, paradoxically, fewer opportunities to gain experience at sea.

The demand for sailors on warships rose from the 1620s, as the Thirty Years' War involved Spain. In 1634, Spain's Atlantic Fleet alone had thirty-three warships (probably about 15,000 *toneladas*), and two years later it needed twice that much, because France had entered the war as an enemy of Spain.[14] The eight years 1639-1646 brought a special urgency to naval recruitment, as Spain prepared fleets to send against the French and the Dutch simultaneously. When government agents negotiated to rent foreign vessels for the war effort, they also recruited foreign crews, in particular from Ragusa, Naples, and Genoa.[15]

The Indies trade remained depressed for much of the seventeenth century, but a slow recovery marked the eighteenth. The Indies trade employed fifty to sixty large ships per year by the 1750s and over 100 by the 1780s, at an average size of over 400 *toneladas*. In other words,

[11]Phillips, "Maritime Labour in Early Modern Spain," 18-19; and Alfredo Moreno Cebrián, "La vida cotidiana en los viajes ultramarinos," *Cuadernos monográficos del Instituto de Historia y Cultura Naval*, I (1989), 118.

[12]Carla Rahn Phillips, "Time and Duration: A Model for the Economy of Early Modern Spain," *American Historical Review*, XCII (June 1987).

[13]Chaunu and Chaunu, *Séville et l'Atlantique*, VI (1), 168 and 337; and Lutgardo García Fuentes, *Comercio español con América (1650-1700)* (Seville, 1980), 417-422.

[14]Carla Rahn Phillips, *Six Galleons for the King of Spain: Imperial Defense in the Early Seventeenth Century* (Baltimore, 1986), 201-202.

[15]AGS, Guerra Antigua, legs. 3176-3178.

by the late eighteenth century, commercial shipping volume had nearly equalled its sixteenth-century peak.[16] Military needs expanded as well, as Spain pursued a more aggressive foreign policy from the 1740s.

At the start of the eighteenth century, the native supply of mariners seems to have met demand one way or another. By the 1720s, however, the situation changed, as both commercial and military needs increased. Before 1750 the navy probably had 125 large warships and an equal number of smaller ships, which would have required close to 35,000 crewmen; the need for merchant mariners would raise the total to about 40,000.[17] In other words, the proportion of sailors in the navy and merchant marine had reversed since the late sixteenth century. The detailed registry of sailors compiled in 1737-1739 (discussed below) included nearly 38,000 men, of whom about 32,000 were fit for service. In 1750 the government noted a serious shortage of sailors for the navy. According to one prominent government official, the shortage resulted from "the scarcity of people, the scarcity of maritime commerce, and the war against the Moors [Algerian and Moroccan pirates], which alarms people and forces Spaniards to put twenty-five men on a ship that the English would man with no more than six."[18]

New ship construction for the navy increased demand further. Between 1750 and 1800 the number of heavy warships built or bought for the Spanish navy increased from seventy-seven to 193, along with ten various classes of smaller vessels.[19] The number of able-bodied sailors

---

[16]Antonio García-Baquero González, *Cádiz y el Atlántico (1717-1778)* (2 vols., Cádiz, 1976), II, 123-137, reports far lower global tonnage figures for the eighteenth century. I used Gárcia Baquero's figures in "Growth and Composition of Trade," 46, but higher figures now seem more plausible.

[17]Carlos Martínez-Valverde, "Trayectoria militar de la marinería de la armada," *Revista General de Marina*, CXCIX (August 1980), 43, estimated a need for 79,000 mariners, but that seems far too high, based on other figures for the eighteenth century.

[18]Cited in Vicente Rodríguez Casado, "La marina," *Historia general de España y América*, X, No. 2 (Madrid, 1984), 198. See also Rodríguez Casado's more detailed earlier article, "La política del reformism de los primeros Borbones en la Marina de Guerra española," *Anuario de Estudios Americanos*, XXV (1968), 601-618.

[19]Rodríguez Casado, "La marina," 187. For a listing of all of the ships built for the Spanish navy in the eighteenth century, by year, see *El buque en la armada española* (Madrid, 1981), 415-425. The life spans of the twenty-eight ships built between 1749 and

required in peacetime ranged from about thirty-two for ships smaller than 100 *toneladas* to 200 for a three-decked ship of 1000 *toneladas* or more.[20] Twenty-two officers, apprentice seamen, marine gunners and pages rounded out the crew. In wartime, the largest ships were supposed to carry about thirty percent more able-bodied seamen and marine gunners, and fewer apprentices.[21]

High manning ratios and rising demand strained reserves, but the situation eased as the population rose from nine million in 1768 to over ten million in 1787. This rise built upon strong growth in the early eighteenth century, especially in parts of the northern and eastern coasts. The northern district held about 10,000 mariners in 1740, the Mediterranean coast southward to Cartagena registered over 14,000, and the south and southwest held 13,000, for a total of 37,000. Registered mariners comprised seventy-four percent of the population of the coastal provinces, though a much larger percentage of coastal towns alone, and a much smaller percentage of the total Spanish population. Only about sixty percent of the registrants were skilled mariners in their prime. The rest were either too young, too old, or too inexperienced to be proper

---

1758 ranged from ten to thirty-five years. Leopoldo Boado y González-Llanos, "Reglamento General de Marina," *Revista de Historia Naval*, I (1983), 47-66.

[20]García-Baquero, *Cádiz y el Atlántico*, I, 288, citing documents in the Archivo General de Indias.

[21]José Ignacio González-Aller Hierro, "El navío de tres puentes en la Armada española," *Revista de Historia Naval*, III (1985), 70.

| | Rule of 1788 (peacetime) | Rule of 1803 (wartime) |
|---|---|---|
| Cannons | 112 | 112 |
| Officers | 23 | 37 |
| Able-Bodied Seamen | 200 | 240 |
| Apprentices | 230 | 200 |
| Superior gunners | 30 | 30 |
| ordinary gunners | 100 | 160 |
| Infantry soldiers | 168 | 200 |
| Infantry gunners | 57 | 75 |
| Pages | 40 | 40 |
| Totals | 848 | 982 |
| Officers, sailors, apprentices, pages, marine gunners only | 623 | 707 |

recruits for the navy. Still, the government found it easier to man seventy-seven warships in 1750 than half that many in the 1720s.

Shortages remained chronic, however, and the government of Charles III (1759-1788) fostered the merchant marine as a nursery for the navy. About 15,000 men formed merchant marine crews in the 1780s, the peak years of Spain's Indies trade. Though the vast majority could not sign their names, they were indispensable to the navy in wartime.[22] Toward the end of the eighteenth century, Spain registered over 51,000 mariners, about 30,000 to 35,000 of whom were fit for naval service. Rules approved in 1788 called for 33,000 men for 110 warships, and another 9000 for smaller craft, for a total of 42,000, well above the number fit for service.[23]

Warfare generated by the French Revolution and Napoleon strained Spain's naval capacity to the utmost and led to its ruin. By calling up all registered mariners in 1790, the navy was able to crew 100 warships and an equal number of smaller ships in three months. Yet in 1793, registered mariners were so scarce that the crown had to rely on forced levies, vagabonds, and even prisoners to man the ships, a rare occurrence.[24]

The battle of Trafalgar in 1805 gutted the navy, and further damage occurred in the reign of Ferdinand VII (1814-1833), when Spain lost most of its American empire. From forty-two ships in good repair in 1808, the number fell to a total of sixteen by the early 1830s, only

---

[22]José M. Delgado Ribas, "La marina mercante española durante el reinado de Carlos III," *Cuadernos Monoqráficos del Instituto de Historia y Cultura Naval*, II (1989), 63-74. Many authors accept General José de Mazarredo's 1801 estimate of 5800 merchant mariners, but he cited no source for that figure. His memorandum is printed in Cesáreo Fernández Duro, *La armada española desde la unión de los reinos de Castilla y Aragón* (Madrid, 1895-1903), VIII, 230-237. Fernández Duro's work remains a classic for Spanish naval and maritime history.

[23]See Angel O'Dogherty, "La matrícula de mar en el Reinado de Carlos III," *Anuario de Estudios Americanos*, IX (1952), 358. Some scholars have estimated that Spain needed 90,000 sailors to man the navy at full strength, but O'Dogherty rightly rejects that overestimate.

[24]José Cervera Pery, "La marina de Fernando VII: Agotamiento, decadencia, crisis," *Cuadernos Monográficos del Instituto de Historia y Cultura Naval*, IV (1989), 81-90; Martínez-Valverde, "Trayectoria militar," 46; and José P. Merino Navarro, *La armada española en el siglo XVIII* (Madrid, 1981), 87.

four of which were fit for service. By then, naval construction had begun to recover, augmented by the purchase of foreign vessels.[25] From 1800 to 1850, Spanish and colonial shipyards built sixty-three vessels for the navy; another sixteen were acquired elsewhere.[26] Though Spain's merchant marine slowly recovered as well, foreign competitors grew more rapidly and usurped larger shares of global trade. In about 1860, 80,000 register tons, almost ninety percent of Spain's total mercantile tonnage, carried cotton from America to Barcelona's textile mills.[27] With the decline of the navy and the merchant marine, and a continuing rise in population, it was much easier to man ships with Spanish sailors. But those same declines left the navy unprepared for the Spanish-American War at the end of the nineteenth century.

**From Where did the Sailors Come?**

In the late sixteenth century, merchant mariners in the Indies trade came disproportionately from Andalusia, the gateway to Spain's American empire. By contrast, nearly half the sailors in military fleets for the Atlantic came from the northern coasts.[28] The northeastern Basque provinces of Vizcaya and Gúipzcoa supplied crews for most of Spain's whaling voyages, which regularly sailed across the Atlantic to Terranova (later Newfoundland and Labrador).[29] Sailors from Spain's east coast

---

[25] Cervera Pery, "Marina de Fernando VII," 82, 88-90.

[26] *Buque en la armada española*, 425-429. Another twenty-two small vessels were acquired outside Spain, but the dates are not listed.

[27] Figures for Spanish mercantile tonnage in the American trade appear in Jesús M. Valdaliso, "La flota mercante española y el tráfico con América en la segunda mitad del siglo XIX," *Revista de Historia Naval*, XIII (1995), 7-9.

| | | | |
|---|---|---|---|
| 1850-54 | 1,746 ships | 398,034 *toneladas* | 226,282 metric tons |
| 1895-99 | 1,032 " | 1,952,368 " | 366,416 " " |

[28] Pérez-Mallaína, *Hombres del Océano*, 61 and 71, notes 71 and 72.

[29] Selma Huxley Barkham, "First Will and Testament on the Labrador Coast," *Geographical Magazine*, XLIX (June 1977), 574-581; and "The Basques: Filling a Gap in Our History Between Jacques Cartier and Champlain," *Canadian Geographical Journal*, XLVI (February-March 1978), 8-19.

manned Mediterranean trading voyages, as well as the crown's galley fleet (augmented by forced labour pulling the oars).

Spaniards filled the vast majority of positions in both the naval and mercantile fleets, but foreigners made up the balance when demand exceeded supply. In 1568 the House of Trade officially limited foreigners to six per ship for security reasons, or about twelve to fifteen percent. Yet when demand was high, as in the late sixteenth century, foreigners could account for twenty percent or more of the sailors on naval vessels, and sometimes a third of the marine gunners. The percentage may have been even higher on merchant vessels.[30] Many foreigners undoubtedly signed on as sailors in order to enter the Spanish Indies, knowing that it was nearly impossible for non-Spaniards to obtain a license to immigrate. Others were simply looking for work they could not find at home. The net result of the availability of foreign mariners was to expand the labour pool and dampen pressure for higher wages, even in times of high demand. When the demand for sailors fell, as in the mid-seventeenth century, the percentage of foreigners on Spanish vessels presumably fell also, only to rise again when demand increased. After nearly two centuries of trying to enforce quotas on foreign sailors, the crown explicitly recognized their value in the decree setting up a mariners' registry in 1737. Although foreigners who wished to gain full benefits under the decree had to meet various criteria, the advantages were sufficiently attractive to make it worth their while.

The foreigners who entered Spanish service were mostly from friendly Roman Catholic countries. In the late sixteenth century, about fifty percent of the foreign mariners in Indies fleets were from Portugal, twenty-five percent were Italian, and the rest were *Levantiscos* from various parts of the eastern Mediterranean, plus some Flemings and Germans. Not surprisingly, very few were English or French, the habitual enemies of Spain in the early modern period. Sailors from the island of Malta, a centre of commerce and corsairing, were particularly prized by Spanish commanders. Maltese sailors served in Spanish fleets for hundreds of years, most notably in the late eighteenth century, when corsairing had entered a decline. At the end of that century, there were about 1600 Maltese sailors on Spanish naval vessels, or three to four

[30]Pérez-Mallaína, *Hombres del océano*, 63-64.

percent of the total crews.[31] Maltese continued to serve in the Spanish navy until well into the nineteenth century, even after Malta had fallen under British control. A sizeable number of Irish sailors entered Spanish service as well, and some of their descendants became prominent in Spain's naval establishment.[32]

## Wages and Other Remuneration

In the late sixteenth century, wages for sailors on Spanish military craft suffered by comparison to many other jobs. Pages made half a sailor's wage, pilots and masters made twice as much, and the wages of minor officers and gunners ranged in between. The value of rations was the same for all, adding considerably to the total, especially at the lower ranks. Prices rose five-fold during the sixteenth century and, although wages of specialized workers in Seville did not keep pace with inflation, they came closer than the wages of either naval sailors or inland workers in Castile. Only when a sailor's wage outpaced that of an unskilled worker on land did naval recruitment benefit. Judging from the prices for a variety of foods in the late sixteenth century, an unmarried sailor who saved his wages could support himself between voyages, but he probably could not support a family without supplementary sources of income.

**Table 1**
**Daily Wages (in *Maravedís*)**

| Year | Sailors in the Navy (wage plus ration equals total) | Seville: masons, caulkers, carpenters | Workers in Castile |
|---|---|---|---|
| 1500-33 | 35 to 45 +10 = 45-55 | 55-85 | 22-35 |
| 1534-66 | 45 to 65 +34 = 79-99 | 85-204 | 35-68 |
| 1567-1600 | 65 to 100 +50 = 115-150 | 204-306 | 68-85 |

*Source*: Pablo Emilio Pérez-Mallaína Bueno, *Los hombres del Océano. Vida cotidiana de los tripulantes de las flotas de Indias. Siglo XVI* (Seville, 1992), 117-118.

---

[31] Cármel Vassallo Borg, "El reclutamiento de marineros malteses en la Armada española durante la segunda mitad del siglo XVIII," *Revista de Historia Naval*, VIII (1990), 25-29.

[32] See Merino Navarro, *Armada española*, 100-102, note 145, for a list of over sixty men from the British Isles working in Spanish shipyards in the early eighteenth century.

The wages of merchant mariners are more difficult to calculate, but a variety of evidence suggests that they were consistently higher than those on military vessels. Wages alone in the last third of the sixteenth century, not including the value of rations, showed ranges as depicted in table 2. The most common wage for the New Spain voyage was sixty ducats. Sailors going to Tierra Firme earned a bit more, because the voyage generally took longer. To replace men who deserted in America, ships' masters often had to pay the equivalent of a round-trip wage for the return voyage alone. A merchant mariner could feed a family with his wages, if he made the round trip in a year or less, because his own food and drink were provided during the voyage. With little chance to save, however, most mariners were poor, barely making a living if they did not rise through the ranks or supplement their income through trade or other means. On the other hand, they were better off than rural day-laborers and poor landowners. The promise of a steady wage as a sailor provided a powerful lure for the desperately poor, Spaniards and foreigners alike.

**Table 2**
**Wages in the Merchant Marine, Late Sixteenth Century**

| Destination | Spain-America-Spain | America-Spain |
|---|---|---|
| New Spain | 50-60 ducats, or 18,750-22,500 maravedís | 25-65 ducats, or 9,375-24,375 maravedís |
| Tierra Firme | 50-104 ducats, or 18,750-39,000 maravedís | 40-60 ducats, or 15,000-22,500 maravedís |

*Source*: Pérez-Mallaína, *Hombres del Océano*, 120-123.

Maritime wages rose over time, but not as fast as inflation. Sailors on warships in the late sixteenth and early seventeenth centuries made about forty-four silver *reales* per month, or the equivalent of about seventy-five *maravedís* per day, including the premium for silver, but not including the value of rations.[33] That wage seems to have held steady for the rest of the seventeenth century. On merchant ships at the end of

[33]Earl J. Hamilton, "Wages and Subsistence on Spanish Treasure Ships, 1503-1660," *Journal of Political Economy* (1929), 430-450. The official wage rates were listed in 1633 in the *Ordenanzas del buen govierno de la armada del mar océano de 24 de henaro de 1633* (facsimile ed., Madrid, 1974).

the seventeenth century, a sailor earned a basic wage of 800 *reales* for a round trip voyage (about 40,800 *maravedís*, including the premium for silver). He could earn additional money in the Indies by working on the ship's careening and repair, plus the proceeds from the sale of his daily wine ration, if he did not drink it on the voyage. In all, a sailor might earn 62,220 *reales* for a round trip, plus his food and any merchandise he might sell. Sailors on both naval and mercantile voyages often carried goods to be sold in the Indies, which could form a more important component of income than the basic wage. Though the practice was criticized in the eighteenth century, it was only prohibited in 1793.[34] A kind of health insurance also supplemented a sailor's income. Even if he fell ill, his salary continued as long as he stayed on board the ship.

The daily wage of a merchant mariner depended on how much time the trip took.[35] A round trip could be made in an average of about eight months, but most ships wintered in the Indies, extending the duration of a voyage to over a year. Even if the round trip took two years, however, a merchant mariner could still earn more than his naval counterpart. If wages were paid monthly, they came in two instalments: three months' wages in advance, which sailors typically left with their families, and the rest once the return voyage began. This schedule was generalized in the eighteenth century to prevent desertions in America.

The rapid mobilizations for war in 1790 and 1793 put great strains on Spanish finances and led to a neglect of the navy. A thorough reorganization of naval recruitment and financial responsibility at the end of the eighteenth century, however, stabilized the budgets for sailors' wages under the Ministry of Finance. In 1800 a sailor's basic wage in the Spanish navy was about three *reales* per day (102 *maravedís*), and the value of his daily ration was five *reales*, higher than wages for comparably skilled workers on land.[36] Nonetheless, sailors' wages were

---

[34]Delgado Ribas, "Marina mercante española," 72-74.

[35]Moreno Cebrián, "Vida cotidiana en los viajes ultramarinos," 121. The average round trip seems to have taken eight to nine months in the late seventeenth century, but individual voyages varied widely. See Chaunu and Chaunu, *Séville et l'Atlantique*; and García-Baquero, *Cádiz y el Atlántico*.

[36]Leopoldo Boado y González-Llanos, "Algunos aspectos de la Marina española en los años previsos al del combate de Trafalgar," *Revista de Historia Naval*, III (1985), 6-12 and 15-16.

often in arrears during the chaotic period of the Napoleonic wars. At the start of Ferdinand VII's reign, nearly three years' wages were owed to officers and men, and the arsenals were virtually abandoned. Spain's navy and merchant marine only recovered slowly from the Napoleonic wars and the loss of the American empire. With diminished demand for sailors and a rising population, maritime wages probably did not rise rapidly in the nineteenth century.

**Recruitment Policies by Governmental Bodies**

Spain relied overwhelmingly on promotive means to crew its fleets, even in the heyday of the Habsburg and Bourbon dynasties. Economic coercion – that is, the lack of viable alternatives – played an important role in an individual's decision to go to sea, but physical coercion was relatively rare. Commercial and fishing voyages relied on the appeal of wages and fringe benefits. The government relied on enticements, persuasion, negotiation, and cooptation to man military vessels. Brute force was considered too costly in both money and good will. Sailors in the navy were not in permanent service. Instead, the crown recruited or levied them for a particular need. Local authorities, whether noble or civil, managed the recruitment process, especially in crises. Working through the local power structure gave a better chance of success, especially since local authorities could often ask favours from the crown in return for signing up sailors. These methods worked fairly well, but they were somewhat haphazard, and they were not popular with the men at risk. The announcement of a levy could spread panic in a local community during wartime, even without the use of force.[37]

Royal governments from the late sixteenth century tried to regularize recruitment to foster long-range planning. In 1607 and again in 1625, government asked all mariners in Spain to register with officials in their home ports, so that government could keep track of them. Despite an attractive list of privileges and exemptions for registrants, voluntary registration failed in the seventeenth century, and government

[37]Adelaida Sagarra and Nieves Rupérez, "La deserción en la Marina española del siglo XVIII," *Revista de Historia Naval*, IX (1991), 66-67.

did not press the issue, perhaps because the slump in commerce lessened the pressure of demand for sailors.[38]

Maritime administration underwent a thorough reorganization in the early eighteenth century, including the creation of three naval administrative districts in Ferrol, Cartagena, and Cádiz in 1726. That year also marked the tentative beginning of a complete, though still voluntary, maritime registry (*Matricula de Mar*).[39] In 1737 the new system began in earnest. Like its prototypes in 1625 and 1726, the 1737 decree sought to create a registry of all mariners, including sailors, gunners, carpenters, and caulkers, as well as officers. Although explicitly aiming to foment commerce as well as the royal navy, the decree clearly had military matters foremost in mind.

All those who registered were exempted from army levies, and their permanent residences were excused from the billeting of troops. Any civil or criminal cases involving registrants fell under the jurisdiction of the Admiralty courts. The king invited foreign mariners of the Catholic faith to serve in the Spanish navy and offered them the same benefits as natives if they married in Spain and maintained their registration. When registrants were needed to man royal vessels, they were paid the customary enlistment bonus, plus travel costs to the port of embarkation. Although registration was technically voluntary, the 1737 decree set up so many restrictions on maritime activities by non-registrants that it was effectively mandatory. Retirement age was sixty, and anyone who remained on the registry for thirty years without desertion could enjoy all the privileges of registration during his retirement; those who served a shorter time could still enjoy many of the benefits.[40]

---

[38]AGS, Secretaría de Marina, leg. 276.

[39]See O'Dogherty, "Matrícula de mar," 347-370, for a detailed analysis of the system; and the classic work of Franciso Javier de Salas, *Historia de la matrícula de mar y examen de vicarious sistemas de reclutamiento marítimo* (Madrid, 1870).

[40]Eugenio de Larruga, "Historia de la Real y General Junta de Comercio," Unpublished manuscript, James Ford Bell Library, University of Minnesota, IX, f. 202.

As a further inducement, the crown allowed registered fishermen to exploit coastal fisheries previously barred to them.[41] The crown ordered officials on land and sea to treat registrants with kindness and consideration, because they were "honourable people" who were willing to abandon the calm of their homes, for love of king and country.[42] Because there were no age limits for registration, many ancient mariners signed up, presumably hoping for rewards for past service, but not expecting to be called to duty. When the need arose, the men fit for service were called up according to a rigorous rotation schedule.

The marine registry helped to meet the rising demand for sailors in the eighteenth century. Nonetheless, the pressure of successive wars from 1770 led to a crisis in the recruitment system, with hasty levies and failures to pay wages on time or to observe promises made to registrants and their families. The crisis eased with better organization in the 1780s and a conscious effort by government to inspire loyalty among the registered mariners.[43] For greater efficiency in the intermittent warfare that marked the Napoleonic period, the marine registry was reorganized in 1802 and placed under the jurisdiction of the navy, so that all registrants, even civilians, were technically part of the military. The three maritime departments were subdivided into a hierarchy of districts, and registration and recruitment came under more centralized direction.

After the Napoleonic threat ended, the Spanish government decentralized responsibility for the marine registry in 1820 and put it under the control of local authorities. The change had a disastrous effect, destroying the structure that had manned the fleets for nearly a century. Recognizing its error, in 1823 the government reinstituted the 1802 system. Spain's voluntary marine registry lasted more or less in that

---

[41]The Duke of Medina Sidonia filed a series of lawsuits from the 1740s protesting the entry of fishermen from around Cádiz and Huelva into his tunny fishery. Luis Urteaga and Ignacio Muro, "Una serie histórico sobre producción pesquera: Las almadrabas de la bahía de Cádiz (1525-1763)," *Estudios Geográficos*, LIV (April-June 1993), 343-344.

[42]José Segura Obrero, "Del Secretario de Marina en la estructura gremial a la reforma marítima de Godoy (1786-1800). (Gremio de Pescadores y Mareantes de Cartagena)," *Revista de Historia Naval*, VII (1989), 52.

[43]*Ibid.*, 48-50, citing documents from the Archivo Histórico de la Armada, Zona Marítima del Mediterráneo (AHAZMM).

form until 1883, when it was replaced by a mandatory registry under military control. In the century and a half that it existed, the marine registry provided Spaniards and foreigners for the navy, while maintaining the principle of voluntary recruitment that was a key element of Spanish naval policy.[44]

## Careers of Sailors: Mobility between the Three Maritime Sectors and Other Economic Sectors

The majority of Spanish sailors seem to have made seafaring a lifetime career, in large part because of the lack of alternatives. The coastal areas were not favoured agricultural zones, and local populations depended on the sea for employment. Though some mariners undoubtedly held other jobs for part of their adult lives, there does not seem to have been much serious competition for their services in agriculture, industry, mining, or other local occupations in the centuries before industrialization. Of course, when seafaring served as a means of clandestine emigration to the Indies, a sailor's career might last no longer than the outbound voyage to New Spain or Tierra Firme.

Areas far inland were also remote from the sea culturally. The lure of regular meals and higher wages may have attracted would-be sailors from the Castilian interior, but their numbers are likely to have been small.[45] Inter-sector mobility may have increased in times of rapid population growth. Yet the marine registry, established in the midst of the eighteenth-century rise in population, included only coastal towns, plus a few river ports such as Seville. Many of the benefits provided for the registrants required a lifetime at sea, and there is reason to think that was the pattern long before the start of the registry. In a special type of career mobility from the early seventeenth century, many infantry officers, whose companies were assigned to warships, took the trouble to learn about ships and the sea. They eventually qualified to be named

[44]Martínez-Valverde, "Trayectoria militar," 51-54. Francisco Javier de Salas published a classic defense of the marine registry a decade before its demise, arguing against critics who blamed it for hampering commerce and fishing and damaging the nation's economy; see *Historia de la matrícula*. See also José Cervera Pery, "Francisco Javier de Salas. Un centenario olvidado," *Revista de Historia Naval*, VIII (1990), 7-18.

[45]Pérez Mallaína, *Hombres del Océano*, 33-43, discusses the poverty and lack of opportunities that drove men to choose a life at sea.

"sea and war captains," expert in both commanding a ship and directing the crew and its infantry company in battle.[46] But this was less a matter of occupational mobility than of the merger of related functions into a new job description.

## Mobility among the Three Sectors or Their Subsectors

Seafaring in Spain included the regular movement of sailors between civilian and military voyages, the former including fishing, commerce, and whaling. Although the crown owned ships, it did not maintain a permanent navy before the eighteenth century. In the sixteenth and seventeenth centuries, private vessels were embargoed and rented by the crown in wartime, and sailors were recruited for military voyages from fishing and merchant vessels. Men involved primarily in coastal fishing or trading did not have experience appropriate for deep-sea sailing, either on merchantmen or on warships, but they were recruited all the same. Given Spain's global commitments, there was no choice. On one warship in 1790, only ten percent of the sailors had experience on the high seas. The rest came from fishing and coastal trade.[47]

Sailors from coastal areas with limited employment opportunities might sign up readily for military voyages. By contrast, coastal areas that regularly launched commercial, deep-sea fishing or whaling voyages, provided attractive options for local mariners, who were much less willing to take a dangerous and lower-paid job on a warship when the crown needed them, which explains the need for enticements in the marine registry.

## Group Formation of Sailors: Culture, Strikes and Mutinies

Sailors in Spain shared a culture defined by their lifestyle and a sense of their distinctiveness from other Spaniards. Even naval officers were prone to argue that Spaniards were not a seafaring people, and they often complained that the government in Madrid had no understanding of their needs. Among the general population, sailors were held in far lower esteem than soldiers, and they tended to be treated much worse on naval

[46]Phillips, *Six Galleons*, 123-128 and 146-147.

[47]O'Dogherty, "Matrícula," 13.

vessels where companies of soldiers were present than on merchant ships. Nonetheless, scholars generally agree that punishment on Spanish ships was lenient, compared to the brutality reported for other nations.[48] Because crews were mostly comprised of free men who had volunteered, they tended to follow orders without being threatened with the lash. Physical punishment did occur, however: officers called *contramaestre* and the "guardian" maintained discipline one way or another, especially among apprentices. Still, there is no reason to doubt the general notion that brutality was uncommon on Spanish ships. Although sailors were held in low esteem, they had legal rights on both naval and commercial voyages. The judicial tribunal of the House of Trade in Seville heard numerous complaints from crews against officers, and the judges habitually decided in favour of crews when the evidence warranted.[49]

Similarly, there are few documented cases of strikes or mutinies among Spanish sailors in the period in question. In the early days of global exploration, several well-documented mutinies occurred, mostly related to the anxieties of sailing in unknown waters. Once regular trade routes were established, however, labour unrest became very rare. This, too, may have been related to the free status of the sailors and their awareness that they had recourse at law. Desertions were much more common. Some men slipped away before they even boarded the ship, after collecting their enlistment bonus. On voyages across the Atlantic, many disappeared as soon as the ship docked. In the heyday of empire, ships might lose twenty percent or more of their crews in the Indies. By withholding wages until the return voyage, such desertions were reduced in the eighteenth century. Naval sailors, however, deserted at high rates in the late eighteenth century, when the crown failed to pay them.[50]

## Conclusions

Though much more work remains to be done regarding the labour market for sailors in Spain, a few generalizations can be advanced at this point. Throughout the period under study, Spanish sailors seem to have

---

[48]González-Aller, "Navío de tres puentes," 71-72.

[49]See Pérez-Mallaína, *Hombres del Océano*, 210-216, for exemplary cases in the sixteenth century.

[50]Merino Navarro, *Armada española*, 88.

enjoyed virtually full employment, as the demand for their services exceeded supply. The main change over time was the growing proportion of naval vessels in Spain's total shipping tonnage. The pay of sailors in the navy tended to stay above that of unskilled workers on land, and the pay of merchant mariners was higher still. Nonetheless, wages did not rise as high as they might have, restrained by the availability of foreigners and the use of forced levies in crisis situations. Spanish sailors were known for their good discipline, especially in combat, and they seem to have been treated less harshly than their counterparts elsewhere. When they had grievances, they tended to desert or sue rather than mutiny. All these characteristics sprang from the relative scarcity of sailors in Spain, a nation whose global empire made enormous demands on its limited seafaring population.

# Notes from an Outsider

Marcel van der Linden

A remarkable and very commendable rapprochement has taken place between maritime and labour historians in recent years. Maritime historians are becoming more interested in the social aspects of seafaring life, while labour historians have started to view sailors as part of the working class. Thus far, the emerging maritime labour history has primarily addressed the period after the invention of steamships. While the era of sailing ships has been less popular among scholars, it has aroused new interest as well.[1]

The essays in this collection offer an issue-oriented approach to additional material for analysing the early modern period. While the data highlight gaps in our empirical knowledge, they also enable tentative interpretations. Publishing case studies from a variety of nations in a single volume shows that the editors and authors aim for more than a medley of bare facts. The focus on a contiguous geographic area (Northern, Western, and Southern Europe) and a continuous temporal period (1550-1850) provides an opportunity to explore comparative and connective elements. This setting may serve as a basis for studying regional instances as articulations of an evolving totality. Such analyses are known as encompassing or incorporating comparisons. They challenge practitioners by requiring "both a mental map of the whole system and a theory of its operation." Fortunately, neither the map nor the theory need be accurate from the outset. "[S]o long as the provisional placements of units within the system and the explanations of their characteristics are self-correcting, map and theory will improve in use."[2]

---

[1]Of course, I am primarily referring to Marcus Rediker, *Between the Devil and the Deep Blue Sea. Merchant: Seamen, Pirates, and the Anglo-American Maritime World, 1700-1750* (Cambridge, 1987).

[2]Charles Tilly, *Big Structures, Large Processes, Huge Comparisons* (New York, 1984), 125. See also Philip McMichael, "Incorporating Comparison Within a World Historical Perspective: An Alternative Comparative Method," *American Sociological Review*, LV (1990), 385-397.

I do not claim to offer an encompassing comparison here, if only because I feel I am venturing into unfamiliar territory as a social historian without specialized knowledge of the maritime industry. Quite possibly, however, my questions and conjectures may stimulate experts toward more substantive work.

## I

The preceding case studies relate to international connections through their clear emphasis on domestic relationships. An encompassing approach, however, requires reversing this perspective to focus on the international system comprising the different countries and regions. Without broaching the controversial issue of whether Western Europe was a capitalist society as early as the sixteenth and seventeenth centuries, we can safely state that a close network of commercial ties existed from Finland to Italy and beyond by the early modern period.[3] Over time, gradual reinforcement of these commercial links boosted the volume of overall trade. This economic expansion occurred alongside an ongoing process of state formation that quickly resulted in territorially circumscribed proto-national states with consolidating national monopolies of violence.[4] Simultaneously, the increasing power and effectiveness of national states ensured that merchants since the seventeenth

---

[3]As is generally known, this assertion is supported by Immanuel Wallerstein's school and opposed by scholars such as Robert Brenner and Eric Wolf.

[4]Recently this process has become the subject of scholarly scrutiny. France and England and their interdependent development have received special attention. For example, see Heide Gerstenberger, *Die subjektlose Gewalt. Theorie der Entstehung bürgerlicher Staatsgewalt* (Munster, 1990); Hilton L. Root, "The Redistributive Role of Government: Economic Regulation in old Régime France and England," *Comparative Studies in Society and History*, XXXIII (1991), 338-369; and Aristide R. Zolberg, "Strategic Interactions and the Formation of Modern States," in Ali Kazançigil (ed.), *The State in Global Perspective* (Aldershot, 1986), 72-106. For important topical work on the Netherlands, see Marjolein 't Hart, *The Making of a Bourgeois State. War, Politics and Finance during the Dutch Revolt* (Manchester, 1993).

century have "laid down their weapons and accepted that the state would protect their business in exchange for regulating and taxing it."[5]

From the mid-sixteenth to the mid-nineteenth centuries, just as during later periods, hegemonic cycles clearly emerged within this system of economic and maritime power. Such cycles are evident from the succession of countries that have occupied the top position in the international hierarchy.[6] The Netherlands emerged from the revolt against Spain as a hegemonic power. The multi-polar situation that followed lacked a clear leader. Finally, Great Britain entered a lengthy period of supremacy in the early nineteenth century.[7] These shifts in the international balance of power coincided with different international "shipping regimes:" openness and free trade prevailed during periods with a clear hegemonic power, while closure and protectionism characterized the interim years.[8] The *mare clausum* doctrine intended to preserve Spanish and Portuguese power made way for Grotius' *mare liberum*, which was followed by the British Navigation Acts that were succeeded by the Free Trade doctrine during the nineteenth century.

Throughout these developments, international seafaring expanded steadily. Although the idea of a Transport Revolution may seem exaggerated, sweeping changes certainly occurred during the period covered here: ships increased in number and became somewhat larger (although opportunities for expansion were quite limited before the use

---

[5]Anne Pérotin-Dumont, "The Pirate and the Emperor: Power and the Law on the Seas, 1450-1850," in James D. Tracy (ed.), *The Political Economy of Merchant Empires* (Cambridge, 1991), 196-227 and 217-218.

[6]Joshua S. Goldstein, *Long Cycles. Prosperity and War in the Modern Age* (New Haven, 1988), 282.

[7]The exact periodization of these stages has elicited extensive debate. See George Modelski, "The Long Cycle of Global Politics and the Nation State," *Comparative Studies in Society and History*, XX (1978), 214-235; and Immanuel Wallerstein, "The Three Instances of Hegemony in the History of the Capitalist World-Economy," *International Journal of Comparative Sociology*, XXIV (1983), 100-108.

[8]Alan W. Cafruny, *Ruling the Waves. The Political Economy of International Shipping* (Berkeley, 1987), 40.

of iron in shipbuilding), and loading and unloading times decreased.[9] This expansion, along with the professionalization of the navies, brought about a growing division of labour between merchant and military shipping.[10]

II

The emerging international system for the allocation of maritime labour power was an essential part of these economic and maritime developments. By "emerging system" I mean that a number of differentiated and often compartmentalized regional or interregional allocation systems arose that gradually established contact with each other.[11] This particular system extended beyond Europe, as it included areas of North America, the Caribbean, Africa, Asia, and Australia.

The emergent allocation system had some distinctive features: it was expansive and slowly came to include an ever-larger geographical area; it gradually became more integrated: from a European perspective, starting with the Dutch sub-system, parts of Germany, Northern Europe, Britain, and other areas eventually followed; and it allocated labour power not only through economic means (supply and demand) but also

---

[9]See the balanced analysis in Russell R. Menard, "Transport Costs and Long-Range Trade, 1300-1800: Was There a European 'Transport Revolution' in the Early Modern Era?," in Tracy (ed.), *Political Economy*, 228-275 and 274-275. In addition to the contributions in this volume and the literary references included, see Werner Sombart, *Krieg und Kapitalismus* (Munich, 1913), 177-187; and Walther Vogel, "Zur Größe der europäischen Handelsflotten im 15., 16. und 17. Jahrhundert," in *Forschungen und Versuche zur Geschichte des Mittelalters und der Neuzeit. Festschrift Dietrich Schäfer* (Jena, 1915), 268-333.

[10]Violet Barbour, "Dutch and English Merchant Shipping in the Seventeenth Century," *Economic History Review*, II (1929-1930), 261-290. The author notes that this change in the naval status of merchantmen "did not release the merchant service from the obligation of self-defence" (262). Piracy remained endemic into the nineteenth century. "To eliminate piracy as a phenomenon...trade monopoly had to be given up altogether. This was a policy toward which England, France, and Spain only gradually moved in the second half of the eighteenth century." – Pérotin-Dumont, "The Pirate and the Emperor," 226.

[11]This allocation system did not include all sea-going individuals. Subsistence fishermen and self-employed coastal fishermen catering to local markets seem to merit a different approach.

through non-economic compulsion. The notion of the "labour market" suggests that the allocation of maritime labour power occurred exclusively through market mechanisms.[12] At times, however, other forms of labour allocation also played a role, such as the English press gangs or the Norwegian runaway prisoners. Finally, in addition to the separate allocation areas, the emerging system was highly segmented in other ways, such as race (Lascars), skill, and status; and it developed in an uneven and combined fashion. Certain parts of the emerging system became central sites of attraction; later, other parts caught up with and overtook the older centres.

## III

Within this system of maritime labour power allocation the following three segments may be distinguished: extractive industry (hunting, fishing); commercial industry (merchant navy, transportation), including short, medium, and long distance activities; and violence industry (navy). This institutional separation of the spheres arose over time. Fine lines always separated trading, fishing, and fighting. Moreover, the allocation of labour did not always conform to the logic of the segments.

War and peacetime differences were crucial. While trade and fishing obviously dominated during peacetime, wars dramatically increased the demand for naval personnel. For example, examining the numbers of British naval personnel between 1750 and 1900 immediately reveals enormous differences from one year to the next.[13] The end of a war always resulted in countless dismissals. Because the new peace often coincided with economic readjustment or recession, employment opportunities in the trade sector often disappeared as well. The conse-

---

[12]Labour markets may comprise two forms of labour power commodification: "Either the labourer may be sold outright, which is slavery; or his services only may be hired, which is wage-payment."John Hicks, *A Theory of Economic History* (Oxford, 1969), 123.

[13]George Modelski and William R. Thompson, *Seapower in Global Politics, 1494-1993* (Basingstoke, 1988), 30-31, based on William L. Clowes, *The Royal Navy* (7 vols., London, 1897-1903).

quence was a major rise in unemployment.[14] Such brief cyclical fluctuations in the demand for labour power need to be interpreted in combination with long-term changes.

We should of course differentiate demand according to skill and status. These notions are fluid, developing over time and varying from sector to sector. Perhaps we could provisionally distinguish three social strata on board: masters and their associates; skilled workers (experienced sailors, carpenters); and unskilled workers. Of course, these distinctions were not relevant to all kinds of seafaring; a real hierarchy emerged only on relatively large ships. Besides, social distance between the various strata could differ markedly. Norbert Elias observed that the social distance between a master and his crew was much bigger in the English navy than in the merchant marine in the early modern period.[15]

In addition to wars, the contributions in this collection suggest that four other factors underlay shifts in labour demand: economics (growth and decline of markets, business cycles); technology (in a broad sense, including social technology: innovations in shipbuilding, more efficient organization on board); exits from the existing labour force (death, desertion, occupational changes); and nature (seasonality: for example, fishermen were able to catch herring, mackerel, pilchard, or sardines only at certain times and in specific areas.[16] Each of these factors has a short-term and a long-term component, and all are interdependent. Technological advances, for instance, may lessen the influence of nature and may entail serious economic implications.

Strategies for recruiting naval personnel varied considerably by country and period. In some cases, such as the Dutch Republic, market forces appear to have prevailed; elsewhere, non-economic coercion also played a role. While this method obviously applied to the galleys in

---

[14]In such situations, as after the British-Spanish peace in 1603, the Spanish-Dutch peace of 1609, or the Treaty of Utrecht in 1713, piracy increased because the ships lay idle and desperate seamen abounded. J.L. Anderson, "Piracy and World History: An Economic Perspective on Maritime Predation," *Journal of World History*, VI (1995), 175-199 and 194.

[15]Norbert Elias, "Studies in the Genesis of the Naval Profession," *British Journal of Sociology*, I (1950), 291-309.

[16]A.R. Michell, "The European Fisheries in Early Modern History," *The Cambridge Economic History of Europe* (Cambridge, 1977), V, 134-184, especially 138.

Southern Europe, the difference between systems of national conscription (France) and impressment (Britain) appears to have been more significant.[17] While the reasons underlying the choice of recruitment system at a given location are unclear, the state's power base and the relationship between authorities and merchants appear to have been decisive.[18]

Recruitment of merchant seamen generally used intermediaries, such as crimps. The preceding essays suggest that middlemen were most important in larger, more international ports. This assumption certainly fits the conclusions in general labour history on subcontractors and mediators. Such literature stresses that middlemen reduced the transaction costs involved in labour recruitment. They always performed at least one of the following three services: recruiting potential labourers in places outside the potential employers' information sphere (if labourers were to be found in a huge urban labour pool or in remote villages): pre-selecting potential labourers and thus reducing the employer's risk of hiring a man or woman inappropriate for the job; and acting as interpreters in case of communication problems due to language or other reasons.[19]

---

[17]See, for example, André Zysberg, "Galères et galériens en France à la fin du XVIIe siècle: Une image du pouvoir royal à l'Age Classique," *Criminal Justice History*, I (1980), 49-115.

[18]The importance of the state's power base seems obvious. The role of the relationship between authorities and merchants may be extrapolated from Nicholas Rogers's observation that the success of impressment was ultimately contingent on a tacit agreement between the government and the employing classes concerning the need to sustain Britain's naval power. Impressment benefitted employers in various ways: "Impressment reduced property crime; it mopped up a migrant male population that might otherwise steal and pilfer, especially in times of wartime scarcities and high prices. It also allowed portside employers the opportunity to reinforce the fabric of authority and labour discipline...Predictably impressment was used to resist demands for better pay... Portside employers also used the gang to rid themselves of unruly apprentices." Nicholas Rogers, "Vagrancy, Impressment and the Regulation of Labour in Eighteenth-Century Britain," in Paul E. Lovejoy and Nicholas Rogers (eds.), *Unfree Labour in the Development of the Atlantic World* (Newbury Park, 1994), 102-113, especially 110.

[19]Morris D. Morris, *The Emergence of an Industrial Labor Force in India. A Study of the Bombay Cotton Mills, 1854-1947* (Berkeley, 1965), 129-153; Dick Kooiman, "Jobbers and the Emergence of Trade Unions in Bombay City," *International Review of Social History*, XXII (1977), 313-328; and Tim Wright, "'A Method of Evading Management:' Contract Labor in Chinese Coal Mines before 1937," *Comparative Studies in Society and History*, XXIII (1981), 656-678.

Middlemen performed these functions on a private basis. Of course, non-private institutions (i.e., local or national authorities) may very well have replaced the middlemen by taking over their functions, as seems to have been the case in France. This observation re-emphasizes the different processes of state formation mentioned earlier.

## IV

The studies gathered here reveal that calculating the number of sailors by country, period, or segment of the labour market is a highly complex operation that comprises many factors of uncertainty. Quantifying the total labour pool – the number of individuals in a certain region and year that are *potential* seafarers – from which these sailors were recruited is even more difficult. An indirect approach will probably yield a rough indication of the size of this labour pool. For each region we could distinguish the people who actually went out to sea in a certain year, albeit only for part of the year; and the age cohort of the entire relatively poor male population between fifteen and forty in that year. The first level is the quantitative lower limit of the labour pool and the second level the upper limit. Systematic subtraction of the subgroups ineligible for seafaring from the size of the relevant age cohort lowers the labour pool's upper limit and reduces the margin of error (see figure 1).

**Figure 1: The Labour Pool's Limits**

Actual Sailors

Lower Limit

Labour Pool

Upper Limit

Relevant Age Cohort

Insight into the size of the labour pool may facilitate interpreting factors such as labour market relationships and wage progression. When calculated for Europe as a whole, this labour pool is simply a statistical unit of magnitude. For concrete analysis, emphasizing the regional and local sources of maritime labour power is probably more prudent. Separate areas of labour supply existed even within the most highly developed countries.

Analyses of the relevant age cohort should of course consider the attractiveness of alternatives to seafaring. Attractiveness combines economic and non-economic motives (wages, danger, etc.), which differ according to the various segments of the labour market (coastal trade is probably less dangerous than joining the navy). Generally, workers clearly prefer certain types of occupations. Accordingly, exchange on the labour market is influenced not only by pecuniary motives but also by many other factors that combine to form a complex package of considerations.[20] This non-material aspect merits closer study. If wages are not the only factor shaping labour markets, identifying the other relevant factors becomes important. Perhaps some youngsters were attracted to seafaring because of the opportunity to see the world; conversely, others may have been afraid to go to sea because of high mortality rates.

The preceding essays repeatedly confirm that sailors tended to be young. This information leads to the suggestion that work at sea was a limited stage in a more extended life cycle. Many sailors apparently came from rural households.[21] This pattern resembles the "discontinuous peasant-worker strategies" mentioned by some anthropologists. Such strategies:

> were discontinuous in the sense that wage-earning activities and the operation of the family farm were separated in time and space. Typically, male labor from rural households was periodically drawn off into extra local employment and then restored to meet household

---

[20]Bruce E. Kaufman, *The Economics of Labor Markets and Labor Relations* (Chicago, 1985), 4.

[21]In principle we should base our analysis not on individual sailors but on their *households*, as such settings are the fundamental budget-pooling units. See my "Connecting Household History and Labour History," *International Review of Social History*, XXXVIII (1993), Supplement, 163-173.

> needs during peak agricultural periods. The result was that through discontinuous peasant-worker strategies rural households became intermittently tied to the wage economy.[22]

Additional research is necessary to determine whether many young sailors indeed played such a role in agrarian households.

Investigating shifts between urban and rural labour supply over time and – if this is the case – tracing the causes would also be very interesting.[23] A related question concerns the options available to sailors upon resuming life on land (agriculture, work on the docks, etc.).

## V

The preceding essays suggest that sailors were paid in many different ways. Some remuneration systems offered money wages, whereas others provided rewards in kind. Some remuneration systems fixed the amount of compensation at the beginning of the job, while others determined the pay on the basis of the journey's results. Figure 2 presents the different wage systems.

**Figure 2: Forms of Remuneration**

| | Fixed | Variable |
|---|---|---|
| Money | | |
| Kind | | |

---

[22]Douglas R. Holmes, "A Peasant-Worker Model in a Northern Italian Context," *American Ethnologist*, X (1983), 737. See also Douglas R. Holmes and Jean H. Quataert, "An Approach to Modern Labor: Worker Peasantries in Historic Saxony and the Friuli Region over Three Centuries," *Comparative Studies in Society and History*, XXVIII (1986), 191-216.

[23]For example, Vogel, *Geschichte der deutschen Seefahrt* (Berlin, 1915), I, 445-446, has asserted that the majority of the crew on German Hanse ships came from the Hanse cities in the fifteenth century, but that the share of the rural coastal population increased dramatically from the sixteenth century.

Of course, remuneration could also embrace multiple forms; theoretically, a single payment arrangement could include all four types. Identifying the combinations selected in certain situations would be quite interesting; such choices could obviously result from negotiations between an "employer" and an "employee." Many factors might affect decision-making: the employer's opportunities for effective supervision; the degree of skill required; the substitutability of personnel; the employees' bargaining power; the share of wages in total operating costs; the stability of the product market; the voyage's risks; and so on.[24]

Remarkably, the data in this volume indicate that nominal money wages decreased rarely. Such stickiness might ensue from the money illusion described by John Maynard Keynes. According to his *General Theory*, "labour stipulates (within limits) for a money-wage rather than a real wage." Keynes explains that "whilst workers will usually resist a reduction of money-wages, it is not their practice to withdraw their labour whenever there is a rise in the price of wage-goods."[25] If nominal wages were in fact rather rigid, real wages were presumably mainly determined by price fluctuations rather than by money wages.[26]

## VI

Quite possibly, the preceding essays have devoted insufficient attention to living conditions aboard the ships. Several means are available to learn

---

[24]Mark Granovetter and Charles Tilly, "Inequality and Labor Processes," in Neil J. Smelser (ed.), *Handbook of Sociology* (Newbury Park, 1988), 175-221.

[25]John Maynard Keynes, "The General Theory of Employment, Interest and Money" in *The Collected Writings of John Maynard Keynes* (London, 1973), VII, 9. Keynes perceived a measure of logic in this type of behaviour among workers: "Since there is imperfect mobility of labour, and wages do not tend to an exact equality of net advantage in different occupations, any individual or group of individuals, who consent to a reduction of money-wages relatively to others, will suffer a *relative* reduction in real wages, which is a sufficient justification for them to resist it." (*ibid.*, 14). Nevertheless, Joan Robinson and others have argued that nominal wages sometimes declined, whether temporarily or permanently.

[26]See Jan de Vries, "How Did Pre-Industrial Labour Markets Function?," in George Grantham and Mary MacKinnon (eds.), *Labour Market Evolution. The Economic History of Market Integration, Wage Flexibility and the Employment Relation* (London, 1994), 39-63.

more about this subject, including some methods, like studying shanties, applied elsewhere.[27] Sociological studies of relationships on board contemporary ships might be conducive to interpretation. While major differences obviously exist between modern-day and historical seafaring, studying modern-day ships may be of heuristic value to historians. An essential aspect of all ships is of course that they are Erving Goffman's "total institutions," comparable to boarding schools, monasteries or barracks.[28] Whether on or off duty, seamen remain at the same location and are surrounded by the same people. "Neighbours" are also colleagues. Personal experiences have repercussions in other areas as well, which probably explains why a captain usually keeps his distance from crew members.

As a detailed discussion of the relevant sociological literature would exceed the scope of this essay, I will provide only one example here. The sociologists Vilhelm Aubert and Oddvar Arner explain the tremendous significance of food aboard ships to seamen:

> The food is a symbol saturated with a variety of partly conflicting meanings. It is a product of work for one section of the ship, the steward and the cooks; for the others it is a private consumption, and at the same time, part of their remuneration. This latter aspect is frequently emphasized on ships, and may explain some of the apparently unreasonable complaints about the food...Deterioration in the food is considered not only as a lowering of the standard of consumption, but also as a lower evaluation of the work put in, and of the occupation. Complaining about the food is also considered good policy in the fight for higher wages. The emotional value of food is enhanced because eating is one of the few activities on board with rich emotional associations from childhood and youth ("mother's meat balls"). The food

[27]An interesting anthropological approach to interpreting shanties appears in Helge Gerndt, *Kultur als Forschungsfeld. Über volkskundliches Denken und Arbeiten* (Munich, 1981), 56-84 and 98-117.

[28]Concerning this point and the following paragraph, see Vilhelm Aubert and Oddvar Arner, "On the Social Structure of the Ship," *Acta Sociologica*, III (1958), 200-219, quotation on 204.

> is a link with the world ashore, as are all small privileges associated with eating and drinking...In this male society, where men prepare the food, but do not visibly pay for it, food has a social meaning which is both more significant and different from what is the case in families ashore.

Such considerations probably also applied to social relationships aboard ships during the seventeenth or eighteenth centuries.

The aspect of social relationships raises the question concerning the extent to which collective protest by sailors on board may be viewed as a form of *workers'* protest. Peter Earle's contribution emphatically casts doubt on this interpretation of rebellion among sailors. I am inclined to differ on this issue. Just as referring to a "trade union" of journeymen in early-modern Lyon is not necessarily an anachronism, a "modern" interpretation of sailors' protest may also have its merits.[29] For example, consider the following cases from the fifteenth century:

> By 1417 the merchant in Bruges complained that the crew members often took advantage of the shipmaster's vulnerability in foreign countries or at sea to force pay raises. In 1480 when the shipmasters complained extensively about the associations of seamen formed by a few agitators who spitefully abandoned their work or forced shipmasters at sea to lay anchor elsewhere than the port of call, most cases appeared to involve coalitions and strikes to obtain higher wages.[30]

---

[29]Nathalie Zemon Davis, "A Trade Union in Sixteenth-Century France," *Economic History Review*, Second Series, XIX (1966), 48-69. Cf. Catharina Lis and Hugo Soly, "'An Irresistible Phalanx': Journeymen Associations in Western Europe, 1300-1800," *International Review of Social History*, XXXIX (1994), Supplement, 11-52.

[30]Vogel, *Geschichte der deutschen Seeschiffahrt*, I, 442. For an enlightening comparison between sailors' and workers' insurgencies, see Cornelis J. Lammers, "Strikes and Mutinies: A Comparative Study of Organizational Conflicts between Rulers and Ruled," *Administrative Science Quarterly*, XIV (1969), 558-572.

While such protest clearly took place within an early-modern moral and religious discourse, the material basis (wage earners protecting their interests) persisted.

Thus far, forms of self-organization among seamen have been a stepchild of historical research, although Karel Davids in particular has conducted studies on this subject.[31] Some types of associations were primarily defensive, such as the "boxes" for mutual insurance, while others were more offensive, like the acclaimed collective petitions known as "round robins." Identifying the organizational forms chosen by different groups in various situations is important. Perhaps such information would reveal the reasons behind the fairly late emergence of seamen's unions (the first was formed in Britain in the 1820s), which lagged behind unionization among other groups of wage workers, including textile workers and miners.

## VII

The fact that experts have joined forces in this volume to answer a series of questions by region sheds light on the course for a wealth of research on economic and social history in the years ahead. Anyone wishing to explain national developments needs to draw systematic comparisons with developments elsewhere; this requirement applies even more to scholars attempting to establish encompassing comparisons. As very few of us have Max Weber's ability to acquire in-depth knowledge of many histories as a means of conducting comprehensive analysis independently, specialists generally engage in collaborative efforts. The present volume is a fruitful example of such teamwork.

---

[31]In addition to his contribution to this volume, see his article "Seamen's Organizations and Social Protest in Europe, c. 1300-1850," *International Review of Social History*, XXXIX (1994), Supplement, 145-170.

Printed and bound by CPI Group (UK) Ltd, Croydon, CR0 4YY
16/09/2026
14963458-0007